THE REMINISCENCES OF
Admiral Harold Edson Shear
U.S. Navy (Retired)

INTERVIEWED BY
Paul Stillwell

U.S. Naval Institute • Annapolis, Maryland

Copyright © 1997

Preface

To use the words that Admiral Hal Shear himself used in describing others, he was a "damn fine naval officer." During his active service he was a tough, no-nonsense individual who did his homework, produced results, and demanded results of others. As the following pages will demonstrate vividly, his forte was a combination of dedication and hard work. He put in a great deal of extra effort, whether it was learning the engineering plant of his first destroyer or learning to speak Portuguese so he could function effectively as head of the U.S. naval mission to Brazil.

As the stepson of a merchant marine officer, young Shear spent his teenage summers in the 1930s on board a fishing boat. That experience instilled in him a love of the sea and the qualities of a seaman. He relished ship handling and operations on board ship. See, for instance, his description of commanding the fast combat support ship Sacramento during the Vietnam War.

Foremost among his sea experiences, Admiral Shear had a distinguished career in submarines, including combat service in World War II, postwar tours in diesel boats, duty as executive officer in the fast attack submarine Trigger under Commander Ned Beach, command of a Guppy, and putting the Polaris ballistic missile submarine Patrick Henry into commission as her first skipper. He subsequently ran Polaris operations for Commander in Chief Atlantic and then served consecutively as head of both submarine warfare and antisubmarine warfare in the Pentagon.

As a four-star officer, Admiral Shear served as Commander in Chief U.S. Naval Forces Europe, Vice Chief of Naval Operations, and NATO Commander in Chief Allied Forces Southern Europe. Again, the emphasis was on long hours and hard work. In the overseas jobs he dealt with diplomatic situations and international crises. While in the Pentagon, he and Admiral James Holloway, the Chief of Naval Operations, quietly worked together to turn back the clock on some of the changes from the previous Zumwalt era that they believed went too far. Following retirement, Admiral Shear used his no-nonsense approach as administrator of the Maritime Administration. He worked, with some success, in trying to bring together two groups often at each other's throats--ship owners and maritime unions.

Barbara Maddux generously volunteered her time to transcribe the interview tapes for the benefit of the Naval Institute. In the course of moving from her initial transcript of the oral interviews to this final version, Admiral Shear and I have done some editing in the interests of accuracy, smoothness, and clarity. I have added footnotes to provide further information for those using the volume. Ms. Ann Hassinger of the Naval Institute's history division has made a significant contribution through her diligence in the overall process of printing, proofreading, and overseeing the binding of the completed volume.

                                                        Paul Stillwell
                                                        Director, History Division
                                                        U.S. Naval Institute
                                                        July 1997

ADMIRAL HAROLD EDSON SHEAR
UNITED STATES NAVY (RETIRED)

Harold Edson Shear was born in New York City on 6 December 1918, the son of First Lieutenant Harold E. Shear, Medical Corps, U.S. Army, and Jane Dillon Shear. Following the death of her first husband, Mrs. Shear married Captain Kenneth H. Payne, a merchant marine officer.

In 1920, as a small boy, Harold Shear moved to Shelter Island, New York, where his grandfather, the Reverend A. Lincoln Shear, was minister of the Shelter Island Presbyterian Church. He attended Shelter Island Union Free School for 12 years, graduating in the class of 1937. He attended the Cochran-Bryan Preparatory School, Annapolis, Maryland, prior to entering the U.S. Naval Academy on 15 June 1938 on a presidential competitive appointment. As a midshipman he was a member of the plebe crew and won his letter in sailing, being a member of the sailing team for three years.

Graduated with the class of 1942 on 19 December 1941 (the course was accelerated because of the national emergency), he was commissioned ensign from that date. He was subsequently promoted with the following dates of rank: lieutenant (junior grade), 1 October 1942; lieutenant, 1 October 1943; lieutenant commander, 3 October 1945; commander, 1 April 1954; captain, 1 July 1960; rear admiral, 1 July 1967; vice admiral, 1 May 1971; admiral, 24 May 1974.

In January 1942 he joined the USS Stack (DD-406), in which he had gunnery and engineering duties during the early period of World War II, participating in North Atlantic convoy duty, the Guadalcanal-Tulagi landings; capture and defense of Guadalcanal; the consolidation of the southern Solomons; the Battle of Vella Gulf; strikes on Buka-Bonis and Rabaul; and the Gilbert Islands operation. Detached from the Stack in December 1943, he received instruction at the Naval Submarine School, New London, Connecticut, early in 1944 and from May of that year until August 1945 served in the engineering and gunnery departments of the USS Sawfish (SS-276). In that submarine he participated in war patrols in the South China Sea, the Leyte operation, and the assault and occupation of Okinawa.

From September 1945 until August 1946 he served in the operations division of the Submarine Administrative Command, Mare Island, California. Having qualified for command of submarines in 1946, he reported to the USS Becuna (SS-319) as executive officer and navigator. He served as communications officer on the staff of Commander Submarines Pacific Fleet during the year August 1948-August 1949, then had a tour of shore duty in connection with plans and policy in the Bureau of Naval Personnel.

In July 1951 he became executive officer and navigator of the USS Trigger (SS-564), then from June 1952 until July 1954 was commanding officer of the USS Becuna (SS-319). He was a student at the Armed Forces Staff College during the five months following, and in February 1955 he reported for duty in the Strategic Plans Division, Office of the Chief of Naval Operations, Navy Department. In August 1957 he joined the staff of Commander Submarine Squadron Two, and in August 1958 he was transferred to the Naval Reactors Branch, Division of Reactor Development, Atomic Energy Commission, Washington, D.C., where he received instruction in nuclear power, ballistic missiles, fire control, and navigation in connection with the Polaris submarine program.

In July 1959 he reported for fitting-out duty in the Patrick Henry (SSBN-599), then being built at the Electric Boat Division of General Dynamics Corporation, Groton, Connecticut. He assumed command of that ballistic missile submarine upon her commissioning on 9 April 1960. Detached from the Patrick Henry in June 1962, the next month he was assigned to the joint staff of the Commander in Chief Atlantic as director of Polaris operations. He had instruction at the National War College, Washington, D.C., from August 1964 until June 1965, then commanded the fast combat support ship USS Sacramento (AOE-1). In October 1966 he was ordered detached for instruction in the Portuguese language at the Defense Language Institute, East Coast, at Naval Station, Washington, D.C., and in April 1967 became chief of the U.S. Naval Mission to Brazil.

In 1969 he was designated Director of Submarine Warfare (OP-31) in the office of the Chief of Naval Operations. He held that job until the summer of 1971, when he became Director of Antisubmarine Warfare Programs (OP-095) on the OpNav staff. Subsequently during Shear's tenure the billet was expanded to become Director, Antisubmarine Warfare and Tactical Electromagnetic Programs. Promoted to four-star admiral, Shear served from May 1974 to May 1975 as Commander in Chief U.S. Naval Forces Europe and Commander in Chief U.S. Naval Forces Eastern Atlantic. In subsequent four-star billets he was Vice Chief of Naval Operations from June 1975 to July 1977 and Commander in Chief Allied Forces Southern Europe from July 1977 to May 1980.

Following his retirement from active naval service on 1 July 1980, Admiral Shear worked from July 1980 to July 1981 as vice president of Norton Lilly International, the largest steamship agency in the United States. Then he was tapped by the administration of President Ronald Reagan to serve from 1981 to 1985 as the Administrator of the U.S. Maritime Administration, Washington, D.C. Subsequently Shear took an active role in the development and running of the Submarine Force Library and Museum in Groton, Connecticut. Included in the collection is the museum ship Nautilus (SSN-571), the world's first nuclear submarine.

Admiral Shear's awards include the following: Defense Distinguished Service Medal; Navy Distinguished Service Medal; Silver Star and commendation ribbon with Combat V; Navy Commendation Medal; American Defense Service Medal with star; American Campaign Medal; European-African-Middle Eastern Campaign Medal; Asiatic-Pacific Campaign Medal with one silver star and three bronze stars (eight operations); World War II Victory Medal; Navy Occupation Service Medal, Asia Clasp; National Defense Service Medal with bronze star; Vietnam Service Medal; and the Philippine Liberation Ribbon with one star.

Admiral Shear is married to the former Elizabeth Perry of Falmouth, Maine. They have two children, Kathleen Shear (born 20 May 1946) and Kenneth Shear (born 22 December 1949).

Authorization

The U.S. Naval Institute is hereby authorized to make available to individuals, libraries, and other repositories of its choosing the transcripts of three oral history interviews concerning the life and career of the undersigned. The interviews were recorded on 9 September 1992, 10 September 1992, and 4 June 1993 in collaboration with Paul Stillwell for the U.S. Naval Institute.

The undersigned does hereby release and assign to the U.S. Naval Institute the rights and title to these interviews, with the exception that the undersigned retains the right to use the material for his own purposes, as he sees fit. The copyright in both the oral and transcribed versions shall be the sole property of the U.S. Naval Institute. The tape recordings of the interviews are and will remain the property of the U.S. Naval Institute.

Signed and sealed this 12th day of January 1997.

Harold E. Shear
Admiral, U.S. Navy (Retired)

Interview Number 1 with Admiral Harold E. Shear, U.S. Navy (Retired)

Place: U.S. Naval Institute, Annapolis, Maryland

Date: Wednesday, 9 September 1992

Interviewer: Paul Stillwell

Q: Admiral, to begin at the beginning, you told me that your notes start in 1918. Could we begin there with your birth, your early years, and what you remember of your childhood?

Admiral Shear: Yes, I've got a lot to tell you, Mr. Stillwell, about my early days before going to the Naval Academy.

As you noted, I was born in 1918, just a month after the Armistice, December 6.[*] My father was an Army officer.[†] He was not a career officer; he came in as an Army medical officer during the war. He was a first lieutenant, and he died in the great flu epidemic of 1918, while he was taking care of troops at the port of embarkation in New York.[‡] So I never knew my father. He died just a couple of weeks before the Armistice. My mother's parents had passed away, so my mother, a young widow, and I went to live with my grandfather.[§] My grandfather was a Presbyterian minister. He'd had a long career as a minister before the war. Then he felt it was his duty to go in the war as an Army chaplain, which he did.

Then after the war, in 1918 or 1919, he went back to the ministry again. He had been preaching in New York and New Jersey for a number of years. His last church before the war was the Presbyterian church of Mattituck, Long Island. After the war he was asked to take over the Presbyterian church of Shelter Island, New York, which is at the eastern tip

---

[*] The Armistice ending World War I in Europe went into effect on 11 November 1918.
[†] First Lieutenant Harold E. Shear, Medical Corps, U.S. Army Reserve.
[‡] In the worldwide influenza epidemic of 1918-19 some 20 million people died, including more than 500,000 in the United States.
[§] His mother was Jane Dillon Shear.

of Long Island, just a few miles from Orient Point and Montauk Point. It's a small island, surrounded by water, between the two forks of Long Island.

So my mother and I went with my grandfather and grandmother. That's how I got established on eastern Long Island. It was a great place to grow up. When I was five years old, my mother married a wonderful man. He was a master mariner, a sea captain, whose family had been on Shelter Island since the days of the Revolution.

Q: What was his name?

Admiral Shear: His name was Captain Kenneth H. Payne, and he was a wonderful man. He was a great stepfather to me.

Growing up on Shelter Island, we were surrounded by salt water. We had a small school there, a 12-grade school. I spent 12 years in one little country school, which is not something many people do anymore. We had small classes, we had great teachers, and it was a great opportunity for me.

Q: How well educated were those teachers?

Admiral Shear: Well, let me tell you. Some of them were college graduates, and a number of them were New York State Normal School graduates.* But they were very fine teachers in the small classes. They did a great job in bringing me up in English, math, history, and science and all that sort of stuff that you get in a normal country high school. We had a group of boys there, all my friends and classmates from high school, and we did everything. We hunted, we fished, we sailed, we did everything good that you could do around salt water. We had a great life together.

---

* A normal school was a preparatory college for elementary school teachers; it was usually two years in duration.

Incidentally, that was in the days of the rum runners, and eastern Long Island was one of the great rum-running centers of the East Coast.* Why? Because it was isolated and had access to good, deep water. Rum runners would run offshore 12 miles and pick up a little rum from the larger vessels coming in from the Bahamas and Canada. They brought the loads in very quickly and unloaded at night. We kids would lay up in the woods and watch them unload, and we knew exactly what was going on. We knew who was involved: who the good guys were, who the bad guys were, and the whole bit.

Q: Did you see the Coast Guard around there?

Admiral Shear: Oh, yes. Oh, yes. Very much in evidence, and fights with the rum runners and at night aircraft flares and machine-gun fire. It was very interesting. The good guys, the heroes, were the rum runners, and the bad guys were the Coast Guard. That was recognized everywhere; that was taken for granted.

Q: Why?

Admiral Shear: Why? Well, many people were involved in the rum running. My family was not, but many of my friends' families were.

Q: It was part of the local economy.

Admiral Shear: It was a very big part of the local economy, because this was the

---

* The 18th Amendment to the Constitution was ratified in 1919 and went into effect in 1920, prohibiting the consumption of alcoholic beverages in the United States. The Volstead Act, enacted by Congress in 1919, spelled out the penalties for violations. The rum runners smuggled alcohol into the United States in violation of the law. In December 1933 the ratification of the 21st Amendment to the Constitution repealed the 18th Amendment and thus ended national prohibition.

Depression.* This was a very serious Depression. None of us went hungry, because we hunted and fished and raised gardens. None of us went hungry, but a lot of us didn't have too much to eat.

Q: Did your stepfather have steady employment?

Admiral Shear: Yes, as I told you, he was a master mariner. His business was in commercial fishing, and he was master of a steam-powered North Atlantic purse seiner. It was a vessel that was about 175 feet in length. It carried about 30 men, because you needed a large crew to handle those huge seines. That industry covered the entire East Coast of the United States, from Maine to south of Cape Hatteras in Carolina.

I went to sea with him every summer, from the time I was ten until I entered the Naval Academy. So I was pretty well shaken down in seagoing stuff by the time I entered the Naval Academy. I learned a great deal, because these men were magnificent seamen. The officers were from Maine, Long Island, and Connecticut primarily: captains, mates, engineers, and pilots. But the working crew--and you had 20 men, 10 men to a seine boat--were principally from Nova Scotia and Newfoundland. So I got to see that kind of a crew in action for ten years before I entered the Naval Academy.

Q: What are some of the experiences you remember from those cruises?

Admiral Shear: Well, the first thing was the massive, massive size of the industry. There were factories all up and down the East Coast, and a typical factory would have about ten steamers. There were a number of large factory owners: the Wilcox family, the Smith Meal Company, the Hayes Company over here in Delaware. Unless you've seen it, it's hard to realize the quantity and size of the menhaden industry. Menhaden are migratory fish; they

---

* Following the crash of the New York Stock Exchange in late October 1929, the United States was plunged into the Great Depression, from which it did not recover until the nation geared up for World War II at the beginning of the 1940s. The Depression was marked by high unemployment and many business failures.

migrate up and down the East Coast according to the water temperature, spring and fall, in vast schools.

It was not uncommon in a single set of a seine to get 250,000-300,000 pounds of fish. A typical good-sized steamer would handle somewhere between 600,000 pounds and a million pounds of fish. Frequently we would load a steamer in a day of good fishing. At other times, when it wasn't so good, you might go three or four days with half a load, but you generally got back to your factory at least once a week. I fished from the Connecticut factories when they were still operating, and I fished from eastern Long Island factories until I went to the Naval Academy.

Q: Was there a ready market for all these fish?

Admiral Shear: All industrial. All industrial. They were cooked, pressed, squeezed, dried into very high-protein meal. They are very oily fish, and the oil was another very important by-product. That went into high-temperature paints and cosmetics and all kinds of fish-oil type of uses. So in those days it was a very lucrative industry. Even in the Depression, when they had some lean years, the menhaden fishery kept going. So we never starved in my house, but no one in eastern Long Island was flush in those days.

In my early years with the boat, I got to know these great crews that we would hire on from Nova Scotia and Newfoundland. They were kind of rough around the edges, but superb seamen and great fishermen. Then along came the Depression, and there was a slump in the industry. You could no longer bring workers across the Canadian border, because there was great unemployment in the United States, and the law was changed so we could not hire people outside of the United States.

So the menhaden industry, which had already been active in this regard in the South, hired almost completely black crews from the Chesapeake Bay area. I fished with those black crews for the last three or four years of my fishing experience. They weren't quite the seamen of those northern Maine, Nova Scotia, Newfoundland crews, but they were fine people, and they were all big men. They were hired because they were big, strong men.

The southern mates always picked out the crews and brought them up to the northern steamers.

When you got a big set of fish, maybe a quarter of a million pounds in a single set of the seine, it was man-breaking work to get that seine pursed up into the bunt and get the fish pumped from the seine, first by means of large bail nets and then later on by pumps. It was backbreaking work, both in the seine boats as you got the seine into a tight knot, and then getting the seine into even a tighter knot as the fish came from the seine alongside the steamer and into the hold of the ship.

The men in those seine boats would sing in unison. They would sing Negro spirituals and hymns. They'd get in a rhythm, they'd bend down, get 20 men together and heave up on that seine and tighten her up. The crew would keep up their rhythm, and hold what they got, and reach down again and get another two or three feet of the seine. They had magnificent voices, those deep tenors and basses. It would make the hair on the back of your neck stand right up to listen to them sing.

Sometimes in heavy fishing you might have half a dozen steamers within earshot of each other, on the backside of Long Island, the Jersey Coast, or the Gulf of Maine. You'd have as many as half a dozen crews on different sets of fish, all singing, working that seine, getting those fish tightened up and into the bunt of the net. When you had half a dozen crews singing, not all together but individually on their own sets, their own seine boats, that was something to hear. That was really something to hear. Some of those men are still alive, and in recent years they've put out a tape, which you can now purchase, of the menhaden chanting of some of those Virginia and North Carolina crews. This is something that I remember very clearly as a boy: how those men worked that heavy seine equipment and how they sang together.

Q: It's a vivid word picture you've painted.

Admiral Shear: It was vivid, very vivid. The voices that those men had, and they were all very strong men. The northern crews sang also when they got a heavy set of fish, but they didn't sing like those southern Chesapeake and North Carolina crews--no comparison between them.

Q: What specifically did you do during the cruises?

Admiral Shear: I started out as a young boy, ten years old. I had a number of older cousins, and they all went a few years before I did. I started fussing at my mother by the time I was about six, but she said, "You can't go menhaden fishing until you're ten years old and you learn how to swim in deep water." Well, hell, I could swim in deep water from the age of three.

So I started out at ten, and I spent the entire three months of summer vacation at sea. My first few years I just learned the business, kept out of the way, and made friends with the cook. They had excellent cooks; they were known as very good feeders. The hardworking men like that, a 30-odd-man crew--boy, they ate, and they ate well. So for the first couple of years I just got around, saw what was going on, and kept out of the way.

By the time I was about 14, I was put on the payroll in a small way, and I would go out in the seine boats. But the last two or three years before I finished high school I was what they called the ship keeper. As the industry changed from triple-expansion steam power plants to diesel plants--oil-fired diesel plants versus coal-fired steam plants--the licensing requirements changed also. You had to have a licensed captain, and you had to have a licensed chief engineer, but you no longer had to have a licensed pilot.

The owners, being anxious to squeeze a dollar or two here and there, didn't require the captains to take a licensed pilot anymore. So for several years I went as ship keeper. That meant I stayed with the steamer while the other men were out in the seine boats with a big set of fish. Then I would come alongside the seine boats and pick them up as the fish were transferred from seine into steamer. So I got to be pretty damn good ship handler before I finished high school. It was great experience for me and a lot of fun, and it was a background you couldn't begin to improve on for coming to the Naval Academy.

Q: It sounds as if your stepfather was a real hero to you.

Admiral Shear: He was--great man, great man. He had served as a lieutenant in the Naval Reserve in World War I. His ship was engaged in laying mines in the North Sea and in sweeping those mines after the war. He let me do everything, taught me a lot. So I had a great youth, really.

Q: How did those triple-expansion engines work?

Admiral Shear: Well, a triple-expansion steam engine is a vertical engine with a high-pressure cylinder, an intermediate-pressure cylinder, and a low-pressure cylinder. As the steam enters the high-pressure end, it drives a piston and expands, then goes into the intermediate-pressure cylinder. There it expands some more and goes into the low-pressure cylinder, where it is then discharged. It goes into the condenser, where it is then cooled into condensate and heated again and becomes steam. And we had the old Scotch fire-tube boilers, which were coal-fired, and it was a very efficient operation.

Of course, in a steam engine, you reversed it by means of what we call the Stevenson reversing link. If you looked around the labs here you could probably find a Stevenson reversing link. I recall a number of years later that I had an engineering exam, and one of the questions was, "Sketch and describe a Stevenson reversing link." Well, hell, half the class didn't know what a Stevenson reversing link was. I'd been playing with one for over ten years, and it was a very efficient engine.

When I started, they were all steam-fired--the whole fleet, several hundred vessels up and down the East Coast. Then, as diesel engines became more refined, they all shifted into diesel, because they were oil-fired and easier. You could have a smaller crew, because you didn't have to carry firemen. For a steam-fired plant you had to carry three firemen just to stoke that coal. So it was an economical situation and a cheaper and more efficient operation, and really the engines were probably better.

Q: You had to have oilers, too, to keep the lube oil in those pistons that were going up and down.

Admiral Shear: Yes, yes. With the diesel plant you still had to have a chief engineer and a second engineer, but you had to have no firemen because they did everything else. So there was a saving there. There was a saving just in the efficiency of the diesel engines. So by the mid-1930s, everything was shifted to diesel except one steamer. The only one that was never shifted happened to be the one my father fished for many years, the old East Hampton. She was the largest in the fleet at that time.

Q: How many tons would you say?

Admiral Shear: Well, let's see. I guess the East Hampton was 175-180 feet long, 1,000-horsepower triple-expansion engine. I would guess she was 500 or 600 tons.

Q: That's a pretty good-sized vessel.

Admiral Shear: Oh, yes. And as I said, they carried the large crews. Then as other refinements came along, more mechanized use, they cut down the size of the crews. By the time I left the industry, each seine boat was carrying only six or seven men instead of carrying ten. Hydraulics and things like that had come along for handling the net. They had hydraulic pulleys and levers and large rollers that did away with much of the manual labor.

Q: Did these crews treat you sort of as a mascot in your early years?

Admiral Shear: That's a very good term. In my early years I was sort of a mascot, and they were all good to me.

Q: Interesting, throwing a young boy in with all these seasoned seamen.

Harold E. Shear #1 - 10

Admiral Shear: Yes, that's right. My stepfather used to say, "If your mother knew some of the things you're exposed to around here, she'd have a fit." [Laughter]

Q: Do you remember any of those things you were exposed to?

Admiral Shear: The weekends there'd be a little drinking. Even if it was the height of Prohibition, there'd be a little drinking. We'd have to go in and lay at a port where the ship could get coal. One of the coaling ports was New London, Connecticut, which is close to where I live now. We also went to New York and Boston, and some of the crew would get pretty well boozed up. But my stepfather always had a couple of men who didn't drink, so when I went ashore I always went with one of the fellows who didn't drink. I liked to go ashore and get a banana split or sundae or something, or go to the movies. That was a big Sunday afternoon.

Q: How would you describe those crewmen in general? They were probably not that well educated, but very good in working with their hands.

Admiral Shear: Very good. Superb seamen. They came from two Catholic provinces, Nova Scotia and Newfoundland. They all had large families. It wasn't uncommon for one of these men to have eight or ten kids. They came down and signed on as a crew members, roughly May to November. That was a normal season on the East Coast. Then they'd go home at the end of the summer and would go offshore in the steam trawler business off the Grand Banks and the Georgia Banks off Boston during the winter months. They were superb seamen, spent their entire lives at sea back then.

Q: I'm curious, why did you aspire to a naval career rather than in the merchant marine?

Admiral Shear: Well, that's very interesting. As I got toward the end of high school in the spring of 1937, I had a chance to go to the New York State Nautical College, as it was then called. It was at Schuyler, New York, at the mouth of the East River. I could have gone there, and I could have gone to the New York State University system. We had a system all through the state of New York, very good system, very high standards. But my stepfather said, "Well, if you want to go to sea, if you want to be assured of a good solid career, you'd better take the Navy over the merchant marine." He didn't force me to do anything.

Q: How strong a background did you have when it came time to compete for an appointment?

Admiral Shear: Well, each year there were a certain number of competitive appointments given to sons of officers and enlisted men who had lost their lives in World War I. Otherwise, I'd never had a chance to get into the Naval Academy. I took my first exams in April of 1937, just before I finished high school. In those days you took the exams every April, and you took six exams for the regular appointment. I didn't have a regular appointment, but I was eligible to take the competitive exams.

When I took the six exams, I bilged two of them. I felt like I could handle anything they gave me, but I failed physics because I had time to finish only seven out of ten questions. What was the other one? It wasn't ancient history; I did fine in history. I think it was one of the math courses; you had to take two or three math courses.

I graduated from high school when I was about 18, so I went to prep school for a year. I got some information about Naval Academy prep schools. There were two here in Annapolis--the Werntz School and the Cochran-Bryan School--and then up the river was the Severn School.* They were all Naval Academy prep schools. I got the literature from all three of them, and I said, "Well, Cochran-Bryan looks pretty good to me." They all had

---

* Robert Lincoln Werntz graduated from the Naval Academy in the class of 1884 and subsequently resigned his commission in June 1890. He then set up his preparatory school in Annapolis for prospective midshipmen and operated it for many years prior to his death in 1931. The Cochran-Bryan Preparatory School in Annapolis was operated by Lieutenant Commander Schamyl Cochran, USN (Ret.), and Lieutenant (junior grade) Arthur W. Bryan, USN (Ret.). The Severn School is in Severna Park, between Annapolis and Baltimore.

pretty good entry records; they advertised the number of students that got into the academy each year.

So I came down here and went to this little two-room outfit out here. It was across from the Anne Arundel Hospital, right in the center of town. Those two men were both retired naval officers. Cochran was out of the class of 1908, and Bryan was out of the class of 1922. They ran that school by themselves with one other teacher. They were good, and they worked our tails off.

Q: What was the method of instruction?

Admiral Shear: Well, we had assignments, and then we had study periods. Then Cochran and Bryan would take us through P-works and get us acquainted with all kinds of problems and all kinds of issues that would come up.* They got us so that we could recognize a math problem or a physics problem of a certain type that sooner or later was going to show up in the exam.

During the last two or three months of that school, just before the exams in April, all we did was take old Naval Academy exams from way back before World War I and go over them, because there was a habit of repeating questions. So we got to know those exams backwards and forwards. We knew what kinds of questions to expect and how to hit them when we recognized them.

In 1938 I had a chance to take the exams again. The age range at the Naval Academy in those days was 16 to 20. As long as you entered before you were 20, you were all right. I went flying through that second time around, no problems. By golly, those instructors were good.

Q: And they were really indoctrinating you to the Naval Academy method of instruction.

Admiral Shear: Yes, they were. Yes, they were.

---

* P-works--practical works.

Q: Who paid for your prep school time?

Admiral Shear: My family did. It was not expensive in those days, only $200.00. I lived with a Naval Academy math professor. All the boys in the school--I guess there were less than 100 of us--lived around town here. The people around town were delighted to get a few extra dollars by boarding a boy, and I lived with a very fine Naval Academy math professor named Eugene Mayer.* He had a boy my age, a boy younger than I am, and a girl older than I am. So I lived right with them as a member of the family. They were wonderful people. So I had a fine year in prep school, and I was fully ready for the Naval Academy when I took those exams.

Q: Did your stepfather see security as the advantage of a naval career?

Admiral Shear: He saw it as a more steady type of a job and one with promotion opportunity considerably better than the merchant marine in those days. That was important, because we were still in the Depression. My younger brother, on the other hand, stayed in the fishing industry all of his life, and he did very well, probably made more money than I did. [Laughter] But that's neither here nor there.

Q: What's his name?

Admiral Shear: Kenneth H. Payne, Jr.

Q: Do you have any other siblings?

Admiral Shear: I have a stepsister and a half brother and myself. So there we are. I should tell you, in addition to my summer fishing, we were working all the time. Every hour

---

* Dr. Eugene S. Mayer taught at the Naval Academy from 1918 to 1948, except for a brief break during the Depression when the faculty was temporarily reduced.

outside of school we had something to do--fall, winter, spring. We hunted, we fished, we clammed, we scalloped, all for sale. And sometimes, while I was in high school, I had a partner. He was a boy named Clark, and we were sort of in business together in those high school days. Among other things, we got a piece of a menhaden seine made into what we called a shore seine for shoreside fishing. So even during the spring run, before school was out and before I went menhaden fishing for the summer, we made some pretty good money.

So we always had something going on, always a work type of thing; at the same time it was play, pleasure too. But it was a hell of a way to grow up. Outdoors every minute, doing something, you know, active.

Q: Did you get involved in upkeep and maintenance on the boat?

Admiral Shear: Not on the big steamers, no; they were laid up in the shipyard for winter. I knew what was going on, but never worked on them. I had a small boat of my own, and there I got plenty involved in upkeep and maintenance. I started out with a 14-foot rowboat; then I graduated to a 22-foot power dory, and that was enough maintenance to keep me pretty busy.

Q: Did you go sailing at all?

Admiral Shear: Oh, yes. Lot of sailing, lot of sailing. One period I worked for a rich summer resident and took care of a sailboat and his powerboat. His father was an avid sailor. I took him out sailing quite a bit, and I did a lot of small-boat sailing. As a result, when I got to the Naval Academy here, the first thing I did was get on the sailing team.

Q: How much did you keep up with world events? The dictators were advancing in Europe during that period leading up to your time as a midshipman.

Admiral Shear: That came about the time I got to be a midshipman, and I'll tell you about that after we get into my early Naval Academy days.

Q: All right.

Admiral Shear: The world wasn't falling apart in the '20s and '30s. We had that tremendous inflation problem in Germany, even before I was able to understand that Germany was just a disaster. That brought Hitler along and so forth in the early '30s.* We were all aware of Hitler, and we were all aware that Lindbergh had gone over there.† We weren't quite sure Lindbergh was doing the right thing by going over to Germany and so forth and so on, but I don't think we got deeply concerned about world events until the late '30s.

Then we got immediately involved as midshipmen. I'll get into midshipman days. In those days every summer you had a three-month cruise to Europe. After you went through your plebe year, then you'd have a cruise in the youngster year.‡ Then, as a first classman, you'd go on another cruise and be gone three months. Well, by 1939 the war clouds were so ominous over Europe that we were not permitted to go to Europe. So we were restricted to the East Coast. We went to Canada and visited a number of ports up and down the East Coast. That's how I met my future wife. I'll tell you more about that.

Q: All right.

Admiral Shear: But we did not get to Europe. Now, I entered the Naval Academy in June of '38. At that time the academy had scattered entries all summer. I was very fortunate, because I came in with the first group, maybe 40 or 50 of my classmates, on the tenth of June 1938. Others dribbled in all summer, up until late August. Well, if you got in early, you really got to know your way around before the rest of the fellows did. We had all the

---

* Adolf Hitler was Chancellor of Germany from 1933 until his death in 1945.
† Charles A. Lindbergh became a national hero when made the first solo flight across the Atlantic Ocean in May 1927. In the late 1930s he visited German aircraft manufacturing facilities. On the basis of his observations, he was visible in subsequent years in the effort to keep the United States out of a war against Germany.
‡ A first-year midshipman is known as a plebe. The first part of his indoctrination to the Naval Academy occurs during plebe summer. The "youngster" or third-class year at the Naval Academy is the equivalent of the sophomore year at a civilian university.

usual things in plebe summer: sailing and pulling boats and rifle range firings and marching and a little bit of academics. Members of the second class were here to indoctrinate us, and they did a good job. You got a fair amount of running, fair amount of discipline. Some people didn't like it, but, hell, I thought it was great. I had a hell of a time.

Q: What are some of the examples you remember of the running?

Admiral Shear: Oh, a whole series of questions that you had to find answers for. There were allegations about cruelty in hazing, but I never ran into it. I got my tail beat periodically, but that was part of the game. You know, upper classmen would stand up on a chair and whack you with a broom. It was kind of hard on your dignity for a while, but it never bothered me much. Some people took great exception to that and fought it. You see, when you fought it, you just got more of it. I used to say, "Hell, I had as much fun running the upper class as they did running me."

Q: How did you run the upper class?

Admiral Shear: We sat at tables, 15 or 20 people to a table. Plebes were in the middle and the upper class at the ends: the first class at one end and second class at the other. Every Sunday night we had to put on a happy hour to entertain the upper classmen. We'd have maybe a half dozen plebes at the table, and we'd get together and we'd decide we were going to put on a little play on what they'd been doing over the weekend. If they'd had a bad date or something like that, we'd work them over. We had some bawdy songs we'd sing to them and tell them what a lousy bunch they were. You could get away with doing that on Sunday evening.

Q: They took that with good humor?

Admiral Shear: Oh, yes, always good humor. Always with good humor. And we would really work them over. We got to be very good at it, my table in particular. We put on some shows that wouldn't stop.

Q: Who are some of the cohorts you remember, especially from that table?

Admiral Shear: One very close friend was H. P. McNeal, who's now retired, living in Virginia Beach.* After he retired from the Navy, he took over his father's big industrial hardware company, which he's still running. And we had a number of other people; we sort of stuck to one table throughout that plebe year.

I had no problems during plebe year. I marched a little extra duty once in a while for some infraction that I got involved in, but the discipline never bothered me. I enjoyed it, and I enjoyed the upper class. But I must say that some people fought it, and some people resigned because of it. I guess you'd probably find some of that today, although the discipline today is nothing like it was then. It was very firm, but I never ran into any brutality.

Q: With your background you were probably much more suited for it than those who came straight out of high school.

Admiral Shear: Yes, coming out of the cornfields of Nebraska or something like that. So I had no problems of that kind.

Q: What do you recall about the academics?

Admiral Shear: Well, a lot of people came in with a year of college, and some came in directly from high school. I didn't have that year of college, but I had several months in prep school. I went to that prep school from September to April and took exams in April.

---

* Midshipman Horace P. McNeal, USN, graduated with the class of 1942 and eventually retired as a commander in 1962.

I must tell you something else about those exams. Commander Cochran at the prep school knew that I was working for a competitive exam based on my father's World War I eligibility. The West Point exams were a month earlier than the Naval Academy exams. He said, "Why don't you take the West Point exams for experience and practice?" I had no idea whatsoever of going to West Point. West Point exams were given over at the old Army Hospital in Washington in March. So he said, "It's not going to cost you anything. You just take those exams--because they cover the same subjects--and see how you do."

So I said "All right." So I went over there and spent three days taking those exams, and I didn't hear anything for months. As I told you, I entered the Naval Academy the tenth of June. About the first of July I got a letter from the War Department, saying on such and such a date I should report to West Point for indoctrination, for acceptance. First thing I'd heard. I was then a sworn-in midshipman. I wouldn't have gone to West Point anyway. So I had the pleasure of writing a short note saying, "Midshipman Shear regrets he is not able to accept this appointment." But the old man was right; it was good experience for me to take those exams. Just a little incident.

Now, as far as Naval Academy academics are concerned, I was never a star man.[*] Every year I stood about the middle of my class. I guess we graduated about 575, and I stood about somewhere between 200 and 250, slightly above the middle.[†] I never had any great problems, but I was never the type of guy that could just max an exam. My roommate was a boy from Seattle, Washington, and he had a year at Yale.

Q: What was his name?

Admiral Shear: Henry C. Field.[‡] Fine man. His father was a timber man on Puget Sound. It was a wealthy, wealthy family, and they had sent him up to Andover, Massachusetts, for

---

[*] The midshipmen who ranked at the top of their class academically wore stars on the lapels of their dress blue uniforms.
[†] The Naval Academy class of 1942 had 564 graduates. Shear stood number 275 in the final rankings.
[‡] Midshipman Henry Callender Field, Jr., USN, graduated from the Naval Academy in the class of 1942 and eventually retired from the Navy in 1968 as a captain.

prep school. Then he'd gone to Yale for a year, and he was a brilliant man anyway. He rarely studied, and he stood three in the class. And here I would be, with a blanket over the lamp while I was studying after hours and so forth, and Field would just scan a book and max an exam. He had a photographic memory. But he was a fine guy, and we got along well. He stood high, and I stood in the middle, and that was it. One of the great things about the Naval Academy is that they take boys from every state and from all walks of life and then turn them into competent naval officers.

Q: Do you think you did as well as you could, to ask the Rickover question?*

Admiral Shear: Admiral Rickover asked me that. I'll get into that one of these days. You could always say, "Well, if I had forgotten all sports . . ." I was on the sailing team, and first year I was on the crew. I didn't worry much about gals; I never did much dragging.† But if you'd forgotten everything, if you'd done nothing except bone and hit those books and do nothing else, you probably could have done better. Rickover would say, "Of course, you could have done better." I was one of the first to get a Rickover interview. I'll tell you about that, but we've got a long way to go before that.

Q: What do you remember about the sports participation at the Naval Academy?

Admiral Shear: I had all that sailing experience as a kid, so I had no difficulty getting on the sailing crew. The Naval Academy at that time was just getting into a sailing program. We bought six fine 44-foot wooden Luders yawls; they came while I was here. We got 15 or 20 of the international lapstrake dinghies, racing class, and we raced those in the intercollegiate competitions all up and down the East Coast. And we did very well. The Navy always had a good team, and I did well on the sailing team, both on the small boats

---

* Admiral Hyman G. Rickover, USN (Ret.), was considered the father of the nuclear Navy. He ran the Navy's nuclear-power program for many years. When he interviewed future President Jimmy Carter for the nuclear program, he asked Carter why he hadn't been the best in his class.
† "Drag" was Naval Academy slang for dating girls.

and on the larger boats. Then in the spring of the year, we'd go up to Jersey and race a Barnegat Bay class, Class E scows for example. Or we'd go up to Marblehead, Massachusetts, and race that particular class up there, the larger boats. So I had a hell of a time on that sailing team.

Q: Do you have any contact with Bob McNitt?[*] He's a very enthusiastic sailor.

Admiral Shear: Bob McNitt had left; he was the class of '38. When I arrived here, '39 was the senior class. But I know Bob well; he's an old submariner and also a destroyer man. He's very proud of the fact that the midshipmen just won this Bermuda race.

I was also on the crew, but I was too light. I was simply too light, so I couldn't make the first boat. Plebe year I rowed second and third boat, but I was simply not tall enough, wasn't heavy enough to be a crew man, so I didn't continue.

Q: How skilled were the coaches in sailing?

Admiral Shear: Very good. Very good. And I must tell you about that. Our first sailing coach was a lieutenant named William Freeman Royall, Naval Academy class of '27. He was back here on duty as a seamanship professor, over here at Luce Hall. He had stood one in his class in seamanship at the Naval Academy. He was a Maine boy, and he was damned good. He had been sailing all his life, sort of like the rest of us. We had him for a year or two, and I must tell you a little bit about Royall, because he's a great guy and he's still alive. We're still good friends, way back from those sailing days.

He was a small-boat expert, and he was hauled out of here before he finished his tour to go over as an observer with the British, because the British were then at war. He came back with how the British were handling small craft for landings and so forth and so on. He had a lot to do with that input as far as our own landing craft development was concerned.

---

[*] Rear Admiral Robert W. McNitt, USN (Ret.), is the author of Sailing at the Naval Academy: An Illustrated History (Annapolis: Naval Institute Press, 1996).

By that time, the regulars were all going to sea. Royall went to that observer's job, then he went to sea. Then they brought in a whole series of reserves. These were experienced reserve officers who had gotten out in the '30s and were brought back in for the war. The next man was a lieutenant commander named DeWolf, a wealthy man who had been sailing.* He was a Long Island sailor, as a matter of fact, up not too far from my home--quite a different scale than I had been serving with. He was a good sailor, and he became sailing coach and also seamanship coach, and he did very well by us. He was a good coach, and the Navy continued to do well both in small craft and in the larger craft. He stayed with us until after I graduated; he was here most of the war.[†]

Other things about the Naval Academy days I remember? Well, I remember those cruises very well. The second-class year we made a destroyer cruise; that was standard. Your youngster year you made a battleship cruise, and I told you we were going to Europe but were not permitted to because of the war.[‡]

Q: What ship was that in?

Admiral Shear: USS New York.[§] It happened to be a triple-expansion reciprocating steam plant, a little bit larger than I had had in the menhaden steamer, but still the same plant. She was twin screw, 15,000-horsepower per shaft, exactly the same engine.** We had a midshipman training squadron--the Arkansas, the Wyoming, and the New York--and we

---

* Lieutenant Commander Maurice M. DeWolf, USNR.
[†] DeWolf left for a time to serve in the crew of the new battleship Massachusetts (BB-59), then returned to the Naval Academy to serve as executive officer of the station ship Reina Mercedes (IX-25).
[‡] The "youngster" or third-class year at the Naval Academy is the equivalent of the sophomore year at a civilian university. The youngster cruise comes the summer after a midshipman's plebe year, his first year at the academy.
[§] USS New York (BB-34) was commissioned 15 April 1914. She had a standard displacement of 27,000 tons, was 573 feet long, and 95 feet in the beam. Her top speed was 21 knots. She was armed with ten 14-inch guns, 16 5-inch guns, and eight 3-inch guns. She had originally burned coal in her boilers but had converted to oil prior to Shear's midshipman cruise.
** The overall shaft horsepower for the New York was approximately 28,000.

went up and down the East Coast. We went to Halifax, we went up to Quebec. As we came down from Canada, one ship went to Boston; another ship went to Marblehead, Massachusetts; and my ship went to Portland, Maine. That's where I met my wife.

Q: Please describe the circumstances.

Admiral Shear: Well, it was very interesting. Our ship was anchored out in the middle of Portland Harbor. The admiral who had the midshipman training squadron was a man named Johnson.*

Q: He was in the New York.

Admiral Shear: Do you know that period?

Q: I interviewed his flag secretary, who was out of '23, a man named Elliot Strauss.†

Admiral Shear: I'll be darned. Well, he was in the New York; that's right. And, as usual in the latter part of a port visit, the admiral threw a reception. He threw this reception on board the New York, anchored out in the middle of the Portland Harbor, and people came aboard. I happened to have the duty, and the duty people had to escort guests around the ship. So a group of people would come over the gangway and cross the deck. Midshipmen in the duty section were lined up as escorts at the beck and call of the officer of the deck. Three gals came across the brow, and I was the head of the line.‡ The OOD asked me over and said, "Would you like to escort one of these ladies around the ship?"§

---

* Rear Admiral Alfred W. Johnson, USN, Commander Atlantic Squadron. The oral history of Johnson, who retired as a vice admiral, is in the Columbia University collection.
† Lieutenant Commander Elliot B. Strauss, USN. The oral history of Strauss, who retired as a rear admiral, is in the Naval Institute collection.
‡ A brow is a portable wooden bridge or ramp between the ship and a wharf, pier, or dock. It is usually fitted with wheels at the shore end.
§ OOD--officer of the deck.

There was a tall, skinny one and a fat one, and a pretty little one. So I made a beeline for the pretty little one.* [Laughter] The guys behind me got the other two. Anyway, we struck up a good acquaintance, and I showed her all around the ship. She invited me out to her house the next day, because we had only about a day before we left. Our relationship went on from there. I found out, among other things, she was an excellent cook, so all during my midshipman days she'd send me food through the mail: cakes, cookies, baked goods. I went back to Maine on leave a couple of times during the next two or three years. If you remember, in those days we had to wait two years after graduation to get married. If you got married, boy, you had to resign, right then and there.

Q: Except for Slade Cutter.†

Admiral Shear: Slade may have sneaked by, I don't know.

Q: Yes, he did.

Admiral Shear: And I know a few others who sneaked by, but you weren't supposed to do it. It was a law. Well, we graduated in December of '41, the 19th of December.‡ I had to report to my ship in Boston the day after Christmas. I would have liked to have gotten married right then, but no way I could do it. I couldn't afford to throw my career away.

By that time the reserves were coming in, in large numbers, and they had taken over half of Bancroft Hall.§ We called them "90-day wonders." They were all college graduates,

---

* The future Mrs. Shear was Elizabeth Perry of Falmouth, Maine.
† Ensign Slade D. Cutter, USN, graduated from the Naval Academy in the class of 1935 and got married prior to the end of the two-year period. He became one of the most successful U.S. submarine skippers in World War II. The oral history of Cutter, who retired as a captain, is in the Naval Institute collection.
‡ The Naval Academy class of 1942 graduated nearly six months early because of wartime manpower requirements. The Japanese attack on Pearl Harbor, on 7 December 1941, had plunged the nation into war.
§ Bancroft Hall is the large multi-wing dormitory that houses Naval Academy midshipmen. It also contains the offices of members of the executive department, including the commandant, executive officer, and battalion and company officers.

coming here for 90-day indoctrination. The law didn't apply to them; they could get married. So it became obviously a very unfair thing for academy graduates. People in Washington recognized it, and they got Congress to rescind the law. The law was rescinded on 1 April '42. The collision of the Wasp and the Stack, which I'll get to later, was on the 17th of March '42--the Ides of March.

That collision was really something. Afterward we struggled into the mouth of the Delaware River, went up to the Philadelphia Navy Yard, and were in there for repairs. As of the first of April, that law was changed, so I begged and borrowed a week's leave, got married the 16th of April 1942, and that was it. Then I was at sea most of the rest of the war. I went down to the Solomons, and then I went into submarines. I guess my first three or four years of marriage I was home a little over three months, but we just had our 50th anniversary here this spring, so it took pretty well.

Q: She was a patient woman, to wait for you.

Admiral Shear: Yes, she was--great gal, great gal.

Q: How did you take to the living accommodations on board the New York? Probably comparable to what you'd known previously, wasn't it--hammocks?

Admiral Shear: No, no, no. I always had a bunk on the menhaden steamer. The ship had 25 or 30 bunks in the forecastle for the crew; everybody had a bunk. The officers' bunks were behind the pilothouse for the captain, mate, the pilot, cook. They had a spare bunk, so I always had a bunk. Not so on the New York. We all slept in hammocks; it was a damn good experience, actually.

We were treated just like seaman recruits in training camp. The first year we all slept in hammocks, and that was a good experience. When we got up at 5:00 o'clock in the morning, we holystoned the decks.* Really holystoned them with a good old-fashioned holystone. The standard Navy breakfast was beans and horsecock, you know, that great big baloney.† We worked hard, and we had quite a bit of studying to do, and we had some good times ashore, like my time in Portland, Maine. That was a fine cruise. We all learned a lot, we had a hell of time, and we came back salty as hell, really salty as hell.

Q: How well did the sailors and midshipmen get along with each other?

Admiral Shear: Got along fine. Got along fine. We had a second class boatswain's mate assigned to our particular portion of the ship. We lived in the forward air castle of the New York, and he was our boss. He was very strict and very firm. We worked for him; we knew it and he knew it. But we never ran into any meanness or anything of that nature. The situation between the midshipmen and the enlisted crew members was never a problem in my ship.

Q: What sort of duties did you have?

Admiral Shear: You had lifeboat crew, where you had to stand by a lifeboat right around the clock, slept right beside it. You had watch-standing duties on the bridge, lookout duties. You had engineering duties down in the engine room with an old 15,000-horsepower reciprocating engine, just like my menhaden steamer. You shifted from department to department. You got indoctrination everywhere, and you stood watches everywhere. It was a damn good, damn good program, old-fashioned way of going to sea and learning what was going on.

Q: Were the lifeboats pulling boats still at that point?

---

* Holy-stoning refers to the practice of cleaning a ship's wooden decks by scraping them with bricks pushed back and forth along the planks by means of wooden handles. It is a laborious operation.
† The baloney was cut from cylindrical rolls several inches in diameter, thus leading to the nickname Navy men have long applied to sliced lunch meats.

Admiral Shear: They were pulling boats, yes, absolutely, pulling boats.* We'd have lifeboat drill; we'd lower them away and put them in the water and man the boats and go out and rescue a dummy that was thrown over the side and things of that nature. It was a very good experience, I must say.

Q: You mentioned the second summer was in a destroyer. What ship was that?

Admiral Shear: It was the Simpson, DD-221, one of the World War I four-pipers, of which we later gave 50 to the British.† I'll tell you something about that. That was a fine cruise. We had smaller groups of midshipmen since they were smaller ships, but it was the same operation. We had a petty officer assigned to us, and we went from department to department and stood watches all over the ship. We got a fair amount of ship-handling experience, because the captain would let us maneuver the ship. We'd go alongside boxes that we'd toss over the side and picked up dummies of people thrown over the side. We got a good feel for things.

Q: Where did that cruise go?

Admiral Shear: That was a coastal cruise. We went to Norfolk, went to Newport, Rhode Island, went to New York. We went up the Hudson River to West Point and showed the cadets what the Navy was all about, took a bunch of them aboard ship. It was strictly an East Coast cruise, but a very good cruise. This one was about a month to six weeks. It wasn't as long as the first cruise, the youngster cruise. Then we came back, and we had to spend the rest of the summer on aviation details. We flew some of these seaplanes we had

---

* This means they were pulled by means of crewmen wielding oars, rather than having engines.
† USS Simpson (DD-221), a Clemson-class destroyer, was commissioned 3 November 1920. Displacement was 1,215 tons, length 314 feet, and beam of 31 feet. Top speed was 35 knots. She was armed with four 4-inch guns, one 3-inch gun, and 12 21-inch torpedo tubes.

in the river at that time, and we had a couple of tours around Washington, around the Naval Gun Factory and around the powder factory at Indian Head, just to get experience and learn something of what the Navy was about on that side of the business.*

Q: What were the living conditions like in the destroyer?

Admiral Shear: We had one of the crew compartments assigned to the midshipmen. They were pipe berths with a thin mattress on them and perfectly comfortable. We ate the same food the crew did, and nobody starved.

Q: Was this typical of those ships in which you had to go up and over to go fore and aft in the ship, no internal passageways?

Admiral Shear: The four-pipers did not have internal passageways fore and aft. There were bulkheads between compartments to provide watertight integrity. The four-piper was flush deck, all the way fore and aft. Then there was sort of a spray shield just below the bridge. You had to open the door to get from the forecastle, but she was a flush deck fore and aft. That was a good cruise.

Then we come to first-class summer. By that time, the Brits had been at war since '39. That destroyer cruise was in the summer of '40. In the summer of '41, if all things had been normal, we would have had another three-month battleship cruise and gone to Europe. Well, by that time the decision had been made that we were going to graduate earlier than normal; they needed us too badly. So our graduation time was moved up from June of '42 to December of '41, and we had a steady stream of academics, essentially throughout the year and into the summer.

We had a month during the summer in which we had YP cruises up and down the bay.† We'd go out there and exercise the formations and flag hoist and flashing light and

---
* The Naval Gun Factory was in Washington, D.C.; the powder factory was at Indian Head, Maryland.
† The YP was a yard patrol craft used for training of ship handling and seamanship.

run up and down the bay and spend a couple of nights in various ports around the bay. That was fun. We took some of the new youngsters with us on that cruise. The first classmen got to be COs of the YPs, and that was fun.* I think we had about one officer to eight or ten YPs, and so we had pretty much the run of things ourselves. So that was a good experience. Among other things, that's how I got to learn something about the Eastern Shore of Maryland, because we went over there and we went to two or three of those Eastern Shore ports: Cambridge, St. Michael's, and places like that.

Q: You mentioned you had had that aviation indoctrination. Did that appeal to you at all?

Admiral Shear: Never did. I had nothing against it, but it never appealed to me. We had the early, early variety of the PBYs, twin-engine PBYs.† They made about 90 knots with a tailwind. Then we had the old Curtiss biplane, two-seat biplane, that we kept anchored here in the river; it was a seaplane. We had an aviation contingent assigned to the Naval Academy with a half dozen pilots, I guess, and we would all have some time flying around in those planes. But I never had any desire to go into aviation or any desire not to go into aviation. I loved ships. I wanted to get to sea in a ship.

Q: What was the mood among the midshipmen as the war clouds gathered more and more?

Admiral Shear: We wanted to go. We wanted to get out of here and get to sea, and there wasn't any reluctance anywhere. We knew that we were in war. Of course, we didn't know Pearl Harbor was going to happen, but when Pearl Harbor happened, the seventh of December, just two weeks before we graduated, that made us even more adamant to get out there and get cracking, get a good seagoing job.

---

* COs--commanding officers.
† The PBY Catalina was a twin-engine flying boat that performed extensive service before and during World War II. Built by Consolidated, it first entered fleet squadrons in 1936. The PBY-2 model had a wing span of 104 feet, length of 65 feet, gross eight of 28,400 pounds, and top speed of 178 miles per hour. Cruising speed was 103 mph.

Q: What do you remember about getting the news of the attack?

Admiral Shear: I remember very well. I was in my room in Bancroft Hall studying for final exams. At that time we had what we called mates of the deck, and they were the watch standers. They were midshipman watch standers. They had one on each deck, normally about third class, and they passed the word. They'd get the word from the main office about anything that had to be passed with regard to uniform or changes of schedule and so forth. It was their responsibility to shout up and down the corridors and get the word out. There wasn't any telephone in those days; you did it by word of mouth.

The mate of the deck came out with a report that Pearl Harbor was under attack, and everybody in the building just ran out to see what was going on. Of course, then we stood around all afternoon and talked about it. The information was very, very skimpy, and there was no information whatsoever on damage; that was very closely held for many weeks. But we knew we were in war, no question. So then we had a two-ocean war on our hands in very quick order.

Q: This is a little out of sequence, but three years earlier you'd had a report that the Martians had landed. Do you remember that occasion?

Admiral Shear: Oh, very well, very well.

Q: What was the reaction to that?

Admiral Shear: That was initiated by one Ned Beach.[*] You must know Ned Beach.

Q: Right, he was the five-striper.

---

[*] Edward Latimer "Ned" Beach, Naval Academy class of 1939, has written a number of books, most notably the submarine novel Run Silent, Run Deep. His father, also named Edward Latimer Beach, was an 1888 Naval Academy graduate who wrote popular fiction for boys.

Admiral Shear: He was the five-striper, and he later became my skipper when I put a new submarine in commission as his exec. I'll tell you about that. Ned Beach heard this thing on the radio, as I recall. Who was the guy that put that on?

Q: Orson Welles.*

Admiral Shear: Orson Welles. Exactly. And Beach assumed that thing to be real, and went tearing down to the main office. I don't recall exactly what word was put out, but Beach was convinced that we were being invaded by Martians. I don't know how long it was before it was called back as a false alarm. But I don't recall getting too much excited about that. I just don't recall anything like a war scare or anything of that nature. I guess some of us probably took it as a joke; we didn't really know. But let me tell you, Ned Beach didn't take it as a joke. You've probably talked to him.

Q: Yes, I have. He's able to laugh about it now.

Admiral Shear: Well, it wasn't any laughing matter that night. That occurred during study hour at night.

Q: You had a number of classmates who became flag officers, including people like Ike Kidd and Jerry Miller.† What do you remember of the future flag officers as midshipmen?

Admiral Shear: I knew them very well; both of them were in my company. Ike Kidd and I were the two in the class who made four stars. Jerry Miller made three; we had a number of three stars. We had about 20 flag officers come out of my class. Our company was in

---

* On Halloween night of 1938, actor Orson Welles dramatized H. G. Welles's futuristic novel War of the Worlds by portraying a fictitious landing in the United States by an Army of Martian invaders.
† Admiral Isaac C. Kidd, Jr., USN (Ret.); Vice Admiral Gerald E. Miller, USN (Ret.). The oral history of Miller is in the Naval Institute collection.

fourth batt, and you should know something about the fourth batt. We had a very famous fourth battalion commander named Beany Jarrett.* Did you ever hear of Beany Jarrett?

Q: Uncle Beany.

Admiral Shear: Uncle Beany, hail to the fourth batt. Magnificent man--pretty tough, but a great guy, and we loved him, just loved him. He was that kind of a guy; you just gravitated to him. He was a destroyer sailor, went out and made flag rank later on. He really had the fourth batt with a spirit that you couldn't describe. He was really up on the step in everything. Of course, he could turn right around and put you on the report like that and frequently did. But he was one hell of a guy, one of those rare guys who just has leadership oozing out all over them, and a nice guy too.

Q: What do you remember about Kidd and Miller in particular as midshipmen?

Admiral Shear: We all knew Ike because his father was a flag officer, promoted just before he was killed.† And, of course, we knew Ike because he was one of the battalion. In your own battalion, you know everybody; you know them very well. Jerry Miller had a great reputation as a ladies' man, suave, good looking, a great dancer, and I believe he played the cornet in the NA Ten, the Naval Academy midshipman orchestra.

Q: A very charming individual, as well.

Admiral Shear: Oh yes, smooth, absolutely smooth. And a good guy, nothing false about him. I believe Jerry had come out of the fleet too.

---

* Lieutenant Commander Harry Bean Jarrett, USN, who eventually retired as a vice admiral. The guided missile frigate Jarrett (FFG-33), commissioned in 1983, was named in his honor.
† Rear Admiral Isaac C. Kidd, USN, Commander Battleship Division One, was killed on board his flagship, the USS Arizona (BB-39), at Pearl Harbor on 7 December 1941.

Q: Yes. He served in the New York before he went to prep school.

Admiral Shear: I don't think he was on the New York that cruise, however, but I'm not sure. You probably have talked to Jerry, haven't you?

Q: Yes. I think he was at the Naval Academy prep school down in Norfolk, probably when you were at the school here in Annapolis.

Admiral Shear: That same year, exactly. I guess we had a dozen or 15 people who came from the fleet. Those people who came from the fleet were good people. They had their feet on the ground, and they had some experience in the fleet, and they had gone to the prep school. They were very solid people. Jerry was one of them. I was just trying to think of something else. If I had my class book here, I could spot them right like that. I should have brought it with me.

Q: I heard about Jarrett from Paul Backus who was the president of the class ahead of you.*

Admiral Shear: Yes, and Paul Backus was in my battalion.

Q: What do you recall about him? He was a temperamental fellow.

Admiral Shear: Yes, he was. But you couldn't tell that much about him. He was a short guy, and he was around. I don't recall anything critical about him. I got quite deeply involved with him later, on a tour at the Pentagon when we got involved in the missile business. I'll tell you about that later. That'll probably be next week before we get to that one.

---

* The oral history of Commander Paul H. Backus, USN (Ret.), is in the Naval Institute collection.

I was just trying to think of other flag officers in my battalion. Mark Woods was not in my battalion.* Bill Houser was another good three-star flag officer, aviator.† As you get older your memory gets bad, I find that more, and my wife says my memory is gone completely.

Q: I wouldn't agree with her.

Admiral Shear: Let me see if there's anything that I missed here that I wanted to touch base with you on. I made some notes here.

I must say that these two men at the Cochran-Bryan Prep School had a big influence on me. They were good guys, and they were hard. They were not mean, but they made you work, made you work. I remember Cochran used to lecture us about what we had to do to do well, and I can remember almost exactly what he used to say. He would say, "The difference between the man who is on top and the man who is just getting by you could put on the head of a pin. Now, dammit, I want you boys to study, and I want you all to be that man on the top!" He'd repeat that about once a month. Pretty good advice.

Q: It obviously stuck with you.

Admiral Shear: I remember that like it was yesterday. I think I hit all the highlights on the Naval Academy. Anything you want to ask me about the Naval Academy other than my classmates?

Q: You just mentioned that you had a limited social life. Did you have any at all?

Admiral Shear: Oh, yes. But I was not one of these guys that wanted to go to every dance every Saturday night. After I had met my future wife in Maine, she'd come down occasionally. But that was a long trip from Maine, and the Depression was on then. Her

---

* Rear Admiral Mark W. Woods, USN (Ret.).
† Vice Admiral William D. Houser, USN (Ret.)

family didn't have much money either. Her father was a good competent lawyer, but he wasn't a wealthy man. So she'd come down once in a while, and I know I met a couple of these local gals for an occasional dance. But I was not a socialite. I didn't have to get to every dance. I'd much rather be out there sailing than I would chasing girls around town.

Q: What do you remember about attending the sports events, such as the Army-Navy football games?

Admiral Shear: Oh, those were always great events. We had the old steam trains. They would come down on the old trolley line, what we called the "Rattle, Ramble, and Bump." Let's see, it used to run to Washington and Baltimore. By the time we got here, the Washington line had been discontinued, but it still ran between Annapolis and Baltimore. Any time you went home on leave, you went on that rickety old train to Baltimore and got your train. The roadbed wasn't too hot, so when we went to football games they backed those steam trains down very slowly across the old bridge right around here at the old Annapolis station. And we'd march down there and get aboard. We'd have to go very slowly until we got off in Baltimore. Then we'd get on the main line, and we could go where we had to go, whether it was Philadelphia or Princeton or Yale or wherever it was going to be. We chartered an entire train. But everybody remembers that "Rattle, Ramble, and Bump" from those days. That was a line of its own.

Q: What do you remember about the pageantry connected with the games?

Admiral Shear: My plebe year I was a member of the drum and bugle corps, because I had played a trombone in the high school band. One of the things you had to fill out when you entered was what kind of a musical instrument you could handle. So I put down that I played the trombone. Well, hell's bells, that made me a candidate for the big bugles, but I wasn't particularly enthralled with that drum and bugle Corps. We had a good bunch in it, and we played pretty well, but nothing like they do today, nothing that fancy. At that time we would always take only half of the regiment. But if you were in the drum and bugle corps you got to go to all of them, so that was an advantage. But I stayed in that drum and bugle corps for only one year. I had things I wanted to do other than that, but I got a couple of extra ball games out of it.

Pageantry. We always marched on the field to perfection. That was always a good thing. We were very good at that. In those days we had cards. You had so many cards to carry, and they had a little gouge on it.[*] They'd given a signal, and you flipped your card, some sort of a designation, a goat or flag or something would show up.

Q: So you'd make a design in the stands.

Admiral Shear: Make a design, yes. I don't know whether they do it anymore or not, but I think we did it every year. Then we always had a few hours off after a game before heading back to the train. Wasn't much opportunity to do much around town, but you had a little chance to walk around, and someone would invite you in for a meal or something like that. Other pageantry than that, we had the U.S. Naval Academy Band, we had the drum and bugle corps, then we had the regiment of midshipmen. I must say we really could march; we were damn good. I always said we were better than West Point, but they were damn good too. On signal we would reverse. We'd salute one side then reverse and salute the other side. That was always very spectacular to the people in the stands.

Q: Did you take part in the inaugural parade in 1941?

Admiral Shear: You know, I don't recall if we did or not. We must have.

Q: That was when Roosevelt began his third term.[†]

---

[*] "Gouge" is a slang term for an instruction sheet or a prepared answer to a problem or examination.
[†] President Franklin D. Roosevelt's third term began with his inauguration on 20 January 1941.

Admiral Shear: That's right. We must have marched in that. I don't think we all marched, might have been half, I don't recall if I was there or not. It doesn't stick with me.

Q: What professors do you remember from your time here?

Admiral Shear: Oh, Webb was a superb math prof. Of course, the man I lived with, Mayer, was very good in math. The pair who wrote the book were very good, talking about math now. Slipstick Willie, the physics prof, everybody knew Slipstick Willie.* Magnificent guy. Then we had [chuckle]--we had Sterile Carroll Alden; everybody knew Sterile Carroll Alden.

Q: What prompted that nickname?

Admiral Shear: He looked like he was just a wisp, going to blow away, very slender little guy. He was known by everybody as Sterile Carroll. He was head of the "Bull" Department.† We had some good bull profs. We had a number of profs who were here that were just one lesson ahead of us, really. They weren't really profs. They had a gouge, and they had to keep ahead of us. But some of them were very good, and they went beyond what they had to do and so forth.

John Sidney McCain, Jr., was one of those who did more.‡ He was then a lieutenant (junior grade), and they called him "Good Goddamn McCain." Every morning he'd come in

---

* "Slipstick Willie" was the nickname given Professor Earl W. Thomson because of his prowess with a slide rule. He taught at the Naval Academy from 1919 to 1959. For details see Shipmate magazine, published by the Naval Academy Alumni Association, June 1982, page 13.
† "Bull" was the nickname for the Department of English, History, and Government. Dr. Carroll Storrs Alden was department chairman.
‡ McCain taught physics at the Naval Academy, 1938-40. He eventually reached the rank of four-star admiral, serving as Commander in Chief Pacific, 1968-72.

the classroom and say, "Good goddamn morning, gentlemen." I've known McCain since then. He was John Sidney McCain's son, who was a great three-star combat aviator.[*]

Q: And the father of the present Senator McCain.[†]

Admiral Shear: Yes, exactly, exactly. Of course, he was a submariner, and I got to know him well in my submarine days. He was also CinCUSNavEur at one time, before I was over there.[‡] When I had the job, he came over and spent a summer over there. We became very good friends. I just mention him as one. Benny Field was another one of our coaching people.[§] Benny Field and Bill Royall were very good in the seamanship department. Then we had Diesel Dan, a professor in the steam department. He was a big damage control man. Diesel Dan--I can't think of his name. Everybody knew Diesel Dan.

We had the civilian professionals. Then we had the naval officers who were assigned here for a tour of duty. Some of those naval officers just got by and sort of kept one lesson ahead of you. Others really dug in and became very competent instructors, and you could spot them very quickly. There was another one who was quite good in the English department, a bull professor, Lieutenant Ben Scott Custer.[**] He became quite well known. Before he retired, he was professor of naval science at Princeton. Captain Fort was head of the math department, and Commander Clarke was with him.[††]

Q: There was a man named A. B. Cook.

---

[*] Vice Admiral John S. McCain, USN, was Commander Task Force 38, the fast carrier task force, during the closing months of World War II.
[†] John S. McCain III, a naval aviator, was a prisoner of war in the Vietnam War. He retired from active duty as a captain in 1981. As a Republican from the state of Arizona, he was subsequently elected to the House of Representatives in 1982 and the U.S. Senate in 1986.
[‡] Admiral John S. McCain, Jr., USN, served as Commander in Chief U.S. Naval Forces Europe, May 1967 to July 1968.
[§] Lieutenant Benjamin P. Field, Jr., USN.
[**] The oral history of Rear Admiral Benjamin S. Custer, USN (Ret.), is in the Columbia University collection.
[††] Captain George H. Fort, USN; Commander William P. O. Clarke, USN.

Harold E. Shear #1 - 38

Admiral Shear: Oh, yes, Allen Blow Cook. He was sort of a fixture in the bull department, and he would make midshipman cruises with us. Matter of fact, some of the others were invited to make midshipmen cruises periodically. But Allen Blow Cook went whenever he had the chance. He was something of a character. I believe he was a Naval Academy graduate.*

Q: I think you're right.

Admiral Shear: But he'd only stayed in the Navy a couple of years. He came back here and made a career as a bull prof.

Q: Roy Benson was highly respected in the navigation department.†

Admiral Shear: Oh, yes. Absolutely. "Ensign Benson," they called him. Yes, Roy Benson was a fine officer. Of course, I got to know him very well later on in years. Eller, who became historian of the Navy, was here, I believe, in the ordnance department, and he had a good reputation.‡ He's the type of guy who would have a good reputation.

Q: He was involved in writing a textbook on ordnance during that period.

Admiral Shear: Yes, that's absolutely correct. Yes. I think he finished that textbook before we left here.

Q: Any of the duty officers that particularly stand out, in addition to Jarrett?

---

* Cook graduated from the Naval Academy in 1921 and retired in 1926 as a lieutenant (junior grade).
† Lieutenant Roy S. Benson, USN. The oral history of Benson, who retired as a rear admiral, is in the Naval Institute collection.
‡ Lieutenant Commander Ernest M. Eller, USN. The oral history of Eller, who retired as a rear admiral, is in the Naval Institute collection.

Admiral Shear: Oh, yes. Yes, yes. The Scoutmaster. [Chuckles] Lieutenant Commander Graham always had a Boy Scout brace on him, 24 hours a day.[*] I think he slept with that brace on. During our plebe year, he was very good at spotting us and putting us on report. Another one that we saw a lot of was Jerry Wright.[†] He was here as a battalion commander. In those days we had four battalions in a regiment of 2,000-odd midshipmen. Others who stood out as far as officers on duty here--when we arrived the superintendent was Wilson Brown.[‡] A man named Milo F. Draemel was the commandant of midshipmen, and he was a very distinguished gentleman.[§] Sort of a picture portrait of what a naval officer should look like and act like. Very fine man. He went on and became flag officer. I don't recall what he did during the war.

Q: He had some health problems, and I think he wound up at the Philadelphia Navy Yard.

Admiral Shear: Could be. I don't recall. I lost track of him, but you must have done some research on all these people.

Q: Well, in his case I met his daughter who lives here in Annapolis.

Admiral Shear: Oh, is that so?

Q: She married a man named Balch out of the class of '39.[**]

Admiral Shear: I remember Balch. Tall, slender guy, isn't he?

---

[*] Lieutenant Commander Roy W. M. Graham, USN.
[†] Commander Jerauld Wright, USN, who later became a four-star admiral and commanded the Atlantic Fleet, 1954-60.
[‡] Rear Admiral Wilson Brown, USN, was superintendent of the Naval Academy from February 1938 to February 1941.
[§] Captain Milo Frederick Draemel, USN, served as commandant, 1937-1940.
[**] Midshipman John B. Balch, USN, who eventually retired as a captain in 1967.

Q: Well, not so slender anymore.

Admiral Shear: I remember Balch in '39.

I got to know Draemel a little bit because of my roommate, Hank Field from Seattle. His folks were fairly close friends of Draemel, and at one period Hank Field's sister came here and spent a week or so with the Draemels. We had a dinner or two together, and I met them in that way. But Draemel himself was a fine commandant and a very popular commandant.

Then the man who took over from Draemel was someone whom we despised, Captain Vossler.[*] Of course, war clouds were coming on then, and restrictions were being imposed on us around the Naval Academy here. We were then scheduled to graduate in three and a half years instead of four. For that last year our academics were condensed, our leaves were condensed, and we started to get a wartime atmosphere around here.

One of the things that Vossler did was to cancel our last Christmas leave. That was at the end of 1940, when we were supposed to have about a ten-day leave. The entire regiment of midshipmen were very unhappy about that leave cancellation. I never knew Vossler himself other than seeing him around in his job as commandant. None of us liked this guy. I don't know if he was that bad or not, but none of us liked him anyway. I had no personal contact with him.

Q: Probably just as well.

Admiral Shear: Probably just as well.

Q: There was an executive officer named Thebaud, who was highly thought of.[†]

Admiral Shear: Oh, very highly thought of. He swore us in to the Naval Academy, got us all there in Memorial Hall and swore us in. Yes, he was a destroyer sailor, and I ran into

---

[*] Captain Francis A. L. Vossler, USN, served as commandant, 1940-1941.
[†] Commander Leo H. Thebaud, USN.

him in Iceland just a month or two after I reported on board the Stack. We were alongside the tender up there for some minor work, and Thebaud was the squadron commander with his flag in the destroyer tender.*

Q: And he literally wrote the book on leadership.†

Admiral Shear: Yep, very fine man. Very correct man. Who else do you remember from those days who I should know?

Q: Russell Willson was the superintendent, I think, during your first class year.

Admiral Shear: Wilson Brown was superintendent when we arrived here. Russell Willson, I guess, was superintendent when we graduated and he had a son in '41.‡

Q: And he had a daughter who married Bob Rice out of '27, later CO of the Drum.§

Admiral Shear: I know Bob Rice, submariner, yes. Matter of fact, I made a wolf pack run with the Drum, which I'll tell you about here before we get through.

Q: Well, he married Russell Willson's daughter.

Admiral Shear: Russell Willson might have had a daughter maybe in her 20s or 30s at that time. Rice was about '27, that's correct. Any other names that you ring a bell on?

---

* As a captain, Thebaud commanded Destroyer Squadron 13 during the early part of World War II.
† Leo H. Thebaud, Naval Leadership, With Some Hints to Junior Officers and Others; a Compilation by and for the Navy, First Edition (Annapolis: U.S. Naval Institute, 1924).
‡ Rear Admiral Russell Willson, USN, was superintendent of the Naval Academy from February 1941 to January 1942. His son was Russell Willson, Jr.
§ Robert H. Rice, who eventually retired as a vice admiral.

Q: Not offhand. But it leads us up to graduation. What do you remember about the ceremony itself.

Admiral Shear: I remember the ceremony very well. Frank Knox was Secretary of the Navy.[*] He came down and made a speech about all the great things we were going to have to do to save the nation. I won't say it was an austere affair, but we didn't have a June Week, so it was fairly cut and dried. His speech is on record around here somewhere.

I remember very well one thing he did. Of course, Ike Kidd's father had just been killed, and when Ike got his diploma, Frank Knox spent several minutes with him, right there on the platform. I think that made quite an impression on all of us.

But we wanted one thing in those days. We wanted to get that diploma and get out of here and get on to the next duty station. Some of us were ordered to ships in Pearl Harbor which were sunk or so badly damaged they couldn't go to sea. So a handful of my classmates went right directly into submarines, without going to sub school.

I'd gotten to know that I wanted a small ship rather than a big ship. So when we graduated I requested a destroyer. You had to draw lots, so your ship depended on where you stood in your lots. You had to put down two or three choices. I got my first choice of a destroyer, and she was one of the Benham class. The Benham class was the 397 class, the fastest class the Navy ever built, if you've looked at the history. They made 40 knots or better. The Benham class included the hull numbers 397 to 408, and I got the Stack, 406.[†] She was built in Norfolk Navy Yard, and she was just a little over two years old when I reported aboard.

I graduated on the 19th. I had to report to the Boston Navy Yard the day after Christmas. I reported in, and I said, "I have orders to Stack."

They said, "Your ship's not here."

I said, "Well, where is she?"

---

[*] William Franklin Knox served as Secretary of the Navy from 11 July 1940 until his death on 28 April 1944.
[†] USS Stack (DD-406) was commissioned 20 November 1939. She had a standard displacement of 1,500 tons, was 341 feet long, and 36 feet in the beam. Her design speed was 38.5 knots. She was armed with four 5-inch guns and 16 21-inch torpedo tubes.

They said, "We can't tell you." Everything was very hush-hush and quiet. They said, "You come back tomorrow." So I went back tomorrow, and I said, "I'm looking for the Stack."

They said, "She's not here. We can't tell you where, but we're going to put you on another destroyer who's going to join up with the Stack."

So I was ordered to Gwin for transportation. The Stack was a 1,500-ton, single-pipe ship, but the Gwin was one of the first of the new two-pipers, 1,650 tons. They had the raised forecastle on them. They were nice ships.

The next day we got under way, and I was out there on the high seas looking for the Stack. We had a section of a convoy deploying from Boston and a section of a convoy deploying from New York and a section of a convoy deploying from Halifax. A day or two at sea we all joined forces, and there was my ship, the Stack, with one of the troopships that joined up. The skipper of the Gwin, a very fine man out of the early '20s, a fellow named Higgins, sent a flashing light over to the CO of the Stack, saying, "We have your man Shear on board."* [Chuckles]

I remember the reply he got back: "I feel sure you will indoctrinate him properly." I was right on the watch list with the rest of them. So we joined up, and we didn't know where we were going. We ended up in Iceland. That was the height of the submarine war, but we didn't lose a ship going up there either. We all went into Hvalfjordur, which was that huge fjord up the coast from Reykjavik. We were in there for a couple of days, and then we split the convoy up. One section went up to Murmansk, and one section went over to the U.K.† I joined the Stack there, and we took the section over to the U.K. and dropped them off just outside of Londonderry for the Brits. Then we came back and picked up another convoy from Iceland and took them back to New York. We spent that entire winter of '41 and '42 in North Atlantic convoys.

---

* Commander John M. Higgins, USN, Naval Academy class of 1922, eventually became a rear admiral and commanded a task force in the Korean War.
† Murmansk is a port in north Russia. The Soviet Union joined the war on the Allied side after the German attack on Russia in the spring of 1941. U.K.--United Kingdom.

Q: Please describe convoy duty.

Admiral Shear: All right. That's very interesting. You had certain types of convoys. You had the general merchant convoys, and they were limited to the speed of the slowest ship. Sometimes those ships went all the way back to World War I days, because we weren't really geared up for the big shipbuilding program yet. They were limited to maybe eight or nine knots, and that was bad because the German submarines would just catch up with them.

Now, the tankers and the troopships were put together in convoys that made better speed, 12 or 15 knots, and that's what we were with mostly, ships I made runs to Iceland and the U.K. We never got ashore in the U.K. We just turned it over to the Brits and turned around and hauled back to pick up more ships. We did lose a Coast Guard cutter, one of the big new Coast Guard cutters, one of our escorts, just outside of Iceland one night.

Q: Alexander Hamilton.

Admiral Shear: Alexander Hamilton. That's right. How'd you know that?

Q: We had an article about it.*

Admiral Shear: Did you? Well, I'll tell you something. We were in that same convoy. I, being an ensign, said they should never have abandoned the Hamilton. They abandoned her when she was still afloat. She was still afloat the next day, and I think they put people back aboard her. But progressive flooding eventually got her, and she sank and was lost. I think if they had stuck with her they could have gotten her into Reykjavik. But who am I to

---

* The USCGC Alexander Hamilton (WPG-34) was torpedoed and sunk ten miles off Iceland on 29 January 1942 while towing a disabled storeship. For a description of the "Secretary"-class cutters, see John M. Waters, Jr., "A Ship for All Seasons," Naval History, Winter 1988, pages 34-41.

comment on that--50-odd years later and a young ensign at the time? But a lot of the other skippers around there felt they shouldn't have lost that ship. But that's neither here nor there.

We had a submarine contact that day and made repeated depth charge runs on it, but I don't know whether we ever had a real contact or not. We never got credit for sinking a submarine, and it was a nervous situation. But we did not lose any merchant ships in that convoy.

Q: Did these destroyers have kind of a sheep dog role, roving around on the perimeter?

Admiral Shear: Both. You had a fixed position, then you had some roving positions, and none of us had radar in those days. The first radars were called the bed-spring type.* They went to the big ships--the battleships and cruisers and carriers. I'll tell you when we got ours; we got ours after that collision. We were in the Philadelphia Navy Yard in April. We had no radar, so how did you keep station on these ships? You got to be very good at using your binoculars and judging distance by the size of the blob in the binocular. This is where you should be and where the merchant ship should be. It's amazing how accurately you could judge that. But sometimes in the morning, after steaming all night in the darkness, you'd find a couple of your columns pretty well scattered out, and you'd have to get out and chase them and get them back into position.

Q: That was the sheep dog job.

Admiral Shear: That's right. We all had to do that. But it's very interesting.

Q: Did you use stadimeters?

---

* This was the CXAM air-search radar. The antenna resembled the metal framework for a mattress.

Admiral Shear: Used stadimeters, yes.* But station keeping at night, the size of that blob in your binoculars was one of the primary means of keeping on station.

Q: And you were probably darkened ship, weren't you?

Admiral Shear: Oh, absolutely, absolutely--always. From the time you left port you were darkened ship. But you could do wonders with that blob. We got to be pretty damn good at it.

Q: How good was your sonar?

Admiral Shear: Old QC ping sonar--wasn't worth a damn. We didn't know it, but it wasn't. When I got into submarines later, that sonar never scared me a bit. We pinged on that thing all the time, had good watch standers. They knew it; they were competent on the equipment, but you just train and ping, train and ping, train and ping. If you picked up anything, it was a miracle.

Once in a while, you'd get a contact, and a few ships were credited with sinking submarines, but what really got the submarine problem under control was the jeep carriers and radar.† And then the vast number of patrol craft that came out, the DEs and the big PCs and, of course, the destroyers themselves that came out in huge numbers as the war progressed.‡ That winter of '41 and '42 was a very bleak winter. Losses along this East Coast were tremendous. We didn't get that North Atlantic submarine threat under control until late in '43.

Q: In retrospect, how much value were those destroyers in escorting the convoys?

---

* The stadimeter is a mechanical device for measuring the range to another ship when the height of her mast is known.
† "Jeep" carriers was the nickname for the escort carriers, CVEs, which were considerably smaller than the large attack-type aircraft carriers.
‡ DEs--destroyer escorts; PCs--patrol craft.

Admiral Shear: Well, they were of value to anyone taking a look at the periscope and seeing that there was a destroyer there or a group of destroyers. We were of value in keeping the convoys assembled. There isn't any question, convoys per se were the proper way to get these ships across.

Q Maybe you had some deterrent value in that the submarines would be more cautious about attacking.

Admiral Shear: Oh, yes, no question, no question. And we kept the convoys closed up and in proper arrangement and so forth. It certainly kept the wolf packs down, but the wolf packs were damn good, just as our wolf packs were very good later, and I'll tell you some more about that. Wolf packs were very good, and they were operating at will there in '39, '40, '41, into '42. Most of their sinkings were on the surface at night--very, very effective, which was precisely what we did later on.

Q: Wolf packs were also the U-boats' Achilles' heel, because they did so much radio communication.

Admiral Shear: That's right, and that's one thing we did have. We could get fixes ourselves when these U-boats were transmitting, and we'd get position reports from the U.K. and from the intercept stations on both our coast and in Newfoundland and Iceland and the U.K. So you could cross bearings and get a general area where they were.

But it took from '39 to '43 to get that German submarine problem under control. They damn near won the Battle of the Atlantic. Anybody who tells you differently doesn't know what he's talking about. Just the productivity of the United States and the new developments, radar and jeep carriers and thousands of merchant ships we kept turning out--if we hadn't, we'd have never got the stuff across. I never made one of those Murmansk runs. Those Murmansk runs were brutal, both from submarines and those twin-engine Focke-Wulfs coming out of Norway. If you got a quarter of your ships through up to Murmansk, you were lucky.

Q: That was considered the worst.

Admiral Shear: That's right. That was the worst.

Q: Well, one thing everybody talks about from those convoys is the weather. What are your recollections?

Admiral Shear: Oh, I remember that weather very, very well. It was brutal, absolutely brutal. You'd just go from one North Atlantic gale to another North Atlantic gale, rolling your rails under most of the time. You have two major lows in the area. You have the Kodiak low and the Icelandic low. The Icelandic low, you might have a 100-knot gale. Then the next hour you'd have a calm. Then a few hours later you'd have another 100-knot gale.

I remember the day I reported aboard the Stack in Hvalfjordur, after we got that convoy assembled up there. We had a 100-knot gale that night. We had two anchors down and were steaming to the anchors, holding our position. That North Atlantic weather is just a brutal situation, trying to get those convoys across. Of course, I guess you got a certain amount of break in the weather in protection from submarines. But the submarines were able to handle themselves pretty well in that weather. The submarines I became very familiar with later; you could just take that water over you and keep right on going.

Q: How did the Stack ride?

Admiral Shear: Like any destroyer, but she was a good, able ship. She had the Mark 33 director, and the next class had the Mark 37 director.* The Mark 37 was a heavier director higher up, and that's the class that rolled very badly. I think that started with the Sims.

---

* These were directors to compute the range and bearing to a target and aim the ships' 5-inch guns accordingly. Initially they relied solely on optics; later fire control radars were added to the directors.

They were still one-piper ships, and at one time they thought they were going to have to reballast those ships, but I don't think they did. Any destroyer in North Atlantic weather is going to roll around a lot, but we never felt unsafe. Took a lot of green water over the bridge, but we never felt the ship was unstable.

I had a magnificent skipper. I haven't told you about that yet.

Q: Well, please do.

Admiral Shear: His name was Isaiah Olch, out of the class of '22.[*] He was a naval officer of the old school, and there couldn't have been a finer man for the first ship a young ensign was reporting to. He called me in a day or two after I got there, and he said, "Shear, I've got something I want you to do. We've got a bunch of reserve ensigns aboard here, and they aren't Naval Academy type. They're good men, but they aren't Naval Academy type. I want you to show them the ropes."

Well, it turned out they were damned good people, so I didn't have to show them the ropes. They were 90-day wonders, and they were fine people. Let me tell you, I learned respect for that crowd very quickly, and we could never have won the war without them. We took them aboard by the hundred of thousands, all over the Navy. There's no way we could have won the war with only the products from the Naval Academy.

Q: Well, especially those early reserve officers, who were almost cream-of-the-crop type guys.

Admiral Shear: They were from the Ivy League group, and they had been down here for 90 days, and they had been up in the old training ship in New York for 90 days and several other places around the country. They were fine people. As the war continued on, we got more and more of these younger fellows. They all turned out to be good people. Get a little experience behind them, they did very well. Did very well.

---

[*] Commander Isaiah Olch, USN.

Q: What else do you remember about Olch?

Admiral Shear: He was one of the finest ship handlers I've ever been acquainted with. Almost as good as my stepfather, who was absolutely superb. But Cy Olch was a great ship handler. He was a naval officer of the old school.

Q: What do you mean by that?

Admiral Shear: He was very correct. He wasn't demanding, he wasn't nasty, but you knew that he was skipper of that ship, and he was as good as they come.

Q: Was there a great deal of formality?

Admiral Shear: A certain amount. A certain amount, but not obsessively so.

Q: Probably less than in a battleship.

Admiral Shear: Oh, yes, absolutely, less than in a battleship. When I left the Naval Academy there wasn't any question, I wanted to go to a small ship. I didn't know I wanted to go to submarines at that time, but I knew I wanted to go to a small ship. Because you got to know everybody very well; you got to know the wardroom, you got to know the crew. And Cy Olch was just the absolutely right guy to start out with.

And we had a good exec, a fellow named Williamson out of '31, and we had John McMullen out of '40, who was the chief engineer.[*] At that time ComDesLant had put out a directive, knowing that so many ships were coming out so quickly, and one of the weaknesses was in engineers.[†] He said there must be two engineers in every destroyer in

---

[*] Lieutenant Francis T. Williamson, USN; Ensign John J. McMullen, USN. McMullen later became well known as head of a naval architecture firm and owner of professional sports teams.
[†] ComDesLant--Commander Destroyer Force Atlantic Fleet.

training. Therefore Captain Olch said, "You're going to be assistant engineer. You'd better learn fast because you're going to have to relieve McMullen, because he's going to leave pretty soon." That was good advice. McMullen got me down there in those bilges, tail down, head up, and I got checked out in that plant very thoroughly, very quickly.

Q: What do you recall about the personalities of the skipper and McMullen?

Admiral Shear: Cy Olch was a pleasant guy. He was a firm guy, he was almost austere, but not in a negative sort of way.

Q: Highly respected, it sounds like.

Admiral Shear: Oh, absolutely, Every man in the crew loved him. But he was not an easygoing type. The crew never took advantage of him; I'll tell you that. And he could be very firm when he had to. But he was a great naval officer. He never made flag. Among other things, he was a communications specialist, and they needed a communications specialist in one of the sea frontiers. He had to take that job rather than going on into higher sea jobs later on in the war.

Q: Well, the collision with the Wasp probably didn't help him either.*

Admiral Shear: That didn't help him either. That didn't help him, but he was not at fault. I'll tell you about that night.

You asked about McMullen. McMullen I had known at the Naval Academy. McMullen, among other things, loved to sail, particularly the bigger boats. We'd race around the Chesapeake with McMullen. Sometimes I'd be in his boat and sometimes another. McMullen was also a crackerjack athlete, but he wasn't quite good enough to

---

* The Stack collided with the aircraft carrier Wasp (CV-7) at 0550 on the morning of 17 March 1942. The ships were part of a task group steaming from Casco Bay, Maine, to Norfolk, Virginia.

make the varsity in anything. I remember he was voted the best B-team football player they had in his class, but he never made the varsity.

He was a very competitive, hard-charging guy. I got to know his parents very well later on. His father ran a marine repair operation in Hoboken, New Jersey, repair of merchant ships. And he was well known in and out of New York where various shipping companies came in to get their ships repaired. It wasn't a shipyard; it was a machine shop-type of operation where he'd send a gang of men out to a ship that needed some work done at anchorage or pier or something like that. He had a very good reputation. And McMullen later took that business over. I'll tell you about that later.

I got along fine with McMullen. He worked me hard; he was pretty hard on his troops too.

Q: In what ways?

Admiral Shear: I think he was kind of demanding, and I don't think he recognized the capacity of his talent as much as he might have. He had some crackerjack people. These were the pre-World War II petty officers. The chiefs and first and second class, they knew their stuff.

Q: They could tell by the sound whether something was wrong.

Admiral Shear: Absolutely. They were absolutely superb. And those chiefs brought me up in a hurry. They taught me all kinds of things. And the first class too. We have a reunion every few years. I still keep in touch with some of them.

Q: I've gotten the impression McMullen was very sound professionally.

Admiral Shear: Oh, absolutely. He stood near the top of his class, crackerjack engineer, knew his stuff backwards and forwards.* A lot of him rubbed off on me, I'll tell you. By the time he left that ship, I knew as much about that plant as he did. We had a good relationship, a very good relationship, and we've been close friends ever since. He came up to our 50th wedding anniversary this spring, and I said, "John McMullen is one of the guys I'm beholden to, because he gave me a week off to get married." [Chuckles]

Q: Did you get ashore in Iceland at all?

Admiral Shear: I never got ashore once in Iceland. That was a wartime situation up there. A few of the officers did. Since I was George, there were more things for me to do in the ship, but I could go ashore just for an hour or so.† That was a fighting operation. You go in there, and first thing you did, you'd fuel up. If you had any critical repairs, you'd have a tender or two there, but normally you didn't need anything. Just needed fuel and get out again, pick up a convoy, headed east to west and there you were. That magnificent huge fjord north of Reykjavik, you could put 200 ships there and lose them. Perfectly protected by those mountains coming right down to the water's edge, critically important piece of real estate for that war.

Q: Did you ever refuel at sea in that ship?

Admiral Shear: Yes, many times. Many times. We got very good at that. Later on, when I had command of the Sacramento, we had it down to an absolute science. I'll tell you more about that. Absolute science. But fueling at sea became routine, both in the Atlantic and Pacific.

Q: Well, it was still relatively new early in the war.

---

* McMullen finished number 43 of the 456 graduates in the Naval Academy class of 1940.
† "George" is the traditional nickname given to the most junior ensign serving in a ship.

Admiral Shear: Oh, yes. Absolutely. Early in the war it was relatively new, oh, absolutely. But by late '42 in the Pacific it was routine.

Q: You haven't talked in detail about the collision. Do you want to discuss that?

Admiral Shear: Sure. This was February by now. We got back to New York from an Iceland convoy, one of those that split up and part went to Halifax and part went to New York. We took the New York element into New York. As we approached, coming down Ambrose Channel, there was a signal light where the net crossed, where the Verazzano Bridge is now, Staten Island to Brooklyn. They had to open the gate to let you get through the net.

We thought we were going to have a few days off to relax around New York. Instead, a flashing light came to the ship: "Stack, fuel immediately and proceed at best speed to Boston." Well, it took a couple of hours to fuel. We went through the East River, and as soon as we cleared the East River, got into Long Island Sound, the captain said, "Okay, open her up." So we went at flank speed and went down the Long Island Sound at 30 knots and went through the Cape Cod Canal. We got to Boston just at dusk.

We came into Boston Harbor, and we saw what our next job was. There was the Queen Mary over in South Boston loading troops, and she loaded 15,000 troops.* We had two ships of DesDiv 15 there, the Stack and the Sterett.† The Sterett had come with us out of New York. So we got under way at daylight the next morning, Queen Mary right behind us, loaded to the gills with troops. Those fast ships didn't go in convoys; they just turned them loose. So we took her 600 or 700 miles at sea, and as soon as she cleared the harbor she'd worked up to about 35 knots. We were patrolling ahead of her, so we were making 40 knots back and forth across her bow. We were using the sonar, even though we knew the sonar wasn't worth a damn at that speed. But at least we were there, we were present; they could see they had a couple of destroyer escorts.

---

* The Queen Mary was a large British passenger liner converted for use as a fast troop transport in World War II.
† DesDiv--destroyer division.

Q: You were there for moral support.

Admiral Shear: Moral support. We got 600 or 700 miles at sea, and we turned her loose. She was headed for North Africa, and they sent us a very warm and glowing message from the CO of the Queen Mary to the CO of the Stack and the Sterett. That was the way those big ships ran all during the war, those 30 knotters, both the U.S. and British ships. They carried hundreds and hundreds of thousands of troops that way. But when you put 15,000 or 16,000 men aboard a ship like that, they are just all over the place, just crawling all over the ship.

So there we were. By then it was late February and we got up to Casco Bay, and we had a big operation out of Casco Bay, Maine. Couple of tenders there all the time, big portion of the fleet in and out of there because that's a magnificent bay, if you know the Maine coast--deep water, well protected by islands. You could put half the fleet in there. The Wasp was there with a bunch of other ships, so we worked with the Wasp in the Gulf of Maine for a couple of weeks getting their flight group in shape--a lot of flight operations and so forth.

Then we were ordered to take her to Norfolk for an important assignment. We didn't know what the assignment was. So the Stack and Sterett took her out of the Casco Bay, Maine, in lousy March weather, absolute pea-soup fog, no radar. The Wasp had one of the early versions of radar; no radar on either destroyer. As we headed for Norfolk, we got down opposite the Delaware Capes. The Wasp was telling the two destroyers over TBS--that's the voice radio, bridge to bridge--what our position was. They were keeping us in position by their radar. We couldn't see a damn thing. We were just running on what we knew to be 25-knot speed, and we had the Stack on one side and the Sterett on the other, two of the Benham-class destroyers. Well, it became apparent that the Wasp was easing over toward us, and we couldn't see anything. We couldn't exactly tell where she was. We could tell that she was easing over, and it turned out later that her gyro was off a degree or two.

Well, the first thing we knew, the Wasp's bow loomed out of the fog, literally feet away, and hit us amidships, right at the forward fireroom, right at the whaleboat davit.* If it hadn't been for that whaleboat davit, we'd have been sunk. So the ship heard the Wasp coming, and it hit us a glancing blow like that. Then the Stack swung like this right across her bow. We were impaled on her bow with her bow sawing on that whaleboat davit, which was right down into the frame of the ship, a good solid piece. The forward fireroom flooded.

The Wasp didn't know they hit us. The smoke from the Stack's stack went forward across the Wasp's bow. The first thing that happened, the Wasp reported fire in the forecastle. They sent my classmate, the junior officer of the deck, Emery Nickerson, forward to take a look at this fire and see what the problem was.† Nickerson got up forward, and his bow lookout was speechless, absolutely speechless. Then Nickerson looked over the bow of the Wasp, and there was the Stack. Incidentally, they had been pushing us for 20 minutes. We were laid over 62 degrees.

Well, Nickerson got this word back to Tommy Weschler on the bridge.‡ In due course, the Wasp stopped and backed clear, leaving us there. Then she continued on at 25 knots. It was the height of the submarine campaign, submarines all up and down the East Coast, so she hightailed it on for Norfolk. When she got down the coast aways, she sent a message saying, "Have been in collision with destroyer believed to have been Stack."

Well, they got this message in fleet headquarters in Norfolk, and they thought the Stack was sunk, because it said, "Believed to have been Stack." Well, we were there dead in the water, lost all power, boilers flooded, forward fireroom flooded, down a couple of feet. Incidentally, while she was held this way across the bow of the Wasp, a second class torpedoman named Wright--I remember like it was yesterday--went aft and in water up to his waist set all the depth charges on safe. He got the Navy Cross for that. If they had gone off under the bow of that ship, that would have been the end of the Wasp.

---

* The collision was at 0550 on the morning of 17 March.
† Ensign Emery M. Nickerson, USN.
‡ Ensign Thomas R. Weschler, USN, was officer of the deck on board the Wasp. Weschler, who retired as a vice admiral, described the collision from his perspective in his Naval Institute oral history.

So there we were, left alone, and the next morning we knew roughly where we are. We started feeling for the mouth of the Delaware Bay. We got in there, and it took us better than a day before we got into the Delaware breakwater and then on up the river. We went on into the Philadelphia Navy Yard, and we had to patch a sizable hunk of that forward fireroom.

Q: Did you have to replace the boiler?

Admiral Shear: No, we didn't have to replace the boilers, but the boilers were all salted up. We just kept going at five or six knots by pouring boiler compound by the barrel into the boiler water system, just to keep within some kind of steaming specs. So we got patched up, and we were in there several weeks, during which time I sneaked off and got married. We got a lot of new things. We got our first generation radar and we got 20-millimeter machine guns, because we didn't have any. And we got a few other alterations.

So that's the story of the Wasp and the Stack. Then they had a court of inquiry. Of course, none of us junior officers were involved in that. The court of inquiry was held in the wardroom of the Wasp down in Norfolk. The captain was ordered down there. From what I was told informally, it was rather a nasty affair. The skipper of the Wasp sort of gave a sort of back-of-the-hand treatment. Who was the skipper of the Wasp?

Q: Black Jack Reeves.[*]

Admiral Shear: Black Jack Reeves, exactly. He just wanted to get on about the business: "Oh, hell, we hit a destroyer, so what?" More or less that attitude. Olch never got any reprimand out of it, but I think obviously it hurt him. The Wasp was then ordered to Scotland, so she could get a load of planes to take to Malta. We were supposed to have gone to Scotland and Malta with her, because Malta was in absolute desperation, just on the verge of falling. So she made a high-speed run across the Atlantic, stopped briefly in

---

[*] Captain John W. Reeves, Jr., USN, commanded the aircraft carrier Wasp (CV-7) from her commissioning on 25 April 1940 to 31 May 1942.

Scotland, then went way into the Med.* She got within range of Malta, flew the planes off, and got her ass out of there before she got in trouble herself.†

The four ships of our division were Stack, Sterett, Wilson, and Lang. She took one or two of the other of our division and went over and made that run with a couple of other destroyers. Then she came right back to Chesapeake Bay, where we encountered her again. By that time it was May. So there we were, and we spent a few weeks up and down the coast there, plane guarding for the Wasp around the Chesapeake Bay and that area.

Then we got together in a convoy, and we headed for the Pacific.‡ I'll tell you who was in that convoy. The North Carolina was in it; our complete division of four ships was in it; the Wasp was in it; a heavy cruiser was in it and a new AA cruiser, the Atlanta class.§ The AA cruisers were magnificent ships, but they had a very poor combat record because they kept getting sunk. Pretty bad thing to do, get sunk. But they had 16 5-inch rapid-fire AA guns, plus all the 40 millimeters and 20 millimeters and so forth. We went down and went through the Panama Canal. Again, we didn't know where we were going.

So we went through the canal, and we went immediately up the coast to San Diego. We were in San Diego less than a week, and we picked up a big convoy of Marines, a full division I believe. They were in our early amphibs, and these early amphibs were the C-1, C-2, and C-3 merchant ships, which were built for the merchant marine in the 1936 Merchant Marine Act. As soon as they came out, they were taken over. They made a few cruises in the commercial business and then were taken over by the Navy.

Within a week, we were headed southwest with that division of Marines, and I guess we had a dozen or so of those first class of amphibs, plus all the rest of our task force and a few other ships. We didn't go to Pearl at all. We didn't know where we were going, and

---

* Med--Mediterranean Sea.
† The Wasp launched the British planes for Malta on 20 April 1942. She then returned to Britain and picked up a second load of planes, which she delivered to Malta on 9 May while in company with the British carrier Eagle.
‡ This convoy left Norfolk on 6 June 1942.
§ The heavy cruiser was the Quincy (CA-39), and the antiaircraft (AA) cruiser was the San Juan (CL-54).

there was all sort of speculation about where we were going, were we going to the Fijis or to the Marquesas. We ended up in Tongatabu. You know where Tongatabu is?

Q: Well, approximately--the Friendly Islands.

Admiral Shear: The Friendly Islands, and it had one of those great big atolls; you could put a fleet of ships in there. We were in Tongatabu for a few days, and then we made some rehearsal amphibious landings for the Marines. We left there, and after a week or two we went down to New Caledonia. We all assembled in that huge outer anchorage in New Caledonia. There was some great speculation about what we were going to do next. This extended into June and July. It was July by that time. The latter part of July we headed north, and there was great speculation that we were going into the Solomons, because the Japs were already there. And that's what we did. We put the Marines ashore the seventh of August of '42.

Q: What do you remember about the day of the invasion?

Admiral Shear: I remember it very well. We happened to be with the amphibs, and we took the amphibs in as close to the beach as we could. They were unloading stuff a mile a minute, piling the stuff on the beach. One of the great problems was just piling up on the beach; you had to get clear of the beach. We had the Wasp for cover, and I think the Saratoga was there for cover also at that time. The most important thing they had to do early was get that airfield, Henderson Field--whack it out of a coconut plantation.

The same day the Marines went into Guadalcanal they went into Tulagi, which was across the bay there. It was difficult for us in the ships to see actually what was going on ashore, but we got reports there was hard fighting on both sides. We stayed there with those amphibs, I guess, a week or more. Then we joined up with the Wasp again south of Guadalcanal, and she steamed back and forth there providing air cover south of the islands. And she stayed in one area for quite a while. We left the Wasp; I think it was to escort a tanker somewhere. She was sunk, and once again I think it was a mistake to keep that ship in one place.

Q: One thing I was curious about: how much of an antiaircraft workup had you had before going to the Pacific?

Admiral Shear: We periodically shot at sleeves, and I don't think we did too much in the Atlantic because we weren't worried about aircraft in the Atlantic. But that week we spent around San Diego, a week or ten days, we had some AA shoots there. Then occasionally a carrier aircraft would drag a sleeve, and the destroyers in the screen would bang away at it. We needed that, because we got in a lot of Jap aircraft attacks down there.

Q: Well, that was more of a threat than submarines, around the Solomons.

Admiral Shear: Oh, yes. Except one submarine got the Wasp.*

Q: Got the North Carolina also.

Admiral Shear: That's right. I forget where the North Carolina was hit.

Q: It was in the same action, the 15th of September.

Admiral Shear: Was she hit the same time as the Wasp was?

Q: Yes.

---

* The carrier Wasp (CV-7) was torpedoed and sunk by the Japanese submarine I-19 on 15 September 1942. For details, see Ben W. Blee, "Whodunnit?" U.S. Naval Institute Proceedings, July 1982, 42-49.

Admiral Shear: We had left that formation, and I think we went off with a tanker somewhere. We had been with them for a week, just steaming back in that same general area, and I personally thought they had stuck too close to one area. By that time I was almost a lieutenant (junior grade), so I guess I rated that comment. I made lieutenant (junior grade) the first of October.

Anyway, this one submarine clobbered her, and we lost her. One of the reasons we lost her was that our avgas systems were bad.* Fires got out of control; there wasn't a damn thing you could do about it. In the later ships, they improved them, but the avgas was always a big problem, and she got some roaring fires. I was not alongside at the time, but people told me that she had.

Q: Where were you during the night battle of 8 and 9 August, when those cruisers were sunk?†

Admiral Shear: We were with the amphibs, away from the landing area. At night we'd button everything up. We took them over on the Tulagi side, which was about 20 miles away. We were not in that battle. We could see it, see the gunfire flashes and so forth, but we were not in that battle. We were with the amphibs, and we took them back the next morning. That was an absolute melee, that battle. Radar was not so hot, and there was great confusion, certainly on our side. One of my later skippers in the Stack was a fellow named Roy Newton, and he had been exec of the Ralph Talbot.‡ The Ralph Talbot was badly shot up that night. He was a good naval officer, but he was a changed man after that night.

Q: In what sense?

---

* Avgas--aviation gasoline.
† On the night of 8-9 August 1942, between Guadalcanal and nearby Savo Island, a Japanese surface force surprised Allied forces and sank four cruisers, the USS Astoria (CA-34), USS Quincy (CA-39), USS Vincennes (CA-44), and HMAS Canberra.
‡ Lieutenant Roy A. Newton, USN.

Admiral Shear: Well, he became very, very nervous, and we were not very kind to him. He came aboard ship, and his nickname was Jittery Jake. He was a good skipper, and we made a Navy Cross run up the Slot several months later.* This goes on almost a year now beyond where we are at present.

We were not in that battle of Iron Bottom Bay, that first battle of Savo Island, and that's the night we lost all those cruisers. That was a disaster.

Q: Did that lead to any changes in doctrine?

Admiral Shear: All ships had bad fires. One of the things that came to light was that we had thicknesses of paint on the ships--half inch of just solid paint. Turned out the paint burned like hell. So the whole fleet went into a major paint chipping, right down to bare metal. You didn't even put a prime coat on, right down to bare metal, and you kept a light camouflage on the exterior. But you chipped paint everywhere on those ships. That was a major directive. Every ship in the Navy just chip, chip, chip, chip.

Q: How did you keep it from rusting?

Admiral Shear: Well, on the exterior you put on a light coat of essentially camouflage paint. But we just took the interior right down to bare metal and left it that way the rest of the war. Now, what other lessons that I would be aware of?

Q: Anything about vigilance or use or radar that grew out of that?

Admiral Shear: I'm just thinking of the lessons that came out of that battle. That Jap first team was a red-hot outfit. That Jap first team was good, whether in big ships or little ships or destroyers. They had those 24-inch torpedoes, among other things. They were a very professional organization, and I think we learned that we were up against a first team.

---

* The Slot was the nickname given to the ocean passageway between the two chains of islands comprising the Solomons.

Admiral Shear: Were you standing your watches all down in main control during this time?

Admiral Shear: No. I was on bridge watches. I normally had the 4:00 to 8:00, because then I'd have the day free for engineering work.

Q: Anything specifically you remember from watch-standing?

Admiral Shear: We were continually using our director for every target of opportunity, whether it was aircraft or ship or what have you. We were manned for battle stations virtually around the clock, and we operated our fire control director all the time against aircraft. Became pretty good with it too. I'm just trying to think of things that--later on as we got into the Slot I can give you more detail. We ran up and down that Slot continually for a long time.

Q: Did you have a PPI scope on your radar?[*]

Admiral Shear: Yes. Early model.

Q: Which was quite an advance over what they had before that.

Admiral Shear: Yes, that's right.

Q: I'm sure there was a heavy emphasis on lookout training, aircraft recognition.

Admiral Shear: Oh, yes, absolutely. For recognition we had those silhouettes, and we studied them right there. The director watch had them right in front of him all the time. We

---

[*] PPI--plan position indicator, a type of radar that presents essentially a geographical picture with one's own ship in the center of the scope and surrounding ships, planes, and land areas shown in their respective positions in terms of range and bearing.

had a major lookout training program for incoming aircraft, major silhouette flash card type of things. We could spot aircraft and identify them as soon as we could spot them. We became very good at that; all ships did.

Q: Well, your lives literally depended on it.

Admiral Shear: Absolutely, absolutely. I'm just trying to think of things that took place right after that battle.

Q: Were you involved in some of those convoys bringing in supplies for the Marines?

Admiral Shear: Oh, yes, yes, constantly. We'd run back to Espiritu Santo, a big base in the New Hebrides, or to New Caledonia and run the convoys with supplies up there all the time. At one time those Marines were very desperate. My ship didn't do it--we were doing something else--but at one time they were running limited amounts of supplies up there on destroyers, just to get stuff up there, critical stuff. By that time, the merchant shipping started to show up in the South Pacific. When you'd go into New Caledonia, for example, you might see 15 or 20 Liberty ships there. They were slow ships that made about 10 knots, maybe 11 knots downhill, but they were big burdensome ships that carried a pile of cargo.

Q: They had those triple-expansion engines.

Admiral Shear: Yes, they did, exactly. Farm-boy engines--you could teach a farm boy to run them.

Q: Did you get involved in any of those surface actions?

Admiral Shear: Up in the Solomons later on, yes. I'm going to tell you about that.

Q: Okay, but not in '42.

Admiral Shear: Not in '42, no. We were with amphibs, we were with the carriers, we had a number of air attacks on the carriers. The Hornet was down there at that time.

Q: She was sunk on the 26th of October.

Admiral Shear: Yes, she was down there, and she was sunk. That's another one, I think our ships sank her after she was hit. That's another one we should not have lost. And by that time I was jaygee. I could say that, I guess. The Enterprise was damaged. She was not sunk, but she had a couple of bombs on her flight deck. She was out of commission. So we lost the Wasp, we lost the Hornet, we got flight deck damage on the Enterprise.

Q: And the Saratoga was out of it.[*]

Admiral Shear: And the Saratoga was out in Puget Sound. Finally she got back, and the Saratoga was the only carrier we had in the South Pacific when she got back there. She was down there almost by herself for a while. Frederick C. Sherman was the task force commander.[†] Fine man. I'm a little bit mixed up on my timing. The Saratoga was there. Then I guess it's almost a year later we get to Bunker Hill and we get the Essex and a couple of those--the first of that class down there, and we get a couple of the converted cruiser hulls, the CVLs. But for a while down there, we were essentially bare. Bare naked. To support the Marines we sent as many of the carrier aircraft ashore to Henderson Field as we could. And let me tell you, those carrier aviators did a great job there in Henderson Field. Flew out of there by the skin of their pants, just operating with nothing, avgas going ashore in barrels. They were all heroes, let me tell you.

---

[*] On 31 August 1942, the Japanese submarine I-26 torpedoed and damaged the aircraft carrier Saratoga (CV-3) while she was operating in the Solomons.
[†] Rear Admiral Frederick C. Sherman, USN.

Q: Living in tents.

Admiral Shear: Living in tents, that's right.

Q: Going in trenches when the attacks came.

Admiral Shear: Yep, yep. They essentially saved the day down there. And they were being clobbered every night from some Japs coming down from the northern Solomons. We were just really hanging on by our fingernails there for five or six months.

Q: Some of those people I've talked to remember a sense of desperation. Did you have that feeling?

Admiral Shear: No, I never had a sense of desperation, but we knew we had a helluva war on our hands. Did you ever run into a fellow named Turner Caldwell?

Q: I've heard of him. I haven't met him.

Admiral Shear: He's an aviator out of the class of '35. I relieved him as OP-095 many years later, in the Pentagon, when I was director of antisubmarine warfare. Turner Caldwell was down there.*

Q: I think he was an SBD pilot.†

Admiral Shear: Yes, he was. But they had a number of those carrier pilots that they put ashore there in Henderson Field, and they literally saved the day down there. Very little to

---

* Lieutenant Turner F. Caldwell, USN, went ashore after being in Scouting Squadron Five from the Enterprise (CV-6). He eventually became a vice admiral.
† The SBD was the Douglas Dauntless, the U.S. Navy's principal dive-bomber in 1942.

work with, running out of ammunition, running out of avgas, and fighting every night and every day. If it hadn't been for them, we would probably have lost that situation there.

Q: Well, the surface ships certainly contributed also.

Admiral Shear: Oh, yes. Yes, indeed. The Japs knew that Slot backwards and forwards. They'd come out of Rabaul and those upper Solomon Islands and come roaring down that Slot at night, and that kept going on for over a year down there before we finally got it under control. My division got deeply involved in that as time went on.

Q: How good was the logistic support for your ship and other destroyers?

Admiral Shear: Fair. Tender time was minimal. If you could get a few days alongside a tender, that was a godsend. But you went for month after month after month with no tenders whatsoever; you were spread very thin. There was a tender at Tongatabu for a while, and they finally moved her down to Espiritu Santo. There was a tender in New Caledonia, and if you could squeeze a few days between missions you'd get alongside a tender and get whatever. You always needed something critically.

When I left that <u>Stack</u> as chief engineer at the end of '43, I was down below 140 pounds. I was just holding that ship together with baling wire. If it hadn't been for the type of crew I had, we'd have had a helluva time. Just had to make do and piece things together, make your own parts in the machine shop. The logistic support was a very tough situation down there. Now, you could always get fuel everywhere you'd go, even Purvis Bay. Right beside Tulagi became sort of a minor logistics center there, and you always had a tanker down there. You refueled every chance you got. You had to keep right topped off in fuel, because you never knew when you were going to be sent off on a 30-knot run somewhere.

There was a vessel named the <u>Erskine Phelps</u>. Did you ever hear of the <u>Erskine Phelps</u>?

Q: Is that the old sailing ship?

Admiral Shear: Yes.

Q: She was essentially a barge.

Admiral Shear: She was a barge; she was a sailing ship. She had a fine sailing career and she was barged. She was owned by one of the West Coast oil companies. She was brought down there into Purvis Bay as our fuel ship, and whenever you got five minutes you'd go alongside the Erskine Phelps and fuel. They had a boatswain in charge of the Erskine Phelps. He was a merchant seaman, and he'd been with her for many years. He knew her like the back of his hand. I knew something about the Erskine Phelps, because she was built in Bath, Maine, and her quarters aft were in surprisingly good condition.

This boatswain would take me back and show me around once in a while. Since I was taking his fuel, he'd show me around the ship. But the Erskine Phelps was sort of our bread and butter for fuel down there, and they kept her topped off. Anytime a destroyer had an extra few minutes, they'd go alongside the Phelps and top off. Because fuel was critical, and I must say, I don't think anywhere down there we were ever that short of fuel. Short of food--we ran low on food for a while down there, and short of repairs, always short of repairs. Always valves that needed regrinding or odds and ends that you always needed in an engine room. Very difficult time.

Q: How good a design would you say that plant was in the Stack?

Admiral Shear: Excellent. Superb. It was a 50,000-horsepower plant, twin screw, 600-pound steam plant.

Q: Those were in the early days of the 600 pounders.

Admiral Shear: That's right. Absolutely superb plant. Those ships were Vinson-Trammel ships.* That was Franklin Roosevelt's rebuilding of the Navy. The first of those ships came out in 1936-37. We came out in '39. They had one and a half pipers such as the Dunlap and the Farragut. Then there was a class of one pipers such as the Craven ahead of us. Then we were the Benham class of one pipers, Benham, 397 to 408. We were all Benhams. That was a damn good ship. They had one slight problem: they were short-legged: They were 340 feet in length, and if they'd been another 20 or 30 feet in oil tanks, they'd have been better ships. You always had to watch the fuel situation.

Q: I interviewed the man who was the first chief engineer of the Mahan, DD-364, and he had very little regard for his plant.† Maybe some of the bugs had been worked out by the time they got to your ship.

Admiral Shear: We didn't have any significant problems except maintenance.

Q: He damned Gibbs and Cox for that design.

Admiral Shear: Now, let's see. They were a 50,000-horsepower plant.‡ They didn't make the speed we did. They were about 35 knots straight out, maybe 33, 35. Mahan was one and a half piper, I think, wasn't she?

Q: Yes, she had one long stack and a shorter one.

Admiral Shear: I knew the Mahan well; she was around there.

---

* Representative Carl Vinson (Democrat-Georgia) and Senator Park Trammel (Democrat-Florida) were chairmen of the respective naval affairs committees. The Vinson-Trammel Act, 27 March 1934, called for the construction of 102 new ships. The new destroyers built under the program--the first to join the fleet since the four-stackers of the World War I era--became known as gold-platers.
† See the Naval Institute oral history of Captain Frederick A. Edwards, Sr., USN (Ret.)
‡ The rated horsepower for ships of the Mahan class was 49,000.

Q: Why was your ship faster?

Admiral Shear: The entire Benham class, one of the fastest classes the Navy ever built. They made 41 knots in sea trials. Now, down in that hot water with hot injection the vacuum which your condensers draw is a factor of the temperature of the water. In cold North Atlantic water you can have a beautiful vacuum, 30-inch vacuum all the time. You get down in that hot water with 70 to 80 degrees injection, your vacuum starts to drop off, and you can't get your top speed. For 31-knot Burke, that's about the best they could get out of those ships.[*] We could make about 35 down there. We couldn't make what we could in the North Atlantic. But that was a first-rate plant, and I don't know anybody who had any great complaints about that plant except she was short-legged, and, of course, we always needed more maintenance time. We just weren't getting enough maintenance time.

Q: Why were you faster? Did you have better hull lines, more horsepower?

Admiral Shear: They were 50,000-horsepower plants. The others might have been a little less than that, but that's a recognized fact, that the Benham class was the fastest class of destroyer the Navy has ever built. Considerably faster than the 2,100s and 2,250s. If they could make 33, they were doing well. I think they had 60,000-horsepower plants, more horsepower, but they were heavier ships, considerably heavier ships. The Benham class was a nominal 1,500-ton ship. As we got all the extra gear, 40-millimeter guns and radar and so forth on during the war, they were up above 2,000, but they were built as 1,500-ton destroyers.

---

[*] Captain Arleigh A. Burke, USN, was Commander Destroyer Squadron 23 in the Solomons during fighting there in 1943. For the origin of the nickname "31-Knot Burke," see E. B. Potter, Admiral Arleigh Burke: A Biography (New York: Random House, 1990), pages 102-103.

Q: Well, that really desperate period of fighting ended about the end of '42. What kind of a role did you get into then?

Admiral Shear: Okay. I told you we'd had some problems with the boilers salting up after that collision. That slowly started to show up in pitting in the boilers. About the end of '42 we had to go back to Mare Island, and we took with us two damaged cruisers, one of which was the Pensacola, and dropped them off at Pearl.[*] We went back to Mare Island for about a five weeks' availability to retube the boilers. While we were back there, we got 40-millimeter guns, which were then coming out. And we got an improved radar. We turned right around, went back, had a few more days of refresher training at Pearl and went right straight back to the Solomons.

Q: Did you get to see your bride while you were at Mare Island?

Admiral Shear: Yes. Wives came out, and we all lived together in a motel there while the ship was in the yard. That's where I got to know a bunch of submariners. They were in the same motel. When we left, a number of the girls got jobs around San Francisco. My wife got a job in the secret mail room at Com 12 headquarters.[†] They rented a couple of houses together, and the wives all lived together. She stayed there until the end of the war. So we had almost a month together in that particular time when we were getting that reboiler job.

Then we went right straight back out--spent a couple of days in Pearl and went right straight back to Solomons. I guess this was probably March of '43. Then we got involved in the usual things down around the Solomons. We were starting to move up the Solomon chain then. We moved up to Rendova, which is the next group of islands. We didn't go into Bougainville until later on. We had the usual routine jobs around New Caledonia. We had a sizable operation in Efate in the New Hebrides and Espiritu Santo, which was our principal place in the New Hebrides.

---

[*] Mare Island Navy Yard, Vallejo, California.
[†] Com 12--Commandant of the 12th Naval District, with headquarters on Treasure Island in San Francisco Bay.

By that time things were pretty well solidified in Tulagi and Guadalcanal, but there were still raids coming down from the upper Solomons. So we got involved running up and down the Slot on a regular basis. That became sort of a historic thing down there, running up and down the Slot. You'd leave late in the afternoon, crank on a bunch of speed, run up the Slot, and hope you'd run into some Japs coming down.

As our intelligence got better and better, several times we took Australian coast watchers up to the Solomons and put them ashore. Let me tell you, those guys were magnificent. They were absolutely fearless. They knew the islands, and they were in the coconut business and so forth. They'd go up there and get right in with the natives, and they'd carry a radio with them. When you got something from a coast watcher, you knew it was accurate. How they weren't all wiped out, I'll never know. Most of them survived, and they were scattered all through the northern Solomon Island chain. When they said a ship was coming down or a group of ships was coming down, those ships were on the way. They were very valuable. Then we had a certain amount of aircraft coverage giving us halfway decent intelligence.

But that Slot run became a standard thing down there. That's where Arleigh Burke made his first reputation, running up and down the Slot. We went up and down the Slot many nights, and it wasn't always a very well organized thing. There were still some melees going on down there. I remember one night we were about halfway up the Slot, and we were attacked by our own PT boats.[*] They fired a bunch of torpedoes at us, none of which hit. But they claimed they'd sunk all the destroyers. We took them under fire with 5-inch, and we claimed we sunk a bunch of those boats. Neither one of us caused any damage whatsoever. Neither one of us had got a hit.

So that kind of thing was still going on. But things got better, and the principal action that I was involved in down there was the Battle of Vella Gulf. We left Purvis Bay, where we were topped off with fuel, right beside Tulagi, and barreled up there with Moosbrugger. Moosbrugger was the commodore.[†] We had three ships from our division:

---

[*] PT--motor torpedo boats.
[†] Commander Frederick Moosbrugger, USN, Commander Destroyer Division 12, embarked in the USS Dunlap (DD-384).

the Stack, the Lang, and Sterett. Moosbrugger had a division of three ships, and we went up there.* He was in the lead. We went up south of the island chain, went through Blackett Strait. If you've read your history, you know we were worried about Blackett Strait.

Went into the Vella Gulf expecting those people to show up around midnight, 1:00 or 2:00 o'clock, and they did.† By that time we had fairly decent radar, so we tracked them and took them under attack, first with torpedo attack and got hits. Then we finished them off with gunfire, and we sank three or four destroyers that night. Some alleged we sank a cruiser, but I never saw any firm evidence that we sank a cruiser. But I can tell you, our division commander was a pretty roughshod guy, but a very competent destroyer man. He was Rodger W. Simpson who later got in trouble at the end of the war in San Francisco, but that's a different story.‡ Moosbrugger was the task group commander in the lead division.

That was a classic night. I don't know whether we got every ship, or whether one or two turned around and got back. It's covered in Destroyer Operations in World War II.§ That was a great victory. They were bringing down troops and supplies, and they had literally thousands of men in the water, literally thousands of men in the water, and we were steaming through them. We saw just bodies of men, vast groups of men. The captain called me to the bridge.** I was then chief engineer, and my battle station was damage control central, right at the forward engine hatch. When he called me to the bridge, he said, "The commodore wants us to take some prisoners."

I said, "Captain, we've been steaming right through bunches of them. We'll do the best we can." So I went down to the damage control party. We threw a whole series of cargo nets over the side and lifelines and life jackets. We steamed through these groups of

---

* His ships were the Dunlap (DD-384), Craven (DD-382), and Maury (DD-401). For details on the battle and the individual ships, see Samuel Eliot Morison, Breaking the Bismarcks Barrier (Boston: Little, Brown, 1950), pages 212-222.
† The Battle of Vella Gulf took place the night of 6-7 August 1943.
‡ Commander Rodger W. Simpson, USN.
§ Theodore Roscoe, United States Destroyer Operations in World War II (Annapolis: U.S. Naval Institute, 1953), pages 233-237. The Japanese lost the destroyers Arashi, Hagikaze, and Kawakaze. The damaged Shigure escaped.
** The commanding officer of the Stack at that time was Lieutenant Commander Roy A. Newton, USN.

men, and you couldn't get them to come forward. You'd toss them a line, practically give it to them, and the cargo nets and so forth; we couldn't get a single one to come aboard.

I sent word back to the bridge and said, "I can't get anybody to come aboard, and I'm not going to put any of our men in the water and lose them." So we went back and forth, and the rest of the ships were going to try and do the same thing, because we wanted to get some intelligence information. Someone might have gotten one or two prisoners, but none that I knew of. I could not get any, and we worked at it for an hour or so. By that time, it was starting to get almost dawn. We didn't want to be caught way up in the northern Solomons there with an air attack from Rabaul coming down.

Now, this is a pretty dirty story that I'm going to tell you. The commodore said, "Okay, we're not going to let these men get ashore. They're within swimming distance of the beach. We're going to take care of them." So we went through those masses of men dropping depth charges--pattern after pattern. I tell you, if anybody got ashore it was a miracle. But that was war. I expect we probably killed several thousand men that night.

Then we got through that, and we headed for Tulagi at full speed. About the time of sunup we got some air cover up, and it just so happened that no Japanese planes came down that night. But that was a helluva night--and a highly successful night. Everything clicked.

Q: What do you remember seeing and hearing during the gun and torpedo phase of it?

Admiral Shear: Well, of course, I knew when we fired a torpedo, because they were right beside the forward damage control center. Those ships, incidentally, were very heavily armed. They had 16 21-inch torpedoes. As we put more armament on, we took off two of the four quadruple racks. We had eight torpedoes, four port and four starboard. They were controlled from the bridge and fired from the bridge with the torpedo director up there. Then we finished them off with gunfire. Reuben Strelow out of class of '43, one year behind me, at that time was the gunnery officer, and he was up in the fire control director.[*]

---

[*] Ensign Reuben E. Strelow, USN.

And we let go a number of salvos fore and aft. But my job was down there with the machinery to keep the ship afloat if she got hurt.

Q: So you were not topside?

Admiral Shear: Oh, I was topside, yes. I was right up there at the engine room hatch. The damage control central was right at the machine shop, which was at the top of the forward engine room hatch on the main deck. I had my group of damage control people there, petty officers and machinist's mates and boatswain's mates who could take care of any damage that showed up. My responsibility was to control the damage if we were hit.

Q: Did you have any problems with night vision from the gun flashes?

Admiral Shear: I don't recall any. I do not recall any. Of course, we had so-called smokeless powder, but it still made a flash. The fires on the sinking ships were clearly visible.

Q: How much emotion did you feel while you were going through something like that?

Admiral Shear: You don't worry about killing people. Whether you're in destroyers or submarines, it's the same thing; you don't worry about killing people. I was worried about the ship being hit, and I was worried about my people. I remember telling them when we saw that stuff, "Listen, we're going to get some of that stuff back, so you'd better be ready for it." So we were really up on the step; we had a well-trained crew; we were prepared for any kind of damage control that hit us. And I really expected we were going to get hit, because those Japs were good people.

Q: Was your ship fired at?

Admiral Shear: We caught them by complete surprise--absolute, complete surprise. I don't think any of us were fired at. They were hit, and it must have been a total shock to them.

Q: I've talked to men who said that, really, the emotion hits them later. At the time of the battle itself, they're so busy doing the job they don't have time to reflect on it.

Admiral Shear: That's a good statement. I don't recall any particular emotion except exultation later on. We got back, running down back the Slot and getting back there in Purvis Bay and Tulagi. God, we thought we were on top of the world. And we were. We'd had a great victory.

Q: Well, Moosbrugger has certainly been acclaimed for his actions there.

Admiral Shear: That's right. And he was the boss. We were all there with him. As I recall, we were in a close formation, about 300 yards apart, and a little bit of separation between the two divisions. We were red-hot destroyer men; we knew what the hell we were doing. It was a great victory. First time that we really had a complete victory of that kind that I'd been involved in. Also, we'd been operating with the carriers a lot, and we had been under all kind of air attacks, and we got pretty good with our AA capability too.

Q: Well, this battle was one of the few times you got to use the ship as an offensive weapon.

Admiral Shear: Exactly. One of the first times that destroyers were used exactly for what they were built for.

Q: What was your reaction to the decision to drop the depth charges among the Japanese in the water?

Admiral Shear: The depth charges were released from the bridge. We had a manual releaser, triggered release from the bridge. I didn't drop those depth charges, but I saw the men, and I knew exactly what was going on down there with the men in the water. There were just thousands of men; when I say thousands, there were many, many hundreds, because I had seen them, right there. I told the captain where they were and what they were doing. You could not get to them. We made a very determined effort to get prisoners aboard, but even if we had, I don't think it would have made a difference. We probably would've gone ahead with that action anyway. I don't think you'll find that written up in books very much.

Q: Did you think that was a good decision?

Admiral Shear: Yes, absolutely, absolutely, because we were in a hell of a fight down there in the Solomons. By that time, it was getting under control. But there was no sense in letting several thousand men get ashore, with or without their weapons. Of course, many of them had lost their weapons, but if those ships had gotten through, they had a lot of supplies along with them.

Q: Was that an individual ship decision, or did that come down from higher up?

Admiral Shear: That came down from ComDesDiv 15, who was R. W. Simpson. Whether he got it from Moosbrugger, I don't know, but we got it from our division commander to our captain, and he executed.

Q: You said that when the skipper came aboard, and the crew was somewhat derisive of him. How were they by this time, when you were in the night battle? Had they gotten past that phase?

Admiral Shear: Yes. See, he joined the ship when we went back for that quick retubing job. He had been with the ship then, oh, a number of months. He never got over his nervousness, but he was a competent destroyer man.

Q: He got the job done, obviously.

Admiral Shear: He got the job done. He had been on destroyers a long time, had a lot of experience. I think we were probably a little bit cruel to him in what we said behind his back. But, of course, we never showed it, and when the chips were down he performed.

Q: What can you say about your role as chief engineer, compared with having been the assistant earlier. What kinds of responsibilities did that bring with it?

Admiral Shear: The main responsibility was that you had to keep that plant running. You had to keep that plant in the best possible shape you could. You had to take every opportunity to shut down your plant, get a chance to let your boilers cool off. You didn't get a chance to do that very often. You would get a few days of tender availability, if you could. Get as much work done as you could with your own responsible petty officers, and you can do a lot with your own people, particularly if you've brought them up right. I just had to make sure that the plant was ready to go, and I could tell anywhere in that ship if there was the slightest problem. I could just tell by the vibration or by the hum that something wasn't quite right, and I could be on it like that. I could wake up at night and tell that something just wasn't right, and I'd be out of my bunk and on top of it in a second.

Q: The worst sound of all is no sound.

Admiral Shear: No sound, that's right. When you start to lose your ventilation, that's a sign you've got problems. Or if your diesel generator kicks on for some unknown reason, then you've got problems.

But that was a hell of an experience for me. Boy, you grow up fast. You get experience in a situation like that you wouldn't get in 20 years normally. Let's see, I made jaygee in October of '42.* I made full lieutenant in October of '43. And I made lieutenant commander in October of '45. That's four years.

Q: That was moving fast.

Admiral Shear: Moving fast, and the responsibility moves fast too.

Q: How much of a factor was fatigue for yourself and your people?

Admiral Shear: You had to grab a chance to sleep whenever you could. You never got long periods of sleep. When you were at battle stations, you had to be at your gun station or damage control station, and you were interrupted all the time. Sleep was important. You had to give your people a break every chance you could. And food was important, and a couple of times we got pretty low on food. You could always get to Espiritu Santo or New Caledonia; you could always find a supply ship there where you could get pretty well topped off. But sometimes between ships you'd get pretty low. I remember one time when we got down almost to rice and that famous canned Spam. I told my wife I never wanted to see another can of Spam in my life, ever. [Laughter]

But we never starved.

Q: I've been amazed at the ability of sailors to sleep in the most uncomfortable places.

Admiral Shear: That's right, you could sleep standing up practically. I could still do it.

One critical item: you always had to be very careful of boiler water, because boiler water was precious. You could go without a shower, but, by golly, you couldn't go without boiler water. Feed water had to be within specifications for the boilers. In that hot

---

* Jaygee--lieutenant (junior grade).

weather, the hot injection temperature, the boilers tended to scale up and the evaporators tended to scale up, so we worked some devices so we could get more efficiency out of our evaporators. But boiler water was something you always had to watch every day, feed water, replenishing what we called makeup feed.

Q: Purer than potable water.

Admiral Shear: Oh, absolutely. Absolutely. Precisely controlled chemicals. You always had to worry about makeup feed water, and that's something I had to keep on my mind all the time.

Q: What precautions did you take to ensure that?

Admiral Shear: Well, we had certain reserve feed tanks that we always kept full, and never touched unless it was a matter of desperation. Then we had some devices that came on, the first of which we experimented with ourselves. Then they came out as alterations to the evaporator, to the distilling plants, with a device which injected oatmeal through a small pump into the system that kept your scale soft. That way, instead of the scale hardening on your tubes, you could brush it off reasonably easy with a wire brush and so forth. That gave you some improvement in the efficiency of your plants. Feed water was always one of the top priority items, particularly in those tropical waters.

Q: Did you have the luxury of training periods during the midst of all this, or was just operating itself the training?

Admiral Shear: The kind of operating we were doing, we were up on the step for just about anything. Now, if we had a chance to shoot our guns, particularly for aircraft training, that was important, to keep up with that proficiency.

Q: What about ASW training?*

Admiral Shear: As the war progressed, and I'm talking about for a year or two, they sent a couple of old 1920s type S-boats down for destroyer training, one of which I remember was based in Espiritu Santo. If we were lucky, operating in and out of there you might have a day of ASW training with a submarine target, and that was important. Fortunately, the submarine threat down there didn't amount to much, although we lost the Wasp and a submarine hit the North Carolina.

Q: Did you have a better sonar there than the one in the Atlantic?

Admiral Shear: No, same sonar. The sonar on those ships never changed until they went out of commission. The Stack went into Bikini Atoll, and then she was sunk after that.† In fact, I went down and had to test some new torpedoes and we sank a number of those ships. I did not sink the Stack, however. That would been a heartbreaker if I had had to do that.

Q: Probably just as well. I'd heard that Admiral Rodgers, who was the CO of the Salt Lake City in the Aleutians, had to preside over her sinking at Bikini and he was really heartbroken.‡

Admiral Shear: When I went down there after the war, I was then exec of a submarine. We went down there with some new design torpedoes, some old torpedoes and some new torpedoes. And we went down there with a squadron of destroyers. The destroyers sank a number of ships by gunfire, we sank a number of ships by torpedo fire. Those ships were

---

* ASW--antisubmarine warfare.
† Operation Crossroads involved the testing by U.S. forces of two atomic weapons, detonated at Bikini Atoll in the Marshall Islands on 1 July and 25 July 1946. The Stack was sunk by gunfire near Kwajalein Atoll in the Marshalls on 24 April 1948.
‡ Rear Admiral Bertram J. Rodgers, USN.

too hot, you were not permitted to go aboard them. The Stack was too hot with radioactivity, so in due course she was sunk by destroyer gunfire.

Well, okay, there we are now. That Battle of Vella Gulf was in August of '43. By the end of that year, the Solomons were getting pretty well consolidated. We were making carrier raids up on Rabaul and, in fact, we made a number of those raids with the carrier task group that was going north of the Solomons and reaching into Rabaul.

Q: I remember the Saratoga made one around that period.

Admiral Shear: Yes, she made several. We operated with the Saratoga for some time, and I mentioned Frederick C. Sherman. He was a fine naval officer.

Oh, I should also tell you something I forgot. Ghormley. Ghormley mean anything to you?[*]

Q: Sure, he was Halsey's predecessor as Commander South Pacific.[†]

Admiral Shear: And he wasn't much. Halsey came down there, and he electrified the place. His personality and leadership; he was gung-ho and "Let's-go-get 'em." He just changed the atmosphere down there completely. You can say all you want about some of his later mistakes, but Halsey was a great naval officer.

After a couple of those raids on Rabaul, I think, his flagship was in Espiritu Santo, and he threw a reception for all of us who had participated in--I forget which raid it was, Upper Solomons or Rabaul somewhere. We'd been there with one or more of the carriers, and he had this reception, nothing but Quonset huts there, go ashore and have a drink or

---

[*] Vice Admiral Robert L. Ghormley, USN, served as Commander South Pacific Area from 29 June 1942 to 18 October 1942.
[†] Vice Admiral/Admiral William F. Halsey Jr., USN, served as Commander South Pacific Area from 18 October 1942 to 15 June 1944. He was promoted to four-star rank in November 1942.

two.* In this particular case Halsey was there to congratulate us on the success of our operations. Well, his aide was introducing people, and it became my turn at the head of the line. I was introduced as Lieutenant Shear, chief engineer of the Stack. Halsey said "Oh, yes, oh yes, Lieutenant Shear, I know all about you. You've done a great job on the Stack." He didn't know me from Adam but . . .

Q: It made you feel good!

Admiral Shear: Made you feel damn good. That's right. That's the kind of guy he was.

Q: I talked to a former enlisted man from the Saratoga, and he said Halsey came aboard and just got them all charged up, telling them that they were going on a pretty risky operation but that it was that important and he was counting on them.† That's the kind of lift they needed.

Admiral Shear: Yep. Halsey was an absolutely great naval officer. He just turned that South Pacific around. You could just feel his personality all through the area. Other people told you that?

Q: Yes, sure.

Admiral Shear: That's what the situation was.

Q: That Ghormley was sort of a defeatist type.

Admiral Shear: Ghormley was a disaster, and I don't know what his problem was. I think he probably looked at the task, and it looked like it was impossible to him. It was damn

---

* A Quonset hut is a semi-cylindrical metal building that can be shipped to an advance base area and erected quickly.
† This is in the Naval Institute oral history of Roger L. Bond.

near impossible. It was damn near impossible. The first six months, as I say, we were hanging on by our fingernails, we were.

Q: Did you ever come to a point of having a sense of relief, that you were not constantly feeling challenged?

Admiral Shear: When you could get a few days off, away from the critical area, either off convoying a tanker or a couple of amphibs or else a couple of days alongside the tender, you could just relax and get a night's sleep. Just the opportunity to get a full night's sleep was something that was . . .

Q: Precious.

Admiral Shear: Exactly, precious. So you knew you weren't going to get hauled out with a battle station alarm or a casualty in the engine room or something else that you had to be up. You'd just forget about it for 24 hours. That's the kind of break I remember. But let me tell you, the experience I got down there, even before I went into submarines, that's something you could never replace, never replace. It gave me a foundation for everything I've done since.

Q: One great thing I've heard throughout all this is teamwork.

Admiral Shear: Absolutely. You had to have teamwork. You had to have a great crew, you had to depend on that crew, and you had to let them know that you had confidence in the men. I was good at that; I took care of my men, and they knew it.

Admiral Shear: Any specific examples you remember?

Admiral Shear: Oh, all the time. All the time. I'd always take the opportunity to slap them on the back, give them a "well done," give an "atta boy". They used to say, "Well, I got an 'atta boy' from Lieutenant Shear today." I used to tell them, three "atta boys" equals one "well done."

Q: They didn't have much opportunity to get into mischief, I would think.

Admiral Shear: No, except, of course, you'd get back to San Francisco or something like that, and you'd get a few people drunked up.

Q: They'd deserve it by then.

Admiral Shear: Absolutely. But down there, those liberty ports--at Purvis Bay, you'd have an afternoon ashore there before a night run up the Slot. You could have a ball game ashore, and they would issue you two cans of warm beer. I didn't drink beer, so I gave it to somebody else, but that's what you got. And that was a chance to get ashore and get some exercise, and we had a softball field right there in the palm trees.

Q: How much opportunity did you have to communicate any sense of what was happening to your wife?

Admiral Shear: Oh, everything was very severely censored, and every piece of mail that left the ship had to be read by the censors. I hated that, you know, because the wardroom officers were the censors. We all had to censor everybody else's mail. You'd have to read about the personal mail of other people in your division and so forth. I didn't like that, but we had to do it; that was the rule.

Q: Well, you were inhibited in what you could say anyway.

Admiral Shear: Yes, you were inhibited, and you don't want to get involved in the personal details of your people, so that was a chore that I didn't like.

Q: But you still probably felt a need to give her a sense of reassurance.

Admiral Shear: Oh, yes. Oh, yes. You couldn't tell exactly where you were or what you were doing, but you could give your family everything they needed to know that you were well and out of harm's way and so forth.

Q: In one sense it's harder for them than for you, because they have to battle the unknown, whereas you know what's happening.

Admiral Shear: That's right. That's right. A little story: my wife, as I told you, worked for Com 12. She worked in the mail room for Com 12. She knew the ships' names and where the mail was being routed to, so if my mail was going to Espiritu Santo, she knew that I was going to pick it up in Espiritu Santo.

Q: She had an advantage over most other wives.

Admiral Shear: Big advantage over most other wives, that's right. So she could tell in general where I was. You were able to tell your families enough so that they shouldn't have to worry about you too much.

Q: We haven't talked about the Stack's participation in the Gilbert Islands operation.

Admiral Shear: All right, we did participate in that. It was in the fall of '43.[*] We went up there with a task force from the South Pacific, and I don't recall what ships were in that task force. I'd have to look it up. We were up there with the carriers and the Marines, and I don't recall the great details of that operation. We put the Marines ashore.

---

[*] U.S. Marines, supported by warships of the Central Pacific Force, invaded Tarawa on 20 November 1943 to begin the capture of the Gilbert Islands.

Q: That was the one when the Liscome Bay was torpedoed and sunk.*

Admiral Shear: I don't recall that she was hit there, not in my vicinity. But we were there with the carriers and the surface ships, and I think mostly we were not close to the shore; we were not right in on the beach, in other words. We must have been with the carriers most of that time. But we were in that operation, and we went from there back to the South Pacific area, around Espiritu Santo and the Solomons. Any highlights there that I should be aware of, that you recall?

Q: Well, just that it was one of the early operations of the Central Pacific campaign and that there were many more ships available than previously.

Admiral Shear: Yes, that's right. There were a lot of ships there.

Q: And the Tarawa operation is especially memorable to the Marines.

Admiral Shear: Absolutely. Absolutely. And, of course, that was a vicious fight. We were not in on the beach. Some ships were in on the beach providing gunfire support, and we had a couple of battleships there that were providing gunfire support. A couple of the older battleships, as I recall.

Q: The Maryland was the flagship.

Admiral Shear: The Maryland was there, absolutely correct, and she was pulverizing some of those dug-in positions. But we were offshore then. I think we spent most of that campaign with the carriers.

---

* The escort carrier Liscome Bay (CVE-56) was torpedoed and sunk by the Japanese submarine I-175 on the morning of 24 November 1943. Of those on board, 624 were lost and 272 were rescued. Among those killed was Rear Admiral Henry M. Mullinnix, USN, embarked as Commander Task Group 52.3.

Q: So probably either ASW or AAW.*

Admiral Shear: The primary concern in that particular area was AAW, but you had to be careful of ASW also. And I don't recall what carriers were there, either. I'd have to check and look that up.

Q: The Essex I know was there, and I think they had some of those Independence-class CVLs.

Admiral Shear: Could well be because several of them were down there at that time. Princeton, I believe, was one that was down there at that time. Ships in a particular spot at a particular time sometimes you get a little hazy on. That's a few years back.

Q: How long did you remain with that ship?

Admiral Shear: Exactly two years. I joined her in December of '41, and I left her in December of '43. That's another interesting story I've got to tell you about.

I left that ship in December of '43 with orders to sub school. I had applied for sub school at least a year before, and orders to sub school had to be granted, because there was a desperate need for people to go into submarines. But the CO did not have to honor those orders unless he had a qualified relief on board. So I was kept on board the ship for many months, because legally he could hold me up until he got a qualified relief.

Well, they had a couple of people come aboard, reserve ensigns, and they were disastrous. I just could not tell the captain they were qualified. Many good reservists could have taken the job, but the one or two that I had just simply couldn't hack it. Finally, I got a Naval Academy guy aboard. He must have been out of maybe '43 or '44. They were graduating in three years in those times, and he turned out to be a pretty good officer. I got

---

* AAW--antiair warfare.

him down in that engine room, and, boy, I kept his head down and tail up and got him qualified as fast as he could.

Q: Sort of like McMullen did with you.

Admiral Shear: Exactly. Precisely the same. So I told the captain, "Captain, he's qualified, and I want to carry out my orders."

By this time, we had a new skipper. He was a former exec, fellow named P. K. Sherman out of '33.[*] And he said, "I don't want you to leave."

I said, "Captain, I've got to go. I've got orders to sub school, and I've stayed with you almost an extra year after I put my request in."

He said, "Damn it, you should stay in destroyers. What the hell do you want to go to submarines for?" By that time, I had gotten to know something about submarines, and I liked small ships. Besides, I wanted to go home to see my wife for three months in sub school. He knew that. So he said, "All right Shear, you've done a good job, go on." So he put me ashore in Espiritu Santo, and I had to wait for a day or two to get one of those big old Pan Am flying boats.[†] They'd been flying cargo down and flying personnel back. I got on top of a pile of cargo in that flying boat, and in there with me was H. V. Kaltenborn. Remember H. V. Kaltenborn?

Q: Yes, he was a radio commentator.

Admiral Shear: He'd been down finding out who was winning the war in the South Pacific. Well, we got in there with a bunch of other officers and H. V. Kaltenborn, and he kept us enthralled with stories all the way back to Pearl. I got to Pearl, and I had to wait to get a jeep carrier to take me back as a passenger to San Francisco.[‡] We got back to San

---

[*] Lieutenant Commander Philip K. Sherman, USN.
[†] Pan Am--Pan American World Airways, which had a long, close association with the U.S. Navy.
[‡] "Jeep carriers" was a slang term for CVEs, small escort aircraft carriers that were slower than the attack carriers.

Francisco Christmas Eve of '43. My wife was there with the other wives waiting from the Stack. I had orders to report to Com 12 for further transportation to New London for sub school.

Q: Do you have any impressions of Kaltenborn from that flight?

Admiral Shear: Very talkative. Very talkative. I had heard the man on radio when you could pick up a radio. He had that very deep voice: it's bad news tonight or it's good news tonight. My impression was that he probably thought he knew more than most anybody else, but that was just based on one ten-hour flight. It was my only contact with him.

The day after Christmas I reported to Com 12. I went to the personnel officer, and I said, "I'd like 30 days' leave, please." He laughed at me, and I said, "What are you laughing at? Everybody who comes back from the Solomon Islands is guaranteed 30 days. That's what the book says."

He laughed at me again and said, "Sub school is crying for qualified engineers. You've got to get on the train tonight and get back to sub school the day after New Year's."

I said, "Look, I'm not a diesel engineer; I'm a steam engineer."

He said, "Doesn't make any difference. You're a steam engineer and you're going back to New London fast." So my wife and I jumped a train that night and got back. That was the end of my destroyer days and start of my submarine days, which continued for damn near 30 years.

I arrived back in New London from the West Coast, a long trip across country by train. I was supposed to get there New Year's Day, and school started the day after New Year's. I was late getting in by one day, because I guess my train was slow. So I reported in one day late, and I explained the circumstances, and I didn't have any problem with that. In peacetime, submarine school had been six months. But it had been condensed to a three-month course during the wartime years. My course ran from the first of January of '44 until the end of March of '44.

It was a very thorough course. We had some excellent World War II skippers, who had done well in the early part of the war as COs of submarines. One of them was Roy

Benson.* Then we had several others, who quite frankly had not done so well and they were sent back to sub school, I guess, to find a spot for them.

These were the more senior people. It was very interesting that the very senior people of the peacetime submarine force were not the hotshots when it came to war. Some were very good, and there were exceptions to that. Mike Fenno was one exception; Weary Wilkins--C. W. Wilkins--was another exception.† They were in the early Twenties--'23, '24, '25--but, by and large, the hotshot skippers came out of a decade from about 1928 year group to 1938 year group. But I'm getting ahead of my story. We had a few of the very fine skippers there and a few of the old fuds who were sort of marking time.

Q: What do you recall specifically about Roy Benson?

Admiral Shear: Oh, he was on top of everything--hard charger. He was a single man. He'd always invite us to visit the nurse quarters, and he'd introduce us to nurses. Fortunately, I was all married myself, but there were a lot of bachelors around, and Roy was the man to see if you wanted a date with a nurse. Roy was a great guy. You could tell he was a great guy. He'd had a great record in the Trigger already, and he was on top of everything. He was good in the attack teacher, simulating attacks.‡ Just a good man to be around. You knew that you had a fine submarine officer when you were talking to Roy Benson. He was a very nice guy too.

Q: Yes.

---

* Commander Roy S. Benson, USN, had been a successful commanding officer of the USS Trigger (SS-237). The oral history of Benson, who retired as a rear admiral, is in the Naval Institute collection.
† Lieutenant Commander Frank W. Fenno, USN, Jr., Naval Academy class of 1925, commanded the USS Trout (SS-202). Lieutenant Commander Charles Warren Wilkins, USN, class of 1924, commanded the USS Narwhal (SS-167).
‡ The attack teacher was a piece of equipment used to train students in making approaches on targets.

Admiral Shear: So we had that very extensive three-month course, and we covered everything. We covered diesel engines. You know, I came back there as a so-called experienced chief engineer of a destroyer plant, which I was.

Q: You were starting over, essentially.

Admiral Shear: I was starting over as far as diesel engines were concerned. But I came back there as a full lieutenant. We had a coverage period there in those wartime years that went all the way from ensign to lieutenant in the courses. So I was fairly senior, having been out in destroyers for a couple of years, and I had a lot of combat behind me. So I thought I was pretty hot stuff. I'd been around.

We had some of my classmates who'd also come back from the Pacific: Jim Osborn, later Admiral Osborn, was there.[*] Pappy Sims was there; Max Duncan, who was with Gene Fluckey in the Barb later on.[†] We had half a dozen of our own class there; then we had a bunch of reserve ensigns and a bunch of others, reserve lieutenants and so forth. We had quite a mixture in that class. I guess there were maybe 250 of us there, give or take.

We had a very vigorous three months, both in classroom work, and then we had the old O-boats of 1920 vintage that we had for learning the rudiments of submarine systems at sea. We'd go out in Long Island Sound for a day at a time, and during our underway periods we'd learn how the systems worked and so forth. Of course, they had nothing whatsoever to do with a fleet boat of the period. They were way, way behind that.

But we studied the fleet boat system, and the fleet boats which we were going to when we finished there were the 1,500-ton submarines that had been developed in the decade before the war, roughly from the 1930 to 1940. It took a full decade to develop, to bring those submarines along to the Gato class, which was the great fleet boat of World

---

[*] Lieutenant James B. Osborn, USN. As a commander, he was commanding officer of the Navy's first Polaris missile submarine, USS George Washington (SSBN-598), when she went into commission on 30 December 1959.
[†] Lieutenant William E. Sims, USN; Lieutenant Max C. Duncan, USN; Commander Eugene B. Fluckey, USN, was awarded the Medal of Honor for his exploits in command of the USS Barb (SS-220) in 1944-45.

War II which fought the war.* Then the Balao class came on a little later, about the same ship with a heavier hull.

Q: Did they have the Marlin and Mackerel there for you?

Admiral Shear: Marlin and Mackerel were there as school boats; they were two of a kind. They were small boats, and they were built with very interesting connotations. There was an element of the submarine force that thought we needed these smaller boats, because they'd be out in the Western Pacific and wouldn't have to go long ranges. Very fortunately, that philosophy did not prevail, so they only built those two. If we had accepted that class instead of the fleet boat that we did build in large numbers, there would have been a disaster, because they were short-legged vessels.

By the time the war came along, we had the Gato class. Well, we went through several designs building up to that, we went through the Pickerels and the Tambors and the P-boats and the T-boats. They had some two-engine boats and some four-engine boats. By the time the war came along, we had settled on the Gato class, and that was a fine submarine. It was as much a surface ship as it was a submarine, and much of our work was done on the surface. I'll get into that more as we go on. But that's the ship that we built in large numbers: at Electric Boat, at Portsmouth Navy Yard, at Mare Island Navy Yard, and then to a lesser degree at Manitowoc in the Great Lakes, and the Cramp Shipyard in Philadelphia, which was pretty much of a disaster. That was the submarine which was being built in large numbers with which we fought the war.

Q: What did you learn about the engineering plants in those boats?

---

* USS Gato (SS-212) was commissioned 31 December 1941. She had a displacement of 1,525 tons on the surface and 2,424 tons submerged. She was 312 feet long, 27 feet in the beam, and had a draft of 19 feet. Her top speed was 20 knots surfaced and 9 knots submerged. She was armed with ten 21-inch torpedo tubes and a 3-inch deck gun.

Admiral Shear: There were two types of propulsion plant, and you had lovers of each one. The Sawfish, which I reported to soon after submarine school, had the Fairbanks-Morse opposed-piston diesel, ten-cylinder engines with a crankshaft below and above, very solid engines. They turned out 1,800 horsepower apiece, and you could run them forever with just absolute solid performance. Magnificent engines. Tough, reliable, run forever. That was half the fleet. The other half of the fleet were the General Motors 16-cylinder V engines, and they turned out just about the same horsepower, about 1,800. In both cases they drove the big generators which provided electric power, either to charge the battery or direct to your electric motors from the electrical control station.

So you had well proven, excellent engines, both General Motors V-engines and the Fairbanks-Morse opposed-piston engines, which just provided superb performance in all the ships. You'd find people that were more partial to the General Motors, because they were a little bit easier to strip down; you could strip down cylinder by cylinder. With the opposed-piston Fairbanks, it was a little bit harder to raise the crankshaft and take out a piston liner and so forth. But they were so reliable you rarely had to do anything with them. So in both cases, the General Motors engines and the Fairbanks-Morse engines came along at just the right time, and they performed magnificently in all the boats throughout the war.

Q: Did submarine school include a section on teaching the enlisted men how to maintain and operate these engines?

Admiral Shear: Yes, it did. Yes, it did. They had pretty good coverage for the officers too.

Q: Would it be fair to say that for the officers in submarines it was more of a hands-on experience than in surface ships?

Admiral Shear: You couldn't have any more of a hands-on experience than I had in the Stack. Some guys don't like to get their hands dirty.

Q: You may have been exceptional in that regard.

Admiral Shear: Well, not really. Not really. The old professional destroyer men from before the war got their hands dirty. They had those old peacetime chief petty officers, who were excellent men, excellent men. We had a lot of those still left in the Stack when I went aboard. They brought me up right. And John McMullen saw to it that I got right down there when they were taking a fine check on the bearing clearance and stripping the pump right down. My hands were right down and dirty as the rest of them. I had a good bringing up.

I think the peacetime Navy, just prior to the war, and then during the war as the war came on, the officers got in there and kept their fingers on things. If they didn't, they got in trouble. None of my people could fool me a minute. In later years, I used to tell my people, "Don't ever come to me and tell me, 'My chief says . . . ' I don't care what your chief says. I want to know what you say. And I want to know what you've done to get down there and get the dirty facts and so forth." I used to impress that on my people.

So I got my hands dirty in destroyers, and I got my hands dirty in submarines. I was always right on top of any problem or casualty or maintenance situation.

Q: Well, that was part of the Rickover philosophy, too, that the officers had to know the equipment.

Admiral Shear: Oh, no question. Of course, that was many years later. But as professional naval officers, we grew up that way. Rickover didn't have to tell us, but he did. I'm going to talk a lot about Rick; Rick did great things for this Navy.

So here we are. We went through this three-month submarine school class, and it was a good, thorough class, with a very full schedule. We worked hard, and we all wanted to go to new construction when we finished. Boats were coming out in every direction, and they needed people for new construction right away. They also needed people in the fleet to replace those who were coming back for new construction. I had a selfish motive.

[Chuckles] I wanted to go to new construction, because I'd get a couple of more months home with my wife. I'd been married for less than two years, and I'd only been home a couple of months. But such was not to be the case.

I finished sub school at the end of March of 1944, and I immediately went out to the Pacific. It's the best thing that could have happened to me. I caught one of those flying boats from San Francisco, flew to Pearl Harbor, and was put in a waiting mode to wait for a submarine, either at Pearl or one of the forward bases. At that time we had just set up the base at Majuro in the Marshall Islands. So I and half a dozen others of my class, including my good friend Pappy Sims, both of us lieutenants, were assigned to the tender Bushnell. After a few days in Pearl, we departed and headed for Majuro.

We arrived in Majuro. We had two submarine tenders there, tending submarines coming back from the Western Pacific for a refit there in the atoll at Majuro. We set up a rest camp ashore under the palm trees on one of those smaller islands, and it was a nice comfortable spot, good food and a place to swim and a place to play softball and we waited for a few days. That was the rest camp there, and boats were coming and going all the time. With two tenders, there was a steady stream of boats coming in for a refit of about ten days, and then two, three to four days of refresher training, and away you'd go back on patrol.

One of the first boats that came in after we arrived was the USS Sawfish (SS-276).[*] She had been built in Portsmouth, New Hampshire, and delivered in 1942. Her first skipper was Gene Sands, and he'd had a good record with her.[†] He was relieved by Commander Alan B. Banister in the class of 1928. Both Sims and I were assigned to the Sawfish after we had been waiting there for a few days on board the tender. Why were we both assigned? Well, at that time, after each patrol you were sending back about a third of your wardroom and about a third of your crew to new construction, so they needed several

---

[*] USS Sawfish (SS-276), was a Gato-class submarine commissioned 26 August 1942. She had a displacement of 1,525 tons on the surface and 2,410 tons submerged. She was 312 feet long, 27 feet in the beam, and had a draft of 19 feet. Her top speed was 20 knots surfaced and 9 knots submerged. She was armed with ten 21-inch torpedo tubes and a 3-inch deck gun.

[†] Lieutenant Commander Eugene T. Sands, USN.

officers. I went aboard as assistant engineer for one patrol; then I took over as engineer. Sims went aboard as torpedo officer. The exec also went ashore at that time, and a reserve named Clark Wilson took over, a very good man, so the three of us, fairly senior lieutenants, went aboard that ship at the same time.

Q: With no submarine experience.

Admiral Shear: With no submarine experience. Well, the exec had some. Clark Wilson had made five or six patrols in Tullibee and was an experienced and competent submariner. Sims had come from a battleship. Sims had been in the Lexington when she was sunk; then he was main battery officer on a battleship, which was a big job for a lieutenant. And I had come from two years in destroyers. So we had all been experienced in war. I had that engineering background in destroyers, which turned out to be very, very important in the months ahead.

Our first patrol was made in the South China Sea as a member of a wolf pack under Commander Warren Wilkins, as the wolf pack commander. We had a good patrol. All the submarines sank a number of ships. And we sank an I-class submarine, among other things.* We also sank several surface ships. We had some very precise intelligence on that I-class submarine. She was coming back from Singapore with a load of German electronic equipment on board. She was headed for the home islands with some important electronic equipment for outfitting the Japanese Navy. We had good intelligence to that effect.

So we had a string of submarines in the South China Sea, waiting for this I-class submarine to come by. She had been sighted down in the South China Sea once or twice, and I think one submarine fired some long-range torpedo shots at her. They didn't hit her. We were very anxious to get this submarine. So ComSubPac had ordered two wolf packs in the northern South China Sea to wait for this submarine and, by golly, to get her when she came through.

---

* The Sawfish sank the Japanese submarine I-29 on 26 July 1944.

We were quite certain she was going through Balintang Channel, which is the northern entrance into the South China Sea from the Western Pacific. So we had our submarines lined up just a few miles apart across Balintang Channel, and, by golly, along she came on the surface. She was actually in sight of two submarines, both making an approach on her. We were the closer of the two, and we hit her with three torpedoes. She disintegrated, and the captain got many big accolades from that. We also sank several surface ships on that patrol. Let's see, damaged a tanker, and we sank a transport, so it was a good patrol.*

You alternated refit places, so at the end of that patrol, instead of going back to Majuro we went back and stopped briefly on the way through Midway Island to fuel and make reports. Then we continued on to Pearl for our refit, which we did with a wonderful week in the Royal Hawaiian Hotel, resting up and getting a good refit. Then we went right back out on patrol to the Western Pacific again.

This time our skipper was the senior commander. Alan B. Banister was commander of the wolf pack called Banister's Beagles. We had with us the Drum, the Icefish, and the Sawfish. We had a patrol assignment in the northern part of the South China Sea, and again we had a very successful patrol. We got into a large convoy in which we got inside the escorts on the surface at night and sank a large tanker. Then we got ahead of them and made a submerged approach the next morning, and we also were able to call in the other ships of the wolf pack. Everybody got a whack at that convoy and did very well. Then we had one or two other individual attacks, and that was a highly successful patrol. Captain Banister got Navy Crosses for both of those first two patrols.

At the end of that patrol we went back to Majuro for a refit there in the Marshall Islands and a chance to rest up in that rather mediocre little rest camp in the palm trees. Then we got a new skipper out of the class of '38, Douglas Pugh.† We made a patrol from there, this time back to the area around Taiwan and the islands around Okinawa. By that

---

* The Sawfish sank the tanker Tachibana Maru on 9 October 1944 and the converted seaplane tender Kimikawa Maru on 23 October 1944.
† Lieutenant Commander Douglas H. Pugh, USN.

time, shipping was getting pretty scarce; we were running out of targets. So we got some lifeguard assignments and picked up several aviators.

I forgot to mention that we picked up several aviators in our earlier patrols too. We picked up an aviator off of northern Taiwan from a carrier raid, and we also had some lifeguard assignments around Okinawa before we went in and invaded Okinawa. But there were essentially no targets left, so we had no ship sightings at all on that patrol except for some small coastal craft, which weren't worthy to torpedo.

We completed that patrol, and we went back to Guam. Guam at that time was just being well consolidated. We went out to the rest camp on the western side of Guam, the windward side, and they handed each one of us a rifle as we went into the rest camp. We said, "Well, what's the rifle for?"

They said, "Don't worry, the Japs will be down tonight." The Japs were then holed up in the hills, and they were hungry, so they would come down at night and poke around for food. We thought they weren't a problem. One of the crews of another submarine went out for a hike behind the rest camp, and they were ambushed by the Japanese in the foothills. They lost half a dozen men from their engine room. So from then on we took a pretty hard look about what we were doing around there.

At the end of that refit we went back on what was essentially a lifeguard patrol. We picked up several aviators, again no targets, and that was it. By that time we were well into '45. We were then scheduled to go back for overhaul on the West Coast. We went back and stopped at Pearl for a few days and went on back to San Francisco for an overhaul. By the time that overhaul was finished, it was August of '45, and the war was over.* So we did not deploy on war patrol after that overhaul.

Q: What can you say about the personalities and styles of the two skippers, Banister and Pugh, of the Sawfish?

---

* Hostilities with Japan ended on 15 August 1945.

Admiral Shear: Both of them terrific people, both very different. Banister was out of the Naval Academy class of '28. He was fairly late getting his command; some of his classmates and even the younger officers had gotten their commands before and made their records. As a matter of fact, he had been on the staff at submarine school beforehand, so he was rather late in getting out and getting his own command. He did very well. He was a fine man. Cool as a cucumber under fire, very friendly man. He showed complete confidence in all of us, even though those of us who had come aboard fairly new in submarines. He knew we were experienced; he knew we were learning fast. We learned very fast, and he put both Sims and me up for submarine qualification after one patrol. And he knew submarining. He had been around that submarine school as an instructor, and he knew how to run their attack teachers, and he knew how to make real attacks. We never had any qualm about him handling a ship.

Q: Sounds as if he was aggressive too.

Admiral Shear: He was very aggressive. I was the diving officer for submerged attacks, and I was the officer of the deck on the bridge for night surface attacks. So I saw a lot of Alan B. Banister right close up on the bridge of the ship at night attacks. For submerged attacks, I was one level below at the diving station. He was in the conning tower.

I can remember like it was yesterday when we got inside the escorts of that big convoy and fired both our bow tubes and stern tubes and got several ships. The ship I remember particularly was a big tanker which broke in two. My responsibility after we made the attacks was to keep the skipper advised, when we were on the surface inside the perimeter of the convoy, as to what the escorts were doing. It just so happened that I was blessed with good night vision, and through my binoculars I could observe the escorts very clearly. I could tell that they had not picked us up because they had large angles on the bow. They had not swung toward us, and I kept the skipper informed all along that we had no particular danger from the escorts. He told me later that it was very, very reassuring for him to know that he didn't have to worry about the escorts. That was my responsibility as officer of the deck--that after we made the attack I had to make sure that we weren't going

Harold E. Shear #1 - 101

to be run down. So if he wanted to stay on the surface and make another attack, he could do so. Many skippers did that during the war, particularly the aggressive skippers.

We had a special code to let our wolf pack know that we'd made attacks and let them know where we were. As I recall, both the Icefish and the Drum were able to get in on the convoy, port and starboard, for attacks that night. I'd have to check the book on that, but I believe that is what happened.

Q: Some boats communicated with the SJ radar. Did you use that?

Admiral Shear: Yes, yes, that's right. You could actually key it with a Morse code, and then you had a two-letter grouping of signals that said, for example, "I'm in contact with a convoy," or, "I've just made an attack." They used a very simple code, which could easily been broken, but for the spur of the moment it was a good thing to use, and each two-letter combination meant something.

Q: It was quick.

Admiral Shear: It was quick, that's right, and we used the SJ a lot. Rarely did we use the actual radio itself. Radio silence was a very strict thing.

Q: You've described two different types of wolf packs, one that had a commodore in charge and one that had a skipper in charge.

Admiral Shear: That's right. Yep.

Q: What comparisons would you draw?

Admiral Shear: When they started the wolf packs, they felt they had to have a squadron commander. Turned out they didn't have to have a squadron commander. Weary Wilkins was a good squadron commander. After a couple of those runs, I think it became obvious to ComSubPac and other senior people on the staffs that a good skipper was just as good a wolf pack commander as having a division or squadron commander on board.

Q: Sometimes the commodore was almost viewed as excess baggage, wasn't he?

Admiral Shear: Well, I wouldn't say that, but it soon became obvious that a skipper could handle it very well, and they did. They did, repeatedly. So I saw both of those. We did not have the commodore on board with us, but it was not a problem as far as the functioning of the wolf pack was concerned.

So those were my four wartime submarine patrols.

Q: Did you come under depth charge attack any?

Admiral Shear: Yes, yes.

Q: Would you please describe that?

Admiral Shear: Well, I must say that we were never very severely depth charged. Some boats were just beat to death, and some boats were lost I'm sure we don't know about, and some came in with dented hulls and everything else. We had some fairly good depth-charge attacks, but nothing that was really an all-out, right-on-top-of-us attack. You could hear the depth charges being armed with sort of a click-click, and you could hear and feel the explosions around you, but during my time in the Sawfish we were never under so severe an attack that it was dangerous. We were shaken up some, but I never felt that we were in danger of losing the ship or anything of that nature.

Now, some ships were heavily damaged, electrical circuits knocked out and various other things and piping, ruptures of piping and valves. Although we had several pretty good attacks, I never had anything of that seriousness. I remember a classmate of mine, Bill

Pugh, was in the Puffer, and they were really beaten to death.* Then another submarine was so badly damaged that she had to come back on the surface, she had to call for help from surrounding submarines, the Salmon.

Q: That was Dick Laning's boat.†

Admiral Shear: Salmon, that's right, Dick Laning was exec. And the skipper was . . .

Q: Ken Nauman.‡

Admiral Shear: Kenny Nauman. Good man.

Q: And the Silversides with John Coye escorted her.§

Admiral Shear: Yes, that's right. I'd forgotten that--Jack Coye later became my squadron commander. But that's correct. You've learned a lot of things.

Q: What is the function of the diving officer?

Admiral Shear: The diving officer controls the depth of the ship. The skipper wants so many inches of periscope above the water. The periscope depth of those fleet boats was 67 feet, and if he wanted just a few inches above the water he might order 66 feet, and, by golly, you hold her there. If he wanted a few more inches he might order 65 feet or even 60 feet if he wanted to take a long look around with a high periscope, or something of that

---

* Lieutenant William M. Pugh II, USN. The ordeal of the Puffer (SS-268) was on 9-10 October 1943, when Japanese escorts held her down for 37 hours and 45 minutes.
† Lieutenant Richard B. Laning, USN. The oral history of Laning, who retired as a captain, is in the Naval Institute collection.
‡ Lieutenant Commander Harley K. Nauman, USN.
§ Commander John S. Coye, Jr., USN. The oral history of Coye, who retired as a rear admiral, is in the Naval Institute collection.

nature. But the diving officer's job in a battle station was a very important job, because he had to maintain precise depth. He had to be able to control the ship when the torpedoes were fired, because when the torpedoes were fired there was a weight change in the ship.

Q: How did you compensate?

Admiral Shear: You compensated with a very competent petty officer at the diving station through a manifold flood and valves, discharge valves with pumps. You could pump to sea, you could pump fore and aft, you could do any kind of rearranging of ballast that you wanted to do.

Q: Did you make any approaches?

Admiral Shear: I did not make any approaches, no. The skipper made all the approaches in my ship. We made practice approaches, training and so forth.

Q: Did you use your deck gun at all in any of the attacks?

Admiral Shear: I never made a deck gun attack. We considered it a couple of times on small craft, but I personally never made a deck gun attack. We were always fully prepared for it. We practiced surfacing very quickly and getting our gun crew on deck very quickly, and we did that frequently. We were prepared for an opportunity. But my ship never made a battle surface and gun attack. A number of other submarines did, and some were successful, particularly in small craft.

Q: Did you have any problems with aircraft?

Admiral Shear: You always had to be alert for aircraft. We were run down a number of times by aircraft, but we were never under a serious attack by aircraft. We were always able to get under and get clear. Alert lookouts were very important in a submarine, as well as an alert officer of the deck. You kept at least three lookouts up there on the periscope shears all the time we were on the surface. But we found, as the war went on, that you could stay on the surface a great big percentage of the time. Much of our success in the Western Pacific and South China Sea was in night surface attacks.

Q: Well, that was a problem early in the war. They didn't know how dangerous the hazards were and tended to overcompensate.

Admiral Shear: They tended to overcompensate; that's quite correct. But by the time I got out there in '44, skippers then in command really knew what they were doing.

Q: And they had good torpedoes too.

Admiral Shear: Yes, and good torpedoes, and that took two years to get cleaned up.

Q: You described Banister. What do you remember about Pugh as a skipper?

Admiral Shear: He was class of '38, a younger man. This was his first command, good man, good personality. He'd been a very good baseball player at the Naval Academy. Tall, slender fellow. Nice fellow. Very competent man. But we didn't have the opportunity to sink any ships; there weren't any targets.

Q: It was a great frustration.

Admiral Shear: We had essentially swept the Japanese from the high seas. Literally. And submarines had much of the responsibility for that. Now, the carrier aircraft had been pretty good, too, but we'd been working on that for several years. The situation we ran into when we were first out there, when they were running back and forth through the South China Sea from the East Indies up to the home islands, you could find targets of every description.

The submarines essentially wiped the Japanese from the high seas, merchant ships, men of war, anything, and all you've got to do is look at the record.

That brings me to the dropping of the atomic bombs.* They caught everybody by surprise, of course. We'd been operating out of Guam during our last patrol. The B-29s at that time were flying out of Guam and Titian, making regular raids on Tokyo and other cities. Of course, we went into Iwo Jima, among other things, to get a field there so that the damaged planes could land.† On those last patrols we did nothing except pick up aviators; there weren't any ships left to attack. Prior to the invasion of Iwo Jima, we generally had a string of submarines south of the island to pick up downed aviators.

Those of us on the scene out there felt that Japan was on its absolute last legs. They had no ships left, they had no merchantmen, wasn't much of a navy left. They were right down to practically no fuel, and they were essentially just prostrated. We felt that they were going to capitulate soon. After the atom bomb was dropped, many of us out there felt that it was an unnecessary thing that we should not have done, because they were going to fall soon anyway. There was great concern about an invasion with heavy casualties, and I think that swayed people, particularly back in Washington--the fear of running up big casualties. I think they would have capitulated in a matter of a few months with no invasion whatsoever. Those raids on the cities, both from the carriers and from the B-29s, were having a devastating effect. Their capability to carry out the war any further was right down to rock bottom.

Q: Well, plus all the mines that the B-29s dropped.

---

* In the first combat use of atomic bombs, U.S. B-29 bombers attacked Hiroshima, on the island of Honshu, on 6 August 1945 and Nagasaki, on Kyushu, on 9 August.
† On 19 February 1945, U.S. Marines invaded the island of Iwo Jima, approximately 660 miles south of Tokyo, and captured it in a fierce campaign. The objective was to provide a forward airfield--an emergency landing site--to support the U.S. bomber offensive against Japan.

Admiral Shear: That's correct. The Inland Sea was fully mined, Tokyo Bay was mined, and fundamentally, they had no oil. They simply couldn't function without oil. The submarines saw to it that they didn't get that oil, in large measure.

Q: They were running their motor vehicles on charcoal.

Admiral Shear: On charcoal, absolutely correct. So I think those of us on the scene out there recognized, more than the people back running the government, that Japan was much further down the stream than was recognized. That's strictly the case.

I think the same thing applied to the Vietnam War, that situation out there that we saw on the scene was much different than what they saw back here in Washington. I'll talk about that a little later.

Q: What do you recall of Pappy Sims as a shipmate in the Sawfish?

Admiral Shear: Great guy. Great guy. He lives here in Annapolis. He was an All-American football player. We were close friends. We'd known each other at the Naval Academy and at submarine school. We were aboard the same ship, and we had a hell of a good wardroom. Good skipper, good exec, good department heads, Bobby Kunhardt out of '43 was one of our shipmates, and we had several good mustang officers.[*] We had two or three good reserve officers, one of whom was a radar expert. He had been sent to radar school, and, boy, he was invaluable. Because he kept our radar in top-notch, peaked-up condition.

Q: I suspect morale was very high in that boat.

Admiral Shear: Morale was very high. We had a good crew and good wardroom, and the camaraderie between the wardroom and the crew was great. Terrific.

---

[*] Lieutenant (junior grade) Robert M. Kunhardt, USN.

Q: What do you recall about the quality of the enlisted men of the crew?

Admiral Shear: Absolutely top-notch, even with that one-third turnover between patrols so men could go back for the new ships. The petty officers that we had on board and the young fellows coming along training were crackerjack people. Chief petty officers and the first class--of course, we had a continual training program going on all the time, particularly for the new kids out of sub school like myself. First of all, you had to qualify in submarines, and then you had to qualify in a particular job, so the qualification process was an ongoing thing right around the clock. We had great crews, and the crews that I ran into in rest camps when we had half a dozen submarines together were the same caliber of people and same caliber of wardrooms.

Q: You mentioned the stop in Guam. What do you remember about the rest periods in general? Any other highlights?

Admiral Shear: Yes. Let's see, I had two rest periods in Majuro, one rest period in Pearl, one rest period in Guam. Pearl, that was paradise. Absolute paradise. I think they charged us 50 cents a day for a suite of rooms at the Royal Hawaiian. Milk, ice cream, and fresh vegetables were what you missed most, and we just loaded up on them. We loaded up enough, everything we could to take to sea, and the fresh stuff lasted about two weeks. From then on we ate frozen and chilled and dried. Submarines always fed well, never had a problem with feeding. We'd load for 90 days every time. Typical patrol would be 60-plus days, but you always loaded out for 90. Every nook and cranny on the submarine we loaded out--chockablock.

Rest camps--period of rest, relaxation, exercise, ball games. Just a good, healthy period to relax and get back to battery and get a suntan. You'd come ashore with an absolute pallor, get a little suntan, relax, read some mail, write some letters, things of that nature. Those forward area rest camps were pretty spartan. We had some Quonset huts, hacked out a softball field, and there were some pretty nice swimming beaches, but that was about it. You had good food, and I told you that one we were one of the first submarines to go into that one in Guam, and the Japanese were still up in the hills.

Q: You mentioned when the tape wasn't on that you saw large labor battalions there, black sailors.

Admiral Shear: Yes. That was later on. We were building up Guam for a fare-thee-well, and that was to be a major base there as we proceeded on up. We had the big airfield out there, Anderson Field. B-29s were flying out of there, as well as Tinian, and we had a big repair establishment going on. We had one of those big battleship docks in Apra Harbor. Lot of repair facilities there ashore in the harbor.

Q: Big supply facility.

Admiral Shear: Big supply facility and those black labor battalions, which I saw a little bit of, because my old friend was there with them. I went to visit my friend a couple of times, and I saw what that operation was. They were just worker bees. I'm not sure we did our best by those blacks, probably didn't.

Q: That was the policy of the time.

Admiral Shear: That's right.

Q: I've talked to any number of submariners who say that there's a special feeling about serving in the boats. How would you articulate that?

Admiral Shear: Every submariner loves his boat.

Q: Why is that?

Admiral Shear: Well, they're small ships, and you know everybody well. You know that submarines are the best in the business, you know you've got a great weapon system, you know you can go out there and fight a war. You got six or eight million tons of sunk shipping to show for it. You know what you did in World War II and the camaraderie and the expertise and the training you get, I don't think you can beat anywhere in the Navy. There's a unique closeness to a submarine organization.

Q: Well, and a degree of informality also.

Admiral Shear: A degree of informality, that's correct. Not undue informality, but a degree of informality and something that you never let get out of hand. And you've got crackerjack people, closely screened before they go to sub school and sub school behind them. If you have any lemons, they'll drop out before they're through. You work with just top-notch people across the board. It was that way in World War II; it was that way before nuclear power; it's that way today with nuclear power. Just the nature of the beast.

Q: Anything more to say on the Sawfish?

Admiral Shear: She was a great submarine, and she brought me up right in submarines. We had two great skippers, and that was important. I had great destroyer days with great skippers, and I had great submarine days with great skippers my first couple of years in the business.

Q: Not everybody was so lucky.

Admiral Shear: Not everybody was so lucky; that's right.
    I served in the Sawfish from April of '44 until August of '45. When the war was over, I went ashore waiting to be exec of another submarine. All the submarines started coming back in large numbers to the San Francisco Bay area, and I was put on the staff as

operations officer of the Submarine Refit and Training Group there. We had the responsibility for taking all the submarines back. We brought back four or five tenders. We set them up in Tiburon, across the bay from San Francisco. We had 50-odd submarines lined up there waiting to be decommissioned.

We had a major operation going on at both San Francisco Naval Shipyard and Mare Island Naval Shipyard, where we had special crews put together to lay these ships up. They put the machinery out of commission, greased and oiled them and so forth, and shielded them so they would not deteriorate when they put them in the reserve fleet. A fellow named Bob Keating was the senior operations officer for the San Francisco Bay area.[*]

We worked for C. W. Wilkins, whose nickname was Weary Wilkins, because he was always busy, busy, busy--busier than everybody. Great guy, out of the class of '24 at the Naval Academy, and he had a good war record himself. One of those few of the early skippers that I said did well. His headquarters were at Mare Island, and we ran the operation for the bay area out of the Federal Building in downtown San Francisco. We had the responsibility for all the operations in and around the bay area. That went on for the better part of a year. That was a very busy period. I made lieutenant commander in October of '45.

That was also the time of the demobilization. The name of the game at the end of the war was by God, get home fast. No matter where you were in the Navy, whether submarines, destroyers, or anywhere, you had a point system.[†] Regulars couldn't go home, but reserves could go home, whether you were Army, Navy, Marine Corps, whatever you were. So we set up a Magic Carpet to bring the boys home. We used amphibious transports, we used any vessel that could carry troops and personnel and we'd run them from the Western Pacific back to San Francisco, back to the West Coast, all up and down the coast, and send them home. We really did this faster than we should have, but there was a personal clamor and a political clamor to get the boys home, so we had to do it.

---

[*] Commander Robert A. Keating, USN.
[†] For the demobilization, the services had a point system to determine individual priorities for leaving the service. Points were awarded for length of service, overseas service, battle stars, decorations, and dependent children. Those with the highest number of points were the earliest discharged.

We drew down the Navy so badly that we had hardly enough people to man the ships. I remember in submarines we were down to a two-section watch. As these submarines went out of commission in the San Francisco Bay area, they took the officers off them, particularly the skippers and execs, and put them on amphibious ships, large passenger-carrying vessels and sent them out to the Western Pacific to bring home the troops. They became skippers and execs of those big ships. They were in that game for a year, year and a half, until we got the boys home. And if you were on a ship in San Francisco Bay and you had enough points, boy, you went home. They couldn't hold you. Some of the ships got stripped right down so they really could hardly keep themselves together. That probably could have been handled better, but it wasn't and it affected everybody. It affected the service ships, it affected submarines, it affected the whole Navy.

After I finished that job, I became exec of a submarine based at Pearl. That was in end of '45, early '46. I went out to Pearl to become exec of the Becuna (SS-319).* That was a period of great relaxation. The war was over, submarines had done well, submarine skippers were practically all heroes, and I in that period had two crackerjack skippers. One was a fellow named Frank Smith out of '35, and the other fellow was named J. K. Fyfe out of '36; they relieved each other.† Both of them had great war records.

We had three squadrons at Pearl at that time, about 25 or 30 submarines. All had similar skippers, and all had similar experienced wardrooms like myself and many others. The skippers couldn't care whether school kept or not. Very interesting relaxation situation. The war was over, they had all done well, they all had great reputations, and they just wanted to relax.

Q: There was nothing more to prove.

---

* USS Becuna (SS-319) was a Balao-class submarine commissioned 27 May 1944. She had a displacement of 1,525 tons on the surface and 2,424 tons submerged. She was 312 feet long, 27 feet in the beam, and had a draft of 15 feet. Her top speed was 20 knots surfaced and 9 knots submerged. She was armed with ten 21-inch torpedo tubes and a 5-inch gun.
† Commander Frank M. Smith, USN; Commander John K. Fyfe, USN.

Admiral Shear: Nothing more to prove. As I told you, we were stripped down in personnel, and in many cases we were down to two sections, couldn't get under way for more than eight or ten hours a day for local exercises. So the skippers essentially turned the boats over to the execs and said, "Just take care of things." That was a great opportunity for us execs, because we ran the whole damn show. When the skipper showed up once or twice a week to look over things, we made sure that everything was in good shape. The skippers were together with their wives for the first time since the war was over.

Housing was very sparse around Pearl, but they made a bunch of Quonset huts available for us, very crudely furnished. We lived in those Quonset huts, and we had a small number of Navy housing units there. The skippers were together with their families, and we got our families over in due course. It was a period of a year, year and a half, when, boy, the Navy just sat back, relaxed, and sort of caught up on itself. I had a ball because--hell's bells--the ship was mine. We had a good ship, we had a good crew.

We lost a lot of people, but we had enough local operations, and then as we gradually built our crews up, we got back into more extensive operations with the fleet. We went out to the Western Pacific for a couple of tours, and operations with the fleet around Japan, Subic Bay, and things like that. We made one cruise down to Truk in the South Pacific Islands, with local operation forces in that area.

But that was a very interesting period, that year or two after the war. I'm trying to give you a feel for what it was like to be in ships at that time. Destroyers were the same way; they were stripped right down, half a crew, things of that nature.

Q: Well, and bigger ships often sat pierside, because there weren't enough people to operate them.

Admiral Shear: That's correct. The Magic Carpet was going full blast at that time, and that came to an end as we finally got everybody home. Some of those people that had been sent off to those ships came back in submarines again.

Q: What was life like for a young married couple in Hawaii?

Admiral Shear: After we had spent the whole war separated, except for a month or two, it was paradise.

Q: Like a long honeymoon.

Admiral Shear: Long honeymoon, precisely. A long honeymoon. It was paradise. We had a little baby girl just a few months old.* Weekends were no particular strain. You'd go out to the beach every weekend and relax and live it up. All those good fruits around the Hawaiian Islands. Living was just very nice, very relaxed. The tempo of operations was not too high, so it was just a very delightful time in my life and the lives of my colleagues and friends. Lots of friends and classmates around there.

Q: Any that you remember offhand?

Admiral Shear: Oh, yes, many, many, many. George Steele and Russell Bryan were a pair of them in my wardroom; they were out there with their families.† And the skippers' families were all out there. Throughout the two or three squadrons that were there we had many friends and classmates. Andy Kerr was one you mentioned.‡ Hugh Murphree, another fine submariner.§ Those classes from about 1940 to 1945--we were all in that category out there, having gone through the entire war together. Just a great living period.

Q: Anything to say specifically about Steele and Bryan in your boat?

---

* The Shears' daughter, Kathleen, was born 20 May 1946.
† Lieutenant (junior grade) George P. Steele II, USN; Lieutenant (junior grade) Clarence Russell Bryan, USN. Both eventually retired as vice admirals. Steele's oral history is in the Naval Institute collection.
‡ Lieutenant (junior grade) Alex A. Kerr, USN. The oral history of Kerr, who retired as a captain, is in the Naval Institute collection.
§ Lieutenant (junior grade) Hugh D. Murphree, USN.

Admiral Shear: Steele and Bryan were great officers. They were very competent officers. The Naval Academy was then on a three-year course, so they graduated in '44, and they got out in time to make, I think, one patrol each. Frank Smith, who became the skipper of the Becuna, had made six good runs in the Hammerhead. He had Bryan with him, and Steele was in the Becuna under Hank Sturr.* So each had made one patrol, and they both became qualified in submarines. They were very competent and very cocky, so I had to sit on them about once a week. They knew I was boss, and if I said something they knew I meant business, but they also liked to run me all they could.

Q: What's an example of how they would run you?

Admiral Shear: Oh, they'd kid me a lot, of course, and I'd kid them too. They knew I had a point beyond which they couldn't go, and they never went beyond that point.

Q: They calculated very carefully.

Admiral Shear: They calculated very carefully, never overstepped it. But they were very fine officers, and you see where they both made three stars. And we had some other very fine officers.

Q: One thing you mentioned, they had confidence. I never noted Admiral Steele to be lacking in self-confidence.

Admiral Shear: Never, never. And, of course, I always gave them plenty of responsibility. I had complete confidence in them, too, as well as others in the wardroom.

Q: The only limitation on your enjoyment of this tropical paradise would be the pay, but at least you got submarine pay to help out.

---

*Commander Henry D. Sturr, USN.

Admiral Shear: That helped a little bit. That's right. That's right. Submarine pay helped.

Q: How was the cost of living out there in those days?

Admiral Shear: In those days it was quite reasonable, quite reasonable.

Q: That would help also.

Admiral Shear: Yes, although the pay wasn't too high. I remember at the end of the month sometimes you'd save five cents a bottle so you'd go to the grocery store to pick up a few items. But nobody suffered, nobody went hungry. It was a very good life.

Q: There was no real mission for the submarine force at the time, just to keep the flame burning.

Admiral Shear: Well, we kept the flame burning. We provided ASW services a lot. As the fleet got back to battery, we'd have fleet exercises, both locally and in other parts of the Pacific. And we'd make periodic deployments to the Western Pacific for three or four months at a time, things like that. Then as time went on, we got more and more involved in the rim of the Pacific with the other navies: the Australian Navy, the New Zealand Navy, the British Navy in Singapore, and things like that.

Q: During that period, how much awareness did you have of the technological developments that were coming down the line--Guppies and snorkels?*

---

* The term "Guppy" grew out of the initials for the postwar modification fitted to World War II fleet boats to give them greater underwater propulsion power (GUPP).

Admiral Shear: We went through the Guppy period, and the first Guppy came out there before I left the Becuna. And a fellow out of '38 was skipper; he's now retired and living out in town here and raises Christmas trees. I'll think of his name in a minute.

Q: Skip Giffen.

Admiral Shear: Skip Giffen.* He brought the first Guppy out to Pearl Harbor from Mare Island. So we saw the Guppies coming along. We had three or four versions of Guppies: the Guppy I, the Guppy IAs, the Guppy IIs and the fleet snorkel, four modifications of the fleet boat of World War II. I was exec of the Becuna when she was a fleet boat. Well, after I left and went ashore to Washington, the Becuna came east and was Guppy-ized as a Guppy IA by the Electric Boat Company. Then, several years later, I came back as her skipper, but I've got two or three intervening chapters before then.

So we saw those technological developments coming along, and we didn't know what was going on with this new class of Trigger and Tang until we actually got there. We didn't know anything about the pancake diesel engine and, thank God, we didn't. I'll tell you a story about that if you haven't already heard it from Ned Beach.

Q: No, I haven't.

Admiral Shear: Then I went ashore from being exec of the Becuna. I was ordered to the staff of ComSubPac, who was then a very fine officer named Ossie Colclough.† He'd been JAG of the Navy; he was a lawyer, brilliant man.‡ I think I'm correct when I say he stood higher than anybody who ever went through George Washington University Law School. That was the reputation he had at the time. I was his communications officer. He was something of a stickler, but he was a very good man, and he treated me very well.

---

* Captain Robert C. Giffen, Jr., USN (Ret.).
† Rear Admiral Oswald S. Colclough, USN, served as Commander Submarine Force Pacific Fleet, 1948-49.
‡ JAG--Judge Advocate General.

Q: Being a lawyer, he would be a stickler.

Admiral Shear: I guess he would, yes, but he ran a good show. And his flag lieutenant was a man named Murray Frazee, out of class of '39.[*] Frazee was a great guy, a submariner, as was Colclough. Colclough had been up in the Aleutians in submarines during the war as a squadron commander.

So I had a great year there.

Q: What sort of duties did you have?

Admiral Shear: I was the force communicator. I was responsible for all submarine force communications, which included communications for the boats, communications for the big staff, documentation of, control of communication publications, and things of that nature. It was a very sizable job, plus we ran the submarine radio station in Pearl, where we communicated directly to our ships at sea through the big VLF station down at Lualualei on the far side of the Hawaiian island of Oahu.[†]

Q: Well, you had no particular communications speciality, so you must have needed some school call.

Admiral Shear: None. None, so I learned in a hurry. But at that time, anything you took on, you learned in a hurry. It was good background for me, because I had not had any of that background. I was a makee-learn. Why they picked me to go up there and become force communicator with no experience, I don't know. I guess it was because I was available and on hand and had some submarine experience.

---

[*] Lieutenant Commander Murray B. Frazee, Jr., USN. During World War II, he had been executive officer of the <u>Tang</u> (SS-306) under Commander Richard H. O'Kane, USN, a Medal of Honor recipient.
[†] VLF--very low frequency.

So I had a great year there. I was two years exec, one year force communicator, then I was overdue for shore duty. I had never been ashore before. SubPac was considered fleet staff duty there. So I was ordered back to Washington. I asked to go back to Washington. People had been telling me up and down the line that, "The thing you've got to do if you're going to go anywhere, you've got to go to Washington." Very sound advice. Lot of guys fight to stay out of Washington, but I always went, and I had eight tours there. I'll tell you about that as we go along. It won't all get done today.

So in the summer of '49 I was ordered back to the Bureau of Naval Personnel in Washington. I went back there and was ordered into a section called training plans. We had the responsibility for determining what schools needed what number of people and what number of people to put into which schools where. All the fleet schools in Great Lakes, West Coast, East Coast--we had a big school system then.

I worked for an aviator named Red McDonald.* A more non-reg guy you'll never find, but a hell of a naval officer. He'd been a B-24 combat pilot all during the war with a great record behind him.† He was not carrier pilot; he was a B-24 pilot, and those were big four-engine bombers. We had a sizable number of them, including the Air Force. People don't realize we had a big number too. They were all over the Western Pacific.

Anyway, I went to work for Red McDonald. Red had his war record behind him too. So he didn't care very much whether the school kept, but he was a good naval officer. He let me run the show there, and we had all these quotas to determine and get people into school and so forth, and it was quite a sizable job.

He lived over here in Annapolis, and he was probably one of the--if not <u>the</u>--biggest Navy athletic fans I have ever run into. He had been manager of the football team which included Dusty Dornin and Slade Cutter and all those greats of the mid-'30s, and they were all his big buddies.‡ He was a great fan of all kinds of Navy sports, and he really didn't care

---

* Commander Harold W. McDonald, USN.
† The Navy version of the Army Air Forces's B-24 Liberator was designated the PB4Y.
‡ Midshipman Robert E. Dornin, USN, and Midshipman Slade D. Cutter, USN, gradated from the Naval Academy with McDonald in the class of 1935 and went on to highly successful careers in submarines. Their oral histories are in the Naval Institute collection.

whether school kept or not, as long as he could get to a football game. But he did a good job, and he let me run things. We did a good job, and we kept our bosses happy.

All of a sudden, things changed--overnight. We were just bringing the Navy down to size. Big de-escalation of everything. School quotas were cut and everything else of that nature. Along came Korea, and overnight we reversed course, just reversed course 180 degrees, and everything we had been doing we did exactly the other way. We beefed up our schools, we beefed up our enlisted quotas, we recruited more people, we got ready for another major war. It was a major war.

Q: You just can't turn on the faucet on these things.

Admiral Shear: That's right. We had turned off the faucet, and then we had to get it turned on again. It took a while, and it took some doing.

Q: And planning, which is the part you were in.

Admiral Shear: And planning, exactly. So that was a totally new experience for me, coming ashore and seeing that personnel downside, then a complete reversal to the upside. That was really quite an experience.

Q: Well, part of it, I would think, would be getting people trained for the ships coming out of mothballs.

Admiral Shear: Oh, exactly. I was all part of it, including recalling reserves. I was not on the officer side; it was all enlisted. The desk next to me was doing the same thing for officers. We had a much larger number, so we really had a bigger job than the officers did.

So that was a great experience.

Q: Well, one advantage you had on those reserves is that they had a fair amount of training already. You had a cadre of people to draw on.

Admiral Shear: That's right, that's right. We did that as much as we could, because World War II was not that far behind. A lot of people were very unhappy about being recalled.

Q: That's right, because they had gotten established in civilian life.

Admiral Shear: Because we did this involuntarily. You got some volunteers, but a lot of it we did involuntarily. If they had so many years of obligation, we hauled them back. There was quite a bit of unhappiness, particularly in the officers.

Q: I've talked to some of those people.

Admiral Shear: But, anyway, that was a big change, and we got back on a wartime footing again. We got the fleet manned, people in training schools, and off they went to Korea. That was a hell of a war, actually. That was a nasty, tough war. Probably as tough or tougher than Vietnam, but you don't hear about it anymore. You talk about a few hundred missing prisoners of war in Vietnam; we've got tens of thousands of them in Korea. As they say, "Different ships, different long splices." Ever hear that expression?

Q: No.

Admiral Shear: Different ways of doing things. Different ships, different long splices. There are half a dozen ways to make a long splice. So there we are. Now I'm involved in beefing up Korea. And we just got that done and everything in good shape, and one day I was called over to the submarine desk. The head of the submarine desk was one Chick

Clarey, then a commander; became four-star Vice Chief and CinCPacFlt.* His assistant was Jim Calvert; you probably have heard of Jim.†

Q: Certainly.

Admiral Shear: Superintendent of the Naval Academy. Both of them great guys. They hauled me over there one morning and said, "Shear, you're about ready to go back to sea again. How'd you like to put the Trigger in commission?" I couldn't believe it. Best damn job I could possibly have gotten. They said, "Ned Beach is going to be skipper and we want you to go up there and be exec."‡ They said, "We think you can hold Beach down." I never told Beach that.

Q: What does that mean?

Admiral Shear: You have to know Beach a little bit. I'll tell you some more stories about that.

So out of the blue I got orders to the Trigger.§

Q: Which suggests that you were certainly considered a front-runner.

Admiral Shear: Well, I guess. I had a good record. I had a good reputation, and a lot of my classmates did too. I was no God or anything of that nature; I was just a hell of a good naval officer.

---

* Commander Bernard A. Clarey, USN. The oral history of Clarey, who retired as a four-star admiral, is in the Naval Institute collection.
† Lieutenant Commander James F. Calvert. The oral history of Calvert, who retired as a vice admiral, is in the Naval Institute collection.
‡ Commander Edward L. Beach, USN.
§ USS Trigger (SS-564) was commissioned 31 March 1952. She had a displacement of 1,615 tons on the surface and 1,990 tons submerged. She was 269 feet long, 27 feet in the beam, and had a draft of 17 feet. Her top speed was 15 knots surfaced and 18 knots submerged. She was armed with eight 21-inch torpedo tubes.

So I was ordered to the Trigger, and the first thing I did was go off to advanced PCO school for about a month, six weeks I guess.* Then I reported to the Trigger in the summer of '51. She was then about two-thirds or maybe three-quarters of the way through new construction at Electric Boat. The Navy built three Triggers at Electric Boat and three Tangs at Portsmouth.† They were all essentially the same class of submarines, although they had some minor differences. They were the first new submarines built since the end of the war, and the first new submarines since the fleet boat. The Guppies were just versions of the fleet boat.

So they had many changes in them. The first thing we had to do was qualify in the new submarine and find out what she was all about, what made her tick, what was new and different in the systems. There were many differences. Probably the principal difference was the power plant. The three ships built in New London had the General Motors pancake diesel engine, and that engine became a disaster.‡ It should never have come off the test stand. It was mounted vertically with the generator hanging under it, if you can imagine a generator hanging under an engine dripping oil. The engine looked like one of the old rotary aircraft engines with the pistons going out around the rotary crank shaft. They were high speed, very high speed, almost three times the speed of a good old heavy-duty Fairbanks-Morse diesel engine of World War II fame. The Fairbanks-Morse were magnificent engines which ran forever.

The pancakes were disasters almost from the start; even on sea trials we knew we had big problems. They would chew up the gears. Sometimes you'd have to go into the crankcase and just rake out the chewed-up gears and valves and bearings with a hoe. We had four of those engines, and you were lucky if you could keep one of them running. We got through our sea trials, and then we had a period of operating up and down the East Coast before the ship went on shakedown cruise. We got the engines halfway settled down

---

* PCO--prospective commanding officer.
† Electric Boat Company: USS Trigger (SS-564), USS Trout (SS-566), USS Harder (SS-568); Portsmouth Naval Shipyard: Tang (SS-563), USS Wahoo (SS-565), USS Gudgeon (SS-567).
‡ The Electric Boat Company is in Groton, Connecticut, across the Thames River from New London.

so we could keep at least half of them running. Beach was just raising hell everywhere about the problems with those engines, as well as some of the other things in the ship he wanted changed. I had to sort of hold Beach down from going a little bit too far, and I was senior enough and had experience enough so that I could do that. Beach had had a command at the end of the war; he had the Piper. Before that, he was with Roy Benson on the Trigger. He had a great combat record during the war.

Q: He was with George Street in Tirante.*

Admiral Shear: George Street in Tirante; that's right. At the end he had his own submarine, the Piper. So Beach is really a great naval officer. But you've got to hold him down.

Q: In what sense?

Admiral Shear: He's smart as hell. He's enthusiastic and very competent. He likes to get the most out of a submarine that he possibly can. But sometimes he gets a little bit too enthusiastic and gets a little bit critical, not juniors but seniors. So I had to be strong enough to say, "Goddamn it, Ned, you can't do that."

Q: You had to be the balance wheel.

Admiral Shear: I had to be the balance wheel. So it was a good thing that I was with Beach at that period. With those engines he'd have gone really half-cocked if I hadn't held him down. As it was, we had enough trouble.

Q: Was he willing to listen to you?

---

* Commander George L. Street III, USN, was awarded the Medal of Honor for his exploits while serving as commanding officer of the Tirante (SS-420) in 1945. Street, whose oral history is in the Naval Institute collection, shares the credit for his success with Beach.

Admiral Shear: Oh, yes. When I sat him down, he listened to me. Sometimes I had to hit him over the head with a two by four, but he listened to me. He had great respect for me, and I had great respect for him. It was during that period when we took Clay Blair away to sea for a week, in that shakedown period up and down the East Coast after we'd put that ship in commission.

Q: This was when he was with Time magazine?

Admiral Shear: Yes, he was with Time magazine.* We also took the Secretary of the Navy with us for a couple of those days, and I think that was a separate time. I don't think Clay Blair was aboard with SecNav. Nice guy, this fellow was. He'd been a naval officer during the war, and he knew his stuff pretty well. Anyway, we took him out, and Beach was going to show him everything his new submarine could do, and she could do a lot, even with her bad engines. He put her into 30-degree dives and angles and dangles and really showed the ship off. And I must say the Secretary was very impressed. We had the Secretary aboard a couple of days, I believe. I think we took him from New London to Norfolk.

Then we had Clay Baird aboard for almost a full week, and we showed him the ship. He and Ned were friends, but I think each one thought that he was a little bit better than the other fellow. You know what I mean? They were good friends, and they were both good authors because by that time Beach had written one of his first books.

Q: He wrote the book called Submarine!, which was about the earlier Trigger.†

Admiral Shear: Yes, that's correct. Then along came Run Silent, Run Deep, which was a little later.‡ But being two authors, they had a few differences.

---

* Clay Blair, Jr., is known as the author of a number of books on military topics, including Silent Victory: The U.S. Submarine War Against Japan (Philadelphia: J. B. Lippincott Company, 1975).
† Submarine! was published by Holt, Rinehart and Winston in 1952.

Q: A little competition.

Admiral Shear: A little competition, exactly.

Q: Where does that term "pancake" come from?

Admiral Shear: Because the engines were flat. Looking up from the generator, you saw the engine above it, radial, cylinders all the way around it. It was also flat when you were looking down at a plan view, with the crankshaft going out of the top and bottom. It looked like a pancake, and it was called the General Motors pancake high-speed diesel engine. It was just a terrible design. It blew all apart, as I told you. And then they put the generator hanging underneath it with all the oil from this terrible old leaky engine pouring down on top of it. Can you imagine oil dripping down into a big generator? It was just a mess.

One of the things we did was take the ship down here to Washington and bring it up the Potomac River. The ship drew 19 feet, and that Potomac River had only about a 20-foot channel. I was the navigator, and I was kind of nervous going up there, but we took her up without a pilot, no problem. We brought her up there to show her off to Congress and show her off to the Pentagon.

When we had the congressmen on board, one of them was Carl Vinson, sort of a Big Daddy to everybody in the Congress in those days, as far as military was concerned-- the Navy in particular.* We had him on board, and we showed him the ship in great detail and took his picture with the periscope and gave him a big dinner, and he was just like a

---

‡ Run Silent, Run Deep was published by Holt, Rinehart and Winston in 1955. It was a popular novel that was later made into a movie starring Burt Lancaster and Clark Gable.

* Carl Vinson of Georgia entered the House of Representatives in 1913 and was appointed to the Naval Affairs Committee in 1917. He became the ranking Democrat in 1923 and chairman in 1931. When the Armed Services committee was formed in 1947 Vinson became chairman and held that position, except for two short periods when Republicans held the House, until his retirement from Congress in 1965.

kid. We told him it was the greatest submarine in the world when we knew damn well it wasn't, particularly with those engineering problems, although it had many other good features. Some electrical features, and some of the torpedo tube improvements were excellent. But, overall, that was not the greatest class we ever built.

So then I got orders to take my first command. That was in the spring of '52, just after we brought the ship back from Washington. When we were back in New London, I got orders to take over the Becuna, which had since been Guppy-ized. She was then a Guppy IA. I mentioned she had a big battery with four engines; with the Guppy II we lost an engine, but the Guppy IA kept her engine, which was a very good thing. That was the best of the Guppies, as far as I'm concerned.

In the Trigger, the chief engineer, Flag Adams, had relieved me as exec.* After I left, they went off on a real shakedown cruise to Rio de Janeiro, Brazil. Did Ned Beach tell you about this?

Q: No. I haven't interviewed him.

Admiral Shear: Oh, I thought you had. Well, when they went off on that long cruise, I knew they were going to have trouble. They barely staggered down to Brazil, keeping one out of four engines going, sometimes two if they were lucky. When they got into Brazil, they had to use every spare part they had on board to get the engines back together. It was just one continual problem with those engines.

They started home after a period in Brazil, and Ned kept getting madder and madder. He was firing off one dispatch after another, castigating the manufacturer, castigating the naval architects, castigating the submarine force for ever accepting those engines. He sent all this stuff back to ComSubLant, and it didn't go over well. I was then CO of the Becuna operating out of New London, Groton, and the ComSubLant headquarters were right there at the submarine base. So I was aware of all these going-ons

---

* Lieutenant Commander Alden W. Adams, Jr., USN.

coming back from the ship, and I suspected that Ned would get a little bit wild about the problem with those engines.

Q: Without you there to hold him down.

Admiral Shear: Exactly. Flag Adams was a hell of a good man, but he couldn't hit him over the head the way I could. So the stuff that he sent off in dispatches was just a diatribe-- deserved, but not the way to do things. When Ned got back, ComSubLant wasn't sure he was the greatest skipper in the world.* I don't think there was any thought of relieving him, but there was much great unhappiness about Ned Beach and those engines in the Trigger. I knew this was coming because I had gotten wind of it, knowing the staff and having been around that staff.

So I went down to be the first guy aboard the Trigger when Ned got back. I just forced myself aboard, and I grabbed him and sat him down in the wardroom and said, "Ned, you're in deep trouble and you'd better face up to reality." I told him everything that was going on and the way his messages had been received as a lead balloon. He then realized that he had far overstepped things. He's been forever grateful to me that I got down there and got to him first, before the staff did, because at least it gave him a little bit of alert time to get his thoughts in order.

Q: Well, getting your own command must have been a great source of satisfaction.

Admiral Shear: It was terrific. I had just left the Trigger, and I'd taken over the Becuna. I relieved a man out of '41 named Fred Ruder, a good officer.† The ship was in good shape when I took her over, and she was in good shape all the time I had her. I had her for a little over two years, and I had a ball. We had all kinds of good operations. We were home-

---

* Rear Admiral Stuart S. Murray, USN, served as Commander Submarine Force Atlantic Fleet from 1 June 1950 to 6 November 1952. The oral history of Murray, who retired as a four-star admiral, is in the Naval Institute collection.
† Commander Frederick J. Ruder, USN.

ported in Groton, Connecticut, and that was one of the units of Submarine Squadron Eight. I had two great squadron commanders. One was Brooks Harral out of '31.* He had a fine war record in his own right. The other was Jack Coye out of '33, who had a great record in his own right.† As you mentioned earlier, he was CO of the Silversides, and the Silversides was one of the red-hot submarines of the war.

So I had great bosses, had a great crew, had a great wardroom, and we had great operations for two years. I operated all over the Atlantic. We had an operation called Springboard in those days. The day after New Year's you'd take the entire squadron and go down to the Caribbean for three months. I did that for several years, and then I went up off Murmansk, up to the Barents Sea on one of those Russian surveillance patrols. We had lost a submarine up there. She had had a fire. She had been lost up there off of northern Norway, and we discontinued those operations for several years.‡

Then I was sent up there with the Becuna as the first of those new operations after that period of hiatus. So I was up there a couple of months. That was a great tour.

Q: What do you remember about those operations?

Admiral Shear: Well, we went up there with modest intelligence. We were up there basically to find out what the Russians were doing. I had the authority to do anything I wanted to do outside of the three-mile limit. At that time we claimed three miles, so that was the U.S. position, three-mile limit for sovereignty. So I could go within three miles of the coast, I could go around the entrance to the Kola Inlet. I could cover the entire Barents Sea all the way over to Novaya Zemlya, which I did.§ Very interesting. There was not too much activity up there. I sighted a few ships here and there. There was no evidence of any

---

* Captain Brooks J. Harral, USN.
† Captain John S. Coye, Jr., USN.
‡ USS Cochino (SS-345) was lost off Norway on 26 August 1949 as the result of battery explosions and fires. For details see the Naval Institute oral history of Rear Admiral Roy S. Benson, USN (Ret.) and William J. Lederer, The Last Voyage (New York: Henry Holt and Company, 1950).
§ Novaya Zemlya is the name for a pair of islands in the Barents Sea, off the northeast coast of Russia.

particular submarine activity, and not too much surface ship activity. So I was up there a couple of months and came back and reported everything I did.

We stopped in Scotland for three or four days of rest and recreation on the way back. That was my first acquaintance with the Firth of Clyde, which I was to become intimately familiar with in my Polaris days. We took the ship all the way up the river, right into the city of Glasgow. We were welcomed with open arms, because the Brits still thought the world of us. This was in the early '50s, and the British were still in pretty bad shape, food and everything else.

We had a fair amount of food on board. As I told you, we always loaded up for 90 days. We'd been on this long patrol up north, and we had quite a bit left. So I got permission from the American consul to take all of our meat and some of our delicacies and make them available to the Brits, specifically to the American community, and let them do what they wanted with the distribution. Well, that made a hit you wouldn't believe. Just a few tons of stuff, but it made a great hit with the Brits, and it made a great hit with our people over there. I don't recall whether I sent a message home to get permission, but I got permission from the American consul to do it. So I did it. Hell's bells, a lot of those people hadn't seen fresh meat for five or six years. We had a good time, and I got acquainted with Scotland. I fell in love with the place--great country. We did some local work for the British submarine people who had a small operation there. Then I went home.

Then we had a number of sizable fleet exercises up and down the East Coast, typical peacetime submarine operation, and I had that job until the summer of '54.

Q: What are the satisfactions that come from being the boss at last?

Admiral Shear: Oh, listen. There's nothing that any seagoing naval officer worth his salt wants more than command. You can take any other job in the Navy, at sea or ashore, and the one job that stands out--and which is a must--is command at sea. A naval officer with any kind of salt in his socks or salt behind his ears will tell you that. You must have heard that from a dozen sources.

Q: Sure. What makes it so appealing?

Admiral Shear: Well, first of all, you're the boss. She's your ship, and, by God, she's under your command. Anything that happens is your responsibility. You do with her what you're supposed to do with her, and you just have one hell of a time. There's no experience anywhere on this earth like having command of your own ship. Anybody will tell you that who knows his stuff.

Q: I've heard a number of flag officers say that commanding a big single ship is more satisfying than being a flag officer at sea.

Admiral Shear: It is to me, and I'm going to tell you about that when I get to the Sacramento.

So I had a ball with my first command. I did well, the ship did well, and the people I worked with knew that we did well. We got many accolades, and I just had a hell of a time.

Q: Did you have any intelligence specialists on board for the trips up north?

Admiral Shear: Yes, I did have a team. I had a team of intelligence specialists, and we had the first of our latest intercept equipment to intercept all electronic signals.

Q: Did you have a language specialist?

Admiral Shear: Yes, we did, a language specialist and several electronic specialists. It was a very interesting operation.

Q: What became of the product that they came up with? Did it go back to the CIA or DIA?[*]

---

[*] CIA--Central Intelligence Agency; DIA--Defense Intelligence Agency.

Admiral Shear: It went back to naval intelligence. I knew what we had seen and done, and I knew what they reported. I didn't know everything they got as far as the electronic intercepts were concerned. I knew the types of thing they got. They got a lot of valuable information. Then, of course, as we got into the nuclear business years later, we became much more proficient and much more aggressive up in those waters. But that's a few years downstream.

Q: How would you describe yourself as a ship handler?

Admiral Shear: I am the best in the Navy. If anyone asks, you tell them I said so. I loved to handle ships. That goes way back to my fishing days. I was damn good then, and I'm better today. I can do anything with a ship, single screw or twin screw. I just love to handle ships. Interesting you should ask that question. Do you ask that of other people?

Q: Usually.

Admiral Shear: Well, what answers do you get?

Q: Well, most people are pretty confident of their ability and that they achieved high rank.

Admiral Shear: If they're any good, they'll tell you they're the best ship handlers in the Navy.

Q: They talk about the currents in the river at State Pier in New London.

Admiral Shear: I can handle those, no problem. A lot of people get scared to death of them; it never bothered me. Any hour of the night or day, any tide, flood, ebb, wind or anything else, I can handle with one hand. Furthermore, I always let my officers do it. It gave them great confidence, great confidence. I always stepped in if they got in trouble, and they rarely did because I made sure they didn't. But I always let them handle that ship in the most difficult situations. It gave that entire ship confidence. It gave the officers confidence. I was one of the few guys that ever did that. God, some skippers would come out of there just wringing wet and scared to death and everything else, but I just loved to handle ships, under any circumstances. I'm not bragging, I'm just telling you.

Q: Just the facts.

Admiral Shear: Yes, just the facts. And my people will tell you that too.

Q: Well, you do have to have a degree of confidence to let that guy do it when he doesn't have the experience you do.

Admiral Shear: Absolutely. When we used to take out submarine school students sometimes; I'd get a week of that. I'd always let the submarine students handle the ship. Nobody else would. I'd let them handle the ship, and I wasn't going to let them get in trouble. But it gave them great confidence. Some of them were very good, some of them were very poor. I never let them get hurt. That's an interesting comment you made.

    I'd go back to sea tomorrow if they'd let me. [Laughter]

Q: I served in an LST under skippers who were inclined to keep it themselves.[*]

Admiral Shear: Worst thing in the world. Can't do that. But it's surprising how your wardroom will come alive when they know you're going to do things like that.

Q: Any particular wardroom personalities you would single out from your time on the Becuna?

---

[*] LST--tank landing ship. The interviewer was an officer in the USS Washoe County (LST-1165) from 1966 to 1969.

Admiral Shear: Oh, I had a number of good officers. I had a good exec, Johnny Wise out of the class of '44; he's dead now, poor guy.* And I had Ned Dietrich, who went on to a very successful career in the nuclear business.† I had a whole series of good people. I had a couple of mustangs who were very good men.‡

Those submarines on the East Coast in that period in the early '50s--we all had World War II experience. Many of my classmates had command at the same time I did. We all had damn good ships. Max Duncan, who lives out in town, had a ship up there. He had been with Gene Fluckey in the Barb. I guess almost my entire squadron was manned by my classmates in that period--all good people.

Q: Well, there's a natural selection process at work, that the best rise to the top.

Admiral Shear: Sure, that's right. We all had a full war behind us, and we were confident in our own right. Someone would get a little bit worried about those tides around there; that never bothered me. But, anyway, we were all experienced people and we enjoyed our ships. Once in a while you'd find somebody who was afraid of a ship, but you've got to enjoy your ship. You've got to have fun with a ship. There have been periods in our Navy when people have forgotten how to have fun with a ship.

Q: Another common thread among the successful skippers is that they are the ones who go throughout the boat and see what's going on.

Admiral Shear: All the time. All the time. All the time. You've got to do that regularly. Make inspections, just wander around, have a cup of coffee, go back and talk to the torpedo gang. You've just got to be seen, visible, and they know you know what's going on.

---

* Lieutenant Commander John P. Wise, USN.
† Lieutenant Edward O. Dietrich, USN.
‡ "Mustang" is Navy slang for a former enlisted man who has risen through the ranks to become an officer.

Q: And that you care.

Admiral Shear: That's right. Doesn't make any difference whether it's a nuclear-powered submarine or diesel submarine or a 60,000-ton Sacramento, or anything else, you've got to get around the ship. They know what you're doing when you get around the ship.

Q: Was some of the glamour fading from the diesel boats by then, with the advent of the Nautilus?[*]

Admiral Shear: Not in my day, no. The Nautilus was launched in '54, I finished my first command in '54. Matter of fact we had our entire squadron, ten ships, lined up in front of EB anchored right off the ways of EB, just 100 yards or so apart, the day the Nautilus was launched, and she was launched by Mamie Eisenhower.[†]

Q: And Ned Beach.

Admiral Shear: And Ned Beach. Ned Beach was very visible in the pictures.[‡] Her keel had been laid by Harry Truman, HST welded into the keel plate.[§]

Okay. So I finished my command on the Becuna, and I had a great command. I've probably forgotten half a dozen incidents to tell you about.

Q: Well, maybe you can jot them down if they come back to you.

---

[*] The USS Nautilus (SSN-571), the Navy's first nuclear-powered submarine, was launched 21 January 1954 and commissioned 30 September 1954.
[†] Mrs. Mamie Doud Eisenhower, wife of President Dwight D. Eisenhower, was the sponsor of the Nautilus.
[‡] Commander Edward L. Beach, USN, was naval aide to the President at the time of the launching ceremony. He was next to Mrs. Eisenhower on the sponsor's platform.
[§] The keel laying was on 14 June 1952.

Admiral Shear: I'll tell you a simple little thing that happened. We were in a big fleet exercise off the East Coast, and I had to make a surface transit to get from one point to another for the next event. Lo and behold, along came the Queen Mary making 30 knots, and here was a United States man-of-war on the surface. The Queen Mary dipped to me, dipped to the Becuna.* As I told you, I had taken the Queen Mary out of Boston in February of 1942 with 15,000 troops on board. Well, here she was with a load of transatlantic passengers, and she dipped to the Becuna. She didn't know who I was from Adam, but she knew it was a U.S. man-of-war. That's the courteous thing to do for a merchant. So I put that in my patrol report and got quite a bit of publicity. [Chuckles]

Okay. So I finished up the Becuna in August of '54, and I was ordered to Armed Forces Staff College in Norfolk, Virginia--a six-month course. That's a joint school. It's the first time I'd been involved in any kind of joint operation. We had Army, Navy, Marine, Coast Guard, Air Force, and State Department people there. That was an excellent course.

I'd made commander just before I left the Becuna. Nearly all of us were commanders or lieutenant colonels. We had a couple of Air Force full colonels, I guess, because they made them early in those days. And we had a few lieutenant commanders, but we were all in that middle bracket of commander-lieutenant colonel, with a few exceptions.

We had a couple of hundred of us there, I guess. The course at the school was excellent, and we took a number of field trips. They were all good, and I guess the most important thing was rubbing shoulders with the other people. It was the first time I really got to know the other services. I found out that they aren't all a bunch of bastards; they're good people. I made friendships there that I still have. That was a very good time for me to get into a joint school.

Q: One advantage that any number of officers have mentioned from that is getting insight into the way their brother officers in other services think, how they approach problems.

---

* To dip the colors involves a merchant ship lowering her national flag about a third of the way down as a salute to a passing warship. The warship then responds by dipping her colors, a means of acknowledging the salute.

Admiral Shear: That's exactly correct. We had good people from all services. I thought the Navy were the best; I thought the Army was second; and I thought the Air Force was the lightest of the three. When I say Navy, I mean Marines and Navy. And we had some good State Department people there. But they were all good people. They wouldn't have gone to that school if they hadn't been good people.

Q: What did the curriculum cover?

Admiral Shear: Oh, it covered various kinds of joint exercises. We got good field trips through the activities of the various services: Army bases, Air Force bases, took them to sea in a carrier, and things like that. We got a good indoctrination to the operational aspects of the other services, all of them. And we made some quite extensive trips around the country.

I remember one when we went down to Eglin Air Force Base in Florida, where the Air Force put on a great demonstration, showing how they could win all the wars with bombs. They had B-36s dropping a string of bombs that went on forever, and they had other aircraft. A hell of a good show. I just use that as one example. The Army put on some very good shows. We went down to that jump school in Fort Benning, Georgia, had two or three days down there and they put on some great shows for us. Got great respect for those paratroopers after seeing them in operation down there. And we put on some good shows for them in the Navy too.

So it was a very good six months, including the classroom work. The lecture series was one of the very best parts. The lecture series and the field trips were the best. We had just a continuous string of top-notch lecturers from the military, national, international, State Department, every description and that was a superb part of that course. Very fine people.

Q: Did you get into nuclear doctrine?

Admiral Shear: Anytime you get around the Air Force in those days the name of the game was, "Nuke 'em. Oh, don't worry about that, we'll nuke 'em."

Q: And they believed it.

Admiral Shear: They believed it. That was their doctrine; absolutely they believed it. Of course, we had pretty good nuclear capability in our carriers at that time, but the Air Force were dyed-in-the-wool nuke 'em will take care of all the military problems in the world. It just oozed out of them; it had been bred into them. Have other people ever told you that?

Q: Oh, sure.

Admiral Shear: That's exactly what it was. I'm not exaggerating a bit. I'll tell you more when I get to Washington in a tour or two. It gets worse.

Q: Did you get into any political aspects, or was it more operational type things?

Admiral Shear: We got involved in some international lecturing on political situations, but this was more an operational type and getting to know the other fellow. When I got into the National War College a number of years later at Fort McNair, Washington, D.C., we got deeply involved in that kind of stuff, and I'll go into that when we get to it. But that was a great six months.

Q: Well, that was really your first introduction to doing staff-type work.

Admiral Shear: That's right. And I must say, there was quite a bit of emphasis there on how to put together a staff study, and put together a staff and work up a plan. That was all very valuable, because I went from there to OP-60 in Washington and got up to my neck in that.

So I finished up there in February of '55 and I was ordered to Washington, my second tour in Washington. I was ordered to OP-60, and OP-60 was under OP-06, the Deputy Chief of Naval Operations for Plans and Policy. And OP-60 was the Strategic Plans Division of OP-06.

OP-06 was headed by a vice admiral named Ruthven Libby.[*] He was a great naval officer and a thinker, a real thinker. OP-60 was headed by a rear admiral named Robert L. Dennison, who ended up later as CinCLant, and I'll tell you more about that.[†] His deputy, deputy OP-60, was Wallace M. Beakley, a gung-ho aviator but a fine man.[‡] My boss was a captain named Stephen Jurika.[§] You may have heard of Stephen Jurika.

Q: Aviator, naval attaché in Japan before the war.

Admiral Shear: Yes. His mother was beheaded by the Japs in the Philippines, a brilliant brain, and he took over OP-603. OP-603 under Arleigh Burke had been OP-23.[**] You remember what OP-23 was?

Q: That was the anti-Air Force organization in the late 1940s.

Admiral Shear: That was the get-the-Air-Force OP, headed by Arleigh Burke. Well, that was put out of business, deliberately, by SecDef.[††] They were out to get Arleigh, and they knew about his shop and they said, "That goes." Well, it didn't go because we had all the files hidden.

---

[*] Vice Admiral Ruthven E. Libby, USN, served as Deputy Chief of Naval Operations (Plans and Policy) from August 1956 to June 1958. Libby's oral history is in the Naval Institute collection.
[†] Rear Admiral Robert L. Dennison, USN. The oral history of Dennison, who retired as a four-star admiral, is in the Naval Institute collection.
[‡] Rear Admiral Wallace M. Beakley, USN.
[§] Captain Stephen Jurika, Jr., USN. His oral history is in the Naval Institute collection.
[**] Burke's recollections of the OP-23 period are in the Naval Institute oral history collection.
[††] SecDef--Secretary of Defense.

Steve Jurika became OP-603, and I was ordered into OP-603, fresh out of staff college, along with a commander aviator my age. I can't think of his name, good guy. We became the right and left arms for Steve Jurika. Steve Jurika was a unique guy; I loved him. He had an ego that wouldn't stop. Arleigh thought a lot of him. One of the things he did for both Arleigh Burke and for Robert L. Dennison was write their speeches for them. Half the time, my aviator friend and I would get a crack. We'd get a paragraph or two in these speeches, saying things that we wanted to say. About half the time it would stick, particularly when we were gunning for the Air Force, which we were most of the time in those days. It was a brutal situation.

So that was my introduction to OpNav and OP-60 and Arleigh Burke who was then CNO, Robert L. Dennison who was a magnificent man, and Steve Jurika.[*] Then Steve Jurika got sent out to be ComFAirWing 14.[†] The aviators wanted to use him as an example of a guy who could make flag without getting an aircraft carrier. He didn't make flag, but he was told he was going out there for that purpose because they knew he was going to make flag.

Steve was relieved by a man named Frank Johnson, a fine destroyer sailor.[‡] And Frank Johnson was relieved by the best of all, another destroyer sailor named Bill Wylie-- Joseph Wylie, nickname was Bill.[§] He was a strategic thinker; you've probably read some of his work. So I had three great bosses there, with two great bosses up the line in the two admirals, Dennison and Beakley. And for a young officer like me, that was unbelievable. All the stuff that I was exposed to, and all the stuff I got involved in, my God, what an education.

Q: What were some of these things you got involved in?

---

[*] Admiral Arleigh A. Burke, USN, served as Chief of Naval Operations from 17 August 1955 to 1 August 1961.
[†] Captain Jurika served as Commander Fleet Air Wing 14 from 1957 to 1959. Under his command were three ships and seven squadrons of patrol planes based in Japan and the Philippines.
[‡] Captain Frank L. Johnson, USN.
[§] Captain Joseph C. Wylie, USN.

Admiral Shear: Everything. Everything. I'd draft JCS papers.* You go down through the JCS system, and they turn flimsy, and then they turn green, and then they get red striped. When they're approved, they get red striped.

One of the things that I got involved in by default was the law of the sea, and I became OP-06's law of the sea expert. How'd I become an expert? Just because I fell into it. I learned a lot about it. We had a big thing going on in the U.N. at that time about extending the territorial waters for sovereignty from three miles to 12 miles.† The U.S. was vehemently opposed to that because it would cut off vast straits and areas around islands. You could hardly get through the Aegean Sea, for example, if you extended it to 12 miles. So we took a very hard-nosed position that we were going to stick with three miles, no matter what. This was coming up for a vote in the U.N.--three miles versus 12 miles--and there were other elements in the world that wanted very much to go to 12.

Well, by default I got involved in this, and I wrote the JCS paper on it. Dennison took it down and got it red-striped, and that became the U.S. position on the Law of the Sea. It started out with me. One of those JAG lawyers was fellow named George Rood.‡ He was a destroyer sailor, but he was a legal specialist and he was in the JAG's office. We worked very closely together on this and we had a man in the State Department named Mr. Yingling. Mr. Yingling was known throughout State as the law of the sea man. We put all this together, and a decision was made that we would go on a round-the-world circuit to gain votes for the law of the sea and our position.

So we sent three teams. George Rood and I hit the Far East and the Middle East; two other officers hit Europe; and a third pair hit the Caribbean and South America. So George Rood and I had the best of all because we went everywhere. This was coming up for a quick vote in the U.S., so they had to get us around the world quickly. So BuPers wrote a set of orders that they say stands to this day giving us authority to go anywhere we

---

* JCS--Joint Chiefs of Staff.
† U.N.--United Nations.
‡ Commander George H. Rood, USN.

wanted to, visit anything we wanted, take any kind of transportation we wanted, visit, re-visit, backtrack. Just do. Just go.

Q: "And we'll pay for it."

Admiral Shear: "And we'll pay for it."

So we started out with just those instructions. Dennison called me up the day before we left and said, "Now, these are your instructions. We expect you to get those votes, and by golly, you get out there." Dennison was a great naval officer; I'm going to tell you a lot about him.

So off we went. Went out to the West Coast, we headed out to the Western Pacific first, and we hit Japan, we hit Taiwan, we hit the Philippines, we hit India, we hit Thailand and Pakistan and Iran, all throughout that Middle East area. Then we got up and went to Saudi Arabia, and we got over into North Africa and went into Sudan, we went into Ethiopia, we went into Libya, we went into Algeria, and at that time, wham, the canal was closed. This was in '56, and there we were when the canal was closed.* Rood and I happened to be in Ethiopia. Everywhere we went, we went to the top levels of the government, talked to the top people, foreign ministers, everybody.

Q: How receptive were they?

Admiral Shear: Very receptive. And we got a lot of votes. I'll tell you what the final vote was. Anyway, along came the canal, the Brits and French had ganged up, and the Egyptians had closed the canal. Bang, closed. The Middle East was in a turmoil, and we

---

* On 26 July 1956 President Gamal Nasser of Egypt announced that his country was nationalizing the Suez Canal Company. Israeli forces invaded Egypt's Sinai Peninsula on 29 October 1956. Britain and France then intervened militarily on behalf of Israel in an unsuccessful attempt to secure the Suez Canal, which was damaged and closed to traffic. Rather than support the British and French, the United States asked for a United Nations resolution to end the fighting. A cease-fire took effect on 6 November.

couldn't get out of there. We couldn't move east or west. So finally we got a local flight. They had local pilots and they had animals in the aircraft, snakes coming out of baskets.

We got from Addis Ababa to Saudi Arabia, and then we got from there to Teheran. We got a flight out of Teheran to Turkey. It took four or five days to get through there because nothing was moving. Everybody was mad at everybody else. We were accused of favoring the French and the British. As a matter of fact, we were taking a hard position the other way. We finally got out, and we got from there to Athens. We finished up in North Africa and we came home.

We got home just a few days before the vote of the U.N. We lost that vote by one vote. By one vote. Then the U.S. representative stood up and said, "We're not going to abide by that vote. The United States position is three-mile limit for sovereignty, and on that we stand." Those were his exact words. So we didn't win, but we got a firm position established worldwide. We lost out by one vote. But that was a hell of an experience for a commander. I went to all these places, had backing to do anything I wanted to do, and we got into top positions everywhere. The U.S. ambassadors helped us in every direction, and it was really some experience for a young fellow.

Q: I would think you would use the approach of how it was in that country's self-interest, not that they were endorsing the U.S. position.

Admiral Shear: Oh, yes, we showed everyone. We took charts with us, showed how it was in their best interests, what would happen if it went the other way. We got a very good reception everywhere. Some of them really didn't understand it all, particularly those without much of a seacoast. But it was some trip.

Q: Why do you think the vote turned out to be negative?

Admiral Shear: There were other elements that were pushing for moving offshore, particularly the oil and mineral business. We had to combat that everywhere. But we lost by one vote, and then we took that position and we held it until just a couple of years ago when we backed off again, which I think was a mistake, but we did. But we held that three miles for 30 years more, from 1956 until just a year or so ago.

Q: Well, as long as you have the right of innocent passage, you don't get some of these dire predictions fulfilled.

Admiral Shear: That's right. And we had to stress that right of innocent passage too. So that was a very interesting thing for a young officer to get involved in. It shows that a young officer can go to Washington and get involved in something. People say, "You go to Washington, and all you do is just flail around and can't do anything." Hell, you can do all kinds of things.

Q: What were some of your other projects?

Admiral Shear: I learned that in my BuPers days, a young guy can get involved and do all kinds of things. I was deeply involved in that one, and I was deeply involved in many of the Air Force and Navy papers. Arleigh Burke and Curt LeMay, you know, were at each other's throats all the time.* I won't say they hated each other, but they didn't have any use for each other. And, as I say, Steve Jurika in particular, did a lot of speechwriting for Arleigh Burke. I got to know quite a bit about Arleigh as a result of those speeches and so forth, how he liked to say things and what kind of sentence structure he liked, what kind of issues he wanted to make a point of. That was a great education.

    I got involved in another thing which was very interesting for a young officer. Burke and Lord Louis Mountbatten were great friends.† I didn't know Lord Louis from Adam. I knew who he was, but I became very well acquainted with him later on. I'll tell

---

* General Curtis E. LeMay, USAF, served as Commander in Chief of the Strategic Air Command from 19 October 1948 to 30 June 1957. He was a lieutenant general until 29 October 1951. The original title was Commanding General, changed to Commander in June 1953 and changed to Commander in Chief in April 1955.
† Admiral of the Fleet The Earl Mountbatten of Burma served as Great Britain's First Sea Lord and Chief of Naval Staff from 1955 to 1959.

you about that tomorrow or the next day. They had a voluminous correspondence back and forth. We had what was called the "Dear Dickie" file. Arleigh called Mountbatten "Dickie;" that was his nickname. OP-60 maintained the Dear Dickie file, which was Arleigh's correspondence file to Lord Louis Mountbatten. I was the holder of the Dear Dickie file in my safe. So I got involved in a lot of correspondence between Mountbatten and Burke.

Mountbatten was always asking for something, anything he could squeeze out for the British Navy. The British Navy was always squeezed for money, you know. Anything he could squeeze out of Burke, he'd work on him. Sometimes we'd draft a pretty negative letter, and Bill Wylie, in particular. Wylie had succeeded Jurika and Johnson and was an excellent writer, but he had a very curt tongue. He drafted some letters I wouldn't even send up to Burke. Very caustic letters about "Louie, I got your message but the answer is 'no'. You can't have it." Things of that nature. Sometimes Burke would sign them, sometimes he wouldn't, sometimes he sent them back. I was always working late around there. It seemed that I went to work at 7:00 in the morning and got home about 8:00 at night.

One night I was all alone in the office when Burke called down. He said, "Do you know anything about the letter to Mountbatten."

I said, "Yes, sir."

He said, "Come up here, I want to talk to you." So I went up to Arleigh's office, and the Pentagon was practically empty. Arleigh was sitting there eating a dish of ice cream; Arleigh loved ice cream. He always had a dish of ice cream late in the day. He said, "Who wrote this letter?"

I said, "I drafted it, Admiral Burke, and Captain Wylie put the final touches on it."

He said, "Yes, I know. And this is what we ought to tell Admiral Mountbatten, but I can't sign this letter. You're too hard on him. I want you to take this back and soften it up a little bit and send it back to me tomorrow." So we did just that and sent it back, and he signed it. But that's the kind of stuff I was exposed to around there.

Q: Why didn't he want to be blunt with Mountbatten?

Admiral Shear: Well, we'd been too blunt. He was perfectly capable of being blunt when he had to be, and he was perfectly capable of being very forthcoming when he wanted to be. But I think in this case both Bill Wylie and I had stuck it to him a little too hard. [Chuckles]

Q: It sounds as if Jurika was a victim on that detailing you talked about.

Admiral Shear: Absolutely.

Q: Not really fair to him.

Admiral Shear: It wasn't fair to him. He retired shortly thereafter and he went to college and got a Ph.D. in geology and geography. And went on to a very successful career as a professor at . . .

Q: Hoover Institution at Stanford.

Admiral Shear: Stanford University. He was a very, very competent naval officer. Among other things, he'd been aboard the Franklin when she was torn up.* He had a lot of impact on saving that ship, because she was badly damaged.

Q: And he was the intelligence briefer for the Doolittle raid.†

---

* On 19 March 1945, while operating 90 miles off the coast of Japan, the aircraft carrier Franklin (CV-13) was hit twice by Japanese bombs. They set off explosions and fires in the ship. Of her crew of 3,450, 724 men were killed, and 265 wounded. No other American warship has sustained such massive casualties and remained afloat.
† On 18 April 1942, Lieutenant Colonel James H. Doolittle, USA, led a raid of 16 Army Air Forces B-25 on a bombing raid over Tokyo, Yokohama, Kobe, and Nagoya, Japan. The planes were launched from the aircraft carrier Hornet (CV-8). Most of the planes crash-landed in China.

Admiral Shear: Could well have been. Yes, I don't recall that, but he could well have been. And, as you say, he'd been in Japan before the war as an assistant attaché. Very, very interesting man. I was lucky to get associated with people of that ilk.

Q: What do you remember about Libby? He was brilliant.

Admiral Shear: Ruthven Libby was a brilliant man. Very interesting, he always wrote his own speeches. We could have written his speeches for him, but he always wrote his own speeches. He knew what he wanted to say, and he said it. He was a tough guy. Not a mean, tough guy but a very firm, tough guy. He'd been out there in Korea, you know, the DMZ, and he was hard as nails with those Koreans.* He used to say, "The only thing they understand, and that's the butt of a rifle. That's the only thing they understand."

Q: His oral history talks about some of the little psychological ploys that the Koreans would pull.

Admiral Shear: Did he give an oral history with you?

Q: Yes. I didn't interview him, but I worked on it.

Admiral Shear: Very impressive man. Of course, he was somewhat remote from me as a commander, and he was the three-star OP-06. OP-06 was next to God--Arleigh Burke, and then you go to OP-06. Incidentally, Arleigh leaned tremendously on OP-06. I think of all his three-star DCNOs, OP-06 was the number-one guy. And he leaned heavily on Dennison, because he thought the world of Dennison.

Q: I got the impression that Libby was sort of an austere type. Is that fair?

---

* DMZ--demilitarized zone.

Admiral Shear: I'd say that's a fair statement, yes. As I say, my contacts with him were limited. He was austere, but he was very competent down in the Joint Chiefs. He wouldn't take any nonsense. He'd take a position, and, by golly, that was his position, period. It was a hard position; he wouldn't budge.

Q: I've heard he was also superb operationally, a side you didn't see. For example, when he was maneuvering a formation, he could do it all on the face of a radar scope.

Admiral Shear: Could very well. He was a brilliant man, but he was rather austere. You didn't see him out drinking a beer with the boys or anything like that.

Q: I gather Dennison was more a genial type.

Admiral Shear: Yes, but he could be withdrawn too. Very interesting thing about Dennison. I got to know very well, because I worked for him twice. I worked for him in OP-60, and I worked for him when he was CinCLant.[*] Dennison didn't care a damn about small talk. You'd see him at a cocktail party, and he wouldn't join in the small talk. He was all business, but he was a nice guy and very smart. People claimed that he was a political hack. He wasn't any political hack. He'd been Harry Truman's naval aide, you know.[†]

Q: But he was astute politically.

Admiral Shear: Oh, very astute. Absolutely. He was very, very astute politically. He knew Capitol Hill backwards and forwards, the White House, the political climate around Washington. This is way ahead of the story, but after he retired as CinCLant, he went back to Washington as Copley's man in Washington, scooping out news leads and things of that

---

[*] Dennison served as Supreme Allied Commander Atlantic, Commander in Chief Atlantic, and Commander in Chief Atlantic Fleet from 1960 to 1963.
[†] As a captain and rear admiral, Dennison served as naval aide to President Harry S. Truman from February 1948 to January 1953.

nature. But he did a great job for Arleigh in OP-60. It was a great experience for me to get to know him, and then to know him again as CinCLant. We ran the Cuban quarantine right from his office. I was deeply involved in that. That's a few chapters ahead.

What else did I do in OP-60? Oh, we spent the complete summer of 1955 in a major war game, a no-holds-barred, really professional war game over at the National War College. We just took over the National War College for three months. This was a major war game, participated in by all the services in order to simulate a major confrontation with the Soviets and to have a nuclear war with them. Steve Jurika and I were sent over there to be part of the Navy contingent. They had a handful of other officers. Steve Jurika and I were the two principal members. I guess we had nearly 30 officers from each service--Navy, Army, Air Force. I think the senior man there was--you'd know him. You'd know him.

Q: Do you mean the commandant?

Admiral Shear: No, no, no. This was outside the school altogether. We just took over the school. The Red commander was an Army major general who was my immediate boss in the game. Steve Jurika was there in a different position. We had a control team. We had the Red team and the Blue team. Who was the rear admiral, destroyer sailor with a bad foot?

Q: Butch Parker.

Admiral Shear: Butch Parker! You're good.

Q: Thank you.

Admiral Shear: Butch Parker.* A great guy. Another one of the great guys I was exposed to. He was over there. And this was really a no-holds-barred, nasty war game. The Air Force wanted to show that they could do everything. They didn't need any Army, and they didn't need any Navy. They could do everything. The guy on top of this was Curt LeMay. Curt LeMay was then CinCSAC. He hadn't taken over as Chief of Staff yet. And he had a bunch of red-hot colonels there and some light colonels, but he had a top-notch team there.

Q: What was the scenario?

Admiral Shear: The scenario was that we'd escalate a nuclear war. We'd throw part of our stockpile; they'd throw part of their stockpile. We'd take out what facilities of theirs we could; they'd take out what facilities of ours they could. Then we'd see who won.

I became the Red submarine commander. That was my job. I had all the assets of their submarines and knew all the capabilities of their submarines, and I could use them any way I wanted to, anywhere in the world. The only ones who could tell me I couldn't do something were on the control team. We had a similar situation for all the forces: surface forces, Army forces, Air Force forces. This wasn't any war college game. This was a very professional show. We had the entire assets of the military establishment to bluff them or get information from or utilize--anything we wanted. It was monitored very closely by the top people in OpNav, top people in the Air Force, top people in the Army.†

I was over there almost three months. Steve Jurika and Butch Parker and 10 or 15 other guys. We more than held our own. Among other things, I was able to use the Russian submarine fleet, which at that time had a number of cruise missile firing submarines. Quite a few, as a matter of fact but no ballistic missile submarines yet. They were ahead of us in the air-breathing missiles. I was able to use them any way I wanted to around the world. Plus their other submarines and so forth and so on. So I was very successful in positioning those submarines to knock out SAC bases at H-hour with a flight time of 15

---

* Rear Admiral Edward N. Parker, USN. The oral history of Parker, who retired as a vice admiral, is in the Naval Institute collection.
† OpNav--the extended staff of the Chief of Naval Operations.

minutes in the missiles, or less. In Europe and North Africa they had all those big bases. And they had bases on the East Coast of the U.S. and West Coast of the U.S. So I had enough submarines to cover those pretty well.

So the balloon went up. Well, within 30 minutes I had SAC knocked out halfway around the world. And the Air Force people went absolutely prompt critical. They went wild. They ran to the control team and claimed, "Foul. You can't do this."

Well, the control people backed me up: "They had the capabilities. They did everything they said they could do. That's what the weapons can do. These are the positions they were in--perfectly legal positions. We back them up. Those losses stand." I became a hero. This word got over to the Pentagon in due course.

But other things went on. It was a tough game. The Air Force won some things, and we won some things. But what it really showed was that those Air Force bases, close to the coastlines around the world, were very vulnerable, very vulnerable. This stood out like a sore thumb.

Q: It helped make the case for Polaris.*

Admiral Shear: Exactly. Precisely.

Just to show you how important this war game was, let me tell you about what LeMay did. This exercise went on for nearly three months. Throughout that time, he had his chosen boys that he'd put in there specifically to watch what was going on. Then he'd fly them out to Omaha every weekend to brief him on that war game. They told him about what had happened, and he briefed them as what he wanted to do next. It was a very interesting thing to see these half a dozen colonels fly back out there for their instructions for the week, every weekend. LeMay kept on top of that thing every minute, because he knew it was a very important game, and it was going to have big political implications. And it did. In due course, SAC knew it was a losing battle and knew we had a going system. But there wasn't a goddamn thing they could do about it, and they didn't like it a bit.

---

* In the late 1950s the Navy developed the submarine-launched Polaris ballistic missile system.

When the war game was over, Jurika and I went back to our jobs in the Pentagon. We had all this massive amount of charts and everything. Nobody wanted it, so we stole it all. Just took it and brought it back and put it up in the big briefing rooms in the Pentagon there and briefed all the OpNav staff about what had transpired and what conditions and the results: "Here's the whole picture right there." God, we had all the senior people in the Pentagon coming around to get our briefings. That was a hell of a three-month period. And here I was, a young commander, up to my neck in all this stuff.

Q: You stuck your thumb in the pie and came out with a plum.

Admiral Shear: That's right. Well, that was a great opportunity. And on a national scale, that was really a very impressive thing. And it shaped a lot of thinking.

Q: Butch Parker then went out to Omaha as the head Navy man on the Joint Strategic Target Planning Staff.

Admiral Shear: Oh, yes. That's right, exactly. And he had all this background behind him. He and I were very good friends. I went out there a couple of times with him.

Q: Jerry Miller was one of his guys out there too.[*]

Admiral Shear: Jerry Miller was one of the first people out there. By that time, Polaris was coming along. I'm not quite ready to get to the Polaris story yet. Let's see.

Q: You had all of that war game, but there were some real-world crises. You mentioned Suez, and they had the Hungarian Revolt. Both of those were in the fall of '56. How much did OP-06 get into those matters?

---

[*] Commander Gerald E. Miller, USN, a Naval Academy classmate of Shear's.

Admiral Shear: That's when the tanks went into the streets to put down the rebels.

Q: Right.

Admiral Shear: We didn't get into the Hungarian thing as much as I thought we should. We were helpless. The United States didn't do anything. Now, you look at it closely, and you wonder how much you could have done. But we didn't do much about it. NATO didn't do much about it.[*] I think NATO didn't do a very good job there. We did a good job later on, but I think NATO could have been much tougher in that time, and the Russians probably couldn't have done much about it. I don't recall that we got deeply involved in that at all.

We did get deeply involved in that Suez situation.

Q: George Steele was over there with a submarine.[†] He told me about that. It was a situation where the United States essentially backed off and said, "Britain and France, we're sorry. We're not going to pull your chestnuts out of the fire."

Admiral Shear: That's correct. That was exactly what we should have done. That was exactly what we should have done, because we made lots of money in the Middle East because of our position there.

Q: I think the U.S. Navy's main role was evacuation of American citizens.

Admiral Shear: Yes, that's right. And it was a very good thing that we didn't step in there and side with the French and British on the Suez Canal. That paid off heavily in later years. But it boxed me up for a week or two over there; I'll tell you that. I couldn't move east or west.

---

[*] NATO--North Atlantic Treaty Organization.
[†] See the Naval Institute oral history of Vice Admiral George P. Steele II, USN (Ret.).

What else did I do in OP-60 that I should have told you about? Oh, early Polaris planning. Sputnik went up.[*] I was there then, and Sputnik caught everybody by surprise. That was one of the things that kicked off the Polaris program. Much of that early Polaris planning was done in OP-60. A lot of people don't know that, but it was. The head guy in OP-60 on that project was Captain Bill Wylie, later Admiral Bill Wylie.

Arleigh Burke said, "Go. Whatever it costs, we're going to go with this Polaris ballistic missile in submarines." Two things happened to make that possible, incidentally. First, miniaturization of the warhead had come along, so you could put it in a missile you could handle. Second, we went from a liquid propellant to a solid propellant. The combination of the two gave us the opportunity to build the Polaris missile, which we did.

There was far from universal opinion in the Navy that we ought to go this way. OP-05 did not support it. Why did they not support it? They saw it as a threat to the aircraft carrier. And the bearded wonder--what's his name?

Q: Pirie.

Admiral Shear: Bob Pirie was quite vocal in his opposition.[†] I don't know this, but I think in due course he was slapped down by Arleigh, and Arleigh said, "March off and carry out your orders." But he was quite vocal. And some of the senior submariners were quite vocal: "Oh, you don't use submarines this way. You can't launch missiles in a vertical area. You launch weapons from a torpedo tube, fore and aft. You can't handle two crews in a submarine; it won't work."

This came out of some very high level surprising players, one of which was Joe Grenfell, then ComSubPac.[‡] As a matter of fact, Joe Grenfell came back to Washington to

---

[*] On 4 October 1957, the Soviet Union launched Sputnik I, the first articial earth satellite. It caused great uproar in the United States, which had expected to be first in space.
[†] Vice Admiral Robert B. Pirie, Jr., USN, served as Deputy Chief of Naval Operations (Air) from 26 May 1958 to 1 November 1962. His oral history is in the Naval Institute collection.
[‡] Rear Admiral Elton W. Grenfell, USN, served as Commander Submarine Force Pacific Fleet from 1956 to 1959.

protest in a conference the way that Polaris was going. My boss, Bill Wylie, did a masterful job, very politely but firmly saying, "Admiral Grenfell, this is the way it's going to go. This is the way it's going to be. It has to be this way. And we're going to proceed." Bill Wylie was a whiz at words, and he could really take care of a guy if he wanted to. And a number of other senior submariners said, "We don't want this system. It's no good. You fire torpedoes."

Now we're getting into a long period. Maybe we better quit.

Q: All right. Great start today, Admiral.

Admiral Shear: We had a pretty good day, didn't we?

Q: I think so.

Interview Number 2 with Admiral Harold E. Shear, U.S. Navy (Retired)

Place: U.S. Naval Institute, Annapolis, Maryland

Date: Thursday, 10 September 1992

Interviewer: Paul Stillwell

Q: Good morning, Admiral. Yesterday we got up to the time at which you went to the SubRon Two staff, so please resume at that point.

Admiral Shear: I finished my tour in OP-60, and I told you what a great tour that was and what great experiences I had there. The people I worked for, my golly, were the finest in the Navy, the top leadership in the Navy at the time.

Then I had a brief tour when I went from OP-60 as an operations officer for ComSubRon 2 in New London.* That was a senior squadron. We had the responsibility for all the local operations in that North Atlantic area.

Q: Who was the commodore?

Admiral Shear: The commodore was Bill Hazzard, out of '35, who was ComSubRon Two and Com Sub Refit Training Group New London.† Very fine officer. He had a good war record. I don't recall at the moment what submarine he had, but it's in the book.‡ He was a fine squadron commander. I got along well with him, the staff got along well with him, and the skippers of the ships in squadron got along well with him. He knew his stuff. He was a very pleasant guy. So we had a fine year up there.

---

* ComSubRon 2--Commander Submarine Squadron Two.
† Captain William H. Hazzard, USN.
‡ Hazzard commanded the USS Blenny (SS-324) during World War II.

In less than a year, I was called down to Washington for an interview. By that time the Polaris program was becoming more and more known. I had been involved in the early stage in OP-60 and so forth, and I was called down for an interview to be CO of one of the first ships.

Q: Did this come out of the blue, or had you expressed any preference?

Admiral Shear: They hadn't come out and asked anybody whether he wanted to be skipper or not. But the program was coming along in rapid style. Those ships went from design to commissioning in two years. We'd never do it today. You could never do it today. Red Raborn and Arleigh Burke--with all the priorities they put on it, they did that--and Rick with the power plant.[*]

There were four of us called down for interviews for the first ships. They were myself, my classmate Jim Osborn, my classmate Pappy Sims, W. E. Sims, and Roy Anderson, class of '40, two years ahead of us.[†] We all went over, and the chief of BuPers, Page Smith, had been having a feud with Rick because Rick had been turning down too many good people.[‡] I was never told this, but it was obvious that he had set up some ringers to send over to Rickover. We were all very experienced, we'd all been through the war, we all had wartime experiences, a lot of combat behind us, and we'd all had command of diesel submarines.

So Smith decided he was going to send some people over there that Rick couldn't turn down. Well, by golly, we all got the usual workover from Rick, not half as bad as people try to make it out to be, but the typical Rickover questions. We all got worked over for two or three hours, and I guess somebody got thrown out and called back in again. But

---

[*] Rear Admiral William F. Raborn, Jr., USN, was director of the Special Projects Office, which developed the fleet ballistic missile system. He held the post from 1955 to 1962, being promoted to vice admiral in 1960. His Polaris oral history is in the Naval Institute collection. "Rick" is a reference to Vice Admiral Hyman G. Rickover, USN.
[†] Commander Roy G. Anderson, USN.
[‡] Vice Admiral Harold Page Smith, USN, served as Chief of Naval Personnel from 31 January 1958 to 12 February 1960.

he selected all four of us, something he'd never done before or since.[*] Everybody was amazed. Four in and four out. All got an upcheck. I think Rick's staff were amazed.

Q: Any specifics you remember from the interview?

Admiral Shear: Oh, yes. "Why did you not stand higher in your class and so forth and so on? What have you done in the Navy?" And, of course, I had a pretty good record in destroyers and submarines. He couldn't find much fault with that, but you always get worked over. But I must say, and I'm going to tell you more about this, those working-overs were nowhere near as bad as lots of people advertised and tried to make them up to be.

Anyway, we were all selected. Anderson turned it down. Anderson was then on Bub Ward's staff.[†] He was actually chief staff officer, and he felt that his role was more important working with Bub Ward in the early phases of Polaris than taking command of one of the first ships.

While I'm talking about the selection process, let me say something else about Rick. He was being severely criticized for the way he was browbeating people and all the terrible things he was asking them, "What's your sex life?" and all that. It was utter nonsense. He was a very tough interviewer, but I never saw him pull anything untoward as far as personal allegations or things like that. The stories about his interviews over the years have been vastly, vastly expanded. Each story gets better. He was a tough interviewer, and I suspect he did ask some pretty tough questions by design. He always asked tough questions. But they followed a routine. But I never saw him get involved in any of this nasty stuff.

---

[*] Commander James B. Osborn, USN, became skipper of the blue crew of the USS George Washington (SSBN-598). Shear became the first CO of the blue crew of USS Patrick Henry (SSBN-599). Commander William E. Sims, USN, became first CO of the blue crew of the USS Theodore Roosevelt (SSBN-600).

[†] Captain Norvell G. Ward, USN, was the first commander of Submarine Squadron 14, which did planning and development work for Polaris. The oral history of Ward, who retired as a rear admiral, is in the Naval Institute collection.

In order to protect himself--because he knew that these wild stories were being bandied around--he decided that he would never be alone. He would always have someone listening to the interview. So whenever anything came up, he could say, "Joe was in there with me, and here is what I said, and Joe will validate it." Well, I was "Joe" sometimes. Each Saturday morning one of us who were then in the training pipeline would have the duty to sit in on Rick and his interviews. I happened to have it the morning Bud Zumwalt came in.[*] I had known Bud slightly, Naval Academy and later years, but I didn't know him well.[†] I had the inner sanctum duty of sitting in the back of the room listening to Rick fire questions at him. He fired the usual number of tough questions, such as, "Why didn't you do better than this?" and so forth and so on. And, "Why do you want to get in this program?" and da-da-da, the typical stuff.

Q: And Rickover didn't like the fact that Zumwalt was an aide.

Admiral Shear: That's right, brought that up: "What are you doing with those loafer's loops?"[‡] and that kind of thing. There was the usual number of questions. And since Bud had been working at the top level, I guess he probably needled him a little bit about that. I don't recall the questions myself at all. But Bud got a little shook up. I think he thought he was being browbeaten, and the standard treatment from Rick was that he'd work you over for a while and then say, "What the hell do I want you--get out of here." And you'd go out and you'd sit in the closet for an hour or two till Rick wanted to talk to you again.

So Bud got thrown out. [Laughter] So he went out and sat in this other corner, an austere little office. I think they called it a dungeon or something like that. When he was thrown out, of course, I went out with him. I went in there, and he was feeling pretty bad. I put my arm around him and said, "Oh, hell, Bud, this is par for the course. Don't get too upset about this." I saw that he had quieted down a little bit. Then he was called back in

---

[*] Commander Elmo R. Zumwalt, Jr., USN. Later, as a four-star admiral, Zumwalt served as Chief of Naval Operations, 1970-74.
[†] Zumwalt was in the class of 1943, which graduated six months after Shear's class.
[‡] An aide typically wears gold-colored loops known as aiguletttes around one shoulder of his uniform to signify his duty.

again in due course, after cooling his heels for an hour or so. That was part of Rickover's game. Of course, I went back in behind him as the listener. Rick worked him over some more, the same line. He asked a bunch of other questions. I don't recall any of the questions right now. And I don't recall whether he was thrown out a second time or not. He might have been. I don't recall that.

Anyway, he finished the interview. You never know when you're finished whether you are going to be selected or not. I think Rickover knew that he had better select this guy. I think Rick knew that. Just like he knew that he better select us when we were sent over there. Because if he hadn't, there was enough horsepower around to make life miserable for him.

I guess Bud went back to the Pentagon after the interview. A day or two later, he was selected for the nuclear program but turned it down. He then had the opportunity to go to a new destroyer, and he went to the Dewey.* But I must say that forever after, he felt that I befriended him and I helped him in that. And I did, I guess. I quieted him down and told him not to get too upset about it. It wasn't the end of the world, and so forth and so on.

Q: You told him it was Rickover and not him, that this was just a standard interview.

Admiral Shear: Exactly, standard: "Don't worry about this; everybody gets this." I sent him out of there feeling halfway decent. Anyway, he never forgot that I tried to help him over there. He has brought it up a number of times over the years. He remembers that incident very clearly. I felt that I didn't do anything out of the ordinary. For anybody else in the same position, I would tell him the same thing. But he was upset over that interview, quite upset, much more than he should have been. But he and Rick never did hit if off, and I guess he probably made that clear to you. You've interviewed Bud, haven't you?

---

* The USS Dewey (DLG-14) was the first of a new type of ship for the U.S. Navy, the guided missile frigate. She was commissioned 7 December 1959. Zumwalt commanded the ship from commissioning until June 1961.

Q: Yes. Well, he really covered that pretty well in his book too.*

Admiral Shear: Yes, he did. I read On Watch a long time ago, and I forget the details of many of his things. But there we are.

So, after Jim Osborn and Pappy Sims and I were chosen for the program, then we went into a full year of very vigorous training. We were selected in early '58. We went into the complete nuclear power training program with all the theory and the academics right there in Rick's office, people around him. He had some superb teachers down there. Then we went out and qualified in the shore-based plant in Arco, Idaho. We'd come back to Washington for more academics; then we'd go out to Arco again. We got the full treatment. We were really checked out in that plant.

Q: What specifics do you remember from the training?

Admiral Shear: We had a complete go-around of everything to do with nuclear power, nuclear physics, reactor theory, shielding, all the best textbooks on the subject and the crackerjack people around Rick who were qualified to teach us. We got a very good academic coverage of nuclear power as it was understood at that time. Then we got the complete operation of the plant. We went out there and went on what they called the double-shift: 16 hours a day. Out there we lived in Quonset huts, and Rick wouldn't let us off the station. It was 60 miles away from Idaho Falls, and we went out there for about six weeks at a time. You'd fly into Idaho Falls and catch a bus to go out to the plant. Then you'd stay at the plant until the day you flew out at the end of that period.

This double shifting had two eight-hour shifts, then eight hours off to sleep and eat, and that was it. I'll tell you, it was thorough. He had a crackerjack staff out there, mostly

---

* Zumwalt's book, On Watch: a Memoir (New York: Quadrangle/New York Times Books, 1976), contains a reconstructed version of his interview with Admiral Rickover, pages 86-95. Zumwalt recalled that he and Commander Raymond E. Peet, USN, were competing to be CO of the nuclear-powered Bainbridge (DLGN-25). Rickover selected Peet for the billet, and Zumwalt opted for command of his own ship rather than going into the nuclear program to serve as executive officer of the cruiser Long Beach (CGN-9).

civilians, running the plant itself. They had a small naval staff out there. We got involved in, among other things, nuclear physics and health aspects of the power plant and things of that nature. They had some very good nuclear-trained doctors out there who were teachers in that regard. So we got a very thorough going-over on nuclear power.

Q: And a great emphasis on safety.

Admiral Shear: A great emphasis on safety and a great emphasis on reliability. By the time we left there after that year with Rick, we knew our stuff. Then we continued on for about three more months under Raborn on all aspects of the missile. We studied the missile, we went out, we studied the launcher system, we studied the fire control system, we spent some time at the fire control plant in Pittsfield, Massachusetts, we spent some time at the Lockheed plant out in Sunnyvale, California, we spent some time with the launchers at Westinghouse. We got to know that system as well as we did the power plant. During that power plant period we also spent about a month at Bettis laboratory in Pittsburgh, where they were actually building the fuel for the plant. So we knew the plant thoroughly, and we knew the missile system thoroughly. By the time we were aboard those ships, we were ready to go.

The plant that we qualified on was the shore-based version of the old Nautilus plant. The plants that went into our ships were the S5W plants, Westinghouse plants of a later version. We got a thorough study program on those plants with the prints and systems laid out, electrical systems and pumping systems and the plant itself.

Q: How did the S5W differ from the Nautilus plant?

Admiral Shear: Quite a bit. It was a much more modern plant, a more powerful plant, about 15,000 horsepower. It was about the third generation of nuclear power plants. Nautilus was the first; it was the one that was set up out there in Arco. Then we had the versions that followed the Nautilus, and they included the Skate class and Sargo class. There was a progressive improvement in those plants. Then came along the S5W, which became the standard for the ballistic missile ships. It was a fine plant, a very good plant, very reliable. I won't say it was simple, but overall it was relatively simple as far as nuclear power was concerned.

Q: How much cooperation was there among the students going through that with you?

Admiral Shear: We went through in batches. In the very early stages of the nuclear power business, which was what we were in at the time, I guess maybe three skippers went through there with me. Then we had three or four others that were going to attack boats. I guess there were six or eight skippers in that category, plus our executive officers. So there was about a dozen or 15 officers there at that time. In due course we all got to know each other, and we got to know those who had been operating some of the earlier nuclear boats after the Nautilus.

But there wasn't any problem with good cooperation or anything of that nature. Sims, Osborn, and myself went to the first three boats. The George Washington and Patrick Henry were built a month apart at EB, and the Theodore Roosevelt was built in Mare Island Naval Shipyard. Then the fourth boat was the Robert E. Lee, built down in Newport News. She came along a little bit later, but they were all right on top of each other. The Robert E. Lee, was commanded by a man named Reuben Woodall out of '43, a year behind us.* The fifth boat was the Abraham Lincoln, built in Portsmouth, New Hampshire.

So those first five boats were all commanded by contemporaries of mine, all of us with long wartime experience and all of us with command of submarines. We all had crackerjack people. We had the best wardrooms you could possibly put together, as far as the power plant was concerned, as far as the missile system was concerned. We had the cream of the crop.

---

* Commander Reuben F. Woodall, USN, was first CO of the blue crew of the USS Robert E. Lee (SSBN-601). The first skipper of the ship's gold crew was Commander Joe Williams, Jr., USN, whose oral history is in the Naval Institute collection.

Q: It must be a skipper's dream to get a wardroom like that.

Admiral Shear: Absolutely incredible. And practically the entire 41 submarines had people of that nature. Because those ships were coming along in rapid succession. I couldn't have had a better wardroom or a better crew. The enlisted people were crackerjack too. It was a CO's dream. The people you had to work with, you couldn't find any better.

Q: Any examples that you'd like to mention?

Admiral Shear: Gosh, it's hard to pick out one and say he was better than the others. I had great people. My chief engineer was a man named Bob Douglass, who had been in either the Saury or the Sargo, crackerjack man.* He's retired near me up in Connecticut now. Dick Wright was the weapons officer.†

Incidentally, we had the two crews, and Bob Long was my counterpart on the Patrick Henry.‡ Bob Long was a year behind me, because he got involved in the training program a year after I did, so the first year I had both crews under me.§ I had the responsibility for breaking in both crews and shaking them down in the operation of the ship and so forth. That was a great break because both Long and I had been in OpNav in the early phases of the program. I was OP-60, and he was then in OP-31, which was the submarine desk working for Fearless Freddy Warder.** You may have heard of Fearless Freddy Warder, great wartime skipper.

Q: Yes.

---

* Lieutenant Commander Robert M. Douglass, USN.
† Lieutenant Richard T. Wright, USN.
‡ Commander Robert L. J. Long, USN, was first commanding officer of the gold crew of the Patrick Henry. The oral history of Long, who retired as a four-star admiral, is in the Naval Institute collection.
§ Each Polaris submarine had a blue crew and gold crew. They alternated with each other, thus enabling the SSBNs to spend the maximum time on patrol.
** Rear Admiral Frederick B. Warder, USN.

Admiral Shear: Fearless Freddy was one of those who recognized the importance of the program, whereas some of the other senior people did not.

So Long and I came to that ship with all that background. We knew the importance of the program, we knew the importance of keeping the ships on station, we knew all the problems of fights with the Air Force on command and control and so forth. We were determined to make that system work, and we did make it work. We were the first ones to exchange crews and so forth. Our indoctrination, I think, rubbed off on the rest of the fleet pretty thoroughly. There were some cases where the two crews squabbled with each other.

Q: Well, since you'd brought up both crews, you wouldn't have that problem.[*]

Admiral Shear: Oh, no, I never had that problem, and many people used to come aboard and look us over and say, "My God, how do things go so well on this ship?" Well, the answer was that we brought the crews up that way. We started out properly, correctly.

Q: What was the source of the squabbles on the other ships?

Admiral Shear: Oh, how can you have two commanding officers and so forth and so on? How can you have two people giving orders? Well, it wasn't that kind of a problem at all. We had formal change of command after each patrol with a formal turning over of the ship, both officers and enlisted. In due course we got so that people were vying to turn the ship over in better shape than they got it. So the two-crew system, when it got going, worked out very, very well. We started it, and we made it work. I think the two of us were largely responsible for making it as smooth as it was. I don't say that bragging; it was just a fact.

Q: What memories do you have of Bob Long?

---

[*] Long said his oral history that Shear bent over backward to be fair in allocation of personnel between the two crews.

Admiral Shear: Bob and I were close friends. Bob was two years behind me in Naval Academy, class of '44. We had known each other in OpNav. We worked together very closely in the ship. As I told you, I had his wardroom along with me for a year, and the officers and crews in both wardrooms were absolutely superb. Bob and I knew the importance of the program. We had a ship that was second to none, and we made sure it stayed that way. We could not have been a better pair. I think a lot of people will tell you that. Shear and Long started the thing out right and made it go.

Q: What do you remember of Captain Ward, the squadron commodore?

Admiral Shear: Bub Ward, great guy. He had a great wartime career as a CO of a submarine. He had the Guardfish for most of his patrols. He was a very thorough man. He was not nuclear trained and didn't have any nuclear background, but he got along reasonably well with Rickover, selected a good staff. Roy Anderson was his chief staff officer. He had Charlie Styer, a good submarine man, and he had Yogi Kaufman.[*] He had a staff of about a dozen people that were all good people, carefully selected.

But--and it's very interesting--none of them knew the ships or the weapon system as well as we did, because they hadn't had that thorough training. So, as Bob Long used to say, in the early days there were no rules. We wrote the book. We wrote the procedures in many cases. We brought the squadron up as to what things had to be and how they had to be done and so forth. I must say that Bub Ward was very good at recognizing that we knew a lot more than he and his staff did. He gleaned a lot from us. But we never tried to take a holier-than-thou situation, that we knew more than the goddamn squadron did. That happens once in a while. We worked very closely with the squadron, and we really brought the squadron up, those of us in the early boats. We brought them up.

---

[*] Commander Charles W. Styer, Jr., USN. Lieutenant Commander Robert Y. Kaufman, USN. Kaufman wrote about Admiral Rickover and the early days of nuclear submarines in his book Sharks of Steel (Annapolis: Naval Institute Press, 1993).

Q: What were some of the things you wrote in this book as you were charting the new waters?

Admiral Shear: We didn't really write a book. In many cases we wrote procedures, or we improved procedures that the factory people had not put down quite properly or didn't know enough to put down regarding the operation of the ship. Of course, we wrote up the organization of our own ships very carefully and very thoroughly: all aspects, the nuclear aspects and the weapon system aspects.

Q: What would be examples of some of these new procedures?

Admiral Shear: Well, just the operation of the ships. Oh, hovering, for example, for firing the missiles. That's something you didn't normally do in a diesel-electric submarine. You had no need or reason to. The missile countdown procedures, things of that nature. Some of that was put together by the plants and the factories, and a lot of it we refined and improved and made sure it worked properly. And we documented all that as we went along.

We had lots of problems with those early missiles, lots of problems. The A-1 missile had some very serious growing pains.[*] The George Washington was one month ahead of us. One of the things we had to do was go down to Cape Canaveral, where each crew had to fire a successful missile before they were they were certified as ready to go on patrol.

The Washington went down in the summer of '60 and fired two successful missiles, one after the other, two crews. Everybody was elated, the system was proven, everything was go--no problems. We went down a month or six weeks later, and we had two missile failures. We fired two missiles. The first missile failed to ignite and fell directly back onto the ship. It was about a 30,000-pound missile, and it made the imprints of the jetavators--those are the control units at the bottom end of the missile--right smack into our deck. We had perfect jetavator dents in the deck of the ship.

---

[*] The first version of the Polaris missile, the A-1, was 28 feet long, 4½ feet in diameter, and weighed about 30,000 pounds. It had a range of 1,200 nautical miles.

We went out a day or two later and fired the second missile. The way the missile functioned was that you ignited it underwater; that fired the first stage. The first stage burned so many seconds, and then the second stage took off and then after that the warhead separated so many miles downstream. The second missile that we fired ignited right away, but the missile broke apart underwater. The second stage ignited with a fury that you wouldn't believe, and the observers outside thought they had lost the ship. They thought we had sunk. The observers were close by in the <u>Observation Island</u>, which was the support ship.

Q: What was your reaction inside the boat?

Admiral Shear: We knew there was a problem, but we didn't know exactly what had happened to the missile. So we surfaced a few minutes later, and, of course, the missile had rolled off the ship by that time. It had actually burned out and gone off in all directions away from the ship. But the people topside really thought that we'd had a tremendous explosion. There was no internal problem with the ship whatsoever. The missile had been counted down properly, it had ejected properly, and as it ignited it just went completely berserk.

So then there was a great review of what the problems were. They found some serious problems with the missile. One was in the ignition systems, and there was also a problem with some separation of the solid propellant from the wall of the stages, and that permitted early burn-through. That was one of the things that they found.

Q: Was this a design defect?

Admiral Shear: I think it was more of a manufacturing defect than a design defect.

So those things had to be corrected. That took a few weeks, and then we went down and fired again, and we had no problems for either crew.

Q: Did you get all your missiles replaced at that point?

Admiral Shear: Oh, no. These were test firing missiles.

We had some other problems. Arleigh Burke came down to observe a firing. The gold crew had just taken over the ship, and I stayed on board. I wanted to keep out of Bob Long's hair, but I stayed aboard for a couple of days. His crew had taken over, and my crew had gone back to New London.

They went out and had a test firing and had a firing problem with their first missile while Arleigh Burke was on board.* Arleigh was disappointed but was very nice about it and congratulated the crew, because everything performed to perfection, counted right down to T-minus-zero, and away she went. I forget exactly what happened to that missile, but it didn't function properly. So there was a further review over that. They made some more corrections, and both crews in due course fired successful missiles. We went on patrol in December of that year.

I'm sort of getting ahead of the story here. I'll go back to where we were when we reported to the Patrick Henry.

When we reported to that ship in the spring and summer of 1959, the program had top priority in the Navy. Red Raborn had unlimited funds. Arleigh Burke told Red Raborn he could select any officers he wanted from the Navy. He gave him a limit; I think the top limit was 70 or 80 officers, anybody he wanted. The system had to go. We were going to take this on, and it was going to be a strategic deterrent. No holds were barred.

Raborn was the man for that job. He was a hard-charger, and he was a public relations man. He selected as his number-one technical man Levering Smith, which was an absolute proper selection.† I don't know if you've ever talked to Levering Smith. Quiet, unassuming, but smart as a whip. He was an ordnance PG.‡ Technically, Raborn depended heavily on Smith, and Smith did everything to perfection. He brought that system along,

---

* Admiral Long's oral history discusses this incident, which occurred in July 1960.
† Raborn's first technical director, prior to Captain Levering Smith, USN, was Captain Grayson Merrill, USN. Merrill's oral history is in the Naval Institute collection.
‡ PG--postgraduate.

even though we had those early problems with the A-1 missile that were part of the growing pains. And by the time those ships went to sea those missiles were in good shape.

I reported to the Patrick Henry when she was about seven or eight months away from sea trials. The sea trials were in early 1960. The missile tubes were in the ship. Just the major components of the reactor plant were in: the reactor vessel, the pressurizer, the main coolant pumps, and a few other big units. Other than that, she was just a wide-open ship. EB worked in three shifts, right around the clock.

As the ship was put together and the systems became completely finished, we had great difficulty getting in the ship to qualify our people, because the ship was just absolutely packed with the yard workmen. On the third shift, which was from midnight until 8:00, the pace eased off somewhat. So we'd go down and do all of our training from midnight till 5:00 or 6:00 in the morning. We had to do that, because it was the only way to get in the ship. And it worked very well. It surprised some people to see that that's what we had to do, but that's what we did. People got used to it. They slept when they got a chance, and we worked our asses off to get those ships ready, and to get ourselves checked out.

Q: Did you have any contact with Andrew McKee, the design man at EB?[*]

Admiral Shear: Oh, yes, a great deal of contact with Andy McKee.

Q: What do you remember about him?

Admiral Shear: Oh, I remember a great deal about Andy. I'm one of Andy McKee's trustees now for the Andy McKee award at the submarine school.

Q: What were some of his contributions?

---

[*] Rear Admiral Andrew I. McKee, USN (Ret.). For details on his remarkable career, see John D. Alden, "Andrew Irwin McKee, Naval Constructor," U.S. Naval Institute Proceedings, June 1979, pages 49-57.

Admiral Shear: Andy McKee made contributions forever. He started out back in the '20s. He was class of '17 at the Naval Academy and stood close to the top of his class.[*] He went to sea and was injured in his first ship when he fell from the rigging. He could not go to sea again, so he went to MIT and became what we now call an EDO.[†] They were called naval constructors in those days, but they were actually naval architects.

He got involved right away quick with submarines, worked very closely with L. Y. Spear, who was sort of the dean of all submarine builders, later became head of EB.[‡] Andy McKee was deeply involved in all of the pre-World War II developments, from the 1920s to the end of the war, including the development of the fleet boat. As the war progressed, we went from the 300-foot boats to the 400-foot boats.[§] Andy McKee was responsible for that. He put heavier frames into the ship and more hull thickness; that's what he did.

He was sort of like Rickover in many ways, not in personality, but in his engineering expertise. He was a very conservative engineer. Anything that Andy McKee designed and manufactured, you knew it was going to work with perfection, with a lot of extra capability. Many boats were driven down by depth charge attacks well below their test depths in World War II, and you can thank Andy McKee that they came back because he was a very conservative designer.

Q: Well, and skippers had so much faith in him that they were willing to go deeper than the test depth.

Admiral Shear: Absolutely. Andy McKee was sort of a god as far as submarines were concerned, and a very nice man. Very nice man. You could go to Andy McKee any hour

---

[*] McKee stood number six of the 182 graduates in the class.
[†] MIT--Massachusetts Institute of Technology; EDO--engineering duty officer.
[‡] Lawrence Y. Spear graduated second in the Naval Academy class of 1890. After transferring to the Navy's Construction Corps, he was involved at the turn of the century in the construction of the first U.S. submarines. In 1902 he resigned his commission to work for the Electric Boat Company. He was president of EB, 1942-47, and then chairman until his death in 1950.
[§] These refer to test depths--that is, the depth to which a submarine could go safely without being crushed by sea pressure.

of the night or day with a problem, and he'd give you the time and sit you down and talk to you about it. I never knew him in his active duty days. But when he retired from the Navy he went to work for Electric Boat and became head of their design section. He stayed there for 20-odd years. I got to know him first when I put the Trigger in commission. He was a design man then, and I got quite well acquainted with him. Then I went back and put the Patrick Henry in commission and I got even more acquainted with him.

Q: What do you recall of him from that period?

Admiral Shear: Oh, he was into everything. Into everything. He watched everything like a hawk. He was involved in making the decision essentially to take the Scorpion class and put a 120-foot section in her. The story goes that they actually pulled them apart on the ways. They didn't do that, but they did put a 120-foot section basically in the Scorpion-class hull. Andy was involved in all that development work. Anything going on in submarine design in those days, Andy McKee was in it with both hands and both feet. He was recognized as an absolute top-notch submarine design man, every bit as great as L. Y. Spear was. It would be awfully hard to say one was better than the other. We were very fortunate to have those men come along in the period of history when they did, because they both made great, major contributions to submarines overall and submarining overall.

I told you how far the ship was from being completed when we got there, but the work was going on every day. You could see additions to every part of the ship: piping, electrical wiring, major components, missile systems, nuclear power plant systems. It just sort of grew in front of you. The speed with which that system was put together--Andy had a lot to do with that, Red Raborn had a lot to do with it, and Levering Smith had a lot to do with it. Harry Jackson, one of our great submarine design men, had a lot to do with it. He had a great deal to do with the designing of the fundamental Polaris hull and weapon system.

Q: Carleton Shugg was there too, wasn't he?

Admiral Shear: Carleton Shugg was head of the plant.* I'll talk to you about Carl Shugg. Carl Shugg and I became very close friends. Carl Shugg came to Electric Boat almost the same day that Beach and I reported to put the <u>Trigger</u> in commission. Fellow named John Jay Hopkins had taken over Electric Boat.

Q: And made it part of General Dynamics.

Admiral Shear: It became part of General Dynamics. The former head of Electric Boat was a fellow named O. P. Robinson. He'd been there for many, many years, and he'd done good work. He was quite an elderly man at that time, and clearly it was time for him to go. He was never the type of guy that L. Y. Spear or Andy McKee was, but he'd been with the boat company for a long time and come up the ranks and he was president. I don't know this, but it must have been clear to John Jay Hopkins that he had to get a new man in there pretty fast.

So along came Carl Shugg. He could not have picked a better man. To follow in the footsteps of L. Y. Spear and Andy McKee, the guy was Carl Shugg.

Q: Also a Naval Academy graduate.

Admiral Shear: Naval Academy graduate and MIT constructor, naval architect, and early history in submarines following right on after Andy McKee. He served as a submarine design man and submarine engineer for about ten years in the '20s. Then he resigned from the Navy and went into private business--private shipbuilding, among other things. At one time he was head of the Todd Shipyards in New York, before he came to EB. After that he was head of the Hanford nuclear plant out in the state of Washington. I think he came to

---

* Carleton Shugg graduated number two in the Naval Academy class of 1921. He resigned his commission in 1929 and went into private industry. His oral history concerning the Polaris program is in the Naval Institute collection.

EB from the Hanford plant, if I recall correctly. I may be off a year or two there, but I think he came directly from Hanford.

So not only was he a great submarine design man, but he had this nuclear power background, and he was a hell of an engineer. He took over that company and, by golly, within 24 hours you knew Carl Shugg was on board. He was into everything. You could see him wandering around the yard with the fedora hat that he wore. He was a nice guy, but he was a very firm, tough, hard-driving individual. He got that yard up on the step, and it stayed up on the step the entire time he was there. As I say, I got to know him initially when I put the Trigger in commission, and I got to know him very, very closely, very well when I put the Patrick Henry in commission.

Q; That may account for this speed of construction that you've described.

Admiral Shear: Well, that was part of it. The priority of the system accounted for that speed. Anything that had to do with the Polaris program just got top priority. Weapons system, electronic system, hull construction, power plant construction--it was top of the line. It went fast. Today you get involved in the DSARC system and the Pentagon and Secretary of Defense and 15 or 20 assistant secretaries of defense, you could never, never put a weapon system together like that today.* Everybody knows it would never happen.

Q: Well, the amazing part is that so many experimental type things had to come together.

Admiral Shear: So many experimental things, and they all came together. And, incidentally, everything was done in duplicate. Raborn insisted on that. Every one of his systems had a duplication so in case one system didn't work properly, you slipped the other one in. American industry came through, and with rare exceptions everything worked. For the navigation system we had the choice between North American and Sperry Gyroscope. Both of them turned out good systems, but the Navy selected North American because it

---

* DSARC--Defense Systems Acquisitions Review Council.

was a little better in a number of ways. Just one example of the two-system procedure that we went through. We had that for practically every system in the ship.

So here we are, rushing that ship to completion. Kept her right on schedule, although when I arrived I said, "We're never going to make it. We're never going to make it." The ship was practically empty. Many systems hadn't even started to go into the ship. I said, "God, we'll never make this schedule." But, by golly, it went together and we did.

Q: How useful was the PERT program in making that happen?[*]

Admiral Shear: Oh, the PERT program was Red Raborn's pet, and it was a good program. When you went into that PERT showroom of his, he had everything up there with red stripes and pins and so forth, exactly where everything was. You could go in and scan that room, and you could tell where it was. It was a very handy system. Red thought it was absolutely the thing that kept everything on schedule. I'm not sure it was quite that good, but it was a very good system.

Q: Useful but not essential.

Admiral Shear: Useful but not quite as essential, I think, as Red thought it was. I think that Levering Smith would probably agree with my comment on that.

So there we are. We finally got the ship assembled, and the ship's company took over the ship in the nuclear power business for all the internal testing themselves. The ship's company did that. So as systems were delivered to us, we accepted the systems--the cleanliness, the electrical checkout, and so forth. Then the ship's company became responsible for them, for all the testing and the filling of the power plant and the testing at low powers, test each system first and then testing the whole power plant itself. We did that. We were checked out and ready to do that.

---

[*] PERT--Program Evaluation Review Technique, a system of milestones for tracking the progress of a program against its schedule.

One of the things that we had to do was to pass periodic inspections by Rickover's senior vice presidents, who would come up and inspect the ship and inspect us. Then, before the ship finally went critical for the first time, ran on its own power, we had an examination that I tell you was some examination. Every nuclear powered submarine got that. Rick had a group of what we called senior vice presidents. They were people who had been with him a long time, some naval officers and some civilians, and they were probably the finest nuclear power people anywhere in the world at that period. They had the responsibility for putting us through the ropes, and when you went through one of Rickover's inspections and did well, you knew that ship was ready to go to sea. The inspection took two or three days by six or eight people really working the officers and the crew over, really thoroughly.

Some people objected to it, thought it was nasty and demeaning. Hell's bells, they were just thorough. They were tough and thorough, and they were going to make sure that they weren't going to send any nuclear power plant to sea or any ship or any crew that wasn't ready to do the job. That was their philosophy, and by golly, it stuck and it stuck to this day. You can thank Rickover for that. On the last day of the inspection Rick would show up. He would go over everything that the inspectors had found and done, give us a certain amount of hell for something that hadn't been done quite right. At the end Rick would always get us together, skippers and execs and his engineers, and philosophize a little bit and give us a little hell. But when he departed, when he knew that we'd gone through the mill of his inspectors, he knew that ship was in good shape and he had confidence.

Q: That gave you a great deal of satisfaction.

Admiral Shear: Oh, yes. That's right. And, incidentally, lots of people objected to what they thought was Rick's nastiness and unnecessary roughness. I had many fights with Rick; we all had fights with Rick. I had as tough as fights as anybody. But I respected that man immeasurably. And as time went on, I could tell that Rick respected me, because I was not a bullshit type, and I took no bullshit from him. Sometimes he tried to lean on me a little heavily, and I just wouldn't have any part of it. He knew that if he got too hard or too rough, I wasn't going to pay any attention to him. Many skippers did not get that knack.

Q: They took it too much to heart?

Admiral Shear: They took it too much to heart; that's right. The terrible interview stories that you've heard about Rick are about 50% accurate.

Q: What were some of your fights with him about?

Admiral Shear: Oh, my goodness, 1,000 different fights--both with the ship and then in my later years when I was OP-31, Director of Submarine Warfare, and when I was Vice Chief. Well, for example, we had a big fight with him over the ULMS. ULMS turned out to be Trident. You remember or ever hear of the word ULMS?

Q: Yes.

Admiral Shear: Underwater Long-Range Missile System. That started when I was OP-31. Levering Smith and Rick and I had some big go-arounds on that, about the power plant that was going into the ship and so forth. Oh, I had 100 different fights with Rick, but all of us that were around him did. One way or another, I had better than ten years of association with Rick. From the time of the ships, Director of Submarine Operations, through Vice Chief of Naval Operations--all of those had very close contact with Rick.

The more I got to know him, the more respect I had. I had respect for him from the start. You may be interested in this. An EB engineer wrote a nasty article in the Naval Institute about what a terrible guy Rickover was.* I wrote a rebuttal to it, and the Institute

---

* H. C. Hemond, "The Flip Side of Rickover," U.S. Naval Institute Proceedings, July 1989, pages 42-47.

published it.* You ought to look it up sometime. You'll see what I thought of Rickover. I tore this guy apart; I went right down the line with what Rickover has done for the Navy.

Q: Would you say Rickover was a fair man?

Admiral Shear: Oh, yes, he was fair. Rickover was Rickover. He was a thorough, tough, no-nonsense engineer, and he demanded perfection. That's what he got. Look at the record. Just look at the record. How many nuclear reactors do we have operating in the Navy today? One hundred fifty, I guess, plus or minus. Never had a serious problem with any of them. He did many other things too. So I'm one of Rickover's fans, and as I became more senior he knew that I was one of his fans. He still gave me hell every chance he got, [laughter] but he knew that fundamentally I was backing him.

He was a great naval officer. Many, many people don't understand that and don't realize that, but he was a great naval officer. I think in this piece that I wrote for the Naval Institute I put him alongside Arleigh Burke, Chester Nimitz, and Ernie King. I said that those men were the great naval officers of the century. And that's true.

So where were we? Okay, we're on sea trials. Now we could finally get the ship under way. That summer of '60 we were operating on sea trials and post-repair trials on down the East Coast and our missile trials down at Cape Canaveral. Eisenhower was President, and Ike was a great golf fan.† He liked to go up to Newport for a week or two of golf. So one day I was asked to take the ship up to Newport and have Ike come aboard and look it over. We'd been having some post-repair trials around EB, and we were out on local operations.

Ike was very proud of the Polaris system, because he felt it was developed in his administration. So we went up and anchored up there off Fort Adams, and Ike's aide was an aviator named Pete Aurand.‡ He was a good guy, but a lot of people didn't understand

---

* Harold E. Shear, "Comment and Discussion," Proceedings, August 1990, page 75.
† Dwight D. Eisenhower served as President of the United States from 20 January 1953 to 20 January 1961.
‡ Captain Evan P. Aurand, USN, served as naval aide to the President from February 1957 to January 1961.

Pete. I worked with him over the years quite closely. Pete came out and looked over the ship, and he wanted to make sure that we were prepared to take care of Ike. He asked a lot of questions about how we were going to handle him and so forth. I said, "We've handled VIPs by the dozen. We'll take good care of Ike, and I'll guarantee he'll leave this ship a happy man." So they wanted to know what I was going to feed him. I said, "We're going to feed him the best submarine chow. We always have good chow on submarines."

He said, "Well, Ike can only eat certain things, and we're going to bring the meat out. We're not going to take any of your meat." So they brought out some special hamburger that had been blessed for Ike's consumption. We were going to give him filet steaks or something like that, I guess. But they were very fussy about Ike's diet. So he came out, and everything that we could feed Ike had to be spelled out.

Ike came out about 10:00 in the morning, and he stayed almost all day. We took him through the ship from bow to stern, and we showed him everything in the ship, every system there: power plant, the missile systems, navigation system, fire control system. He was just an absolute kid in his enthusiasm. We took pictures of him all over the ship. I've got some of those pictures of him at the diving controls and so forth that he was just tickled to death with. We sent some of those out to his museum in Abilene, Kansas. He had a hell of a day.

He sat down and talked to us informally in the wardroom and told us how proud he was of the system and so forth. He said he personally had been the guy that decided to name the ships after American heroes, because, "In years ahead they're going to be the primary deterrent of the United States, and they should be recognized for all these great names we put on them." Ike made that selection himself.

Then we took him topside, and we fired two dummy missiles for him. In order to make sure that they didn't hit the ship on the way back, they were what we called sabots. They were a wooden shoe type of thing. But they were launched just like a regular missile. We had this big gyroscope system that was put in the ship to stabilize it in a heavy seaway for regular missile firing. You could precess that gyro and actually lean the ship over 15 or 20 degrees. So we heeled her over with that big gyro, and then we fired these missiles with

Ike up on deck astern of the missile tubes so he wouldn't get wet, because they went up with a big blast of water.

With him were Bub Ward and Red Raborn and myself, and the exec was on the bridge. On my signal he told the weapons officer to fire the missiles. They went off. Ike thought that was the greatest thing in the world, because he could see that that system functioned. He'd been all through the ship, and he saw intricate details of everything we had down there. Then he saw the system work. It made a big impression on him.

We had a huge picture of the ship, a very good picture, and I had every man in the crew sign it. We presented that to Ike on deck as he departed. He thought that was great. That's now out in Kansas in the museum. So Ike had a great day. He really got a good indoctrination as to what the system was about. He made a public statement shortly thereafter, after he had seen the condition of our ship and he knew that Washington was a month ahead of us. He said that there would be two Polaris missile submarines on patrol before the end of 1960. I guess he did that some for political purposes and some because he wanted to scare the Russians a little bit. But he made that as a public statement. From then on, we knew that--come hell or high water--we were going to be on patrol before the 31st of December.

Q: Well, one of the issues in the presidential election campaign that year was the so-called missile gap.[*]

Admiral Shear: Oh, yes, it was a lot of bullshit. It was something that Kennedy tried to make a big thing out of. There wasn't any missile gap. But anyway he made that statement. So the Washington went on patrol in early November, and we went up on patrol the following month. Patrols at that time were 60-odd days in length. We had only the two ships operating at that time. The Roosevelt and the Robert E. Lee were some months

---

[*] In the general election of 1960, Eisenhower's Vice President, Richard M. Nixon, was running for President against John F. Kennedy. The Democrats argued that the United States had a "missile gap" vis-a-vis the Soviet Union. After Kennedy won the election and the Democrats took office, they acknowledged that there was no such gap.

behind us. So we were the two operational ships, and we had to relieve each other on station until the other ships came along.

So we deployed on the 30th of December. We were then out patrolling in the Norwegian Sea, because we had to be within range of the targets. We went out and relieved Washington. No communications between us; we just got there on the station, and they knew from their radio traffic that we'd arrived on station, just by the schedule. So then they returned to New London for the first refit alongside the tender.

At the end of our first patrol, which was the seventh or eighth of March of 1961, we went directly to the Holy Loch.* By that time Dick Laning and the Proteus had been there about a week ahead of us.† She was anchored bow and stern, and we came alongside.

We were met by Bertrand Russell's "ban the bombers," and that was a big thing in the U.K. at that time.‡ He was a big anti--anti-nuclear guy and a radical--but he had a big following. We were met by several thousand of these people. They tried to block us from going into the Holy Loch. They lined the entrance to Holy Loch with small craft: rowboats, canoes, and so forth. We just steamed on through them, and I think we had some fire hoses on deck to blow them away from the ship. Then we went alongside the tender. Then we had a big press conference with well over 100 reporters there, because this was a very big thing as far as the U.K. was concerned, the fact that we were going to operate ballistic missile submarines from their ports.

I'll go back a little bit. It had been a big thing with regard to setting up this replenishment anchorage. It had been a big political issue with the Scots and the British. It was quite an element that was opposed to our being there--really opposed to it. We had to demonstrate to them early on that we were not going to be any danger to them. We said that we were going to be a big attribute to them, and that's how it turned out. We had this big group of reporters, and Bob Long came over to relieve me, and we answered questions,

---

* Holy Loch, Scotland, was the first overseas base for deployed Polaris submarines.
† Captain Richard B. Laning, USN, was the commanding officer of the submarine tender Proteus (AS-19), which had been modernized to service Polaris submarines. Laning's oral history is in the Naval Institute collection.
‡ Bertrand Russell (1872-1970) was an English mathematician and philosopher. He was awarded the Nobel Prize in literature in 1950.

I guess, for an hour or so. Bub Ward was there, of course, and we got vast coverage in the press all over Europe.

All of those first patrols had come off to perfection, so there wasn't any question that we had a system that was functioning. And by that time the whole world knew it. We went into this two-crew rotation that we had set up in the very earliest days. The oncoming crew would take over the ship, and the two crews would be together about a week, turning everything over to them very carefully. We set that system up, and that's the way it worked. And it works that way today.

Then the off-going crew went home for a couple of months for training and rest and recreation, and then we came back and relieved again. Well, I didn't get to go home. They hauled me down to London. Page Smith was then CinCUSNavEur.* I had to brief Page Smith, and he wanted me to go over and brief all the NATO people. So I had to go around Europe for about two weeks briefing all of NATO staffs about how successful the system was. That went off very well and made quite an impression with the NATO nations.

After that NATO trip, I had to go to Washington to brief everybody's brother there. I briefed Admiral Burke, and I briefed some people in the Congress. After I briefed Burke, he said, "I want you to go down and brief General LeMay." [Laughter] By that time, LeMay was Chief of Staff.†

I said, "All right. Are you coming down with me, Admiral Burke?"

He said, "No, LeMay knows you're coming."

So I saluted and said, "Okay." So I went down, and in the outer office there was a colonel there, and I said, "I'm Captain Shear. I've just come back from Polaris patrol in the Patrick Henry, and Admiral Burke tells me that he wants me to brief General LeMay."

The colonel said, "Oh, yes, General LeMay knows you're coming." Burke obviously had got him on the phone and said "Shear's coming." So, all right, I entered this big office,

---

* Admiral Harold P. Smith, USN, served as Commander in Chief U.S. Naval Forces Eastern Atlantic and Mediterranean (CinCNELM), U.S. Commander Eastern Atlantic, and Commander in Chief U.S. Naval Forces Europe (CinCUSNavEur) from February 1960 to April 1963.
† General Curtis E. LeMay, USAF, served as Air Force Chief of Staff from 30 June 1961 to 31 January 1965.

and here was LeMay at a desk at the far end of the office, way down in the end. There wasn't anybody else in there, so the colonel in the outer office followed me in to take notes.

So I marched down the length of this long office and stood at attention in front of General LeMay's desk. I said, "General LeMay. I'm Captain Shear, and Admiral Burke has asked me to come down and brief you about the success of the Polaris patrol." I gave him a good rundown on everything we had done: how successful everything had been, how well the ship worked, the status of the missiles and so forth. He grunted when I arrived. He acknowledged my presence [grunt]. After I had talked to him about 20-30 minutes, I said, "Do you have any questions, General LeMay?"

He said one word: "Communications." Well, I had already told him about the communications, but I went over in detail with him about the way we had for receiving messages, because that was one of his points--that you couldn't communicate with submarines. So I explained carefully to him the redundancy we had and then the complete coverage of the area by VLF radio stations and so forth.

And I said, "Are there any other questions?"

"No, that's all."

And so I turned to go, and I said, "Anything else, General LeMay?" [Grunt] I turned around and left the office. So I would say that it wasn't an unfriendly meeting, but it wasn't a very friendly meeting either.

Q: You had done what you were told.

Admiral Shear: He knew damn well that Burke had set me up. Because he knew damn well that we'd had a good patrol and that Burke was going to go down and rub it in to him. [Laughter] It was a very interesting thing for a young Polaris skipper to have that experience. In due course I got home and had my usual rest and recreation and training.

Q: Could you discuss, please, what was involved in the patrol routine?

Admiral Shear: Yes. You had to be within range of your targets. You were given a sizable chunk of ocean in which to patrol, and you would go from one portion of that patrol area to another on a semi-fixed schedule. It was absolutely vital and important that you kept complete, steady communications all the time because if you got the "go" signal, you had to get the word and fire. So we had multiple communication systems. We had a towed buoy, which towed just below the surface for the receipt of VLF radio transmissions.[*]

We built several big new VLF transmitter stations, one in Cutler, Maine, and one down a little later in Australia for the Pacific coverage. We already had certain VLF stations. One was in Panama, and one was right out here in Annapolis, just across the river. Why VLF? VLF is a very low frequency, covers from 15 to 25 KC, which means they have very long radio waves.[†] That VLF frequency span or spectrum has the unique capability of being able to penetrate the salt water down to X number of feet. With a powerful transmitter sending the messages, you could copy a signal down to 30 or 40 feet.

So we had a fixed loop on the top of our sail; it's the highest part of the submarine. We had a trailing wire which trailed on the surface, and we had this towed buoy. All of these could receive the VLF signals. It gave us good coverage--in that period--in the Norwegian Sea. Then we had the high-frequency standard radio reception, which had to have an antenna exposed to receive. So we never used that, because it was for a dire emergency, last ditch, if everything else failed.

You didn't want to have to expose any part of the submarine, because once you went on patrol and you closed that hatch, you were submerged completely, broken off from the earth's atmosphere for 60-odd days. You manufactured all your own atmosphere. You had atmosphere oxygen generators. You had CO_2 scrubbers. You had your hydrogen burners, and you kept the atmosphere in that ship better than the atmosphere you're breathing right here today. Everything was precisely controlled. So once you closed that hatch, you were underwater and completely submerged until you surfaced back in the Holy Loch.

---

[*] VLF--very low frequency.
[†] KC--kilocycles.

That communication system was vitally important to make the system work. If you got a go signal, you had to fire. Because we were on a 15-minute alert all the time. The missiles were counted down to 15 minutes. We kept them on a 15-minute readiness throughout the entire patrol. If we got a go signal, those missiles were going to be on their way in 15 minutes, with a flight time--depending on the target--of 20 or 30 minutes. There you were--bang, the world is blown up.

Now, those first missiles were nominally 1,200-mile missiles. The Polaris A-1 was 1,200; the Polaris A-2 was 1,500; the Polaris A-3, I think, was 2,000. Along came the Poseidon, which was about 2,500, a few years later. Actually each missile had a specific range on it, and they weren't all 1,200. Some of them might be 1,150 or even 1,175. But you knew the range of that particular missile, and some of those targets were right at the far end of that range. You had to fire across Norway to get off those missiles. In order to cover all your targets, sometimes you had to get right hard up on that Norwegian coast. Norwegians didn't know this at the time, but we were right hard up on their coast. We were in international waters, but sometimes you had to put the periscope on low power just to push the coast away, literally.

We called those early patrols with those short-range missiles the mud-flat patrols. Well named. That coast was not mud flat; it was all rock and mountains, but we called them the mud-flat patrols, because you had to really squeeze up there to get your most distant target coverage, both military targets and city targets. But those early patrols went on to perfection. The other boats came along a few months apart, and in due course we had the entire Squadron 14, ten ships, operating out of there.

Q: Much has been made of the need to avoid detection while on patrol. What things did you do keep from being detected?

Admiral Shear: You operated generally at slow speed in your quietest mode. You kept away from traffic. There was a fair amount of traffic in the Norwegian Sea, particularly as you close in the coast. And we had to close the coast to cover our targets. Near certain areas, around the Lofoten Islands, for example, there was a wealth of Scandinavian fishing activity. So we had to be careful and avoid that. You operated in a routine manner. Of course, you didn't penetrate the surface of the sea at all. You never surfaced. You never opened up the ship for ventilation. And you operated in as quiet a mode as you could. There was no particular need for speed; you had plenty of time in your patrol areas.

Sometimes you would shift from one area to another as another submarine came on the scene and to fill in the area behind you or something of that nature. But non detection was no particular problem. You had to keep alert sonar watch. There was a certain amount of concern that Soviet submarines might come out looking for us. It was easy for them to put 25 or 30 submarines, either diesel or nuclear, into the Norwegian Sea and just go poking around. We never had any problem of that kind.

Q: Are you talking about passive sonar?

Admiral Shear: Passive sonar, yes.

Q: How much latitude did you as the skipper have in where you would operate?

Admiral Shear: We had quite sizable areas assigned. The Norwegian Sea was split up, and, of course, initially we just had a couple of boats on patrol. Then, as we got a larger number of boats, areas were divided up into various sections. Initially we had essentially the entire Norwegian Sea to operate in, as long as we kept within range of our targets. As we got more boats out, then you had areas assigned, and you stayed within that area. Then you moved from one area to another area on a time scale, a certain day of the month and so forth. But we never had any particular restrictions about sea room. We had plenty of sea room, and we never had any particular problems about avoiding contacts. I never had any particular evidence that the Soviets were out there looking at us, looking for us thoroughly with their own submarines. Once in a while there would be a naval exercise out there with Soviet ships. But we had no trouble in avoiding such exercises.

Q: What do you remember about the day-to-day life submerged? How did you keep men from becoming complacent in that environment?

Admiral Shear: Day-to-day life, which some people thought was going to be a big problem, I assure you was no big problem. We had a very vigorous on-board training program on younger people, unqualified people.* We had a very good education program. We started out with Harvard University for the college courses which you could take and get credit for. As a matter of fact, I took the first one of those at sea, put together by Harvard. Other universities put together other ones later on. We had various recreational activities--tournaments, chess tournaments, chess games and cribbage games and things of that nature. You never had a problem keeping your crew busy and occupied. Despite what some people may think, that was never a problem.

Of course, you always miss mail; you always miss being in contact. We sent off in the very earliest days what we called family grams. And the family could go in so many times on a patrol, write a short message, and take it to the squadron office. You had a word limit. The squadron office would put it on the submarine radio schedules, and it would come out as a decoded message a day or two later. That was a very good thing for morale, and the families used that quite frequently. We had to limit the number of words and so forth, but that was a very popular thing.

Q: What measures did you do to take care of the welfare of the families back in the home port?

Admiral Shear: We had a very good system, and I must say Patrick Henry set it up. Bob Long and I assisted on it. We did a good job. We set up a system of blue and gold crews taking care of each other, both officers and enlisted. The off crew would make sure that everything was in good shape with the deployed crew and with the deployed crew's families, and it worked very well. We kept good track of each other, and it paid rich dividends. The

---

* This refers to crew members who had not yet completed the submarine qualification program.

families were at ease. They knew that if they ever had any problems, they could turn to the opposite crew that was back there for refit and training, and they would get action right away.

Q: What sorts of things did they do for each other?

Admiral Shear: Well, any kind of emergency we'd have teams all over. Anything serious we'd take care of it immediately. But they had social get-togethers, and they kept in contact verbally, phone calls, chains, and things of that nature. The officers' wives of the Patrick Henry wardrooms had blue-and-gold banquets which the wives would throw to the off crew and so forth. And they had the same sort of thing with the enlisted wives. And we had senior enlisted wives as points of contact. We had points of contact all down through the crews, so a message could be gotten out quickly, and we could take action quickly if anything came up. It was a very good system. It was very helpful toward the peace of mind of the families.

Q: Let's say a washing machine broke down. Would somebody from the opposite crew go out and fix it?

Admiral Shear: Absolutely! We had that rigged so we could get a maintenance man out there, a machinist's mate in the off crew and so forth. That would be fixed.

Q: Sick child?

Admiral Shear: Sick child needed hospital attention or doctor. The off-crew doctor was right there, and we had the hospital. Anything of that nature, we took care of. And each crew knew that the other crew was going to do the same thing. It started out in the way we set it up, and as far as I know it continued on all the other boats. But we made that work, and it was a very healthy thing.

Q: What do you remember about the support provided by Dick Laning in the Proteus?

Admiral Shear: Absolutely superb. Dick Laning was a very unique guy, as you must know already. I'm a great fan of Dick Laning. He was two years ahead of me at the Naval Academy. He had a great submarine career of his own right. He was CO of the Seawolf, the second of the nuclear-powered ships. She had a sodium-cooled reactor which had many problems, and eventually we did away with that. But Dick was her skipper.

Q: He had the Harder before that.

Admiral Shear: He had the Harder before that, and so I knew him from my Trigger days. The Harder was the second or third ship built there at EB. Well, I'd known Dick for a long time; I knew him during the war. I had great respect for Dick, and we were good friends.

He ran a fine ship in that Proteus, as only Dick Laning would. The Proteus, you know, was cut in two, and she had a section put in her to carry the missiles and some other equipment. He took her over down at the Charleston Naval Shipyard, where that job was done, and he deployed with her to the Holy Loch. I think he first brought her up to New London for that first refitting of the George Washington, which I mentioned.

Then he deployed to Holy Loch and got there just one week before we came in from our first patrol. Right from the start, that was a gung-ho, can-do tender. Anything you needed, that tender did it and did it very well, as only Dick Laning would run a show. He had an excellent crew, he had a top-notch repair officer. One of his early repair officers was an ED named Kenny Wilson, who was a qualified submariner.* But everything about that ship--officers, wardroom, machine shops, equipment--was absolutely top-notch. They were geared to run a Polaris replenishment anchorage, and they did it to perfection.

---

* Lieutenant Commander Kenneth E. Wilson, Jr., USN. Wilson eventually became a rear admiral and served in the late 1970s as Vice Commander and Chief of Staff, Naval Sea Systems Command.

In that regard I should tell you something. In the early planning stages, Bub Ward was deeply involved in this. It was decided that we were not going to get involved in any sort of a big base establishment for the Polaris. It was to be a Polaris replenishment anchorage, and it was to be done strictly by the tender. We went over there, and we put a buoy at her bow and a buoy to stern and anchored her fore and aft. In due course, we brought over a dry dock for periodic dry-docking of the ships. That's all we had. We had a number of small craft to go with it, but we had nothing ashore.

Unfortunately, over the years--and many of us early people were very disappointed in the way that came about-- they built up a shore station. They built up a housing area. They built up a commissary, and they built up an exchange--all the things you have in a typical base. That was never the intent. We were to live on the economy; we were to live amongst the Scots. But, as in so many cases around the world, we got involved in a U.S. base, and I didn't like that one bit. I resisted it and fought it, but by osmosis it just kept growing and growing. It was not the way to go.

A number of us old-timers went back for that fond decommissioning ceremony we had back there, and we all said, "This should never have grown up this way." We had an austere, hard-working, ready-to-go operation. We could move out of there in a few hours' notice, as we did in the Cuban Missile Crisis, and go somewhere else. That was the way it was supposed to be. We let our hearts dictate some things that we shouldn't have let happen. We just got a little bit too soft in things we wanted ashore.

Q: Well, that must have been to support the crew of the tender rather than for the submarines.

Admiral Shear: That's right. Exactly. The crew of the tender was about 1,000-1,200 men.

Q: Did you get involved in any of the public relations efforts with the Scottish people besides the press conference you've mentioned?

Admiral Shear: Oh, yes, a great deal, a great deal. Every time I was over there in refit I would make a series of speeches around Scotland. I'd get invited to many places. I always stressed the importance of our being there and the importance of the friendliness of the Scottish people and how well we'd been treated. I really laid that on pretty thick, and I got a lot of good results out of that. The Scots recognized the importance of the program. They recognized the importance of our being there, and they recognized the fact that we knew that we were beholden to them. I really laid that on very hard. I guess I did as much public speaking over there as anybody, because I had been involved right from the earliest days. I made a point of taking every invitation I could get around Scotland, sometimes east coast, sometimes west coast. And I think that paid off.

Q: Did you get to go around as a tourist at all?

Admiral Shear: Times were very tight. In those early days, I wanted to make sure that ship was ready to go. So I stayed right aboard most of the time and just watched that refit progress. I went ashore once in a while. I'd go ashore and make a speech or two now and then, as I told you. Once in a while I'd take a short ride in the afternoon up in the highlands, but most of the time I kept right close to the ship. Some people later on took a little bit more relaxed attitude, but I never did.

I wanted to make damn sure that ship was ready to go for the next one. Because, as I told you, once we took on those targets, we were never going to give them back to the Air Force. Arleigh Burke made that clear from day one. So if we had a ship that didn't make a commitment, somebody had to take on those targets because they had to be covered on the SIOP.* If it wasn't another SSBN to take them on, they were going to go back to the Air Force, and we weren't about to let that happen. Not about to. I don't know all the statistics from those later years, but I don't think we ever missed a deployment.

---

* SIOP--Single Integrated Operational Plan.

Q: How much did the people in the ship have to do with aiming the missiles and targeting them?

Admiral Shear: We had a fire control system. We had a card system initially, and that became more sophisticated for a particular missile for a particular target. And we had a program that told us which targets we were responsible for. We could count those missiles down to T minus a few seconds in drills on patrol. And we did periodically, but, of course, they were various solid ways to prevent launch. We had a very careful two-man system, skipper and exec and weapons officer and so forth. But those missiles were targeted for a series of targets. We knew all the time, wherever we were in a patrol area, what targets we were responsible for and what the ranges of those targets were. It was a ready-to-go operation and had been ready to go right from day one. When I say 15 minutes readiness to shoot, we were that way all the time, all the time.

Q: Was there a psychological screening of crew members to find people who could accept the fact that they might have to cause such destruction?

Admiral Shear: I don't know about psychological screening for that per se, but in all the submarine programs, going to submarine school and so forth, you have a good screening process. At one time, as a matter of fact, we had two Navy doctor psychologists who made a patrol and wanted to make sure that we were stable at the end of patrol as we were at the start of patrol. They poked around the ship and asked a lot of questions, and they made a couple of studies which were eventually put on file. I read one or two of them. Being psychologists, I guess they found what they thought were a few problems, but we never had any problems. I never had the slightest problem with any man in the crew, about worrying about the job he was performing or anything of that nature.

Q: Was this ever an issue in your discussions with the crew?

Admiral Shear: Not particularly, no. Were we afraid to push that button if we had to do it? No, we were ready to push that button. Once in a while, someone in the press or somewhere would ask, "Well, with all this responsibility, are you going to be in a position to push that button without the authority from on high and so forth?" The answer to that was absolutely not. We had a good command-and-control chain of command. We had a chain with regard to a two-man rule, with regard to making the weapons ready to launch, and so forth. That was never a concern. It was not something that bore on your mind at all.

Q: Well, you get focused on doing the job, and that's part of the job.

Admiral Shear: Exactly, exactly. But we were focused in keeping everything in absolute top-notch perfect shape, both on patrol and in refit. If anything, that became the obsession. You wanted that ship to be perfect. You got in good competition with the crews. Each tried to turn that ship over to the next crew in as good or better shape than when she came in. That was a very healthy attitude.

Q: Could you assign a percentage figure to the reliability of the ship and the weapon system?

Admiral Shear: Pretty close to 100%. You have some gadget out of commission with a problem for a short time. It didn't put the system down. Pretty close to 100%. And you know that the two-crew system was built around the concept of keeping the ship at sea for the biggest percentage of time. You could get better than two-thirds coverage of operating time with two crews. About the best you could do if you just had a single crew--the very best you could do--and you couldn't do that around continuously, would be about 50%. But with two crews you could keep that ship deployed and with plenty of rest for each of the off crew a full two-thirds of the time or a little better. That's why the system was put together that way. It was a big saving in numbers of the ships, for example. Because you got essentially two ships for the price of one. Because that ship was out there on station ready to go.

Q: Captain Laning is a very innovative individual. What innovations were needed in maintenance and repairs and so forth for this new system?

Admiral Shear: Everything that he needed to take care of the weapon system and the missile system and the nuclear power plant was incorporated in the modifications of the Proteus. And Dick, of course, being there when the ship was being modified, made doggone sure that everything he needed was put into that ship. I recall one thing. In the early stages of computers they had a computerized stores system so you get a spare part very quickly and keep track of your inventory very quickly. That was just one minor thing. That tender was a converted one from World War II. She had a good reputation in World War II, and she was the first Polaris tender, and she did a great job in getting us things. From then on we built new tenders dedicated to the Polaris/Poseidon system, and they were even more sophisticated than the Proteus. The Navy named one the McKee, and we named one the L. Y. Spear.* Shows you the regard in which we held those fellows.

Q: Right. And I suspect that Polaris had absolutely highest priority in the supply system.

Admiral Shear: Yes, it did. Yep.

I was with the ship three years. I made two years of patrols out of the Holy Loch. Then I went to work for Robert L. Dennison.† He'd been my boss as a two-star as OP-60 and by then was CinCLant.‡ He wanted an experienced Polaris skipper to run his Polaris office for him in his staff, so I was called back to take that up. As I told you before,

---

* USS McKee (AS-41) was commissioned 15 August 1981; USS L. Y. Spear (AS-36) was commissioned 28 February 1970.
† Admiral Robert L. Dennison, USN, served as Supreme Allied Commander Atlantic, Commander in Chief Atlantic, and Commander in Chief Atlantic Fleet from February 1960 to April 1963.
‡ CinCLant, Commander in Chief Atlantic, was--and still is--a joint-service U.S. command.

Dennison knew me well. I don't know whether he asked for me by name or not, but I was called back to take that job. I really left the ship earlier than I should have, because the pipeline was pretty thin in those days. That's one of the problems that we had with some of Rick's non-selections; the pipeline was awfully thin.

Long before that occurred, before they were all deployed, I went back and took over the office called J-34, which was Polaris operations on the staff of CinCLant. You should understand something about that, because it was set up specifically to handle Curt LeMay. Curt LeMay made a big pitch to the Chairman of JCS and the White House and Arleigh Burke to put all the Polaris submarines under him. He was the strategic king. He was Mister SAC. He had all the planes under him, all the nuclear bombers, and so forth. Why shouldn't he have the nuclear Polaris submarines under him as part of the forces, because they are all part of the SIOP?

SIOP was what Jerry Miller and Butch Parker were involved in out there in Omaha. That's the Single Integrated Operational Plan for nuclear targets. As Polaris submarines came along, they were integrated right into that plan, ship by ship. Well, this became a cause celebre. You can bet your boots that Arleigh Burke wouldn't turn any ships over to Curt LeMay. Curt made this big pitch to the White House and the Joint Staff, "I've got much better control than the Navy does, because my chain of command goes from the JCS to me to my aircraft with the bombs."

Burke said, "We can take care of that." He and Dennison and several others got into a huddle and said, "We aren't going to put up with that bullshit. We're going to have a system just as good. So our chain of command is going to read from the JCS to CinCLant to the ships. The only guy in the chain is going to be CinCLant, just like LeMay is the only guy in his chain."

That became a very critical and very important and very argumentative issue, because the submariners didn't like it. They didn't like it one bit. They said, "By God, we control our submarines. We did it all during the war, and we ain't going to put it under anybody else." Well, Dennison, having been OP-60 in all those early days of the planning, knew the importance of it, and he knew all the innuendoes of problems with Curt LeMay. He took on that job, and he said, "This is the way it's going to be. Shear, you're my man, and the chain of command goes from the White House to JCS to me. You're right in my office, Shear, and you run the show."

Joe Grenfell was ComSubLant.* I've got to tell you how Joe Grenfell got to be ComSubLant.

Q: He created the job for himself.

Admiral Shear: Yes, and got three stars out of it. But I'll tell you how he got it a little later. Joe Grenfell was irate. He didn't like this goddamn Polaris skipper over there telling him what to do. I wasn't telling him what to do. I was working for Bob Dennison. Bob Dennison was telling him what to do. But Grenfell never could understand the importance of a streamlined chain of command. And until he retired he never could understand, didn't like it. Although he was civil to me, let me tell you, he was never warm and friendly. I'd known Joe for many years, beginning when we were on a staff out in Pearl after the war. I always got along well with him, and I got along with him in that job. But let me tell you, he didn't like the situation one bit. But that was the way it was set up, and that's the way we maintained it right until we cleared the Holy Loch.† Then, of course, the Trident submarines work along the same lines at the present time.

So that was a very interesting period. I had to do the dance around on my toes a little bit on the staff at CinCLant, but Dennison always backed me to the hilt. So I never had any official problems. Then along came Page Smith, another great guy.‡ He'd been CinCUSNavEur, and he knew he was going to become CinCLant. He was just so damn anxious to get back and get that job, he could taste it. He'd call up every once in a while. He didn't talk to me, but he would say, "When is Dennison going to retire? When is he going to retire?" He wanted to get back there, and I guess he talked to Beakley.

---

* Vice Admiral Elton W. Grenfell, USN, served as Commander Submarine Force Atlantic Fleet from 2 September 1960 to 1 September 1964.
† In 1992 the Navy ended its 31-year presence in Holy Loch, because the longer range of the Trident missiles no longer required overseas bases for the submarines.
‡ Admiral Smith served as Supreme Allied Commander Atlantic, Commander in Chief Atlantic, and Commander in Chief Atlantic Fleet from 30 April 1963 to 30 April 1965.

Beakley was Deputy CinCLantFlt, three-star, and he had been OP-60. So I had a front office there that knew me, and they supported me right down the line, anything that came up, and made my job very easy. But I never abused their power, never. I never used my influence with them with Joe Grenfell or anything of that nature. I worked for them, and I did the job. But I never showed that I was their boy or anything like that. I was just the man who ran the show.

Page Smith, was another great CinCLant, great naval officer. He'd had the Missouri before she went aground, you know. Then they hauled him back to take command of her, to get her off the beach and take her to sea again.[*] I was in BuPers at the time.

Q: Admiral Smith is a very polite and cordial man but very firm at the same time.

Admiral Shear: Oh, absolutely. Do you know Page?

Q: I've interviewed him, yes.[†]

Admiral Shear: Great guy. I must go back a little bit now to my first term at BuPers. I was assistant planning officer for all enlisted training. I mentioned that the next desk over was the officer training plans. I worked for an aviator named Red McDonald. I can't recall the name of the captain who was the head of the officer planning, but his assistant was Lieutenant Commander Harvey Hall, a very fine naval officer.[‡] We became very good friends. Harvey Hall had been Page Smith's navigator on the Missouri before she went aground. They hauled Page Smith back after they got her off the beach. Of course, the Air

---

[*] The battleship Missouri (BB-63) ran aground near Norfolk, Virginia, on 17 January 1950. Her commanding officer, Captain William D. Brown, USN, was relieved on 3 February 1950 by Captain Smith, a previous skipper. For Smith's recollections of the event, see "The Value of Confidence," Naval History, Fall 1991, page 36.
[†] Admiral Smith's Naval Institute oral history covers his service in the USS Arizona (BB-39) in the 1920s and command of the Missouri, 1949-50.
[‡] Lieutenant Commander Harvey W. Hall, USN.

Force had been clamoring and making nasty noises: "The Navy can't keep off the beach," and so forth.

Finally, Page Smith said, "All right, I'm going to take that ship. I want Harvey Hall back as my navigator." So on one day's notice Harvey said, "I'm going back to sea." He disappeared, went back to the Missouri, and stayed with Page until Page was relieved the second time. He was a fine naval officer, and Page knew it. He was a hell of a navigator. So he said, "By golly, if I take that ship, I'm taking Hall back." So away he went. Like that. Overnight. I just bring that back as a little interlude.

But now before Page Smith took over, we went through the Cuban Missile Crisis, and I was in the middle of that.[*] We were getting some very good intelligence that those missiles were ashore. We had naval intelligence aircraft that were flying right over them-- some at high level, some at low level. We were getting cold, hard intelligence. We knew where that stuff was and what it was. The thing kept getting hotter and hotter. In due course, the decision was made to really lay it down with Russians and put a so-called Cuban quarantine around the island. It wasn't a quarantine; it was an old-fashioned naval blockade, almost 1,000 miles of sea. Dennison ran that entire thing.

The CNO was George Anderson, a fine man who in due course unfortunately got fired.[†] Anderson and Dennison worked very closely together. Anderson's executive assistant was my classmate Ike Kidd.[‡] And I was down there running the Polaris show for CinCLant. When the balloon went up, we established that blockade, and the guy that Dennison picked to run that show was Alfred Ward, who had been the ComPhibLant and

---

[*] In mid-October 1962, U.S. reconnaissance plane photographed a Soviet nuclear missile site in Cuba and the presence of Soviet bombers. On 22 October President John F. Kennedy went on national television to announce a naval quarantine of Cuba, to be implemented on 24 October. On 28 October Premier Nikita Khrushchev of the Soviet Union notified President Kennedy that he was ordering the withdrawal of Soviet bombers and missiles from Cuba.

[†] Admiral George W. Anderson, Jr., USN, served as Chief of Naval Operations from 1 August 1961 to 1 August 1963. Anderson's Naval Institute oral history describes his firing.

[‡] Captain Isaac C. Kidd, Jr., USN, later a four-star admiral and CinCLantFlt himself from 1975 to 1978.

then became ComSecondFlt.* A fine officer, and he'd been in OP-60 when I was there. So I knew him from those days.

They had all that top talent up there at that time. So he became essentially the quarantine commander, and they set that ring 1,000 miles at sea.† The day the decision was made that we were going into condition one, which was the highest condition before getting into a shooting situation with nuclear weapons, we cleared the Holy Loch. Dennison told me to get those ships out of there, get them on patrol in nothing flat. And we did that. Page Smith was still over in London, and we didn't even tell Page Smith what was going on. We cleared the Holy Loch overnight. I think we had three submarines alongside at that time. We got out of there in less then 24 hours, sent them on patrol.

Some of them had repair work going. We got that repair work thrown back together. We got the ships out of there on patrol, and we sent the tender to sea so the Holy Loch was empty. We simply sent the tender way up through the Minches up in northwest Scotland, into one of those big sea lochs, and hid her. Well, let me tell you, there was a Soviet intelligence cell in Glasgow. You could drive right around the shore of the Holy Loch, and they were keeping a daily monitor of what was going on there. That really set them back on their ears. When they knew that all Polaris submarines were cleared at sea on patrol, they knew that the United States meant business.

Q: So it was good for them to know that.

Admiral Shear: You bet. It was good for them to know it. And through our intelligence channels we knew very well that they took that aboard very quickly.

Corky Ward was down there running the blockade, and we set up a big battle staff--Army, Navy, and Air Force--around the clock there at CinCLant headquarters. Once I got the Polaris submarines at sea, hell, I was essentially free. It was a 24-hour-a-day battle

---

* Vice Admiral Alfred G. "Corky" Ward, USN, commanded the Second Fleet from October 1962 to August 1963. His oral history is in the Naval Institute collection.
† For details, see Forrest Johns, "The Cuban Missile Crisis Quarantine," Naval History, Spring 1992, pages 12-18.

staff, fully manned with anybody that you needed for a particular answer to anything that required an answer. We had about 20 to 30 men on the battle staff. I became one of the battle staff commanders, and that was a hell of an experience. Because I had nothing else to do, they grabbed me and said, "You're one of the battle staff commanders."

Q: What kind of issues did you deal with?

Admiral Shear: There was intelligence, status of ships in the North Atlantic. Soviet or Bloc ships--where they were, what they were doing. Where our ships were, what they were doing. Were we or were we not prepared to board a ship? And that became a big issue, whether we were going to actually challenge the Soviets at sea and board a ship.* I think we boarded a bloc ship that didn't physically have missiles on board. But we knew where every ship was, coming and going, and those that had missiles on board and those that didn't or those that had missile components on board.

We really were essentially ready to go to war. Wasn't any question about it. And Dennison ran that superbly. I must say that the White House kept their finger in it pretty thoroughly. The White House would go to George Anderson. George Anderson would pick up the phone and go to Dennison. The White House, of course, was nervous as an old cat. Frequently, Ike Kidd, who was George Anderson's executive assistant at the time, would get me on the phone. He knew I was down there, so he'd pass something on to me that wasn't quite as high as CNO to CinC--something that I was told to do. We had a good relationship that way. But that was a very interesting period in history. It was a great experience for me to be right in the middle of it, from the Polaris end on in to the battle staff end.

Every day you had to brief a steady parade of VIPs, including Kennedy. We took Kennedy through the war room and briefed him thoroughly. And we brought in a Polaris submarine and had him go aboard, one that was not ready to go on patrol yet. The Thomas

---

* On 26 October 1962 the destroyers Joseph P. Kennedy, Jr. (DD-850) and John R. Pierce (DD-753) halted and boarded the Soviet-chartered, Lebanese-flag freighter Marucla. After the Americans inspected her cargo, she was permitted to continue to Havana, Cuba.

Edison was just working up for the missile firings and post-overhaul availability up and down the coast.* She happened to be within a day's steaming, so we brought her in. Kennedy had a bad back, and he couldn't get up and down the hatch. So we made a special metal container, fit it around him, and we lowered him right down the hatch. We got that. It's up in our museum in New London right now, so that was an interesting little aspect.

What else would have been with the Cuban Missile Crisis? Well, I think I'll just give you something aside here. I think that Dennison ran that thing so absolutely perfectly, I thought that he might have a chance as the next CNO.† He would have made a great one, but he was simply too senior. He was simply too senior. He was more senior than George Anderson, and you never go down.

Q: Yes, he was four classes ahead of Anderson. He was in the class of '23.

Admiral Shear: Yes, he was a classmate of Arleigh; Arleigh's '23. And Anderson got fired and went over and became ambassador to Portugal. I forget the details of how he got fired. You probably remember that from some of your interviews. I can't talk about it. I don't know why he was removed, but he was.

So then along came Page Smith. And Page Smith was just as great a guy to work for as Dennison was--different type of guy, but a very fine guy. Great seaman, and a nice fellow to work for. He soon found out that I knew what the hell I was talking about, so I gained his confidence; he got great confidence in me. On anything that had to do with Polaris, by golly, he went to me and got the answer before he did anything. So we had a very good working relationship. I guess I was with him over a year.

He understood the importance of command and control, keeping the Air Force out of the way, just as Arleigh Burke had done and just as Dennison had done. So we kept that

---

* The USS Thomas A. Edison (SSBN-610) was commissioned 10 March 1962 and began her first patrol on 7 November 1962.
† In his Naval Institute oral history, Admiral Dennison said that when the Kennedy Administration took office in 1961, he was sounded out about becoming Chief of Naval Operations. He declined, saying he preferred to be commander in chief of the fleet, because it was an operational billet.

arrangement, just exactly the same as we set it up. A few times we had tiffs with Joe Grenfell, but Page Smith understood why the system had to be that way, and he made things very clear to Joe. We didn't have any problems.

I don't recall any particular international episodes that came on when Smith was there. We ran the Polaris system in a routine manner. Oh, yes, one did come along. There were 41 submarines authorized, and they were coming out in a steady stream. So we had to set up another site. That site had to be within range of targets, just as the Holy Loch was in range of targets. So we set up a site in Rota, Spain.

Q: Phil Beshany talked quite a bit about the establishment of that site.*

Admiral Shear: I was deeply involved in setting that up. On my way from the Patrick Henry to that J-34 job for Dennison, I was asked to go via Rota and look over the situation down there. We had good relationship with the Spanish, and we'd given the Spanish a number of ships. A pretty good little Spanish Navy, thanks to the U.S. Navy.

I had never been there before. We had a sizable air station there. We had a good harbor, which was essentially a man-made harbor, and we had a good pier. There was a little bit of a problem with the surge, but it wasn't significant. They had a very good rock breakwater built around most of the harbor. Good water in the harbor, good approach channel, plenty of space in the harbor to put the tender alongside and a couple of submarines. So I came back with a very glowing report that we ought to grab that base and build it up and put the ships in there. And politically it was not that difficult. I think we'd have had a much more difficult problem if we had tried to put the ships inside the Med somewhere.

Now, as we grew in numbers of ships, we had to expand our coverage into the Mediterranean. Now, I'm going to tell you about this, because a lot of international politics got involved. After the Cuban Missile Crisis there was a deal made, and I don't know the details of the deal in exact precise point. But there were some allegations that we and the

---

* See the Naval Institute oral history of Vice Admiral Philip A. Beshany, USN (Ret.).

Russians had come to an agreement, i.e. Kennedy and Khrushchev, about missile coverage.* One of the deals was that we would take the liquid-fueled Jupiters out of Turkey, where they were a visible threat to the Soviets, and replace them with something else. And we also took them out of Italy. The Jupiters weren't anything.

Well, the southern European nations didn't want to be left bald-face naked. So we said, "All right, we'll agree to take those missiles out of Turkey and Italy. But we'll replace them with Polaris submarines." Which we did. In order to make that chain complete within the time frame we're talking about, we had to operate a chain of submarines from Holy Loch down into the Med, which we did until we got Rota established. So some of the submarines would go up and patrol the northern waters, and some would patrol the southern waters down in the Med.

You had to get pretty far into the eastern Med to cover some of your targets, just as you did up against the Norwegian coast. To demonstrate to the southern nations that we had, by God, done this, we sent the first of the ships that went into the Mediterranean for a port visit in Izmir, Turkey. And we had all the Turkish military and political types come down and see the ship visit there. It was the Sam Houston. The skipper was my good friend and classmate Bill Willis.†

So that was a very interesting political and military ploy. First, it put the ships in the Med for target coverage down the southern flank, to replace the target coverage of the Jupiters in Italy and Turkey, and then to show politically that, "By golly, the Unites States is there with those ships. Take a look fellows; there they are." And we kept that chain up once we started, kept up like we did up north, for many, many years. It was rather inefficient time-wise running that chain out of the Holy Loch. So as we got established in Rota it became much more efficient. Just go around the corner and go through Gibraltar, and there you are. So that worked out very nicely.

---

* Nikita S. Khrushchev served as First Secretary of the Communist Party, 1953-64, and Premier of the Soviet Union, 1958-64.
† Captain William P. Willis, Jr., USN, was the first commanding officer of the USS Sam Houston (SSBN-609), which was commissioned 6 March 1962. In the spring of 1963 she became the first ballistic missile submarine in the Mediterranean and the first to make a port visit during a patrol.

Q: Going back a little bit, you said you would tell me how Joe Grenfell became ComSubLant.

Admiral Shear: Do you want this on the record?

Q: Sure.

Admiral Shear: Not too many people know this. ComSubLant was a man named Dan Daspit, class of `27.* Pretty good man, quite tough. He was known to everybody as Danny Daspit. He was ComSubLant with headquarters in New London. Joe Grenfell was ComSubPac with headquarters in Pearl Harbor. Joe as a two-star came back to Washington and became OP-04B as a two-star, OP-04 being a three-star as head of logistics.

As the Polaris program progressed, the one about which Joe Grenfell was very lukewarm in early days, it became apparent that that was going to be a really gung ho, going program and it was going to develop into a three-star job. Dennison wanted to make sure that ComSubLant was at his beck and call beside him down in Norfolk, even though he was going to run the show as CinCLant from CinCLant headquarters. He felt that for Polaris he wanted the submarine force commander at his side, even though that submarine force commander was not in the command-and-control chain. The submarine force commander, however, did have logistic responsibility for the upkeep of ships during refit.

So the decision was made to move ComSubLant from New London--actually Groton--to Norfolk. Dan Daspit didn't want to go. He had commitments around New London, and I think his wife wanted to stay in New London. I don't know this for a fact. But Dan Daspit made it clear that he did not want to move to Norfolk. Well, SubLant was going to move, period. If Daspit had made the move willingly and immediately as Dennison

---

* Rear Admiral Lawrence R. Daspit, USN, served as Commander Submarine Force Atlantic Fleet from 13 January 1960 to 2 September 1960.

had asked, I feel personally that he would have remained ComSubLant and gotten a third star.

Joe Grenfell saw his opportunity. He became quite aware of Daspit's reluctance to move from Groton to Norfolk and stepped into the breach and made it quite clear that he was the senior submariner of ComSubPac, and he ought to be the man to go down there and take over ComSubLant, a three-star billet for Polaris. That's exactly what happened. I know the facts--that Dan Daspit bucked and resisted that move. If he had played it the other way, I feel fairly sure that he would have gotten the job. That's just a little sideline.

Q: One topic we mentioned at lunch and hadn't put on the record was the idea of putting Polaris missiles in merchant-type ships. What are your recollections of that?

Admiral Shear: I recall in the very earliest days, before we had perfected the miniaturized warhead and the solid propellant that permitted great reduction in size in Polaris, that we had considered this, putting in a version of the Jupiter liquid-propelled missile in merchant ships. We had done some fairly detailed studies about size and spaces, what ships they would put into, merchant hulls, what holds they'd put into, and so forth. But with the dangers of carrying a liquid-propelled missile in a seagoing hull, being what they were--because that was a very unstable type of propellant--we never went very far with it. George Miller, who was always a strategic thinker, at that time was in OpNav.[*] He was pushing that concept hard, but it never really got off the ground. Along came Polaris--smaller missile, smaller warhead, much easier to handle in a maritime environment--so we went that way.

Q: Plus the advantage of stealth.

Admiral Shear: Plus the advantage of stealth. And our studies showed that even with the number of merchant ship hulls, you could keep track of those hulls--if you really wanted to

---

[*] Rear Admiral George H. Miller, USN.

put the effort on it. With the Polaris submarine that stealth issue was very important. For example, we had hardened bases out in North Dakota, but the Russians knew precisely where they were, and they could target them. You could not target Polaris. You could not target the entire ocean area. That's why we went for the long-range missiles as they came along. It just increased our operating area. A very fundamental fact. It increased our targeting coverage, and it increased our operating area. Now here we are today with a 5,000-mile Trident with vastly increased targeting capabilities and vastly increased operating areas--essentially anywhere in the world.

Q: And eliminating the need for overseas basing.

Admiral Shear: Exactly, exactly.

Q: You've mentioned in broad terms the business of working for Admiral Dennison and the operational chain. Specifically how did you carry out that responsibility?

Admiral Shear: I had a small staff, very good officers. In the chart layout of the organization of CinCLant, J-34 had a block as Polaris operations. I had the responsibility for preparing all the operation orders for the submarines to conduct their patrols. Before each patrol, the crew would be in the final stages of their upkeep and refit and training; the off crew would be ready to take the ship out. They would always come down to Norfolk for briefing. I would brief them thoroughly about where their patrol was going to be, what they were going to do, what the targeting assignments were, and deliver their op order to them. We had briefings that encompassed two or three days.

We were flying back and forth, initially out of Quonset Point, Rhode Island, to Prestwick airfield in Scotland, near the Holy Loch. First we had contract aircraft; that's another story. Some of those aircraft were barely able to get off the ground. But we were flying the crews back and forth, and I briefed them for the next patrol and delivered their op order, and away they'd go. That operation was run entirely by CinCLant; that was Dennison's job. The chain of command, as I said before, went from the JCS to CinCLant to the ship, period. Nobody in between. Curt LeMay had to live with that. He didn't like it, but he couldn't fight it.

Q: When you were working for Admiral Dennison, how much interchange did you have with Omaha and the strategic target planning staff out there?

Admiral Shear: We had our people out there. We talked about Butch Parker and Jerry Miller. Then, as soon as we could get enough of a background to take some of the people off the ships, we sent some of our best weapons and fire control officers, and put them on the Joint Strategic Target Planning Staff. Once we started getting our people in there, they were able to demonstrate what Polaris could do. They were on the scene to answer Polaris questions. They were part of the formal joint staff out there. It took a couple of years before we were in the position to get any significant number of people out there. We did that as soon as we could, because that was very important.

Q: Did you communicate with them on a regular basis?

Admiral Shear: Yes, both formally and informally. And we had ways of getting back and forth with the Air Force without any stunts and so forth. We kept pretty close track of what was going on.

Q: How much interface in that job did you have with Admiral Grenfell and SubLant since he owned the boats?

Admiral Shear: A lot, a lot. The operations office for his staff was right next door to mine. He was physically in the CinCLant compound, in another building, but his operations offices were actually in CinCLant's building, and his typical national submarine operation job was done there by his operations officer. When I was there, it was Commander McCauley.[*] A

---

[*] Commander James E. McCauley, USN.

good man, an experienced submariner, but I had no formal responsibility to him or him to me, even though we were just a room apart.

Q: Well, you'd have to coordinate on schedules, for example.

Admiral Shear: We coordinated very closely on schedules--for refits and when the ships would be ready to go and so forth and so on. But the schedule we set up--so many days at sea on patrols, so many days in port--was adhered to religiously, religiously. Because if you didn't, you got your whole chain bollixed up.

An interesting little sidelight. When we first set up that 60-day patrol and so many days in port, it became a rotating situation such that every year it came up at the same time. So if you were on the summer patrol, you were on patrol every summer. If you were on patrol on Christmas, you were on patrol every Christmas. It went three years that way. As soon as I got to J-34, I changed that schedule. We had to keep the ships on patrol a full two-thirds of the time. But I rearranged that a little bit so that you had a few more days on patrol and such that it didn't repeat every year.

Q: Sort of like dogging a watch.

Admiral Shear: That's right, dogging a watch. I think we went from a 60-day patrol to a 66-day patrol. And we added one or two days or subtracted one or two days from refit so that you were moving forward. Moving forward each patrol so that you didn't repeat precisely every time. If you were away from home once, you were away from home forever. That turned out pretty stale. For instance, you were away when it was summer vacation for kids and you were away for Christmas. And that wasn't much fun. Everybody thanked me profusely for making that change. Having been subjected to it for three years, I made damn sure that we modified it. It didn't hurt the program a bit, and it helped the rotation of the crews.

Q: Well, since Admiral Dennison was the big boss, then it was up to SubLant to adhere to your schedules.

Admiral Shear: Oh, absolutely, yes, which they did. There was never any question about that.

Q: Did you have much connection with the shipyards as they were producing the new ships, or was that SubLant's job?

Admiral Shear: That was SubLant. Of course, we watched the schedule of ships coming out, because that was very important as far as targeting was concerned. That was what enabled us to take on more targets from the Air Force and things of that nature. We had to know when a ship was ready to go. And I must say that the four yards did great work in keeping those ships on schedule. We had Portsmouth, Electric Boat, Newport News, Mare Island, and those ships came out in rapid succession once we got rolling. That program had a priority which we haven't had since and probably will never see again.

Q: Did the level of talent stay as high as more and more ships came into commission?

Admiral Shear: Stayed very high. But the base of our pyramid didn't catch up for a long time. What did that mean? We were not putting enough people in, so we had to keep people in the ships longer and make more and more patrols. And we had to send skippers back for a second ship. The only reason I didn't go back for a second ship was I had to take that operations job with CinCLant. Otherwise I would have gone back and put a second ship in commission. My counterpart Bob Long put a second ship in commission, as did many others.*

---

* Commander Robert L. J. Long, USN, commanded the gold crew of the Patrick Henry (SSBN-599) when she was commissioned in 1960. In 1964, as a captain, Long was first skipper of the blue crew of the Casimir Pulaski (SSBN-633).

So the base was not broad enough. Some of that was Rickover's fault. He didn't take some very good people that he should have, and as a result that base did not expand as quickly as it should have. Just too narrow when there were so many ships coming out. They were on a roll, and we just had a repeat performance with good people going back to second ships. Not only skippers and execs but some of the other people--engineers, weapons people, and so forth. So that's one area where Rick could have done better.

Q: And that put heavy demands on family life.

Admiral Shear: Very heavy demands. That's one of the reasons why our resignation level at one period was too high. Pure and simple.

Q: Anything else on the job in Norfolk to mention?

Admiral Shear: No, I mentioned the transfer to Page Smith and what a great guy I thought Page Smith was. Fine relief for Dennison. One thing I did do: I took Page Smith out to Omaha once. They gave him a royal treatment out there, because they knew he was running the show, and they knew they weren't going to change that. But they gave him the typical SAC professional glad hand, which they had down to perfection. They had professional briefers that had stayed in the job for years, and they knew exactly what to say and what emphasis to put on each syllable. But--let me tell you--nobody snowed Page Smith, just like nobody snowed Dennison. He knew what was going on.

I have to say that that SAC establishment out there was something. That was really a professional show, the command post and the targeting situation and so forth. He wanted to physically see that, because he was responsible for part of the SIOP. When he took on those missiles, that was his responsibility. He just wanted to see that physically and wanted to see the staff that was working the problem. He wanted to see the CinCSAC command post. Of course, CinCSAC wore two hats. He was CinCSAC and he was commander of the Joint Strategic Target Planning staff. So we out there for a couple of days, and we got a very thorough going over.

Q: General Power had that job for quite a while, and he was a very parochial Air Force man.*

Admiral Shear: They all are. Rarely do you find one who isn't. It's sort of bred into them. But you could never find anybody more parochial than LeMay. But I must say they were very competent people; they knew their stuff. As narrow as it might have been, they knew their stuff.

Anyway, I had a hell of a tour there at CinCLant: Cuban Missile Crisis, two great CinCs to work for, and all the Polaris operations expanding rapidly. It was touch-and-go; I was on my toes every minute.

In the August of '64 I went to National War College, which was at Fort McNair in Washington. At that time that was the senior of all war colleges. I had never been to the Naval War College, because I never had time to fit it in. One of the problems you get in this nuclear business, you're just tied up. As I told you, the base wasn't broad enough. So I could never take time off to go to the Naval War College. But I did have that time after I left Norfolk to go to the National War College, which was important that I did because that was a crackerjack school.

It was a mixture of Army, Navy, Air Force, Marines, Coast Guard, and State Department. And State Department had a few CIA guys that they called State Department, but they were CIA guys. So it was a great cross-section at a more senior level than the Armed Forces Staff College. That had been at the commander level, and this was at the fairly senior captain/colonel level. It was a ten-month course, a great course. The lecture series was superb, somewhat of a higher level than we had down at Norfolk earlier. The top people of the nation and the world were there to lecture us three or four times a week.

---

* General Thomas S. Power, USAF, served as Commander in Chief of the Strategic Air Command from 1 July 1957 to 30 November 1964.

Q: Any names you remember?

Admiral Shear: Oh, it was just one magnificent name after another. For one, Page Smith came up. I remember that he was still CinCLant. But the top levels--military and civilian, state ambassadors, all naval forces or all military forces of the United States, number of foreign dignitaries, number of foreign military men. It was just an absolutely superb list of one fine lecturer after another.

We also had a good vigorous program of committees and so forth, and we worked on a number of international problems. Then we all went off for an international trip that lasted a month to six weeks. It was much more extensive than we had at the Armed Forces Staff College. The world was divided up into parts: Middle East, South Asia, South America, Europe, and Africa. My group had the eastern Mediterranean and the Middle East as far as India.

Those trips were terrific. We saw all the top people, military and civilian, of the countries. We learned a lot about the countries. We learned all about the political problems. We went to India, Iran, Israel, Jordan--all through that Middle East area. Some of that area, I had covered when I was in that Law of Sea deal, so I had been to some of those countries twice. Also, we went to Pakistan. That was a very good tour.

Q: What are some of the highlights you remember from that trip?

Admiral Shear: We had some very good ambassadors out there in those days. They were good people, and they knew their stuff. We got a good feel for the political situation. I personally learned a lot about Israel's situation. I thought that the Israelis were hard-nosed, unrealistic, unreasonable, and the major problem in the Middle East. And I think all my classmates came away with the same opinion. Every problem in that Middle East rotated around the Israelis. You could say that Jordan was hard-nosed, the Saudis were hard-nosed, and they hated the Israelis, but every problem in the Middle East, the Israelis were at the heart of it. That came through loud and clear. It also came through loud and clear that they had political leverage in the United States, and they weren't going to let loose of it.

Q: You can say almost the same thing today.

Admiral Shear: You can say precisely the same thing today, precisely the same thing. Rabin was chief of staff at that time.* We got to meet him, and I was impressed with him. I thought he was a professional military man who knew his stuff. He spoke good English, among other things. I thought he was a first-rate individual.

Q: Well, he's taken a more reasonable approach now that he's head of the government.†

Admiral Shear: Yes, exactly, yes.

Q: Did you meet King Hussein in Jordan?‡

Admiral Shear: Yes, we did. Yes, and I want to say that he was quite impressive.

Q: Well, he's got a tough job, surrounded as he is by all those hostile countries.

Admiral Shear: Exactly. He has to watch his step. It's quite apparent in the Persian Gulf situation.

Q: Right.

Admiral Shear: I don't recall all the personalities at the time. But it was a hell of a tour, and it was a great education, great education.

---

* Yitzhak Rabin served as Chief of Staff of the Israeli Army, 1964-68, including the period of the Six-Day War against the Arabs in June 1967.
† Rabin served as Israel's Prime Minister from 1992 until his assassination on 4 November 1995.
‡ King Hussein I has been Jordan's head of state since 11 August 1952, when he was 16 years old.

Q: Did you get to Iran?

Admiral Shear: Yes, and, of course, Iran at that time was our fair-haired boy. Iran was our anchor to windward. We were building up Iran for a fare-thee-well: major industrial development, major military development, major communications all over the country. Iran was our boy. Did we ever flub the dub on that. We just blew that, blew it, blew it, and one man is responsible for it--Jimmy Carter.[*] And you can put that on the record as my views.

Q: In what way?

Admiral Shear: He abandoned the Shah.[†] The Shah was a sick man, but Carter abandoned the Shah and all of his people. And the radicals took over. And, of course, I was deeply involved in Iran as CinCUSNavEur, and that's a couple of chapters down. We may or may not get that this afternoon. This was after I had been at the war college.

I knew the Iran situation in the mid-Seventies very well. Iran was our boy out there. The Shah was our boy. I knew all his military people, and they were our people. We were building that country up for a fare-thee-well. That had started back in when we were out there during our war college tour. Just really getting moving at that time.

Q: What was your perception from that trip of the value of the U.S. Middle East force?

Admiral Shear: It was a small force. It was a show-the-flag force, but it was important because they had a program assuring them of visiting all the countries. They'd have dinners; they'd have receptions. ComMidEast Force got to know all the senior people out there. I

---

[*] James E. "Jimmy" Carter, Jr., a Naval Academy graduate in the class of 1947, served as President of the United States from 20 January 1977 to 20 January 1981.
[†] Mohammad Reza Pahlavi (1919-1980) became Shah of Iran (or Persia, as it was then known) in 1941. He held office until his regime was ousted in January 1979 by the Ayatollah Ruhollah Khomeini, who seized power and declared the nation to be an Islamic republic.

think they played a very big role. Furthermore, all it was a small presence in the area. The Brits had more or less abandoned the Middle East by that stage, and our ships were there and our flag was there.

We operated out of Bahrain, and the little Emir of Bahrain has always been a friendly little guy. We were able to use his facilities, even though we weren't supposed to have a base out there. The MidEast commanders got to know the Shiites, the Saudis, and they got to know the heads of government in the countries all around that Persian Gulf and Red Sea perimeter. I think it was very important that we had that point of contact, even though we had only a couple of ships, and their actual significance as a military force was pretty small.

Q: Well, it's a symbolic presence.

Admiral Shear: It was a symbolic presence, very important. I'll get into that symbolic presence when I get into my CinCUSNavEur days.

Here we are at the National War College. In addition to the college year, George Washington University had a program for a master's degree. If you took so many outside hours, you qualified for a master's degree. I took that program. We had a particular professor assigned to us, and he was superb. I can't think of his name now, but internationally he knew his stuff backwards and forwards.

At the end of the school year I had to make a decision, because you had to stay six weeks to two months beyond the school to finish the course. I had to make the decision as to whether to do that or whether to take Sacramento. And I had a hell of a time getting to Sacramento, because those personnel types over in BuPers said, "Oh, you're a damn submariner. We're just going to give you a submarine tender."

I said, "No, I don't want that. I want the Sacramento." Because I knew she was available. The first skipper who put her into commission was about to take over a destroyer squadron, and I wanted that ship because I knew a lot about her. I went over to BuShips during my school year and learned a lot about her. She was a magnificent ship, and I wanted her so bad that I could taste her.

Q: That was a real dilemma.

Admiral Shear: So I hung on. I fought and argued with the personnel detail desk. They offered me an amphib. They offered me a submarine tender. And they offered me a couple of deep-draft vessels. I said, "No, sir. I want the Sacramento." They wouldn't give it to me for a long time.

The last couple of weeks of the school year, they said, "All right, Shear, goddamn it, you can have the Sacramento."

So then I said, "All right, I got the Sacramento. I'm not going to finish this course." So I just dropped out. And I have never regretted it. We talked about command at sea being everything, and every naval officer worth his salt wants to have command at sea.

After all my great days in submarines, that Sacramento was a magnificent command. She was a brand-new ship, first of her class, 797 feet in length, 60,000 tons, 40-foot draft, 29 knots.[*] She was designed specifically to provide all the logistic support for a carrier task force. She had multiple products; she had vast capacity; she had high speed. She could probably feed a task force at sea for weeks at a time. And her design was absolutely superb. I got her.

She was homeported in Seattle, Washington. And she was going through a refit. She'd had one deployment under Mark Gantar, a fine destroyer sailor.[†] Mark was being relieved by me, and he was going to take over a destroyer squadron, which he did. We both ended up in the South China Sea in Vietnam. The ship was practically brand new.[‡]

The power plant in the Sacramento was one half of the Kentucky's. The Kentucky was to be a battleship of the Iowa class. She was never completed, but her power plant was

---

[*] The USS Sacramento (AOE-1), classified as a fast combat support ship, was commissioned 14 March 1964.
[†] Captain Mark M. Gantar, USN.
[‡] For a pictorial treatment of the ship, see William Case and Robert Moeser, "USS Sacramento (AOE-1)," U.S. Naval Institute Proceedings, December 1967, pages 88-102.

in her.* She had four of those 53,000-horsepower units--boilers and steam turbine installations. They put half of that plant into the Sacramento and half of that plant into the Camden, which was the second ship of the class. That was a power plant that wouldn't stop. It just ran forever. Six hundred-pound steam, magnificent plant, absolute solid reliability. She was designed to make 26 knots, and she made 29. She was designed to keep up with a fast carrier task force, which she could easily do.

We developed the logistic capability of those ships; we could do anything. We'd take ships alongside, port and starboard, give them everything they wanted as fast as they could take it. We could take the carriers alongside at 25 knots and never even stop flight ops. It was just resupply, resupply, resupply. And the ship just performed to absolute perfection. We would have a typical situation where we would be out in the Tonkin Gulf or Market Time along the Vietnamese coast for about three weeks.†

Then we dashed back to Subic for three or four days and get a full load and dashed right back out there again.‡ Everything was at high speed. We took on everything that came alongside, anything that needed any help logistically we just took them alongside and gave it to them. In the whole South China Sea, when they saw the Sacramento, they knew they were being taken care of. They knew that anything we had, they could get. We didn't worry about paperwork; we didn't worry about requisitions. Send your flashing light saying, "We need such-and-such." They got it.

Q: Well, you have to do the paperwork at some point but not necessarily right away.

---

* The keel for the Kentucky (BB-66) was laid 6 December 1944. Construction was suspended 17 February 1947, when the ship was 72.1% complete. Her uncompleted hulk was sold for scrapping in 1958.
† In the summer of 1965 U.S. ships and craft began working with the South Vietnamese Navy to establish the Market Time patrol off the coast of South Vietnam. Its purpose was to monitor coastal traffic and thus to prevent North Vietnamese craft from infiltrating South Vietnam to deliver weapons and other supplies to Viet Cong forces. See the Naval Institute oral history of Rear Admiral Norvell G. Ward, USN (Ret.).
‡ Subic Bay, on the island of Luzon in the Philippines, was the site of a major support base for the U.S. Navy during the Vietnam War.

Admiral Shear: That's right, we had a supply guy that could make paperwork talk, maybe a week or two later. He didn't worry about it. You have can-do supply officers, and you have can't-do supply officers. I had the supply department staffed with three or four can-do supply officers, and they could do anything.

Q: Another man who has a very important job in that kind of ship is the boatswain.

Admiral Shear: Boatswain. And I had the best boatswain in the Navy. He was a mustang lieutenant named Dan Gill.[*] Anything that ship could do replenishment-wise, Dan Gill could do. We had 15 replenishment stations on that ship, nine port and six starboard, and we could keep all those stations going. We could take a carrier alongside with five or six stations sending over oil, goods of every description, ammunition, provisions. We'd have a destroyer or cruiser alongside the other side doing the same thing. Unlimited capacity and flexibility that were unheard of before. We broke every logistic record that had ever been established by anybody, and we did it with ease.

We had a crew that was very interesting. We had a crew that included a lot of reserves recalled for Vietnam, a lot of mustangs, a good nucleus of regular Navy people. Practically all of the wardroom were mustangs, but very good men. Long experienced like Dan Gill. The weapons officer was a fellow named George Black, a mustang.[†] Most of my wardroom were mustangs. I had a fine exec, ex-reserve but a regular Navy exec named Jim Burnett.[‡] I had one Naval Academy ensign, a fellow named Ed McCann.[§]

Q: He probably felt out of place.

Admiral Shear: He didn't feel out of place. I put him down there, and I got him checked out and qualified. He turned out to be a hell of an officer. I put him under Dan Gill, and let

---

[*] Lieutenant Daniel J. Gill, USN.
[†] Lieutenant Commander George E. Black, USN.
[‡] Commander James C. Burnett, USN.
[§] Ensign Edward F. McCann II, USN.

me tell you, Dan Gill took that boy by the ear, and he turned him into a seagoing naval officer in about nothing flat. But we had a ship that could do anything. We had a crew that could do anything, and they knew it. I made damn sure they knew it.

I gave responsibility to the whole team. Each of those 15 stations had a rig captain and about a dozen men. And I had a number of blacks. I gave them full responsibility like everybody else, and they knew that they were damn good. They knew that they were the best in South China Sea, and it showed. They had a morale that wouldn't stop. I gave them everything I could in the way of rest and recreation when we got back to Subic. Raise a little hell in Olongapo and so forth.* We'd get up to Japan about once every six months and into Hong Kong about once every six months. Let them blow off a little steam. That was some ship. I had an absolute ball with her. I never wanted to leave her.

Q: Those guys deserved a break, because they worked very hard when they worked.

Admiral Shear: Hardest people, working all the time. Everything at high speed. We could carry immense loads. Sometimes I had to put an extra 5,000 tons just on deck, and so I'd leave Subic drawing 43 feet, which was two or three feet above my legal draft. I had to be damn careful to watch the weather so I didn't run into a typhoon.

You always ran out, and you knew what your demand was going to be. You knew what your first priority items were going to be. Every time you went out with a full load, the first thing that hit rock bottom was JP-5 fuel for the aircraft. After that it was low-drag bombs. The amount of ordnance we were sending ashore in Vietnam at that time was unbelievable, just unbelievable the tonnages.

Q: I'd like to hear more about the mechanics of replenishment, ship handling, and so forth. Would you describe a typical replenishment?

---

* Olongapo is a town that was adjacent to the U.S. naval base at Subic Bay. Olongapo was noted for offering a variety of diversions for sailors on liberty.

Admiral Shear: Sure. You could make an approach on a ship to be replenished, or the ship which wanted the replenishment could make an approach on you. You had to set a steady course and speed, and you had to signal what the replenishment course was going to be and what the replenishment speed was going to be. Normally that would be about ten knots on a steady course, which was a rather perfunctory thing. But we were in a high-tempo wartime situation, and we had to educate some people. Destroyers didn't like to come alongside at 20 knots. But we said, "Okay, romeo corpen is such and such, and the romeo speed is 18 to 20 knots." They found out they had to come alongside that way if they were going to get anything from us. And they found out it wasn't as difficult as they thought it was going to be. Ship handling was not that difficult.

Q: Why did you prefer the high speed?

Admiral Shear: Because of time. If you had a carrier alongside you, it had to make about 25 knots for flight operations. And frequently you would have a carrier alongside conducting flight ops and a destroyer alongside the other side getting her ammunition and fuel. At the same time we would be giving fuel and ammunition and provisions to the carrier. We carried two of the big CH-46 helicopters. We could vertical replenish and we could alongside replenish. Sometimes we could be replenishing two ships alongside and replenishing a ship over the horizon with our helicopters. Those helicopters could carry 5,000 or 6,000 pounds. They would sling nets out underneath the body. It was a regular going thing. And we'd take ships right around the clock, any hour of the night or day.

Q: What were the extra demands and concerns at night?

Admiral Shear: Night vision, of course--handling lines and winches in darkness. You had a color-coded system of wands so that you could let the other ship know what you were doing with regard to your winch and your lines, whether they were going in or going out. And we were concerned about the length of the lines and the distance between ships. It was a tidy piece of seamanship, but we reveled in it. Everybody did a good job. And it became routine. We had ComSeventhFlt aboard once, because he wanted to see the ship. What was his name?

Q: Hyland?

Admiral Shear: Hyland, Johnny Hyland.* You have the timing very well. He said when he came aboard, "Oh, I've heard all about the Sacramento, and I want to see her in operation."

I said, "Okay, Admiral Hyland, we've got some ships coming alongside here in the next hour or so, and we'll show you both big ships and small ships." We took him all through the ship and showed him what we had in the ship itself, in our holds and our replenishment systems and our way of moving cargoes around. Then we replenished a couple of ships right alongside. He left impressed, and he left convinced. So he wanted more ships of the AOE type out there as fast as he could get them. Unfortunately, they were slow in coming along. They built four of that class. The Camden was second, the Seattle third, the fourth was Detroit. They were terrific ships. Then we built the poor man's AOE, which was the AOR. They weren't as fast, and they didn't have the capacity, but they were pretty fair ships.

That Sacramento class was the gold-plated replenishment ship. She could do anything. As I say, we could take ships alongside night or day, 24 hours around the clock. We could go up to Tonkin Gulf, get destroyers at midnight, 1:00 o'clock in the morning. We would barrel down at 25 knots and pick up ships on Market Time, along the Vietnam coast. Pick up a carrier down in the southern station and turn right around and go and pick up the carriers again the next day at the Yankee Station up north.†

---

* Vice Admiral John J. Hyland, USN, served as Commander Seventh Fleet from 13 December 1965 to 6 November 1967. The oral history of Hyland, who retired as a four-star admiral, is in the Naval Institute collection.
† During the initial stages of involvement in the Vietnam War, the U.S. Navy maintained aircraft carriers on two stations based on Civil War designations--Yankee Station off North Vietnam and Dixie Station off South Vietnam. The latter, which began on 16 May 1965, was dropped 15 months later once airfields were available ashore in South Vietnam.

We just had a continual stream of ships alongside. I forget the number we replenished by the time we went back at the end of that deployment, but they were numbers that no one would ever believe and tonnages that people wouldn't believe. So those ships were designed and they paid off. The Bureau of Supplies and Accounts had made quite a bit of input on the early design of those ships, because they knew what had to delivered. They requested such and such be put on the ships, and it was. The first of those ships was built at Bremerton Naval Shipyard, and they did a good job. The second one was built at New York Ship at Camden, and by that time that jackass Wolfson had taken over.*

Q: I think the Camden was the last ship they built.†

Admiral Shear: Yes, I think she was. They had trouble getting her out of there on time. Then the Seattle was built in Bremerton, and I forget where the Detroit was built. Might be Bremerton.

Anyway, that was a great tour, a great ship, and it revolutionized logistic support afloat. It absolutely revolutionized it--big ships, little ships, anything.

Q: Were you the first to take the ship on a combat deployment?

Admiral Shear: Mark Gantar took her out for her shakedown. Then, after being in the yard for some post-shakedown availability, he made one deployment before I took over the ship.‡

---

* The New York Shipbuilding Corporation, Camden, New Jersey, was founded in 1899. It was liquidated in the autumn of 1967 by its parent firm, Merritt-Chapman & Scott, which was headed by Louis Wolfson. For a summary of the events surrounding the closing of the yard, see The New York Times, 3 September 1967, Section 5, page 13.
† The attack submarine Pogy (SSN-647) was under construction as the yard's business dwindled. Soon after she was launched on 3 June 1967, her contract was cancelled and the unfinished ship was towed to Philadelphia for temporary berthing. She was subsequently assigned to Ingalls Shipbuilding, Pascagoula, Mississippi, for completion.
‡ Under Gantar the Sacramento made a 175-day deployment to the Western Pacific, beginning on 28 November 1964.

Q: What kind of demands did that deployment put on your stamina?

Admiral Shear: Every chance I could get, I would take a 30-minute nap. You would have ships alongside until midnight. The next group would come alongside at 4:00. You'd grab a couple of hours' sleep. And if I had a break in the afternoon for an hour or two, I would grab an hour of sleep. At sea I never left the bridge and the sea cabin. I'd go down on deck with the crew, but I never left my sea cabin and went out and relaxed. I had a very comfortable sea cabin just immediately aft of the bridge. So if I had 30 minutes, I'd go back and take a nap, or an hour I'd take an extra nap.

I must tell you a little story. We'd had ships alongside until midnight. We had the next ships scheduled about 4:00 in the morning, and I was taking a nap in my sea cabin right behind the bridge. A messenger came in; there were some messages for me to look at, dispatches. He woke me up, and he said, "Captain, I've got some messages for you."

I said, "All right, just put them on my desk. I'll look at them when I get up for replenishment." So I turned over and went back to sleep. But I could tell that the kid was still standing there; he wasn't leaving me for some reason. So I rolled over and I said, "Yes?"

And he said, "Captain, the flag selection list is here."

I said, "All right, put it on my desk and I'll look at that in the morning." I was kind of getting a little snippy because I was tired. I said, "Put it on the desk; I'll look at it."

He said, "Captain, your name's on that list." [Laughter] So that was the end of that nap. [Laughter] I had been scheduled to take command of the cruiser Providence, which was the Seventh Fleet flagship, but this meant I wouldn't.

Q: That's a happy reason to be deprived of a command.

Admiral Shear: That's right. That's right. Hell, I'd have stuck with the Sacramento forever. I was having a great time with that ship.

Q: You said you had more replenishment stations to port. Why was that?

Admiral Shear: We had nine stations to port and six to starboard. The port side was the big-ship side. We had six big fuel-replenishment stations. We had several ammunition-replenishment stations. With a carrier alongside you might be transferring from as many as six or seven stations on that port side at once. On the starboard side we had six stations of about the same capacity, although we didn't have as much fuel capacity as we did for carriers. You could take a destroyer alongside and be delivering fuel, ammunition, and groceries all at the same time in three or four different stations. The Sacramento was a very, very flexible ship. And she had quite a sizable crew; we had over 500 men to man all those stations and operate the ship.

Q: Any special precautions for handling ammunition to mention?

Admiral Shear: We had elevators in our ammunition holds and in some of our regular cargo holds too. They all had elevators and very high-capacity and high-speed elevators. Everything was palletized, and we had electric forklift trucks to move cargo around fore and aft. You could go fore and aft of that ship with big wide spaces very easily. You could run back with that cargo for the helos on the flight deck and move it all around the ship very simply. Very well laid out and spacious. She was absolutely spacious.

Then we had a special weapons hold for nuclear weapons, which you had to be careful about that, and we always were. But as far as the type of ammunition we were handling, by the tens of thousands of tons, we could move that around, get bombs over to the carriers or get ammunition to destroyers, very simple. We had that down to a science. For example, we could flood a carrier with more stuff than she could take at one time. We could keep ahead of anything alongside and frequently did.

Q: You were ringmaster of a three-ring circus during some of these replenishments.

Admiral Shear: Exactly, exactly, a lot of fun. The ship handling was very important, and we became very good at it. We could take the carriers alongside and get all that rig over. Once in a while you would have a casualty. It happened either in your ship or the ship alongside. You had to go through what we called an emergency breakaway. You had to break your rigs like that [snap sound]; otherwise you get in trouble and hit another ship or something. We didn't have to do that very often, but when we had to do it, we could just [snap sound] break away like that. Once that first lieutenant saw a problem or I saw a problem, we gave the signal for emergency breakaway. Then things came apart in a hurry, but we never had a serious problem. And we never had a man injured all the time I was aboard, which I thought was a pretty good record.

Q: I think Camden bounced off another ship when Joe Moorer had her.*

Admiral Shear: I think she did; I think she did. I remember Joe having a problem. But I don't think he got in any trouble over it.

Q: Well, he made three stars.

Admiral Shear: He made three stars; that's right. Ship handling is an art, and you had to be on your toes every minute. And you had to watch out for the other guy, too, because sometimes his ship handling might not be as good as yours. During a carrier operation, you know, with a variation in the wind the carrier has to be prepared to change course. The carriers and I got that down to a science, both of us. Because I would wear the headphones on my ship, and the skipper of the carrier would wear the headphones for a telephone we sent back and forth. We got so that we could keep each other informed and make course changes with ships alongside and never even slow down flight ops. Keep on replenishing, make a course change of 5, 10, or 15 degrees, because the wind would tend to make little

---

* Captain Joseph P. Moorer, USN, younger brother of Admiral Thomas H. Moorer, USN, who was CNO, 1967-70.

shifts of that nature. You always had to keep that wind coming properly across the flight deck. We got so we could do that, no problem at all.

That was something else we hadn't done much of before. It was fun working out all these things.

Q: I didn't realize until you mentioned it that you could replenish during flight ops.

Admiral Shear: Oh, yes, sure. Yep, we developed that. Of course, with the slower ships you couldn't do it because you couldn't keep up the speed. The carrier normally wouldn't go much above 25, 26 knots in flight ops. We could handle that with ease and still have reserve in the boilers.

Q: Was there any problem with rules of road, or were other ships obligated to keep out of the way?

Admiral Shear: Well, in any sort of encounter with a merchantman or so forth, you had to obey the rules of the road, but as far as replenishment was concerned the task force commander made sure that he didn't have other ships that were going to be interfering with the task force.

Interesting point. The Soviets kept a couple of surveillance trawlers up in the Tonkin Gulf all the time, all the time. They were always poking around looking at us. Sometimes, when we were replenishing, they'd get pretty close aboard, just kind of snooping around. But I never let it bother me; I had ships alongside and just kept on going. I don't think we ever had any big fights over the right of way, but they never bothered me. I never had any particular problem. They did get close aboard a number of times and took a good look at us. Among other things they recognized we were pretty damn good in underway replenishment. I think they took that story home pretty thoroughly.

Harold E. Shear #2 - 227

Q: But they didn't do any deliberate harassment, I take it.

Admiral Shear: I never saw anything that I could call deliberate harassment. They came pretty close aboard a couple of times but nothing that caused me to take action to avoid them.

Q: Well there were some incidents about that time when they were hitting destroyers.

Admiral Shear: There were more in the Med than anywhere else. It did not occur in the South China Sea any time I was out there.

Now, before we leave Vietnam, I want to say a few more things about the Sacramento and Subic Bay. Subic Bay was absolutely indispensable for that operation. It was a major logistic support base. It was a major repair base. It was absolutely vital to that Vietnam operation. In my particular case, we'd be out on Yankee Station for three weeks or more. We'd dash back at high speed to Subic, get a complete reload in about three days, and get right back out there on Yankee Station again and Tonkin Gulf and the Market Time area. If we hadn't had that capacity in Subic Bay, we would have been in deep trouble. So Subic Bay, from a logistic point of view, was absolutely critical to the United States Navy in the Western Pacific at that time.

And it really is today, although the threat has changed, of course. I think it's a big mistake for the Philippine Government ever to force us out of Subic Bay.[*] I think they will regret it in years ahead. It was a stupid thing for them to do. They're going to try to make it into a big commercial establishment now, and I predict they'll probably bollix it up in one form or another. They aren't very good at that sort of thing. So it was very foolish for the Filipinos to force us out of there. Subic played a very great role in that war. And being in the Western Pacific, you say you can fall back to Guam. Guam is 1,500 miles in the other direction. Whether you're going to be in the Indian Ocean or the Western Pacific, Subic

---

[*] Because of the Philippine Government's unwillingness to extend base rights, the U.S. Air Force vacated Clark Air Force Base in November 1991, and the U.S. Navy left Subic Bay in the autumn of 1992.

Bay had a big role to play and should be having a big role today, but politics have taken different courses.*

Q: Did you have to take any special precautions to try to keep your crew out of mischief there in Olongapo?

Admiral Shear: Olongapo is a den of iniquity. Since you bring it up, whenever I was in port I was normally the senior skipper. Because of my length of time in the nuclear business and my time at CinCLant and my year at the war college, I was fairly senior when I got that ship. I was even senior in most cases to the carrier skippers, which meant that every time I got into Subic Bay, I would get responsibility for the shore patrol.

The commander of Subic Bay at that time was Admiral Pinky Baer, an old submariner, whom I'd known ever since the war years. D. G. Baer, Pinky Bear, everybody knew him as Pinky; he was a redhead.† Pinky knew that if he gave me the shore patrol duty that I wouldn't let anybody get in trouble. Because he knew that I was going to rule them with an iron hand. And my shore patrol officer was a man I already mentioned, Dan Gill. And Dan Gill was ruthless. He could take 5,000 sailors on the beach and keep them in line and keep them out of trouble. Well, by the time they got back to pier and going aboard ship, he'd keep them out of trouble. A lot of them would be drunk; they'd be chasing women all night. So the shore patrol problem around Subic could be pretty critical. But we ran that thing, because nearly every time we were in port we had that responsibility. I had people I could put ashore. I knew that we were going to keep peace in Olongapo. We had to be on our toes, because sometimes a couple of carriers might even have 6,000-8,000 men ashore.

Olongapo was a sailor's paradise and a den of iniquity. I think many of the sailors liked Olongapo as much as they did Hong Kong. Hong Kong was on the more

---

* While reviewing this transcript in early 1996, Admiral Shear added the following, "In hindsight, Subic is developing into a major commercial shipping port. I didn't think they could do it, but great progress is being made."
† Rear Admiral Donald G. Baer, USN, commanded U.S. Naval Base Subic Bay, 1964-66.

sophisticated scale, but it was the same type of liberty port. But in those days Olongapo had a big role to play in rest and recreation. Not necessarily a completely healthy role but a big role to play. So in my patrol responsibilities, once in a while I would make a patrol just through the town to see what was going on out there. I got to know Olongapo and see how it operated, and it was a very interesting situation.

Well, I want to say one thing about being out there in Yankee Station so much. We were on either the Yankee Station or Market Time all the time. We went back to Subic just long enough to get a full load and get back out there. One of the things that I was able to do out there in Yankee Station and at the mouth of the Tonkin Gulf was to see the amount of traffic which was headed in and out of Haiphong and Hanoi. It was a vast amount of merchant shipping: Polish, Soviet, British, various other nations. The amount of stuff that was going into North Vietnam in merchant hulls was really quite phenomenal. And every time that I would see a ship fairly close aboard, I would speak him. You know what I mean by speak a ship?

Q: No.

Admiral Shear: Speak him by flashing light or flag hoist. What ship, where from, whither bound? Normally a reasonable merchantman would came back and give you the answers. Captain Iran from Odessa to Haiphong. I would always ask him, "What cargo?" I would never get an answer on cargo. But I got a very good feel of the amount of traffic and the nations that were involved out there.

We let quantities of material into that North Vietnam which were absolutely incredible. Which we could have stopped like that [snap]. We could have stopped it very simply by putting a quarantine across the mouth of Tonkin Gulf, but we simply refused to do it. We could have done the same thing we did in Cuba, and I'm convinced that the Soviets would never have challenged it. As it was, we let war material of every description get through there in huge quantities and just helped the VC no end.* And we could have brought that to a grinding halt way back in '64, '65 and made it stick.

Q: It could have been done with mines also.

Admiral Shear: It could be done with mines. We didn't mine early enough. We didn't stop traffic at all. And we could have brought that war to a grinding halt in a very short time. I think that is going to go down in history as a terrible, stupid error that we blundered. And we had good people out there trying to make that point. John Sidney McCain was one when he was CinCPac.† Ulysses S. Grant Sharp was one when he was CinCPac.‡ All of them recognized that picture very well, but to get political action out of Washington, no way. It was just a stupid, stupid situation which we ran into, which we could have handled differently and brought that war to a successful close. Historians will, I hope, recognize that in the future and make a big thing of it.

Q: Well, the other part of it is on that Market Time patrol the North Vietnamese were able to make an end-around and bring things in through Cambodia.

Admiral Shear: Yes, they were. Not in the quantities that they were in the Tonkin Gulf but still fair quantities. But I, as skipper of the ship being on the scene out there, saw that almost continuously for more than a year. I could see what was going on, and I could see what we could do to stop it, but it didn't happen. It just didn't happen. As a result, they got logistic support and military supplies of every description, and they were able to continue

---

* VC--Viet Cong.
† Admiral John S. McCain, Jr., USN, served as Commander in Chief Pacific from 31 July 1968 to 1 September 1972.
‡ Admiral Ulysses S. Grant Sharp, USN, served as Commander in Chief Pacific from 30 June 1964 to 31 July 1968. His oral history is in the Naval Institute collection.

that war on indefinitely, until we had the terrible task of hauling ass out of there. George Steele's told you a lot about that.* I guess he was the guy on the scene.

Q: He said one of his big challenges as Seventh Fleet Commander was to refocus on the Soviet threat. Because the Seventh Fleet had gotten so in tune with fighting the Vietnam War, it had forgotten about the Soviets.

Admiral Shear: I think to a degree that was true. I agree that was true. Anyway, the end of that war was a national disaster. It didn't have to be that way. It didn't have to be that way. If we had been able to handle that war in a military fashion, we could have brought it to a successful close years earlier. Those of us on the scene could see that very clearly. Flag officers out there and the COs of ships could see that very clearly. Marines ashore--everybody could see it very clearly.

I'll tell you a little sea story here. I got fairly well acquainted with the Marines at Chulai. They would fly out on their helicopters and come aboard ship, and I would give them whatever I could spare. We let them scrub up, get a shower and a hot steak and so forth. One day they flew aboard, and they asked me if I had any beer. I said, "No, we don't carry beer."

They said, "Well, when you go back to Subic can you bring us some beer out?"

I said, "I'm not authorized to carry beer in the supply system. But I can purchase this on a cash basis and put it in a bonded storeroom. But I've got to do it on a cash basis."

They said, "All right, here's the cash. We want you to bring 50 cases next time." Every three or four weeks I swung by, I'd finish up the carriers in the Tonkin Gulf, and I'd swing down Market Time and take care of everybody in that area, gunfire support ships and so forth, and I'd pass right by Chulai. So next trip out I brought them 50 cases of beer that I paid cash on the barrel head for. They said, "Thank you very much." The next time we want 100 cases of beer."

---

* Vice Admiral George P. Steele II, USN, served as Commander Seventh Fleet from 28 July 1973 to 14 June 1975. His oral history is in the Naval Institute collection.

I said, "Okay, same deal, cash on the barrel head, and I'll bring it out to you." I could not show it on the supply records or anything like that, but I did have authority to carry it in a bonded storeroom. So the next time I brought 100 cases out, and I would alert them about 25 miles out that I would be zipping by at 25 knots. I would alert their helicopters, and they would come tearing out, pick me up, load the beer, and fly back. The next time they said, "We would like 200 cases."

I said, "You really mean 200 cases?"

They said, "Yes."

"I've got to do cash on the barrel head."

"Here's your cash." So from then until the time I left the ship, every time we swung by we delivered by helicopter 200 cases of beer to the Marines. And they were forever grateful. The Sacramento to them meant one thing, beer. [Laughter] And they were a thirsty bunch of Marines. Shoot, I was right on the coast there, so no trouble for me to get the stuff ashore. I could fly it either in my helicopters or their helicopters. But that became sort of a joke in South China Sea; the Sacramento, the Marines, and the beer. But it made for hell of a good rapport for Marines and damn good morale for them too.

Q: They needed it, because that was kind of a godforsaken place.

Admiral Shear: It was.

Q: I was there a number of times. I was in a LST, so we went there a lot.*

Admiral Shear: You went there regularly, sure. It was a godforsaken place, sort of isolated by itself there south of Danang.

Q: It was either a mud hole or a dust bowl.

---

* The interviewer served in the tank landing ship Washoe County (LST-1165) from 1966 to 1969.

Admiral Shear: Yep, one or the other. That's right, depending on the time of the year.

Q: Anything else to say about the Sacramento?

Admiral Shear: Great ship, great command, and I had a ball with her. I didn't keep her long enough. But I was called off to other things.

Q: Well, after you were selected for flag did you then go to charm school?

Admiral Shear: Charm school at that time was three days. Now it's gotten to be two or three months. When you passed through Washington, you got three days of orientation around the Pentagon, JCS, and so forth. But I got orders in a matter of days, to come back to Washington to go to the Foreign Service Institute to study Portuguese. I remained in the ship long enough to bring her back and take her into Bremerton for a refit at the end of a long deployment. We'd been out there for almost a year.[*]

Then I was ordered back to Washington. I had my orders before I got back there. I was supposed to go to this foreign language school and then go down to Brazil as Chief of Naval Mission. I didn't want that job. I didn't want to go. I wanted to stay at sea, and I wanted to stay out there in the Southeast Asia where the action was. And I really wanted to get Fred Janney's job as Commander Task Force 73, which had the logistic responsibility for all the area.[†] So I went back and complained. I knew damn well that I wasn't going to win. But I went to see David McDonald, who was CNO.[‡] I said, "Admiral McDonald, I've had a great tour out there in Vietnam, and I want to stay out there. There's a lot of war going on yet. I want to be in it. I want to get a seagoing job in the South China Sea."

He smiled. He said, "Young man, I've got lots of billets I've got to fill around the world. I've got to fill this Brazilian billet, because they're our friends and we've got to keep

---

[*] The deployment began from Long Beach on 14 October 1965 and ended at Seattle on 17 July 1966, a period of just over nine months.
[†] Rear Admiral Frederick E. Janney, USN, Commander Service Force Seventh Fleet.
[‡] Admiral David L. McDonald, USN, served as Chief of Naval Operations from 1 August 1963 to 1 August 1967. His oral history is in the Naval Institute collection.

them happy. So you're going to Brazil." I knew he was going to tell me that, but I had to ask him anyway.

Q: "Aye, aye, sir."

Admiral Shear: Yes. So then I went to the Foreign Service Institute. At the Naval Academy I had studied French, and in high school I had studied French, so I had four or five years of French. I had a reasonable knowledge of French, although I was not proficient. But they put me into this complete-immersion course, and my wife went with me, I must say, and she did very well. She did better than I did in some cases. We studied Portuguese around the clock for 12 weeks. I had one more month of getting indoctrinated around the State Department, around the Brazilian embassy, and so forth.

Then off I went to Brazil. I was told, "By God, Shear, you be proficient in Portuguese when you get there." Well, I wasn't proficient, but I was pretty damn good. I made up my mind that I was not going to speak any English in Brazil. I wanted to make sure that I was completely fluent in Portuguese by the time I left there. We went down first class as a courtesy of the Brazilian Navy on board a Moore-McCormick passenger liner. They were still running to the east coast of Brazil at that time. We boarded the ship in New Orleans. We had two or three cargo stops; it was almost a two-week trip down there. Those are long distances down that South Atlantic, better than 5,000 miles.

There was a Brazilian admiral on board who had been the attaché in Washington. I had gotten to know him in Washington before I left. So we had two weeks together, and I'd had that school behind me, and all we did was talk Portuguese all the way down. He just worked me out thoroughly. I was reasonably proficient when I left the school although by no means good. I was a lot better by the time I got to Brazil after concentrating with this fellow. When I arrived in Brazil, I was not totally fluent but speaking pretty decent Portuguese. So I was greeted with open arms by the Brazilian Navy.

The naval mission down there had been established in 1922. It was established by the President of Brazil, who had been up to the United States for an official visit. We sent a battleship down to bring him up and take him home, and he became thoroughly impressed with the American Navy. So he set up the naval mission down there in 1922, and we kept a sizable staff down there, training and essentially operating much of his Navy all those years.

They were really a second U.S. Navy down there. They were thoroughly indoctrinated in the U.S. Navy and U.S. Navy ships. We had given them a number of ships after the war: a number of submarines, a number of cruisers, a number of destroyers. They had a first-rate little navy, and they were very professional naval officers. We had that mission as a fine, going thing since 1922. I relieved Larry Geis, a very fine guy out of '39--aviator, carrier skipper.[*] But I must say that Larry had not done very well in becoming proficient in the language. He could scuttle by, but he was by no means proficient.

When I arrived there, I had my formal introduction to the Naval Minister and the Chief of Naval Operations called O Chefe Maior da Armada, Chief of the Highest Order of the fleet, which is what they call their CNO. They had sort of a ceremony to introduce me to all their senior people, and I made a speech in Portuguese. God, they were amazed--pretty good Portuguese. They recognized that they had a guy that was going to work with them closely, that I had taken the job seriously and I had done my homework. So from then on I refused to speak any English for two years.

The Brazilians love to tell jokes about each other. They used to tell the joke about this crazy American admiral who speaks no English; he speaks only Portuguese. They'd tell that all over Brazil. But I stuck to that, and I spoke nothing but Portuguese down there for two years. I spoke English to my own staff and so forth. But by the time I left there I was completely proficient. I could give an hour lecture in Portuguese in the Brazilian War College, for example, and frequently did.

Then I had an aircraft assigned to me, an old C-47, DC-3.[†] The DC-3 was a workhorse of the 1930s. This was a U.S. Navy plane assigned to the U.S. Naval Mission to Brazil. I had two broken-down aviators assigned to me, both of them passed over. They had no interest in life whatsoever except being in the cockpit. They loved to fly, and that's

---

[*] Rear Admiral Lawrence R. Geis, USN.
[†] The Douglas DC-3 was a superb plane for carrying cargo or passengers; its design in the 1930s was quite innovative for its time. The DC-3, which was widely used in World War II, carried the Navy designation of R4D and the Army Air Forces designation C-47.

all they ever wanted to do. I had a little maintenance crew and these two aviators, and I went all over Brazil in that aircraft. Brazil is a big country, bigger than the United States. I went to every airstrip, grass strip, frontier, and far distant corner you could think of. Today I know Brazil better than most Brazilians.

Among other things, the Brazilian Navy had the responsibility for their huge river systems. The Amazon is just one of a number of big river systems. They make the Mississippi look like a trout stream. The Sao Francisco, the Tapajos, the Xingu, the Negro, the Salamoines, the Parana--they're all huge river systems. The Navy had all patrol responsibilities up and down those river systems, because most of them border on other countries, and they had to keep those borders checked out pretty thoroughly. So I got to get all around the country. I got to patrol those rivers with the Brazilian Navy, and I flew in every back corner you could think of.

Everywhere I went, I would always make a welcoming speech in Portuguese, and I would make a departure speech in Portuguese. That word got all over the country--about this crazy American admiral that speaks no English and then makes Portuguese speeches. I tell you, it made a tremendous impression on them. They knew that I was one of them. They were very fond of the United States, and they use to call us their brothers, "Nasso Irmour de Norte," which means "Our brothers to the north." They were very sincere, you know. They had fought with us in two World Wars. In World War I they had a division in Europe, and in World War II they had a division in Italy which performed with great distinction. And they had their Navy fully committed both in the North Atlantic and the South Atlantic. So they were good allies.

Q: Admiral Jonas Ingram had done a lot to solidify that relationship.

Admiral Shear: Absolutely. Jonas Ingram was ComFourthFlt, and his quarters were in Recife, up in the bulge of Brazil.[*] Jonas Ingram was sort of a god down there. They

---

[*] Vice Admiral Jonas H. Ingram, USN, served in South America from February 1942 to November 1944. His billet had several titles along the way, including Commander South Atlantic Force and, later, Commander Fourth Fleet.

thought the world of Jonas Ingram. He had the Brazilian Navy right fully integrated in his staff; half of his staff were Brazilian officers. The Naval Minister was a man named Rademaker.* He had been a member of Jonas Ingram's staff, and he thought the sun rose and set on Jonas Ingram, as they all did.

I had a couple of unique experiences down there. I got Tom Moorer to come down, because the Brazilians invited him, and I urged him to take the invitation, which he did.† We had him down there for ten days, and I showed him all around the country. We went all around Rio and Brasilia, and I took him down to San Paulo, which is the manufacturing center for Brazil. He was absolutely amazed at what they had down there in the way of an industrial base. I knew it very well by that time, and I showed him all the surrounding big manufacturing cities, the city of Sao Paulo, which is the biggest city in the southern hemisphere. He came away with a very unique appreciation for what Brazil was all about.

Then along came Paul Ignatius, Secretary of the Navy, and he got an invitation to come down.‡ I urged him to accept it, and, by golly, he did. So he came down there, and I showed him the same type of things I had shown Tom Moorer, took him all around the place. He went back very impressed. Then, of course, the CNO and the Naval Minister were both invited to Washington at different periods. And that was a typical visit for a senior naval person like a CNO. They could bring them up for a week or ten days, give them a series of briefings and social activities around Washington. Then they would give them a plane and take them around the country--the West Coast and most anywhere they wanted to go.

Q: Did you go along when they went to Washington?

---

* The Minister of the Navy in the late 1960s was Admiral Augusto Hamann Rademaker Grunewald.
† Admiral Thomas H. Moorer, USN, served as Chief of Naval Operations from 1 August 1967 to 1 July 1970.
‡ Paul R. Ignatius served as Secretary of the Navy from 1 September 1967 to 24 January 1969.

Admiral Shear: Oh, yes--both times. And by that time my Portuguese was in pretty damn good shape. And a very interesting thing--this Naval Minister, Rademaker, was a fine gentleman of German extraction. There are a lot of Germans in southern Brazil. He got up there in Washington. OP-61 was the one who took care of foreign dignitaries, and the liaison officer in OP-61 asked him if he needed an interpreter. Rademaker didn't speak much English--just the little bit he had learned from Jonas Ingram's staff--but he said, "Oh, no, I don't need an interpreter; Admiral Shear is my interpreter."

Well, let me tell you, that made an impression on the OP-61 people at that time. So I was the interpreter for all the social functions. The CNO always presents them with a medal, and I was the interpreter for that ceremony. And the Secretary had a big affair for him, and I was the interpreter for that ceremony. He'd speak, and I would interpret, and they'd speak, and I would interpret back to him. It went off to perfection. Let me tell you, that made an impression around that E-ring, a big impression.[*] I wasn't trying to; I was just doing my job.

Q: Right.

Admiral Shear: But they got the picture that I knew what the hell I was doing down there. Then the same thing happened when the CNO came up a few months later. "Do you need an interpreter, Mr. CNO?" He was Admiral Moreira Maia, double name, which is frequent down there.[†]

He said, "Oh, no, Admiral Shear is my interpreter." [Laugh] Well, by that time they had seen me work with the Naval Minister, so they knew that I could handle this guy with no problem. Which we did. Both of them had superb visits. They were believers before they came up, and they went home just bubbling about the United States and the United States Navy. So we made a lot of progress down there.

---

[*] The Pentagon has lettered corridors, going from A at the innermost to E at the outermost. E-ring offices, which go around the perimeter of the building are considered the most prestigious.
[†] Admiral José Moreira Maia.

Q: Did you get involved in these Unitas exercises?

Admiral Shear: Oh, yes, yes, of course I was not in that sea command, but they all worked through me.

Q: Well, Commander South Atlantic Force runs it, but you have to have liaison.

Admiral Shear: Oh, yes, I did all that. One of the commanders of the South Atlantic Force was one Fritz Harlfinger, whom you have heard of before.[*] Fritz did a good job down there. You know, he was a garrulous, talkative type, and that went over well. They had two or three ComSoLant commanders; Fritz was one and another one was Jim Dare.[†] He had been in the Polaris program as commanding officer of the Compass Island--fine man out of '39.

He was a very fine guy, and as a hobby he raised orchids. And orchids in Brazil are everywhere, 100 different varieties. So the Brazilians became aware that he was an orchid collector, and orchid raiser and that made a big hit with them. Jim Dare had a lovely wife named Jean. He did a great job as ComSoLant, better than Fritz, I think. Fritz was sort of the jovial type. That went over well, but not necessarily completely well. But they both did good jobs. But as SoLant you made a swing around South America. It was very important to those South American navies, particularly the big three, the ABC countries: Brazil, Argentina, and Chile. The rest of them you could throw in a hat, but they were three good professional navies.

Q: What was the substance of your work? You certainly had to maintain good relations, but did you get into specific issues?

---

[*] Rear Admiral Frederick J. Harlfinger II, USN.
[†] Rear Admiral James A. Dare, USN.

Admiral Shear: Oh, yes. I had quite a sizable staff. We got involved in maintenance. We got involved in training. We got involved, of course, in updating their equipment.

One of the things that both the Naval Minister and the CNO wanted when they went to Washington was some replacement cruisers. We actually went up to the back channel in Philadelphia and looked over the cruisers. As far as our CNO was concerned, he would have been delighted to have them take a couple of those cruisers. They already had a couple from the World War II Brooklyn class.[*] Brazil, Argentina, and Chile each had two of those 6-inch cruisers. Brazil wanted to renew those cruisers with ships we had in the back channel, as well as getting some updated World War II destroyers we had laid up. We were perfectly willing to give them. But McNamara was SecDef and the Assistant Secretary for International Security Affairs was Paul Warnke, a jackass that everybody despised.[†]

He said, "No way are we going to give those dictatorships any more military equipment." Well, democracy in Brazil is a lot different than democracy in the United States, and Brazil was then being run by the military, because they had to throw Goulart out.[‡] Goulart was about to take the country Communist. It was within a hairline of going Communist. The military threw him out. So the military was running the country all the time I was there, as they had to.

As I say, democracy down there is a lot different than democracy up here, and frequently the military has to step in and run things. When they get things settled down, they turn it over to the civilians again, which is what happened in recent years. It now looks like this current president is in very deep trouble. Mello is being accused of all kinds of

---

[*] In January 1951 the U.S. Navy sold two mothballed cruisers to Brazil. The former USS Philadelphia (CL-41) became the Barroso and remained in service until 1973. The St. Louis (CL-49) became the Almirante Tamandare and remained in service until 1975.
[†] Robert S. McNamara served as Secretary of Defense from 21 January 1961 to 29 February 1968. Paul C. Warnke served as Assistant Secretary of Defense (International Security Affairs) from 1967 to 1969.
[‡] In 1964 Brazilian Army troops, led by General Humberto Castelo Branco forced out President Joao Goulart because of a fear that his economic polices would open the way for a Communist takeover of Brazil.

things, half of which are probably right; half are probably exaggerated.* He may get fired. He may get booted out of office. Whether the military takes over again, I don't know. I hope they don't. I hope they leave it in the civilian process, but if things really come apart, the military will take over. They'll run the country well--much better than the civilians will.

Now, as a result of our reluctance to be forthcoming and trying to help the Brazilians to update their military because of this attitude of SecDef under McNamara, they turned to the Brits. They went to the Brits for new ships, and they went to the Brits for several other things. They still loved the United States, but they said, "Well, we can't afford to hang around. If we're not going to get any cooperation from the United States, we've got to go elsewhere." So they went to the Brits.

Then Jimmy Carter came along. And instead of going to Brazil himself or to South America himself to make the rounds, he sent his mother. Furthermore, he took a very hard-nosed attitude about these non-democratic dictatorships throughout South America. That went over like a lead balloon. It undid all the good we've done down there for 50 years. If you say "Jimmy Carter" in South America today, you'll be spat upon. He just showed his total lack of appreciation for the status of world affairs. Jimmy Carter in South America in toto became a disaster. He set us back for everything we'd been doing down there for a long time. I don't I can't remember whether he sent his mother or his wife, but I think he sent his mother to represent him. Now, I'll have more to say about Jimmy Carter as we get into Europe.

Q: Did you get involved in any of Brazil's strategic planning when you were there?

Admiral Shear: Oh, yes. Yes, yes, yes. Deeply involved in everything their military did: Army, Navy, and Air Force. Even though I was the naval mission commander, I got involved in everything else that was going on. There was a MAAG there with a two-star Army general, senior to me, and a one-star Air Force general, who was junior to me.† But

---

* Fernando Collor de Mello served as President of Brazil from 1989 until his impeachment in 1992.
† MAAG--military assistance advisory group.

neither the Air Force or the Army had a naval mission per se, which was something that the nation of Brazil had requested and established. So I was much closer to the Brazilians and the Brazilian military than these other Americans were, because I was one of them.

Q: Even though they were passing out the goodies.

Admiral Shear: That's right. I was one of them. The Brazilian Navy carried me on their lineal list as one of their flag officers. They had done that as long as the naval mission had been there.

Q: I think that started with an officer named Vogelgesang, who had a destroyer named after him.[*]

Admiral Shear: Vogelgesang was down there at one time. I don't recall whether he was the first one, but he was chief of the naval mission at one time--exactly correct--a long, long time before me. So that was a very interesting tour, both politically and militarily. I got to know that country backwards and forwards. I got all over it; I made a point of getting all over it.

Q: Did you pass information to ONI on what you learned?[†]

Admiral Shear: We had some intercept sites down there which we were working with the Brazilians on. There was a lot of Soviet activity, particularly over along that African coast. From that northern bump of Brazil that extends out of Recife the distance to Africa is only 1,500 miles. So we kept pretty close track through the Brazilians. And the Brazilians,

---

[*] In November 1922 Captain Carl T. Vogelgesang, USN, received orders to organize and lead the U.S. naval mission to Brazil. He was soon promoted to rear admiral, to date from 16 October 1922. He completed his mission to Brazil in January 1925. The destroyer Vogelgesang (DD-862) was named in his honor.
[†] ONI--Office of Naval Intelligence.

through the Portuguese nations of Angola and other places over there, knew exactly what was going on on that coast. They kept the Brazilians pretty well informed, and we passed that back to Washington.

But I never abused my privilege by spying on the Brazilians. That was not my job. The Brazilians would have given us anything we asked for anyway. If we wanted any information that they had, all I had to do was ask for it. They'd have given it to me. So that was never a problem.

Q: Did you file regular reports with somebody in Washington?

Admiral Shear: No, that was not my responsibility.

Q: I see.

Admiral Shear: I kept Washington informed as far as what I was doing as Chief of Naval Mission and what the Brazilian Navy's desires were as far as improving and updating, but the attaché in any nation is responsible for intelligence reports.

Q: In other words a separate attaché?

Admiral Shear: Totally separate. He had nothing to do with me. He was in the embassy, just like any other embassy around the world.

The ambassador down there was a man named John Tuthill during my day.* Good professional ambassador, experienced. He and I became very good friends, and he worked closely with me. But he knew very well that I was much closer to the Brazilian military than he would ever be, and he respected that. He never pushed me for something beyond which I should have gone. But every once in a while, if I knew something that was going

---

* John W. Tuthill served as U.S. ambassador to Brazil from 1966 to 1969.

on politically that I thought he ought to be aware of, I'd cut him in on it. He always appreciated that.

The political officer, the number-three man in the embassy was a man named Frank Carlucci. The embassy always has a political officer, and he was responsible for keeping track of the political situation in the country. Frank Carlucci and I became very good friends. Frank had a very interesting background. He had a couple of tours in Black Africa. And he was an FSO-1, which is pretty high up in the State Department hierarchy.[*] And he was the youngest guy on record--if I'm correct, and I believe I am--in making FSO-1. A brilliant guy. A little bit touchy at times, but he and I had a very good relationship.

When I got back to Washington, he showed up in two or three Washington jobs, one of which was coordinator of that bad flood they had out in Pennsylvania a number of years after I got back here. I had some contact with him on that, I had some contact with him on some surplus real estate, and I had some contact with him as he got further up the line in OSD.[†] In due course he became SecDef himself.[‡] I always had the situation where I could go to Frank any time I needed to talk to him, and he didn't hesitate to talk to me.

Then I had some contact with Frank in the 1980s when I was Maritime Administrator. We found out some stuff was being shipped to foreign countries, and they were charging excess shipping prices. I had a little sleuth who worked for me who pinpointed that stuff. I got it all compiled, and I took it over to Frank, and I said, "Frank, this is what's going on. It's illegal, and your people are involved in the International Security Affairs. I don't know whether there's anybody who is legally guilty, but there's a bunch of illegal stuff going on and a bunch of money being transferred improperly. Some of the shipping companies are involved, and you better, by God, do something about it." I didn't get the reaction out of him that I wanted. He took some action, but he wasn't tough enough. We eventually got it stopped, but I know that some of his people were involved. Turn it off. I'll tell you one.

---

[*] FSO--Foreign Service Officer. Frank C. Carlucci III served as a naval officer, 1952-54, and then entered the Foreign Service in 1956.
[†] OSD--Office of the Secretary of Defense. Carlucci became Deputy Secretary of Defense when Caspar Weinberger took office as Secretary of Defense in 1981.
[‡] Carlucci served as U.S. Secretary of Defense, 1987-89.

[Interruption. Tape recorder turned off.]

Q: Well, I get the impression from what you're saying that you enjoyed that job in Brazil.

Admiral Shear: Yes. I didn't want to go, but then I had a ball. I had a hell of a time down there. I got to know the Brazilian nation. I got to know the Brazilian people. I've got a million friends in Brazil today. I got to know the Brazilian military backwards and forwards. I have great respect for them; they were thoroughly professional people. It's a great nation; they've got 130-odd million people down there.

They've got lots of problems. They have great poverty, terrible poverty of the worst kind. And then they have great wealth. They have a modest size middle class. But they have those slums around the cities, where people come in from the countryside just destitute, in the northeast part of Brazil where the sugar cane country and other agricultural products is very poor.

Then you get down into the southern states from Sao Paulo on south, and you have a totally different nation, a temperate nation which is absolutely thriving, just thriving. Vast farms, vast ranches, vast manufacturing facilities. Big German, and big Italian, and big Japanese influence in the southern part of Brazil. There are over a million Japanese in Brazil. It's the biggest colony outside of Japan. There's quite a bit of intermarrying between the Brazilians and the Japanese. You might think it's strange, but there's quite a bit going on. I knew a number of families with a Japanese husband or wife and a Brazilian husband or wife. It seemed to work out really well.

There's a huge Brazilian shipyard down there called Ishikawa-jima do Brazil which is Ishikawa-jima of Japan. They can build a 200,000-ton tanker for you down there and do very well at it. They build their own ships. They build their own engines. They build a ship for one-third of the price you can in the United States. They're very good in heavy industry. They have a big steel industry. They have absolutely unlimited mineral resources, every description. They have unlimited timber resources. They have unlimited agricultural resources. The only thing they are shy on is oil. They have some oil but not huge quantities. They have virtually unlimited precious and semiprecious stone assets down there, some of the finest in the world.

It's a great nation with all sorts of potential. One of the old stories is, "Well, they've got all the potential, and they always will have." But they're making progress. Not as fast as they should, and they got deeply in debt from buying too much Russian oil for one thing. They've got inflation problems that they never have gotten under control, and they are still rampant today. But they have a lot going for them and a lot of industrial capacity, probably the biggest industrial capacity in the southern hemisphere, without question, including Australia.

Q: Does the fact that the Brazilians speak Portuguese rather than Spanish set them apart from the rest of South America?

Admiral Shear: To quite a considerable degree. When you go down to the Uruguayan or the Argentine border, both sides can understand each other, and neither will admit that one is speaking Portuguese and one is speaking Spanish. They will sort of go out of the way not to speak the other fellow's language, but they understand very well what each is saying.

Over history there were great battles between Argentina and Brazil for example, big battles. But that's all sort of like our Civil War; that's in the distant past. When I arrived down there, they still had three divisions of cavalry down on the southern border. And there's still enough feeling between Brazil and Argentina so that they had armed forces down on each other's border.

I went down to make an official visit on the city of Uruguaiana, which is a pretty good-size city right on the Argentina border. They had one of their divisions of cavalry stationed there. I arrived in my old C-47 at this dusty grass strip airfield about ten miles out of the city. They knew I was coming for an official visit, and they met me at my plane with a full 10,000-horse mounted cavalry division. The general was there. He gave me warm greetings, and then they took me in this official car, and they put a horse at each wheel. They took me into town, escorted with these four horses at the wheels, with the entire 10,000 division of cavalry behind me. Went right into the middle of town, stopped in front

Harold E. Shear #2 - 247

of the one hotel in town, and disembarked, and the cavalry went back about their business. One of the most impressive sights I've ever seen in my life.

Q: That's a lot of horses.

Admiral Shear: Yes, and that was a great show of courtesy for me, I'll tell you. But they had three active cavalry divisions. Except for Saudi Arabia, it was probably one of the last in the world, and I guess the Saudi Arabians are out of it now. That was just one of the many, many interesting things I got involved in down there.

Q: Did the United States keep supplying spare parts for these old ships?

Admiral Shear: Yes. They had a good capacity of their own; they had a good naval shipyard right there in Rio. And they built a new naval shipyard while I was there, up at Bahia, near Salvador. They had good base capacity up and down the coast. They were very competent engineers. They'd sent enough people to our schools, large number of people to our schools. They sent people to MIT, naval architect courses, things of that nature, graduate engineers. As a matter of fact, the president of Ishikawa-jima do Brazil, which is the big Japanese yard there, was headed when I was there by a retired admiral--I can't think of his name now--who was a graduate of MIT, naval constructor's course, who had been sent there by the U.S. Navy.

So we've had a very close relationship over the years. And they are very proud of their support of the United States in World War I and World War II. That Brazilian Army division that served in Italy with great distinction is known all over Brazil. They have a special club; of course, it is getting smaller now as they get older, but all the members of that division are recognized as heroes throughout the country. I forget the name of it now; I can't think of it. But I've been to several of their reunions and receptions and, boy, those guys are still fighting the war in Italy. They had a great division that got involved in all kinds of combat out there and served with great distinction, fine people.

So that was the job I didn't want to go to, and I got there and I had a ball. Shows what you can do when you make up your mind that you're going to have a good time. I was there from April of '67 to April of '69, exactly two years, almost to the day. Then I was ordered back to Washington and OpNav, where I became OP-31. I relieved Phil Beshany as Director of Submarine Warfare.

Q: You probably didn't argue against that job.

Admiral Shear: No, I didn't. I was tickled to death to get that job. [Laughter] As I said before, "One thing you've got to do in this Navy--if you're going to go anywhere, you've got to get back to Washington, time after time." I'd known Phil Beshany well over the years and relieved him in good order. He went on up to another job in OpNav, and I had a great two years in OP-31. Later on, OP-31 became OP-02 and was upgraded to a three-star billet. But that was one tour after I left.

But I had it as a two-star, and OP-03 was boss. That was the Deputy Chief of Naval Operations for Operations. It was J. B. Colwell, a destroyer sailor, three-star when I took over, and he was relieved by Ralph Cousins a three-star aviator. So my immediate bosses before the CNO were first a destroyerman and then an aviator. And history is repeating itself. This new reorganization, which is just being put in effect right now in OpNav, knocks those three-star barons, as they're so called, the surface-ship baron, the submarine baron, the air baron. They're all being cut down from three stars to two stars. So it's going back to very much like it was when I took over OP-31 in 1969.

I can see why that is being done. There have got to be some big cuts--cuts that we haven't even thought about it yet, and they're going to come. I understand they're going to come--more than anybody even wants to think about or admit at the present time. It's got to be that way. Because the world has changed; the world has changed dramatically.

All right, I took over from Phil Beshany, and at that time we were at the height of the SSN construction program.* We'd gone through several classes of SSNs. We had the

---

* SSN--nuclear-powered attack submarine.

594 class, the 637 class. We built several other individual types. We built the NR-1 underwater surveillance submarine.* We built the Tullibee, which was one of a class, special sonar equipped unit. We'd been getting pretty good support. McNamara cut us down on the number per year for a while there, and we had to fight like hell to get one or two per year. Then things improved, and I remember one year I was able to get five new submarines through the Congress. When I say I, it was my effort from OP-31 and my support by the CNO. So we were doing pretty well in the submarine business, both ballistic and attack.

Of course, by that time the ballistic-missile submarine program was about finished. Forty-one were completed. We had gone through the Polaris A-1, A-2, A-3. We had gone into Poseidon, and then we were thinking about going into the Trident missile. The Trident was going to be back-fitted into the later of the SSBNs which were already built and were in due course back-fitted. So that program was starting up.

Then along came the very earliest phases of the Trident, which we called ULMS. I was deeply involved in that. Under Phil Beshany, Jim Wilson had made what they called the Strat-X Study.† Yogi Kaufman was involved in that, I was involved in it, and that moved on. We had not yet gotten to the construction phase.

There was a big argument about the number of missile tubes. Big argument. That went back and forth between Navy and OSD for months. As I recall, Johnny Foster was the head of research and development in OSD, and we argued whether it was going to be anything from 12 tubes up to 24 tubes per ship.‡ As I recall, Johnny Foster made that decision it would be a 24-tube ship. We argued about whether we could build a larger number of submarines with a smaller number of tubes and give them more to operate around the world. But in the interest of economy and the fact that the long-range missiles are going to be able to operate most anywhere they want to anyway, the decision was made

---

* The BR-1, a nuclear-powered, deep-submergence research and ocean engineering vessel was delivered to the Navy on 27 October 1969.
† Captain James B. Wilson, USN.
‡ Dr. John S. Foster, Jr., served as Director of Defense Research and Engineering, 1965-73.

to build 24-missile ships. That decision stuck, so we've been doing it throughout the Trident program.

Then there was a big argument about the size of the ship and about the power plant and about whether it was going to be single-screw or twin-screw. That became a big knockdown affair between Rickover and OpNav. Levering Smith and I were in the middle of that. As I mentioned earlier, we had a several sessions with Rickover about the size of the power plant, what he wanted to build for a power plant.

Rickover was always trying to get a test vehicle for a power plant he wanted to try out. He had done that several times in the past. Probably the best example is the Triton, the radar picket submarine which Ned Beach put in commission.* Then in due course we settled on the fact that the next SSBN was going to be a single-screw ship, and we settled roughly on the horsepower of the plant and went ahead with that decision. I don't recall at the moment the exact power plant that we decided upon, but it was not the one that Rickover wanted initially. We had a big go-around three or four times about that.

Q: What can you say about selling Trident or ULMS to Congress? Yogi Kaufman was involved in that.

Admiral Shear: Yes, he was. The Polaris program had been fantastically successful, right from start to finish. I think we as naval officers recognized that the Soviet Union was then at its height as a major military power of the world. That was something we were going to have to be prepared to handle under any circumstance. We knew that we needed to keep ahead of the power curve technologically, and we needed a longer-range missile and more sea room. We were always looking for sea room. Even in the earliest days of Polaris, we were looking for increased sea room in which to operate, both for the operation area for the

---

* In the spring of 1960, the USS Triton (SSN-586), commanded by Captain Edward L. Beach, USN, made the first submerged circumnavigation of the world. Commissioned in November 1959, she was ostensibly a radar-picket submarine but actually a test ship for a two-reactor propulsion plant.

submarines to magnify the ASW problem, and also to give us much improved target coverage from the entire perimeter around the Soviet Union.

So missile range and an increased operating area were always factors, even from the early planning days. By this time we had gone through 41 ships and four classes of missiles--A-1, A-2, A-3, and Poseidon. We wanted to go to a longer range. Then there was a lot of argument about the number of warheads it was going to carry: whether it was going to be a single warhead or whether it was going to be a multiple warhead. That went on for many months. Yogi is probably more up on this than I am. I don't recall too much about the arguments that we took to Congress and the priority which we took to Congress to get the ULMS initiated.

I worked very closely with John Warner on this. John Warner was first Under Secretary of the Navy; then he became Secretary of the Navy.[*] Every time I see John, he says, "Oh, yes, I remember our days together when we were selling Trident." I had a very good relationship with Warner on a whole variety of submarine projects and later on antisubmarine projects.

Q: Any specific impressions of him?

Admiral Shear: I liked John Warner a great deal. Some people thought he was kind of a dilettante, sort of a ladies' man. He was a fellow who cut quite a swath around town at one time, but I thought he was a pretty good man. He was a very wealthy man, both in his right and his wife's right. I think he found his niche very well as a United States Senator. He went through that period of Elizabeth Taylor.[†] I won't get involved in that. I think he probably married her to get elected as much as anything, but don't quote me on that. That was a short episode in his life.

---

[*] John W. Warner served as Under Secretary of the Navy from 11 February 1969 to 4 May 1972 and as Secretary of the Navy from 4 May 1972 to 8 April 1974. At the time of this interview he was a U.S. Senator from Virginia.
[†] Warner was married to actress Elizabeth Taylor when he first ran for the Senate.

I thought John Warner was a pretty good man. Some people thought he kind of a lightweight as a Secretary, but I thought he was a quite reasonable Secretary. I don't remember very much about Warner and I marching up to Congress selling the Trident. We worked very closely about getting the Trident put together as a weapons concept: bigger ship, bigger missiles, and what she was going to do as an operational platform and so forth. I don't recall which year that we got authority for the first ship.[*] I just don't recall. It was sometime after I had left OP-31. Yogi was probably more deeply involved than I was.

Q: Did you get involved in setting up the base structure for the Trident submarines at Bangor, Washington, and Kings Bay, Georgia?

Admiral Shear: Oh, yes, yes, yes. I was deeply involved in that, deeply involved in that.

Q: How much of a factor did politics play?

Admiral Shear: Not as much as you might think. The deep-water strategic aspects of the area played a much bigger role. We examined every possible location up and down the East Coast and up and down the West Coast. We looked at places such as Casco Bay, Maine, and we looked at places such as dredged out Cape Canaveral, Florida. We looked at Kings Bay, Georgia, and we looked at that magnificent site in the deep water of the Hood Canal in Puget Sound, which turned out to be such a natural thing for a number of reasons. That was the one we selected on the West Coast and the one we built.

We built that base from the ground up, and we did it just right. I had gotten to know Bangor very well, because that's where I loaded out my ammunition loads when I had the Sacramento, for deployment to WestPac. So I knew the Bangor geography, the Bangor depth of water, and the Hood Canal. You know, you could have 100 fathoms of water practically up against the beach. It had all those great assets. Furthermore, the decision was made to put the first Tridents into the Pacific Ocean, where we had that vast ocean area

---

[*] The first of the Trident submarines, USS Ohio (SSBN-726), was authorized in the fiscal year 1974 building program.

in which to operate. Because with those long-range missiles you could get good target coverage of practically the entire Eurasian continent and all the principal Soviet targets. So the decision was made to go for Bangor, which we did.

I left OP-31 just about the time that decision was made, before the base was built. As we progressed with the Trident submarine, the decision was made as to how were we going to put that ship together and how we were going to put hatches in her big enough to jerk out complete units that needed replacement and put in another complete replacement unit, sort of like you do with a gas turbine unit in one of the destroyers today. You can just jerk it right out and put in another. We had that kind of concept together for a quick refit of Trident. This worked out very, very well--just as we had planned it would. All that was worked into the concept of how we built that base at Bangor and what that base had to be prepared to do.

Before that really got going, I had moved on up to OP-095 as Director of Antisubmarine Warfare. Warner was involved in the selection of Trident. We made this complete base study in Trident, and Puget Sound stood like a sore thumb as the way to go. And on the East Coast Kings Bay stood out, although Kings Bay had a lot of problems. They had some depth-of-water problems, had a lot of dredging to do. And we had a little squabble with the Army, because that was the major Army ammunition load-out place. But we solved that without any great problem. So today we have two magnificent bases, which were planned from the ground up and built from the ground up, just as they should be, on each coast. If you have been to those bases you could see that they are terrific bases. You ought to visit both of them.

Q: I haven't been to either one of them yet.

Admiral Shear: We can get it arranged to get you down there to look them over. Because that was something that was planned well, developed well, and built well. That was done in a much more deliberate scale than Polaris was, because Polaris was a crash program. It came out beautifully, but it was a crash program from start to finish. This was not a crash program. It's been a very well laid out program, the bases have come along beautifully, the ships have come along beautifully, the missiles have come along beautifully. And these Tridents are 18,000-ton ships. A typical Polaris submarine is around 6,000 tons. These are huge underwater cruisers.

We've just commissioned the Maryland, and she's in here this coming weekend, in Annapolis.[*] They made me the chairman of the commissioning committee, because I had contacts with Maryland, I had contacts with Connecticut, and I was physically on the scene. The ship needed some help in getting its commissioning ceremonies set up and their parties and so forth. And it took a lot money. So they made me the chairman of the commissioning committee. I worked pretty hard and got that organized for them the last six months, kind of a fun job.

Q: Even though the governor snubbed you.

Admiral Shear: We had a hell of a time with the governor of Maryland.[†] He refused to come to the commissioning. I think we're going to get him out aboard ship for breakfast this coming weekend. At the moment it's on his schedule, and I'm supposed to go up there with him. The ship's going to meet him, of course, and give him a fine tour, but it will be the first time he has seen the ship or stepped aboard. He sent us his alter ego, his comptroller, Mr. Louie Goldstein.[‡] Let me tell you Louie Goldstein did a great job of replacing the governor. Louie Goldstein is a great speechmaker and a great politician. He had the entire crowd of 4,000 or 5,000 people in the palm of his hand.

Q: I understand that Goldstein has been a member of the Naval Institute for years and years.

---

[*] USS Maryland (SSBN-738) was commissioned 13 June 1992.
[†] William Donald Schaefer, a Democrat, was the Governor of Maryland, 1987-95. He did not attend the Maryland's commissioning ceremony because General Dynamics, the conglomerate that owned Electric Boat, relocated its corporate headquarters in Virginia rather than Maryland.
[‡] Louis L. Goldstein.

Admiral Shear: I did not know that. But I like Louie; I've known him for a long time. He did a good job representing the state of Maryland up there commissioning that ship. And we're finally going to get the governor aboard this weekend, I think.

Q: Well, that's because the ship is here rather than him having to go to General Dynamics.

Admiral Shear: Oh, absolutely, absolutely. He would never have gone up there. We had enough trouble getting him organized and getting him brought out here just for a breakfast. He put off making a decision on that until the last minute; finally got him in the corner and twisted his arm. [Laughter]

Q: How much support did you get from the CNO, Admiral Zumwalt, on the Trident program?*

Admiral Shear: [Pause] I'm thinking. Bud was never a great lover of submarines or submariners, but he was not a hindrance either. He never gave me any problems. He took over as CNO about halfway through my tour as OP-31.

My relationship with Bud Zumwalt was always very good. I didn't agree with many of the things that Bud Zumwalt was doing, but I was a loyal member of his staff for four years and I worked hard for him, although I disagreed with him vigorously on some issues. I didn't have any particular problem selling submarine programs to Bud. Bud tried to save personnel and money in some of his concepts on ships. He wanted to limit the size of ships. For instance, he wanted to build small carriers.

His FFGs were one effort to cut down the size of destroyer-type ships.† And I must say that turned out pretty well--a single-screw ship with somewhat limited armament and very limited crew size. He put Vice Admiral Frank Price in charge of the program, and he

---

* Admiral Elmo R. Zumwalt, Jr., USN, served as Chief of Naval Operations from 1 July 1970 to 29 June 1974.
† The Navy eventually built 51 guided missile frigates of the Oliver Hazard Perry (FFG-7) class. The first of them was commissioned in December 1977.

did a good job.* That's just a little bit about Bud's thinking about ship size and ship manning. He had a dedication to keep ship manning as low as possible, because personnel are expensive. Personnel are much more expensive than people realize. They cost you. They cost you a great deal--just handling personnel and paying personnel and taking care of personnel and making ships comfortable for personnel. Bud recognized that, and he recognized that you had to cut down numbers of people wherever you could.

I didn't have any particular problems regarding submarines. I didn't have any particular problems I recall selling numbers of submarines. And I don't recall Bud getting much involved in Trident. My memory gets a little hazy there. But obviously he did, because along came Trident during that time frame, the initial phases of Trident. I never had any major confrontations with Bud on numbers of submarines and why we had to have so many submarines and so forth. He didn't go out of his way to support me, and he didn't go out of his way to throw roadblocks in front of me.

Q: How did you react to the Zumwalt initiatives overall, and some of the many changes he brought about?

Admiral Shear: Well, since you bring it up, I'll talk about it now. I was going to bring it up a little bit later on here, when we get into my Vice Chief days. I was on his staff for four full years: one year as Director of Submarine Operations and three years as Director of Antisubmarine Operations. Somebody asked him once why he made a submariner Director of Antisubmarine Warfare. He said, "Well, it takes a thief to know one." [Laughter] He made that statement. I had good relationships with Bud, and I supported him. I worked hard for him, but I didn't agree with many of the things he was doing for the U.S. Navy. I thought he hurt the U.S. Navy pretty badly, particularly in the personnel area.

He was well meaning. He wanted to make some changes that were very necessary. The Navy had been dragging its feet with regard to race relationships, for example. I think

---

* Rear Admiral Frank H. Price, Jr., USN, was chairman of the Ship Characteristics Board and coordinator of the new construction destroyer program. He was subsequently promoted to vice admiral and became Deputy CNO for Surface Warfare.

he made some big improvements there, long overdue. However, I think he permitted an informality to develop in the Navy which was wrong, just wrong. The Navy got too lackadaisical; it got too sloppy. He was well meaning, but once you start letting down the bars, the things go to hell in a hand basket. As far as I am concerned, Bud let down the bars too far. Many of his ideas were good. Some of his Z-grams were good; some of his Z-grams were very poor.*

On the ship side he had obsessions with small ships. If he'd had his way, we'd have built some of these small carriers, and we wouldn't have been able to carry out our function with the big aircraft that we have today in the inventory. He was never enthusiastic about the big carriers such as the Nimitz and the Eisenhower--ships of that nature. He wanted to save personnel everywhere he could, and that's a good objective, but you've got to be realistic about it. He was successful in that one example of the FFGs. He did a pretty good job, although the ships were quite limited in their offensive capabilities.

We had a number of arguments about nuclear power. I remember going to a number of conferences in my OP-095 days with Rick and Zumwalt and all the hierarchy in the E-ring about nuclear-powered cruisers versus gas-turbine cruisers. If Rick had had his way, he would have built them all nuclear power. Well, that would have been ungodly expensive. We had a number of squabbles, some with me and Rick and Bud on that subject. Bud was no lover of Rickover, going back to the time Bud was interviewed for the Bainbridge.

We're now just about finished up with OP-31. And I will probably think of a number of incidents that came up in the two years of submarining that I should have told you about.

---

* Z-grams were consecutively numbered policy directives from Chief of Naval Operations Zumwalt that attempted to deal with such issues as enlisted rights and privileges, equal opportunity, and Navy families. Junior personnel viewed them much more favorably than did their seniors. See U.S. Naval Institute Proceedings, May 1971, pages 291-298.

Q: Well, you started in on the attack submarines, and you didn't really pursue that. This was at a time when the 688 was coming along.[*] Rickover got some information from a test in which the Enterprise had a race with one of the Soviet submarines as a justification for building in more speed.[†]

Admiral Shear: I don't recall that. We had a little side group of senior experienced submarine skippers that was put together to do some design work as to what there ought to be in the attack center of a new submarine and so forth. Joe Williams was deeply involved in that, among others.[‡]

We had a number of very good skippers, sort of working on the side in offices semi-attached to mine. They were actually in a different building, not the Pentagon.

They did some very good work, and in due course much of it was incorporated in the 688. Their main contribution was in the fire control area and the arrangement of the attack center. They also did some work with regard to some of the systems and capabilities that ought to be incorporated into the ship. It was very helpful work; it was good work. I think Yogi was involved in part of that also. You can ask Yogi the next time you see him.

Q: Were you involved also in selling that to Congress?

Admiral Shear: Anything to do with submarines we got involved with the Congress on. We had a full-scale wooden mockup of that ship built up at Electric Boat in New London. I remember taking a number of parties up there--and I don't recall who was in those parties--to go through that. You could get a pretty good feel for it by going through it and seeing the arrangements where equipment was set up and so forth. We've been doing those

---

[*] The keel for the USS Los Angeles (SSN-688) was laid 8 January 1972. She was the lead ship of a large class of attack submarines.
[†] See the Naval Institute oral history of Vice Admiral Kent L. Lee, USN (Ret.), who was the commanding officer of the Enterprise (CVAN-65) at the time of the race. The race is also covered in Patrick Tyler, Running Critical: The Silent War, Rickover, and General Dynamics (New York: Harper & Row, 1986).
[‡] Captain Joe Williams, Jr., USN. The oral history of Williams, who retired as a vice admiral, is in the Naval Institute collection.

full-scale mockups ever since Polaris days. They were very helpful in design work, putting systems together, making sure they fit in the right places, right size, and so forth.

I must say that my memories of congressional contacts in those two years in OP-31 are somewhat hazy. I got over to Congress frequently and even more so in my OP-095 days. One of the things about Congress was that you never had too much trouble selling submarine programs. They seemed to be oriented toward submarines. You always had a handful of anti's, but by and large the congress was pretty good in accepting submarine programs. In many cases much more so than SecDef.

Q: As long as Senator Jackson was there, you had a strong proponent.

Admiral Shear: Senator Jackson was a good proponent.[*] I got to know Senator Jackson very well, and so did Yogi. He was a great Navy supporter and a great submarine supporter. And we had another one, a representative from New York, whom I used to brief on the sly all the time--Sam Stratton.[†] Sam Stratton was a great help over there. I would take Sam over intelligence briefings about what was going on in the submarine world, things we were finding out about the Soviets and so forth. I probably wasn't authorized to tell him some of the stuff, but I did anyway.

Sam Stratton was always a very strong supporter and a very good supporter. I got to the stage where he knew me very well. He could call me up if he wanted to know something, and I would go over and tell him all about it. I guess Stratton and Jackson were probably the people I knew best over there at that particular phase. But I don't recall running back and forth too much trying to sell submarine programs to the Congress at that particular time.

Ask me a couple of questions; maybe it will bring something to mind.

---

[*] Senator Henry M. "Scoop" Jackson (Democrat--Washington)
[†] Representative Samuel S. Stratton (Democrat--New York). Stratton was a Naval Reserve officer, eventually reaching the rank of captain.

Q: Well, I've heard about this process of murder boards and what have you for preparing for testimony--that you get asked the hard questions in advance so you'll be able to anticipate them.

Admiral Shear: You always do that. You always do that. Anytime you get ready to go to a congressional briefing, particularly if it's appropriation-type meeting where you're trying to sell a product, you have murder boards. That's standard. You have a bunch of questions being fired at you. That's just the way you prepare yourself. No matter what part of OpNav you're in, if you're going to sell a program to Congress, you better, by God, be ready for it. You better know what you're talking about, and you better be ready for a series of questions. We've been through that dozens and dozens of times, routine thing to do.

Q: What sort of contacts did you have with SecDef?

Admiral Shear: Mel Laird was a good man, and I had a lot of contact with Mel Laird, particularly in the OP-095 area after I left OP-31.* I didn't have much contact with him in the submarine days. But Mel Laird was a sympathetic ear for the Navy. Bud Zumwalt got along very well with Mel Laird. Let's see, when did Mel Laird leave?

Q: Well, he stayed till the end of the first term of the Nixon administration.† Then Elliot Richardson came in for a while.‡

Admiral Shear: Yes, I remember when Elliot Richardson was there. Eliot Richardson and I had worked on the law of the sea together, so I had a point of contact with him there.

---

* Melvin R. Laird served as Secretary of Defense from 22 January 1969 to 29 January 1973.
† Richard M. Nixon was President of the United States from January 1969 until his resignation in August 1974.
‡ Elliot L. Richardson served as Secretary of Defense from 30 January 1973 to 24 May 1973.

Q: Schlesinger was there for a while.*

Admiral Shear: Schlesinger was an excellent man, sharp as a tack. Mel Laird was a good guy, but he was a political guy. Absolute superb politician; he wasn't a technical man at all. But he was SecDef, and he knew how to sell programs in Congress. I don't recall much contact with Mel on the submarine arena. But I remember a lot of contact with him in the antisubmarine arena.

Q: What are your impressions of him?

Admiral Shear: Oh, I liked Mel Laird. He was easy to talk to, easy to talk to, listened to you. And he wasn't afraid to spend some money. I remember a black program that I can't tell you about.† We were asking to proceed with a lot more money in the black program. I went down and briefed Mel on the status of it: what we were doing, what we were not doing, and how much more money we needed. He said, "Oh, hell. Don't worry about that. We've put more money than that in lots of dry holes. Get your money and proceed." That's almost verbatim what he said.

Q: He had a deputy who was highly regarded, Packard. Did you deal with him at all?

Admiral Shear: Oh, yes, Packard, superb man.‡ He was the technical brains behind Laird. My good friend and former shipmate who put the Trigger in commission with me was Jim Wilson. He became one of Packard's aides. He thought the world of Packard, and Packard thought the world of him. They had a very close working relationship. So anytime I had to get anything to Packard that I really had to get to him, I'd go down and see Wilson. Then Wilson would either slip it to him with a paper or tell him about it. They had some fine

---

* James R. Schlesinger served as Secretary of Defense from 1973 to 1975.
† In this context "black programs" are those involving intelligence gathering and are generally highly classified.
‡ David Packard, co-founder and partner in Hewlett-Packard, served as Deputy Secretary of Defense from 1969 to 1971.

people in OSD in those days, top-notch people. You couldn't get any better man on the face of the earth than Packard. Schlesinger, although a different type of man, was equally competent. Both highly competent technical people.

Anyway, after I took over OP-31, in '69, I don't recall too many issues that I had to take up with Laird in the submarine area. Anything that I would have to take up, I would pass up to Tom Moorer, who was then CNO, and Moorer would carry it down to Laird. Sometimes he might have taken me down; sometimes he might not, depending on what he wanted to do. My memory is kind of hazy there. I remember very well getting involved in the early stages of developing ULMS, which became Trident some years downstream.

I'm trying to think of any major highlights that I forgot in the OP-31 area. I haven't done very well by you there. If I think of any, I'll jot them down and update it in the future.

Q: All right.

Admiral Shear: Okay, let's talk about OP-095. OP-095 was set up a number of years before me, because there was a feeling in the Navy and a feeling outside the Navy that we needed an antisubmarine czar. The Soviet submarine threat was increasing significantly, and we had to put more emphasis and attention on it as a centralized location in the Navy Department. The first OP-095 was Charlie Martell.[*] He was relieved by Turner Caldwell, an aviator of Henderson Field fame down in Solomons, a fine man, a very fine man.[†] And I relieved Turner Caldwell in the summer of 1971.

Antisubmarine warfare was getting a lot of emphasis. The Soviet submarine threat was increasing. We were getting a lot of good intelligence back from our forward air patrols and our submarines, which were pushing very heavily at that time up off the Soviet coast. We knew that they were getting better all the time. They were making improvements in quieting their own submarines, and we knew that we had to really get on

---

[*] Vice Admiral Charles B. Martell, USN, Director, Antisubmarine Warfare Programs in OpNav.
[†] Vice Admiral Turner F. Caldwell, USN.

the ball and keep pushing antisubmarine warfare hard. We got plenty of support from all areas within the Navy and outside the Navy, in the Congress, for antisubmarine warfare.

One of the things that happened early in my period in OP-095 was the consolidation with the electronics branch in OpNav. It had been headed by Vice Admiral Fred Bardshar.[*] I don't know if you have ever heard of Fred Bardshar.

Q: He was a carrier man.

Admiral Shear: A carrier man. Fred Bardshar and Bud did not get along at all well. So essentially what happened was that Bud disestablished Fred Bardshar's job. He put all of Fred Bardshar's responsibilities in OP-095, and I was told to take them over. So OP-095 became a sort of an electronic warfare OP and an antisubmarine warfare OP, combined together. In many respects they dove-tailed together because electronic warfare had a great deal in common with submarine warfare, and in many cases you used the two to get your antisubmarine warfare results. I had a good staff, and I took over some of Fred Bardshar's staff, and we had a lot of talent around there.

One of the most important things that I did in OP-095 was to stress and press hard for passive sonar improvements. Surface ships had practically none; they were pingers and not very good pingers at that. Our best surface sonars were not particularly good in the passive mode. Submariners were passive-sonar types most of the time anyway, but their sonars needed a lot of improvement passive wise also.

So we put great stress into towed arrays. The importance of towed arrays is that you can increase your acoustic aperture. You have a series of hydrophones along a big length of towed wire, for example, or along the entire length of the ship, attached to the hull. That gives you a long frame with which to receive incoming signals. You can increase your range tremendously, and you can increase your bearing accuracy tremendously.

I had a team that was very good at that, and we stressed both towed arrays for submarines and towed arrays for surface ships. Probably the single most important thing I

---

[*] Vice Admiral Frederic A. Bardshar, USN, Director, Tactical Electromagnetic Programs on the OpNav staff.

did of my entire three years in OP-095 was to put that emphasis on passive sonar, particularly towed arrays. We put a great deal of emphasis on increasing our underwater surveillance, our fixed underwater surveillance, which we had all over the Atlantic and Pacific oceans. And that was a very important improvement.

Some of the other things that we did at that time. We put a great deal of emphasis on electronic intercepts, and we built a whole new series with the best of industry working with us on improvements of interception of electronic signals with antennas that fitted both on surface ships and on submarines.

I think I told you that when I took the Becuna up in the Barents Sea many years earlier that we had one of those first type of intercepts on board and the team to go with it. By this time we had gone through three or four generations of that type of equipment, much more sophisticated and much more complex, and we stressed that throughout my time there. We got approval and built a whole series of new intercept receivers, both with regard to frequencies coverage and in regard to accuracy of intercepts and identification of certain type of signals and so forth. I guess that's probably the second most important thing I did in OP-095. Again, I had a team on my staff that was very good at that.

But one of the things that I forgot to tell you--it went over from 31 to 095--was torpedo development. I got deeply involved in torpedo development in OP-31. We went from essentially our World War II torpedoes into the first Mark 46 antisubmarine warfare torpedo, which applied to both OPs, and then to the Mark 48 long-range heavy explosive weapon, an improvement over World War II torpedoes.

We had a very competitive situation between the Westinghouse Corporation and Gould in Cleveland, Ohio. And it was very keen competition, and both of them turned out a good torpedo, but we selected Gould, which was a reciprocating engine. That was sort of a half OP-31 job and half OP-095 job, because it was an ASW weapon as much as a submarine weapon. So we were very deeply involved in that.

We made the selection with Gould, and we had a very good team of Navy professionals put together. I think the head of that was my classmate Parker Armstrong and also my ordnance specialist classmate Mark Woods.[*] They were both deeply involved in the selection of that torpedo. We had a very good, careful team. It was touch and go as to which one we selected. Quite frankly, I didn't know which one it would be until I got the report from our team. But we selected Gould, and we probably could have selected Westinghouse and done almost as well. They were that close in their capabilities and characteristics in the weapon. But we selected Gould, and we had some very good people working on it. I'm trying to think of some of the flag officers working on that besides Mark Woods and Parker Armstrong. One was Jeff Metzel, another very good submarine man.[†] That was a very important thing that we did in those years in OP-95. And that is our standard major submarine torpedo today. And it also has capabilities in surface ships.

We had some black programs that I'm not going to talk to you about. But they were very important black programs; some were quite successful, some were very successful. Some had a submarine connotation, some had an antisubmarine connotation. They took a lot of time and a lot of money--a lot of money in some of those black programs.

Q: On the aviation side you had the P-3.

Admiral Shear: P-3 update.[‡] Deeply involved--we were deeply involved in that.

Q: The S-3 was coming in.

Admiral Shear: The S-3 was coming and we had responsibility for that.[§] Even though it was an aviation platform, we had the responsibility for the weapons system that was

---

[*] Rear Admiral Parker B. Armstrong, USN, was Commander Antisubmarine Warfare Systems Project Office, Naval Material Command. Rear Admiral Mark W. Woods, USN, was Commander Naval Ordnance Systems Command.
[†] Captain Jeffrey C. Metzel, Jr., USN.
[‡] The P-3 Orion has been the Navy's main land-based antisubmarine warfare aircraft for many years.
[§] The S-3 Viking began joining carrier-based ASW squadrons in the mid-1970s.

installed in the aircraft. We worked very closely with OP-05 on that, and we had a very good aviator over on the material side of the house named Ed Waller.* Ed Waller, very good man. After he retired, he went to work for Lockheed, but he was my technical man on the P-3s. He was recognized as the number-one P-3 man; he was very good.

So we went through the updating of the P-3s, the P-3B, the P-3C, and each time we improved the suit inside the aircraft. We improved the sonobuoys. Sonobuoy improvement was a big endeavor when I was in OP-095. We did a lot of improvement there, both in the active and passive sonars. Increased ranges, increased sophistication and so forth.

So we had a lot going on in the overall ASW arena, and I never had any great problem in getting funding. I think it was the recognition in Congress and the recognition in SecNav that, by golly, we had to emphasize ASW. Because, by God, at that time that was a threat. We knew that we did not have a full handle on it, particularly those of us who were on the scene and doing the job. Some people thought that we had ASW by the tail. We did not have it by the tail. We had a long way to go to get that Soviet submarine threat under complete control. We never did get it under complete control, and anybody who thinks that we did is just dreaming. They were getting better and better all the time. They weren't anywhere near as good as we were, but they were very first-rate submarine navy, and we had to put a lot of emphasis in it.

Q: Well, that was the strong suit of the submarine.

Admiral Shear: That's right it was, and throughout my career in OP-095, and before and after, in my Vice CNO days the number-one priority of the Navy was getting that ASW threat under control. It remained the top priority of Navy really up until the end of Carl Trost's tour as CNO.† Because that was the one thing that we had to get under control if we were going to be able to take on Soviets in the sea environment. We made a lot of

---

* Rear Admiral Edward C. Waller III, USN, Commander Antisubmarine Warfare Systems Project Office in OpNav. The oral history of Waller, who retired as a vice admiral, is in the Naval Institute collection.
† Admiral Carlisle A. H. Trost, USN, served as Chief of Naval Operations from 1986 to 1990.

progress, but we never did have it fully under control. I think as we learned more, we may have had more under control than we recognized. But the Soviets still were very first-rate professional submariners and they were turning out first-rate products of high technical capability.

Q: One of the developments about that period was the phasing out of the antisubmarine specialized carriers, and bringing in the CV concept.

Admiral Shear: That's right. We had the CVSs, and they carried, first, the S-2s and then the S-3s. And they had the small capability of attack aircraft. They were essentially Essex-class hulls and they had a great period, roughly from about 1950 to about 1970, I guess, as an ASW endeavor. I worked with them all the time when I had command of the Becuna, for example. A CVS was part of the ASW hunter-killer group, as it was called, but it had a submarine or two assigned with it as a target, and then we'd go off two or three months and just operate together.

Q: Jimmy Thach had really developed the tactics when he had Task Group Alfa.[*]

Admiral Shear: That's correct. But those hunter-killer task groups were not very effective, and don't let anybody tell you that they were very effective. I loved to put green flares on the flights deck of carriers, and I did it repeatedly with a diesel-electric submarine.[†] The honest people knew that they were not that effective, and we submariners knew very well that we could penetrate a target of that type and get a good attack off about any time we wanted to. The destroyers were not that good. The dipping sonar was not that good. The S-2 aircraft were not that good. It was an effort, but it wasn't a particularly successful

---

[*] Rear Admiral John S. Thach, USN, commanded antisubmarine Task Group Alfa in 1958-59. The oral history of Thach, who retired as a four-star admiral, is in the Naval Institute collection.
[†] In the course of an exercise, a submarine fires a green flare to simulate torpedoing a surface ship.

effort. And we knew it very well. We had no particular concerns about the ASW capabilities against us.

Nonetheless, knowing that and then putting that thief in to run the program, I knew what our weaknesses were. I knew, by God, that we had to get something going. Because I knew very well that if we got in a shooting match we were going to have a mess on our hands. We were going to have very heavy attrition and heavy losses. I made that clear time after time around the Pentagon, and I think Bud understood that. I made that very clear to Bud repeatedly.

Q: Well, the fact that you got the money indicates that you got the attention.

Admiral Shear: I think so, yes. And it was general knowledge that we needed to put a lot more emphasis into ASW. And my predecessors had pushed that hard too. Charlie Martell had pushed that very hard. He was a very competent man, and so was Turner Caldwell. But I think in my three years in OP-095 that my emphasis on things that had to be done in the antisubmarine arena paid off today and right up until this period, particularly in those areas where I mentioned. Electronic warfare and towed arrays and long-range passive sonar and things of that nature were big improvements, big improvements.

Not too long ago, I talked to some of my people who had worked for me. One of them is a Vice Admiral Kinnebrew.[*] I used to call him Killebrew after the baseball player.[†] We sat down and he said, "You know, everything we worked on in OP-095 in those early days came to pass as a very important ASW weapon system." He was absolutely right. We had some very good people working for us. They knew the problem, and they knew what we had to do to solve it, and we put a lot of effort into it.

Q: The main emphasis you've talked about is on hardware. What about tactics. Was that an area for improvement?

---

[*] Commander Thomas R. Kinnebrew, USN. He eventually retired as a vice admiral.
[†] Harmon Killebrew, who played for the Washington Senators and Minnesota Twins, is in baseball's hall of fame.

Admiral Shear: Passive sonar was something that the surface forces had rarely used before. They weren't used to passive sonar, and I think they didn't have much confidence in passive sonar. So they had to get used to it. They had to get used to what a towed array could do for them. And we had some of the very earliest generations of towed arrays. We put them on some ships and sent them over to the Mediterranean, for example, and showed them that, by God, they could track submarines with those things. We put them on submarines. Even the earliest ones on submarines we deployed showed them we could track at great ranges with passive sonar. And then we tracked them on our fixed underwater systems too. We improved them and showed how effective they could be for long ranges, over vast reaches of the Atlantic and Pacific.

Q: So it was a challenge of education too?

Admiral Shear: A challenge of education, absolutely. And a challenge of getting out there and operating and showing what you could do. Then we came along with this concept of utilizing a small ship, almost a trawler capability ship with a long towed array on it, a specially trained crew, and just covering the ocean and keeping track of deployed Soviet submarines. We built several classes of ships that do just that, we call them the T-AGOS. That was all started in my time in OP-095, and it proved highly successful over the years.

As we got that and then we became more successful, we also became more and more aware that the Soviet signatures were improving. Their sound signatures were getting better and better, and our program was just becoming more and more difficult. As time went on, they were getting better and better and we had to keep up our own technology, or we were going to lose that capability to track passively. So we had to work hard at improving what we had. If they came out with new arrays, for example, we had to get the most sophisticated systems we could. The industry came through pretty well on there too.

With the slim-line arrays and people like AT&T and Raytheon and those with great electronic experience came through with some big improvements.*

Q: You've got to have good inputs from the intelligence people too.

Admiral Shear: Yes, absolutely, and you've got to know those signatures. You've got to know what the spikes are which you can read in a Soviet submarine output, for example. That's why the submarine's role in that forward area surveillance is so important. We'd come back with the detailed information that would make you stand right on your ear. We'd get right up on top of them and read them out in minute detail. Record everything they were putting out, and we got the stuff. There wasn't any question we knew what was going on. We needed that kind of input in order to modernize and keep a generation or two ahead of what we had to put up with. That was a very interesting job. It was a challenging job, and it was a very good job for a fellow with some submarine background who really understood what the problem was all about. I think Bud recognized that we had a damn good team there. Because I had some crackerjack officers: destroyer sailors, aviators, submarine sailors. I had a fine team there.

Q: Well, it was some of that same set-a-thief-to-catch-a-thief philosophy that he put George Steele in charge of an ASW group.†

Admiral Shear: That's exactly correct, that's right. We had a very good team over in NavMat with Parker Armstrong over there and Ed Waller and some of those other people, some of the program managers of the commander type were top-notch people, top-notch people.

Q: What about the LAMPS program.‡ Do you remember your involvement in that?

---

* AT&T--American Telephone and Telegraph.
† Rear Admiral George P. Steele II, USN, served as Commander Antisubmarine Warfare Group Four, as he described in his Naval Institute oral history.

Admiral Shear: Oh, yes, deeply involved, deeply involved. Because it became obvious a long time ago that a destroyer had to have some legs. Passive sonar was just coming along for destroyers in those days. They had to be able to get out and reach, and they had to have a manned LAMPS that could get out there and drop a sonobuoy pattern and get something out of it and hang on to it.

We worked very closely with the Canadians on the LAMPS program. The Canadians were ahead of us for some time in LAMPS on the sterns of destroyers. We worked with them with regard to what the helicopter should be, what the helicopter equipment should be, ASW-wise. We had several LAMPS generations. We got the last one in production before I left OP-095. LAMPS and destroyers became synonymous with ASW. LAMPS destroyers, towed arrays, electronic improvement--all that tied into a package that you could get your hands on to go out there and get this guy.

Q: Well, LAMPS became especially important as the CVSs were phasing out, because it gets those dipping sonars out there.

Admiral Shear: Yep. That's absolutely correct. What did I want to say? Something else to do with helicopters. It slipped my mind at the moment.

So we had a lot going for us in OP-95, and I think we made some major contributions to antisubmarine warfare in that period. As a matter of fact, I know we did. We made some big contributions that are paying off even today.

Q: Were there any improvements in non-acoustic detection areas?

Admiral Shear: We put a lot of emphasis in non-acoustics, and we got involved in some very deep black programs in non-acoustic. I'm not going to tell you much about them but to say that we worked hard at it. The results, at best, were not what I would have liked to

---

‡ LAMPS, which stands for light airborne multi-purpose system, is an antisubmarine helicopter carried on board destroyers and frigates.

have seen. I thought we could have done much better than we did. We made some modest breakthroughs, but we didn't make the major significant breakthroughs that I thought we might be able to at one time. Bud thought we might have some big opportunities in non-acoustic ASW. We did have some, but it never came through as a major breakthrough of the type that was going to solve the opaque ocean, if you will. It just wasn't in the cards.

From anybody's point of view who knows his stuff, the submarine is still a pretty damn good place to operate without being detected, and I tell you that straight out. Anybody who thinks they're going to lick the submarine program with a few easy answers, it's not in the cards. That vast ocean area in which you have to operate and the problems of antisubmarine warfare, the submarine is going to have a very good place for a long time in history, both from an attack point of view and from a strategic weapon point of view, deterrent point of view.

Solving the problems of what's going on underneath the surface of the sea is a very, very big problem. We're going to be working on it for generations. Don't let anybody tell you any differently. It's not easy. We made some vast progress, and we made some big improvements in equipments and so forth. Systems oceanography has come a long way. But we have by no means whatsoever solved the antisubmarine warfare problem per se. We made progress, we made steps, but it is still a huge problem, a huge problem.

What's happened with regard to the problem? The enemy has gone away. Now, it hasn't gone away, but it is a completely different nature. It's still there in the back channels if they ever want to bring it forth. It will take a lot of doing to bring it forth again. And you have the forthcoming problem of small numbers of submarines and a whole bunch of third countries, for example, that can be a big pain in the neck and cause you major problems. For example, during the war in the Persian Gulf, that could have been a major problem out there with a handful of well-handled diesel-electric submarines. A country like Iran could have given us fits out there. So we've got to be prepared to handle that sort of thing. So antisubmarine warfare is not going to go away. I mean, you've got to keep working on the problem, and you've got to keep working on improvements. Because it can tie you in knots just like mine warfare can tie you in knots if you aren't prepared to handle it.

Q: The Chinese, for example, could come up with something.

Admiral Shear: The Chinese could do it. I must say this is not my particular area of expertise of what I want to cover. But I might say the Navy has done very poorly over the years in neglecting mine warfare, both anti-mine warfare and mine warfare per se.

One thing we did get involved in was the CapTor mine.[*] I got deeply involved in that in OP-095. That is an antisubmarine warfare weapon. That's the mine that you moor, and a torpedo comes off and activates and takes off and sinks the target and so forth. I guess you could call that a semi-success. It never turned out to be the world-beating weapon we thought it might be, but that was the type of thing you could use to put a barricade across something like the Greenland-Iceland-U.K. Gap with fairly narrow passages through which submarines had to pass. The CapTor mine was designed to be moored in places like that and to detect and strike any submarine passing through. We put a lot of emphasis into that program too, with, I'd say, modest success.

So we had a lot going on. There was never a dull moment. A whole series of programs going on both in the electronic area and the sonar area and in the weapon area. A great three years. It gave me five years in a row in the Pentagon. And I'm not particularly proud of that record. [Laughter] But, as I said before, you got to be in Washington if you're going to know what is going on. So I had five years in a row, two years in OP-31 and three years in OP-095. Five full years in the Pentagon, and I was ready to leave when I did. That's when I went over and became CinCUSNavEur in London.

Q: That's a good note to end on for today. A great session today, Admiral.

Admiral Shear: I'm going to have a lot to tell you about CinCUSNavEur and about Europe and about the Vice Chief and about NATO and CinCSouth. Lots of stuff to cover there,

---

[*] CapTor--encapsulated torpedo.

both political and military. Because I got up to my neck in a whole series of things that a naval officer never anticipates getting involved in.

Harold E. Shear #3 - 275

Interview Number 3 with Admiral Harold E. Shear, U.S. Navy (Retired)

Place: U.S. Naval Institute, Annapolis, Maryland

Date: Friday, 4 June 1993

Interviewer: Paul Stillwell

Q: Admiral, we had just finished up last time with the discussion of your long tour of duty in Washington, D.C. You spent five years in the Pentagon in OP-31 and OP-095, and now we're ready to embark on your time in London as CinCUSNavEur, please.[*]

Admiral Shear: All right, Paul. It's nice to be back with you again after a break of some months.

Q: A pleasure to see you also, sir.

Admiral Shear: Let's start out. I was a just finishing up at OP-095, which at that time was the Director of Antisubmarine Warfare and also Director of Electronic Warfare. The Vice Chief of Naval Operations at that time was Jimmy Holloway. He was soon to move up and become CNO, relieving Bud Zumwalt.[†] I don't recall whether Holloway called me in or Zumwalt called me in, but one of them said, "We're going to send you to London to relieve Worth Bagley." Bagley had had a very prominent role in Bud Zumwalt's tour as CNO, where he'd been, among other things, OP-090.[‡] He was a very close, very close intimate of Bud Zumwalt's, and he had only been in London, I guess, for about a year.[§] They called me

---

[*] Admiral Shear served as Commander in Chief U.S. Naval Forces Europe and Commander in Chief U.S. Naval Forces Eastern Atlantic from May 1974 to May 1975.
[†] Admiral James L. Holloway III, USN, served as Vice Chief of Naval Operations from 1 September 1973 to 5 June 1974. He became CNO on 29 June 1974.
[‡] OP-090 was Director of Navy Program Planning. It was frequently a stepping-stone to four-star rank.
[§] Admiral Worth H. Bagley, USN, served as CinCUSNavEur from August 1973 to May 1974.

and said that I was going over to relieve him. Then he was going to come back and be Vice Chief of Naval Operations for Jim Holloway.[*]

I had known Worth Bagley very well, because he was there on Bud's staff for most of the time that I was there. I was delighted to learn that I was going to get my fourth star and go over to London. It was great opportunity and a great challenge. They told me, among all the things, that since I was four star I would have my own plane. I could fly away to London with my wife and as much of my gear as I could put in this four-engine plane. That was what I did. I arrived on the scene over there, and after a couple of days I took over from Worth those magnificent headquarters on Grosvenor Square.

That was probably the best real estate deal that has ever happened to the United States Navy. That deal was arranged by Lord Louis Mountbatten right at the end of World War II, when he wanted to make sure that the U.S. Navy stayed there in London. That had been Eisenhower's headquarters on Grosvenor Square, a five- or six-story building.[†] It was that old architecture of that part of London, a beautiful old building. He said, "I'll arrange for a 99-year lease for one pound a year if the United States Navy will stay here." So we did; we've been there ever since. The lease runs for a good many more years, and I guess we are still paying a pound a year.

Q: What made the headquarters magnificent?

Admiral Shear: Well, it was in the very finest part of London, right across the street from the U.S. Embassy, and right there in that beautiful garden we had at Grosvenor Square. It was convenient to everything, and, of course, we had all of our communications facilities there, so we had everything we needed. There was a magnificent flat on the third floor, where I lived. They had also a country home, but I was so busy there that I rarely got out to the country home. I spent most of the time right there in the flat in Grosvenor Square,

---

[*] Admiral Bagley served as VCNO from 5 June 1974 to 30 June 1975.
[†] General of the Army Dwight D. Eisenhower, USA, was the Supreme Allied Commander in Europe in 1944-45.

right above my office. We had the entire staff there; we had a superb staff. Captain Barber was there, among others, at that time.* That's how we were set up.

Incidentally, they had magnificent quarters for entertaining there. There was a huge, huge, huge dining room there where you could seat 30 or 40 people. I used it for conferences, and I also used it for entertaining officials, both military and civilian. It came in to be a very handy situation. Occasionally I would go out in the countryside there in that beautiful home on the golf course outside of London and spend a weekend there and then do some entertaining out there. But principally I stayed right there in the headquarters, because things had a nasty way of demanding my time right on the scene there most of the time. So I stayed.

If I wasn't on the road, in the Med or Europe or somewhere else in the Middle East, I stayed right there at the headquarters and ran things from there. A whole series of things came about during my year there. When I was sent over there by Jim Holloway, I thought we were to be there for three years. Well, as my wife recounts, I was there 27 days less than one year--to her great disappointment. Then I was pulled back to become Jim Holloway's Vice Chief when Worth Bagley retired early, quite unexpectedly. So I was there, for all practical purposes, a year. A great deal happened that year. There were great problems in Africa. There were great problems in the Med. There were great problems in the Middle East. I was deeply involved in all of those.

Q: Well, maybe we can take those one by one, please, starting with Africa.

Admiral Shear: At that time the Soviets were in Africa in great strength. They had their Cuban troops spread all over that continent. They had sizable strengths in Angola, they had sizable strengths on the other side--in places such as Mozambique. They had sizable forces in up there in Somalia, where they have that big field up there in the horn of Africa.

They had even more influence in Ethiopia, where they had essentially taken hold of the country.† The fellow who overran the king was nothing more than a Soviet puppet.‡

---

* Captain James A. Barber, Jr., USN. Following his retirement from active duty in 1984, Captain Barber became executive director of the Naval Institute.

We had there one of our most important radio stations in the world; it covered the entire Indian Ocean. It was Asmara on an escarpment, about 3,000 feet above the Red Sea. Well, it was actually on the edge of the city of Asmara. We had over 1,000 people there running that station, and eventually we had to evacuate. They were threatened over a period of several months by fighting going on between the new government and Eritrea, a northwestern province that was trying to break away from Ethiopia itself and at the same time keep the Russian influence out of there.

That was a nasty situation; there was fighting going on night and day, and there were raids into the radio station at night. In due course we set up a command post in London, where it was manned around the clock either by myself or by my deputy, Rear Admiral Don Engen, who was a magnificent officer.* One of us was in that command post continually during this period of a month or more, just watching that situation there.

Q: So you got a background in international affairs very quickly.

Admiral Shear: Very quickly. That happened very shortly after I got there. As I recall, the Soviets had 28 ships in the Red Sea, and I had two destroyers of the Middle East Force under my command at that time. About all those destroyers could do was patrol up and down and let me know where Russians were and how many there were. The Russians at that time never came ashore. Oh, they used the port of Mesewa, which is just below Asmara, regularly as a visiting port. But they never came ashore and put their troops up in the communication station, which is 3,000 feet above Mesewa.

---

† On 12 September 1974 military leaders overthrew long-time Emperor Haile Selassie I in a bloodless coup in the capital of Addis Ababa. They set up a military government pledged to make Ethiopia a socialist state, with government control over the economy. Selassie died under house arrest 11 months later.

‡ General Aman Andom, first post-imperial head of state, was killed by opponents in November 1974. In 1977 Lieutenant Colonel Mengitsu Haile Mariam consolidated power in Ethiopia.

* Rear Admiral Donald D. Engen, USN. The oral history of Engen, who retired as a vice admiral, is in the Naval Institute collection.

But the fighting was going on, and I kept an open circuit with the CO of the station who was an LDO commander, terrific guy.[*] I could pick up the phone and talk to him directly anytime I needed to. He kept me on the phone and told me what the raid was doing and said, "Well, now we've got tracers coming through the windows," things like that. You know, they were attacking him every night. So we got the dependents out of there early on, and then it became obvious that we just had to evacuate the station. We had a dirt runway there, which we used to get the C-130s with the short landing capacity in there, and we destroyed as much as we could and then we got our people out.[†] That station was quite a loss, because it covered that entire Indian Ocean and entire Middle East. And it was a backup for the Polaris submarines in the Western Pacific.

Q: Was it your perception this was deliberate harassment on the part of the Soviets to get the U.S. Navy to leave?

Admiral Shear: No question. I don't think there was any question about that. That coverage was eventually replaced by the big new station down in Australia, which was not complete at that time. It was a big VLF station which was designed to provide among other things the strategic coverage for that entire part of the world.

Q: Where there ever any diplomatic efforts to get the Soviets to back off?

Admiral Shear: If there were, they weren't successful. The Soviets at that time were running pretty wild throughout Africa. I guess overall they had 10,000 Cubans here, 10,000 Cubans there. I think there were about 15,000 or 20,000 Cubans in Ethiopia before they were through.

---

[*] LDO--limited duty officer, a former enlisted man whose duties are related to his enlisted specialty.
[†] The C-130 is a large, propeller-driven cargo plane.

Q: The conventional wisdom of the time was that America had lost its will after Vietnam and was probably not going to challenge them.

Admiral Shear: That's just about correct. This was in 1974-75. So that was the first crisis I had.

I guess the second crisis, if you want to call it that, was the exchange between Al Haig and Goodpaster.* Al Haig had come out of the White House, as you know, and had been running the place essentially when he left there.† Goodpaster had been in the White House under Eisenhower, in a powerful position not unlike Haig's. Haig wanted that SACEur job very badly. He didn't want to be Chief of Staff of the Army after having been in the White House. He could have had that, but he chose SACEur. I guess he just said, "I want SACEur," and Kissinger and others arranged for him to get it.‡ He was very close to Kissinger, you know. It was not due for Goodpaster to leave over there yet. So Haig essentially gave Goodpaster a bum's rush, and that did not sit well. They were not on speaking terms, and both of them made it plain that they weren't very happy with each other.

Goodpaster was my boss. He was over there, and he at that time was SACEur and CinCEur, a dual-hatted job, still is. Of course, I had good relationships with him; I had no problem. I'd go back and forth and visit, and he would come over and visit me in the early part of my year over there. We got along fine.

But it was clear there was going to be fireworks when Haig arrived. Haig first came and stopped in London, and he spent the night with me. I had known him only slightly before that. Well, I made sure he was very well taken care of, and I had a very delightful dinner party for him and invited a number of the diplomatic people and a number of the

---

* On 1 November 1974, at Stuttgart, Germany, General Alexander M. Haig, Jr., USA, relieved General Andrew J. Goodpaster, USA, as U.S. Commander in Chief Europe. On 15 December 1974 at Supreme Headquarters Allied Powers Europe, in Casteau, Belgium, Haig relieved Goodpaster as NATO Supreme Allied Commander Europe.
† Haig was the White House chief of staff during the last months of the presidency of Richard M. Nixon, who resigned in August 1974 as a result of the Watergate coverup.
‡ Haig had worked for Henry A. Kissinger when Kissinger was the President's national security adviser. Kissinger later served as Secretary of State, 1973-77.

British military. I made some very nice comments about what a fine person he was to be going over there, and he never forgot that. He never forgot that I met him on the scene and treated him royally and started off a friendship that I think continues to this day. I'm damn glad I did that, because the situation across the channel was anything but nice.

I went over for the change of command, and by that time they had made up publicly. They made a big display of showing how they had made up at the change of the command, where they shook hands and threw their arms around each other and all that stuff, but it was strictly for show. So began my relationship with my new boss, SACEur/CinCEur, Al Haig. So I was there a few months with Goodpaster, who was also a superb man, before Al took over. That was the second little crisis--well, it wasn't really a crisis but something I had to take care of in kind of a delicate way.

Q: Did you have the feeling that if you embraced Haig that you would not have as good a relationship with Goodpaster after that?

Admiral Shear: Goodpaster was going; he was retiring. But that never entered my mind; I just did what I thought was the proper thing to do for an incoming new SACEur, and I never gave it a thought that whether I was going to hurt one feeling or the other feeling. I just treated the guy the way he should have been treated. As I recall, when Haig arrived across channel, Goodpaster never met him officially on his arrival. It was kind of a dicey situation.

Q: Well, it's easy to understand Goodpaster's bitterness.

Admiral Shear: Oh, yes, it is. He was essentially being booted out of there prematurely. And he'd had a great career and he was doing a great job as SACEur. So much for that.

As for my relationship--see, Al Haig was my boss in his national role as CinCEur.[*] He was both CinCEur and SACEur, but I did not wear a NATO hat as CinCUSNavEur.[†] I

---

[*] In his role as U.S. Commander in Chief Europe, Haig had control of the joint U.S. forces in his theater.

wore a national hat. And throughout the rest of my time there my relationship with Haig was superb. We had a lot of business with the Greeks and a lot of business with the Turks, which were pretty tough and pretty nasty, but Haig always supported me 100% with things we had to do. I'll get into that as we get along here.

I'm just looking at my notes here; I put some of this stuff together hurriedly.

One thing that you should realize and should recognize is that the Army and the Air Force had one thought and one thought only in NATO. That was the Central Front of Europe. They were absolutely mesmerized with the Central Front. They could not care less about what happened in the Northern flank; they could not care less about what happened in the Southern flank. They were mesmerized with the Central Front. That held their entire attention. They looked at Germany as their territory--to the victor belongs the spoils.*

It was a lush setup: magnificent facilities, magnificent clubs, magnificent golf courses, magnificent hotels. Anything you wanted over there the Army and the Air Force had. I personally thought it was gross, but I never said so publicly. Every time I had to go over there, I could see that it was a different life, and I didn't think it was a very pretty life. The Germans didn't have much to say about it, but the Germans obviously must have been very, very disgruntled with the attitude and the atmosphere of our U.S. Forces in Germany at the time. You may have heard this from some others.

Q: No, I hadn't. It sounds like an army of occupation being perpetuated.

Admiral Shear: That's precisely what it is--Army and Air Force of occupation being perpetuated, and, by God, they had the best of everything. That was the attitude and the atmosphere. But it didn't hurt my operation, my responsibilities. My bosses were all over there, and I went back and forth frequently. I had the best relationship with the Army and

---

† NATO--North Atlantic Treaty Organization.
* Allied forces had been stationed in West Germany since the end of World War II in 1945.

Air Force over there, CinCUSAFE and CinCCUSArEur, and they were my four-star counterparts on the national side.*

We got along very well, and we understood each other. They were good, competent people, but let me tell you--whereas I had to look at everything from Norway down to the Middle East, they were just mesmerized by Central Europe. They were so intent on that Central Front that it was funny. It was obvious that the Russians weren't going to come charging across that Central Front. If they were going to get involved in anything, they were going to get involved in the flanks. Which is how things developed over the years.

Q: You mentioned that the situation was hot in Africa at the time.

Admiral Shear: Exactly.

Q: You mentioned the Middle East before. What crises or other situations do you remember in that area?

Admiral Shear: A whole lot. At that time the water part of the Middle East came under me. The Red Sea and the Persian Gulf were all part of my command.

Q: And the Mediterranean, of course.

Admiral Shear: And the Mediterranean, of course, and the Baltic and the Black Sea. All the water was under CinCUSNavEur. This was before they had a Central Command or before the Pacific came out and took over any of that. It was all CinCUSNavEur.

I had this small Mideast Force out there, headquartered in Bahrain, and we had a big operation going on in Iran. They were our great allies at that time. And Henry Kissinger

---

* CinCUSAFE and CinCCUSArEur--Commander in Chief U.S. Air Force Europe; Commander in Chief U.S. Army Europe.

among others had made it so. He set up Iran as our major anchor to windward out there, to oppose the Soviets coming down from the north.

We had put industrial developments into that country you wouldn't believe. We had major factories, we had huge military establishments. We had a huge military base at Bandar Abbas on the shore of the Strait of Hormuz. And we had big airfields, both Navy and Air Force. We had big training operations going on with them, and we had U.S. industry in there and all kinds of sophisticated factories. The Shah's ideas were great, although his execution wasn't always the best. The Shah's ideas to modernize his nation were really most impressive.

He had unlimited funds, so he put a lot of money in it, and we put a lot of money in it. We had a huge operation going on over there. I would get down there occasionally, because I had the responsibilities for the their Navy and for their naval bases and Bandar Abbas. We had a big P-3 airfield right outside of Bandar Abbas. We had a complete navy yard there, with a complete dry dock, a complete facility for really a pretty good-sized Navy.

We had a lot of retired U.S. naval officers over there supervising it and assisting it. One of them was Vice Admiral Ralph Shifley, who had been OP-04 a number of years earlier, excellent man.* He sort of headed up the naval development area as a civilian for some of those huge contracts. The contracts we had over there were huge, big industrial companies. Westinghouse had a huge contract, and I guess AT&T had a huge contract, and they had a lot of military contracts. Iran at that time was just jumping. We were delighted at the way things were going out there until the roof caved in with Jimmy Carter and the abandoning of the Shah and so forth.

On the other side of the Persian Gulf we had a big endeavor going with the Saudis. We were building up a nice little navy for the Saudis. We had operations at Jidda on the Red Sea, and then we had operations around the corner in a number of ports there north of Bahrain. We had a very good relationship with the Saudis, and we had good relationships with the Kuwaitis. I would go out there and I'd make a swing of those countries. I spent

---

* Vice Admiral Ralph L. Shifley, USN, had served as OP-04, Deputy Chief of Naval Operations (Logistics), prior to his retirement in 1971.

most of my time around Iran. Then I would swing by the Saudis, and I would swing by Kuwait. I never did get into the states along the gulf coast there, the United Arab Emirates, although we had some good relationships going on then.

We had some relationship with the Sultan of Oman, because he owned the island of Masirah, a big island off his coast, and we wanted to get an airfield in there. He would come up to London once in a while because he liked London. I remember once he came up there, and Kissinger was in town and they had a long confab, and I was in on the edges of that. I got to know Qabus, a nice little fellow who was the ruler of Oman at that time; I guess his family still is.* So we had good relationships all through that area up there.

Q: Was Iraq a factor at that time?

Admiral Shear: I never got to Iraq.

Q: This was before the war had started.

Admiral Shear: Before the war between Iraq and Iran.† I don't really recall much about Iraq, except that it had this common border with Turkey and with Iran and Syria. We wanted to make sure that if anything happened there, it was something that could be in our interest. Really our emphasis was on Iran. Iraq was sort of a secondary issue at that time, because if the Russians were going to come south they would be coming through Iran to get to the Persian Gulf.

Q: Well, of course, the Soviets subsequently moved into Afghanistan, which was next door.‡

---

* Qabus bin Sa'id became Sultan of Oman in a coup on 23 July 1970.
† The war began in September 1980, when Iraqi forces invaded Iran. It became essentially a stalemate and ended with a cease-fire in August 1988.
‡ The Soviets intervened militarily in Afghanistan in December 1979.

Admiral Shear: Exactly, exactly. This, of course, was a few years before Afghanistan. But there wasn't any question in my mind--going ahead now a number of years--that it was their intent to go into Afghanistan. And because of the developments between Iran and Iraq, it was natural for the Soviets to get fully established in Afghanistan and then the next step would be just a nice push into Iran. They already had the Tudeh Party, which was the Communist Party in Iran. The next step would have been just to get in there and put the Tudehs in command, and then they would be right smack on the Persian Gulf. That'll never happen, but that was clearly a goal.

Q: What are your impressions from visiting Iran. Did you visit with the Shah?

Admiral Shear: I never personally visited with the Shah. But I visited with all of his four-star Army, Navy, and Air Force military subordinates. I thought he had damn good people there. I thought what he was doing for the country was very impressive.

Q: The picture was of a very plush high level, and a great gap then to the working man and the implementers of his modernization.

Admiral Shear: There was work everywhere. There was just a beehive of activity. Going back to my days in Brazil, you know, you had that upper echelon of 2% or 3%; then you had a lower echelon of 15% or 20%. And then this mass in the middle at the bare living. I'm sure you had a lot of that out there, but the Shah's goals were absolutely in the best interests of the nation. He was going all out to develop a really modern, progressive nation, and he had unlimited oil money to do that with. It was moving in the right direction, until things all fell apart.

He became ill, and then the Carter regime came along in due course. Our official position became very wishy-washy out there, and things just fell apart. Every once in a while I mention to someone that our real problems out there started with Carter. And they say, "That's very interesting." Not many people realize that, but there isn't any question that's where our problems started. Absolutely no question whatsoever. Our interest and our prestige and objectives in that era fell apart with Jimmy Carter. Some of this is jumping ahead, but that's what happened.

Q: Speaking of presidential changes, was there any spinoff from the Watergate business over in London, where you were? At the time there was talk of alerts and what have you.

Admiral Shear: No, none whatsoever, none whatsoever. I know that there was never any thought on the part of the U.S. military of stepping in and going to war on the Watergate. There simply wasn't any such thing going to happen. As far as being over there and Haig coming over and the smell of Watergate along with him, obviously some of that smell must have been attached to his coattails, but it never surfaced, never surfaced. It never came up as something that I had to face up to or anywhere or anybody in the continent had to face up to. It just all went away.

Q: Maybe you could speculate that he demanded the SACEur job just to get out of Washington.

Admiral Shear: I could speculate that might well have been. Clearly, he did not want the Chief of Staff of the Army. He could have had it. All he had to do was ask Henry. Henry was running the show. I'm sure he did not want to go from the White House over to the Pentagon and run the United States Army with that nice job over there in SACEur, and that SACEur normally was a six-year job. I forget how many years that Goodpaster was there. But that was normally a six-year job, and he stayed there for a full six years. When I came back here as Vice Chief then went back as CinCSouth, Haig was still there.[*] He was my boss again, and it turned out to be a terrific relationship. We got along very, very well together. But we're jumping ahead now.

---

[*] CinCSouth--Commander in Chief Allied Forces Southern Europe, a NATO command.

Q: During the time you were in London, what was your relationship with CinCSouth? Both of you had differing responsibilities concerning the Sixth Fleet.

Admiral Shear: Yes, CinCSouth at that time was Means Johnston.[*] We had no problems. There were problems later, however, with Stansfield Turner.[†] I don't know how much you know about Stansfield Turner, but he is not held in particularly high regard by the professional Navy. And Haig had trouble with Stansfield Turner. This is again jumping ahead. Stansfield Turner had not yet arrived on the scene when I was in London.

Means Johnston and I got along very well with each other. We'd known each in the past and had no problems. He didn't try to take over the Sixth Fleet in the NATO hat. I had the responsibility for the Sixth Fleet in the national hat, and Sixth Fleet actually was a subordinate of mine. It was only a subordinate of his when war came along. I would get down there periodically to visit the Sixth Fleet and visit Means, and he would come up to London and visit me. We had a very good interchange with each other. I never had any problems at all with Means, and I certainly didn't give him any problems. So we had good working relationships.

Now, we had a number of problems going on in the Med. The biggest and the most touchy during my year there was the situation between the Greeks and the Turks. The Greek colonels were essentially running the country at that time. And they had this radical Greek Orthodox clergyman who was essentially their pope. He was in cahoots with the colonels, and they were causing all kinds of problems in Cyprus, all kinds of problems. Cyprus had been divided traditionally between the Greeks and the Turks. Finally the Turks got so fed up with it that they invaded Cyprus with sizable force, and then all hell broke loose.

I knew that something was going to happen, so I had the Sixth Fleet stationed just south of the island in case we were called to get in there and do anything. I was never given

---

[*] Admiral Means Johnston, Jr., USN, served as Commander in Chief Allied Forces Southern Europe from November 1973 to September 1975.
[†] Admiral Stansfield Turner, USN, served as Commander in Chief Allied Forces Southern Europe from September 1975 to March 1977.

any particular instructions about what to do with the Sixth Fleet. I just had them there if I was ordered to do something. The Sixth Fleet commander was Dan Murphy.* He later had a job in the White House. He was a good man, a competent man, and we got along well together. I never had to tell him anything more than once. He did a good job in this situation between the Greeks and the Turks.

Although the Turks legally owned the northern half of Cyprus, they essentially took over the entire island. This was a cause celebre between the Greeks and the Turks and the rest of Europe. But the Turks didn't back down and are still there. And the Turks caught all kinds of hell for doing this. I couldn't show my loyalties, but let me tell you, the Greeks made it so hard for them, so nasty for them that they didn't have much choice. Of course, there was a very effective and strong Greek lobby in the United States, and there was a zero Turkish lobby. That Greek lobby became very, very noisy and claimed everything about what the terrible Turks had done. The facts are that the Greeks had brought it on themselves. A lot of people don't want to admit that or they forget it, but that's what happened.

Q: Great irony here, that on a national level they were squabbling, and in NATO they were supposed to cooperate.

Admiral Shear: That's right, and I'll tell you a lot about that in the next job, when I got down there to the NATO job at CinCSouth.

So that brought up another thing. One of the things Bud Zumwalt had pushed very hard was overseas home-porting. He put it out in the Pacific, where it worked out quite well. He had done that just at the end of his tour as CNO, but the situation in Greece became intolerable. Our people were not well treated there. We had a carrier division staff

---

* Vice Admiral Daniel J. Murphy, USN, commanded the Sixth Fleet from June 1973 to September 1974.

there and six or eight destroyers home-ported there.* Petersen was the carrier task force commander--very good man.†

I was persona non grata in Greece at that time. I was not encouraged to get down there. As a matter of fact, the ambassador told me to keep the hell out of there. The ambassador and I talked to each other, but he didn't want me in Greece.

Q: What was the basis for your being declared persona non grata?

Admiral Shear: I guess we were blamed for what was going on in Cyprus. Anyway, the situation became very bad with regard to the home-ported people there. So to see firsthand what was going on, I went down there in civilian clothes with a civilian passport. I could get into the country that way. I just wanted to poke around and take a look at what our people were doing, how they were living, and what the situation was. There was harassment of all descriptions. There were incidents going on. After looking it over and talking it over with Petersen, who was the senior guy home-ported there, I said, "Pete, we've got to backtrack on this. It was a mistake, and I want you to understand that I am going to tell the CNO that we've got to pull our home-ported people out of here." He agreed with me.

You must understand now that Worth Bagley was the Vice Chief. I went back to London and had some phone conversations with Holloway and said, "Look, Jim, we've got to cut this home-porting situation in Greece, because it's not going to work." Well, Worth Bagley had been one of the predominant people who had convinced Bud to set it up, and here he was sitting as Vice Chief. So that caused a little furor, but I said, "Look, you've got

---

* In 1973-74, the U.S. Navy home-ported six destroyers in the port of Elefis, Greece, near Athens. They were part of a plan that envisioned putting a carrier task force of up to 30 ships in the port. Before the remainder of the program could be implemented, it was cancelled because of strained relations between the United States and the Greek Government. See The Washington Post, 30 April 1975, page A2.

† Rear Admiral Forrest S. Petersen, Commander Carrier Group Two and Commander Attack Striking Force, Sixth Fleet.

to back me on this. We simply can't let it go on this same way any further. We're doing very well in Italy, and I'll back you fully on that, but we've got to get out of Greece."

So the CNO said, "Okay, get out." So we got them out of there just as fast as we could. It's a good thing we did, because it was going from bad to worse. I forget exactly what month we pulled them out of there, but shortly after my arrival in London it became obvious that it was not going to work.

Q: Well, the rationale for that program was so sailors could spend more time their dependents.

Admiral Shear: Precisely. Save money and keep more time with the ships and families.

Q: But if these sailors and dependents were getting harassed by the host country, it was not working.

Admiral Shear: That's exactly what the problem was. And there were very difficult housing situations, far away from the center of the city and things like that. It was just a bad thing to do. Now, in Italy, however, in that remote island of Sardinia, over at La Maddalena, the northern tip there, everything was going beautifully. Our people were integrated, we had a good situation with the ships, we had a good situation with the people, we had good facilities ashore. They were living on the economy, but they were welcomed by the Italians with open arms. It's probably the Italian nature; they are just great friendly people. And that worked beautifully and is still working beautifully. We just had an exchange of tenders out there within the last couple of weeks. We're still there, and that has been a model situation from day one.

Q: Well, that pumps dollars into the local economy.

Admiral Shear: Everybody was happy. People were happy. Families were happy. The Italians were happy. The dollar situation was good, and it worked out just right. Now, if the Greeks had really wanted to do so, they could have done the same thing. But the Greek nature is such that it is not that way; it's never going to be that way. The Greeks are sort of a race unto themselves. I guess it goes back 2,000 or 3,000 years. They have been fighting with the Turks for 2,000 or 3,000 years.

Q: Did Admiral Bagley fight you on this?

Admiral Shear: He certainly was not happy about it. But I just told Holloway, the CNO, that we just had to do it, and Bagley fussed because he and Bud had been predominant in setting it up. But he was not in the position to really stand up and say, "You can't do this." It became so clear that we just had to do it.

Q: Well, there are any number of things that Admiral Zumwalt had initiated that got turned around during Holloway's watch and subsequent ones.

Admiral Shear: I'm going to talk to you a great deal about that.

Q: All right.

Admiral Shear: Later on in my Vice Chief role. Okay, what else happened in the Med?

Q: Is there anything more to say about Admiral Murphy and your relationship with him?

Admiral Shear: No. Murphy did a good job. He was somewhat of a political appointee, because he was a great friend of Mel Laird. I can't say that Mel said, "Put Murphy in that job." But it was known that Murphy had close connections with Laird. But that never became an issue, never came up with me and my relationship with Murphy. He was my subordinate, and we worked very well together. I had no problem whatsoever with Murphy. As far as I'm concerned, he did a good job.

He was relieved by Fox Turner.* He was also a good man. I knew Turner, I guess, a little bit better than I did Murphy, although I knew both of them very well. I had known both of them from Washington days.

The next big thing was the Suez Canal. Suez Canal had been closed for a long time. I guess it had been closed since the '67 war.† So when I took over, it had been closed six or eight years, and then things settled down with Egypt. By that time the world had changed. Other nations had built these 200,000-ton tankers to bypass the canal and go around Africa. It was a totally different situation in maritime transportation until we cozied up to Egypt again. They decided to open the canal, and the canal was a mess. It had debris and sunken ships from one end of the canal to the other. And guess who they asked to clear it up? They asked the United States and they asked CinCUSNavEur to clear it up for them. I was given that task.

Q: Brian McCauley ran that program.

Admiral Shear: Part-time. And then he was relieved by Carroll, the fellow who really did the job.‡ I had the job of clearing the canal, and they reported to me. It was a 95% U.S. effort; there was just a minor token French and British effort. I don't think the Egyptians cared whether they ever saw a Brit or a Frenchman, because that old '56 feeling was still there. But they were there nominally to show that it was a multilateral affair. But it was probably 98% U.S. effort. We had a hell of a job clearing that canal. I first had two captains down there. I had to fire one, and I had to fire the other.

Q: What was the problem?

---

* Vice Admiral Frederick C. Turner, USN, commanded the Sixth Fleet from September 1974 to August 1976.
† In the June 1967 Six-Day War, the Israelis scored a sudden, dramatic victory over their Arab opponents.
‡ Rear Admiral Brian McCauley, USN, Commander Task Force 65, ran the operation until 3 June 1974, when he was relieved by Rear Admiral Kent J. Carroll, USN. For details, see J. Huntly Boyd, "Nimrod Spar: Clearing the Suez Canal," U.S. Naval Institute Proceedings, February 1976, pages 18-26.

Admiral Shear: They just weren't getting the job done, and they were falling behind schedule. McCauley was down there, and he did a good job. And Carroll, who followed him, did an even better job. In due course we got the canal cleared. U.S. effort cleared that canal. And the Egyptians were so delighted that they asked me if we could have the Sixth Fleet flagship take the first convoy through the canal. I had mixed emotions, because I think they wanted the Sixth Fleet flagship to be a mine tester, to see whether there were any mines left. [Laughter] Fox Turner was in the Sixth Fleet flagship, and he took her through.[*] Let's see, who was President of the Egypt at that time?

Q: Sadat.

Admiral Shear: Sadat was President.[†] He went through on the flagship, and we had a big show. First convoy, series of military ships, and Egyptian ships, led by the Sixth Fleet flagship. I must say that Fox Turner put on a hell of a show. He just treated those guys royally and steamed them through the canal. We got great accolades for the great job the U.S. had done in clearing that canal. It solidified our relationship with Egyptians no end. Shortly thereafter it became obvious that they had to improve that canal. So they went into a major widening and deepening endeavor which exists to this day. But that was quite a show. Took us a long time to get that canal cleared. I guess of all the jobs I had to do, that was the most significant in that one-year period. But we got it done, and it came off beautifully.

Q: We haven't talked about Israel. Did you have any relationships with that nation?

---

[*] On 5 June 1975, the USS Little Rock (CLG-4), the Sixth Fleet flagship, was the only foreign naval vessel in the official flotilla that made the first transit of the Suez after it reopened. The clearance operation officially ended on 23 July.
[†] Anwar el-Sadat served as President of Egypt from 1970 until he was assassinated in 1981.

Admiral Shear: I didn't have much relationship with Israel. There was no reason why I shouldn't have, and I don't think I ever visited Israel.

Q: Well, of course, we had done that massive resupply effort for them in '73, during Yom Kippur.*

Admiral Shear: Yes, that's right. I did visit Israel once. At that time you could not go from the Arab side to the Israel side. I visited Israel, and then I went over to visit King Hussein. In order to do that, I had to go up and land in Turkey and then take off from Turkey and go down into Jordan. So I did make an official visit to Israel and to Jordan. Jordan was of interest because of the Gulf of Aqaba and things of that nature. I was treated very kindly in both places, but when you go on the border they had their ramparts manned with soldiers and artillery and so forth. They weren't shooting, but they were prepared, as if to go to war. I thought it was hell of a mess right there. Supposed to be good neighbors but at arm's length with each other.

But we had no incidents during my time. I don't think we had a single incident. Everybody was as nervous as hell. I remember the Jordanian Army, which had been British trained. They were damn fine people, damn fine fighting force. They took me out in the field; they gave me a great big dinner and in one of those great big tents, you know, they have in the field and so forth and I was the guest of honor. I had to eat the traditional lamb's eye. [Laughter] I didn't give a damn about that lamb's eye. But here they made a great show of presenting this lamb's eye to the guest of honor. I had to eat the damn thing. [Laughter] Well, I gulped and swallowed and got that lamb's eye down one way or the other without having any great difficulty, but I wasn't very enthusiastic about it.

Of course, the Israelis had a tough fighting force and the Jordanians had a tough fighting force. The Israelis were best, hands down, as far as aviation was concerned. But there weren't any flies on the Jordanians either.

---

* The Arabs and Israelis fought a war in the autumn of 1973.

Q: Well, they're in an untenable position geographically because they are surrounded by so many nations that squabble with each other.

Admiral Shear: Sure, exactly. You can talk all you want, but you're never going to get the Arabs and the Israelis in a love match. It is never going to happen. It hasn't happened in 5,000 years, and it ain't going to happen in another 5,000.

Q: How much dealing did you have with U.S. diplomatic personnel in these various countries?

Admiral Shear: A lot in all the countries. I became very close to a number of the ambassadors. The ambassador to Turkey, I knew very well. The ambassador to Greece I knew very well. The ambassador to France I had a very close relationship with. You see, by that time France had withdrawn from NATO, but they were permitted to let their armed forces participate in NATO exercises.* I developed a very good working relationship with the French Navy: their Mediterranean forces, Toulon, and other forces up and down the coast. The Italian ambassador I had a good relationship with.

The Maltese ambassador I had a good relationship with, and Malta is another problem. This crazy ruler of Malta at the time was a madman.† Malta was a continuing problem. But I knew the ambassador; he spent some time with me. As a matter of fact he spent a weekend with me, I think in London. We got to know each other very well. He was the ambassador when Teheran was overrun. Later he became the assistant commandant at the National War College here in Washington.

Q: Bruce Laingen

---

* Charles de Gaulle served as President of France from 1958 to 1969. In 1966 he decided to withdraw French forces from NATO and to remove the NATO headquarters from France.
† Labour Party leader Dom Mintoff was Prime Minister of Malta from 1971 to 1984.

Admiral Shear: Bruce Laingen.* Damn fine man, a superb man. He was at Malta at that time, and I got to know him very well. So you ask if I had a lot of contact with the ambassadors and their staffs. Yes, I had a lot of contact. I had a political adviser, polad they called them, who was actually assigned to my staff, a fellow named Don Gelber. He had a lot of Turkish background, had a couple of tours in Turkey. His wife was a Turkish girl. He's now ambassador to Mali in Africa. He was a great help. He had very good relationships with all the embassies.

Q: In what ways did he help you?

Admiral Shear: Introducing me and advising me on the political issues, situations within the countries and so forth.

Q: So a lot of background.

Admiral Shear: A lot of background, yes. He was an official member of my staff, and so he had complete entrée into the embassies themselves. Many of them he knew himself, and others we got to know together. So we had a very good close working relationship, not only in the Med but in the Baltic countries and up in Norway. All those people I got to know very well. That's one of the areas where in the normal chain of things you don't necessarily get too involved in Navy life. I got deeply involved in the course of dealing with such things as the Russians in Ethiopia and the Greeks and Turks in Cyprus. That's a little bit outside the normal run of Navy stuff. And the same thing in Iran. So I got a really across-the-board experience in that one year there in the political arena.

    I recall an experience that involved one of my official visits to France and an official call on the U.S. ambassador. I went over there on a military plane with this political

---

* L. Bruce Laingen was U.S. ambassador to Iran at the time militants seized the embassy in Teheran in November 1979. He and the other hostages were finally released on 20 January 1981. For Laingen's memoir of captivity, see Yellow Ribbon: the Secret Journal of Bruce Laingen (Washington, D.C.: Brassey's [U.S.], 1992).

adviser, Don Gelber. He was superb as a State Department officer. He taught me a great deal, and he kept me out of trouble on many occasions with regard to the political intricacies of Europe. On this occasion Don was with me and we went to Europe. We went to Paris to make an official call on the ambassador. On that same day, within an hour of our arrival at the airport, Henry Kissinger was due, and the press was out there en masse to meet Henry.

Well, they saw this little fellow in glasses, Don Gelber. He looked quite a bit like Henry, and they thought it was Henry. Don and I were in the back seat, and they immediately surrounded my car with all kinds of vehicles, motorcycles, and so forth. They provided us this welcoming committee, thinking they were looking at Henry and trying to get some comments from us through the car window. They followed us all the way from the airport to the U.S. embassy, which was quite a trip. They were literally hard up against the sides of the car all the way into town.

I don't know how we didn't kill two or three of them on the way. But they were convinced that they had cornered Henry in the back of my car. I was just sitting here getting a big kick out of this. I don't know whether we ever said anything to the press or not, but they thought for sure that they had cornered Henry, and they were going to get to him before the ambassador did. As I recall, we arrived at the embassy and were swished inside and the press could not follow us. So I don't know whether they ever got a word out of Gelber or not, but that was an interesting little incident.

Q: How cordial were the relations with the French inasmuch as they had dropped out of military side on NATO?

Admiral Shear: I mentioned before that I worked very closely with the French in the Mediterranean. The French senior people down there were good people. I had a close working relationship with them, and they participated with us in practically every NATO exercise in the Mediterranean. I also made an official visit on the armed forces chief of staff in Paris, as well as the Army and the Navy CNO. So on the personal basis, even though they were officially not on NATO, my working relationships with them were very excellent.

Q: Well, that was General de Gaulle's initiative, trying to set an independent course there.

Admiral Shear: Yes.

Q: Did you ever encounter his son? He was a naval officer.

Admiral Shear: No, I did not. I knew he was, though I never encountered him.

Q: Had your time in South America helped prepare you for this job in London?

Admiral Shear: I suppose it had, because I had a very close relationship with the embassy and the staff there and also with some of the surrounding countries: Argentina, Uruguay, and things of that nature. I know it was very good background.

Q: Who handled the fort when you were out on these various travels. Was that Admiral Engen?

Admiral Shear: Admiral Engen.

Q: Please tell me more about him.

Admiral Shear: Let me tell you, Admiral Engen is a naval aviator. Among other things, after he retired he ran the FAA.[*] He ran the FAA when I was maritime administrator. For my money, he's a four-star, four-star individual, and he should have gotten four stars. He did an absolutely superb job for me. At the time he was my two-star deputy. Any time I left that staff and went outside London, I had no qualms whatsoever, because I knew things were going to be run right. And, of course, when I was in the field I'd touch base with him

---

[*] FAA--Federal Aviation Administration.

by message or by phone on a daily basis. But I never had any qualms whatsoever. He was an absolutely superb person. It's interesting that Worth Bagley was not high on him, and he was not high on Worth.* [Laughter] I just pass that on to you.

But let me tell you, we had a relationship that was absolutely superb. I had great confidence in the man, and we had a team that clicked over there--just clicked beautifully. I had strengths all down through my staff. So it was a very solid situation there.

Q: Any more staff members and their functions that you'd like to discuss?

Admiral Shear: You know, when you have a big staff of commanders and captains and so forth, they sort of fade into a group and I can't really pick out individuals. Well, let's see, I did have a very good man there in the communications intelligence area, a captain who stands out. I can't think of his name. He made flag. I can see him and his wife standing here in front of me. But I had a lot of good people. I had strength all up and down that staff, just solid strength. Some came while I was there, and most of them were there at the time I got there. But that staff had been well supplied with good people by the Navy personnel system. I didn't go out and ask for a particular handful of strong people, but they were there or they came while I was there. So I had no complaints whatsoever about that staff. Jim Barber was there with me for a short time; he did a good job. He was my administrative assistant. That was a strong staff, and under Don Engen's leadership I never had a problem. There couldn't have been a better situation.

Q: That billet later was downgraded to three stars and made subordinate to CinCSouth.

Admiral Shear: Yes.

Q: What can you say about the merits of it being a four-star billet?

---

* Admiral Engen discussed this relationship in his own oral history.

Admiral Shear: That was a very controversial issue. It came to pass under Bill Crowe.[*] It had been in the Department of Defense reorganization ideas. Every year or two, they'd send a team around the world to look at changes and consolidations that should be made or should not be made. They had been recommending such a change for a number of years. These civilian experts out of DoD would come out and make a field tour and say, "We ought to eliminate this; we ought to eliminate that." In some cases they were correct. They had already recommended two or three times before that CinCUSNavEur and CinCSouth be consolidated. In due course they were consolidated. I did not support consolidation, the British did not support consolidation. CNO didn't support consolidation.

We had a good working relationship as we were. We specifically didn't want to put ComSixthFlt under NATO. In other words, we wanted to keep that as a national responsibility, because frequently we had to respond to things that were not NATO, the African situation and so forth. That was one of the primary reasons why the CNO wanted to make sure that ComSixthFlt kept a national hat and CinCUSNavEur kept a national hat. That was one of the arguments that we went on. There were a number of these proposed consolidations. In due course it lost out, but I guess that discussion and review went on for over ten years. It was finally consummated under Bill Crowe, and Bill Crowe then became CinCSouth and CinCUSNavEur. They kept his Deputy CinCUSNavEur in London in the old headquarters as a three star. But the boss CinCUSNavEur/CinCSouth was Crowe in Naples. It's that way today.

Q: Another argument for keeping it separate was to have a four-star Navy representation to deal with the British. Was that a valid argument?

Admiral Shear: It was valid argument and one that the Brits were very strong on. They wanted to have a U.S. four-star presence there to work with and to have physically present.

---

[*] On 1 January 1983, in a realignment of command structure, the position of Commander in Chief U.S. Naval Forces Europe was assumed by Admiral William J. Crowe, Jr., USN, the four-star officer serving as Commander in Chief Allied Force Southern Europe, based in Naples. Effective that date, Vice Admiral Ronald J. Hays, USN, assumed the title of Deputy Commander in Chief U.S. Naval Forces Europe, based in London.

Q: How would you describe your dealings with the Royal Navy and the British defense establishment.

Admiral Shear: My personal dealings were excellent. I got to know them all well. I made sure I kept in close contact with them. I kept them informed on everything I was doing, as much as I could within the realms of intelligence. But we had a very good intelligence exchange between the Brits and the U.S. So I never had any problems with having to hold back anything from them. Our relationship with the First Sea Lord and with the Army and Air Force were excellent across the board.

The one year I was there, I went through two First Sea Lords.[*] Then, when I was down in Naples I went through two or three more Sea Lords and Army and Air Force heads. My relationship with the Brits was very strong. The Brits were diminishing rapidly. They were just essentially getting out of a powerful military situation. They just couldn't afford it, and the country was not doing well when I was there. They had 25% inflation, for example. The British Empire had gone, and Britain itself was not in good shape. They knew it and the British military knew it, but they put up a strong front.

George Brown used to be Chairman of the Joint Chiefs of Staff, a great man.[†] He was Air Force, one of the best generals it ever had. He'd say, "Well, the British are right down to their bands, but they've got some of the best bands in the world." They did. But my relationship with the Brits was excellent across the board. We worked very close with them, and we got to know each other, and I have close friends in that senior hierarchy today.

Q: I suppose the downgrading to three stars might also be a recognition of that diminished capability on the part of the British.

---

[*] Admiral Sir Michael Pollock, RN, served as the United Kingdom's First Sea Lord and Chief of Naval Staff, 1971-74. Admiral Sir Edward Ashmore, RN, held the office, 1974-77.
[†] General George S. Brown, USAF, served as Chairman of the Joint Chiefs of Staff from 1 July 1974 to 21 June 1978.

Admiral Shear: I'm sure it is, no question about that. And I'm sure the British did not want to see that, but it happened. Not much they could do about it.

Q: What can you say just about the business of living in England and dealing with British on a people-to-people level. Getting out and touring perhaps.

Admiral Shear: We had a handful of quarters available for our people but nowhere near enough. So the majority of my staff were on the economy, and they faced some pretty high prices. But living was good over there in spite of the inflation. We had our own commissary, but it was not too difficult living on the economy over there. Once in a while, when things were quiet, I would take a weekend and take a swing around the area or go down and visit some of the British establishments on the south coast. I'd get out to Wales, or get out to Land's End in Cornwall. Then Holy Loch was up there, where I had taken in the first ship. I'd get up to see them every once in a while.

Q: So that was probably an emotional pleasure?

Admiral Shear: Emotional, that's right. Just on a side issue here, I went over there to close it down last year after we'd been operating in there for 31 years. So in a sort of a farewell gesture, I went over and closed it down since I took the first ship in there. I must say it was a very emotional experience with us, the Scots, the Brits. They were truly hurt to see us go. But the world has changed. We went in there with 1,200-mile missile; we now have a 5,000-mile missile, and there's no longer any need to operate out of there. But it had been a tremendously successful operation from day one.

Q: Did you have any operational or administrative connection with the boomers there at Holy Loch while you were CinCUSNavEur?

Admiral Shear: Nope. They were under CinCLant, not under CinCLantFlt, and not under ComSubLant. As I told you before, they were specifically set up that way by Arleigh Burke.

Q: Well, it finally changed with the establishment of the Strategic Command.[*]

Admiral Shear: Yes, that's correct. It changed just last year. But that's how it was set up and that's how it worked for over 30 years. It worked beautifully.

So I had no official responsibility there, but I did have a very close working relationship with CinCLant, who at that time was Ralph Cousins.[†] Ralph Cousins and Bagley had not gotten along well with each other. And, quite frankly, Ralph Cousins didn't know why. But Bagley was kind of short and nasty with Ralph Cousins. I knew this before I went over, and the CNO knew it. One of the few directions that Jim Holloway told me was, "When you get over there, one of the first things I want you to do is to clear up this relationship between CinCLant and CinCUSNavEur." Hell, it took me 30 minutes to do that.

See, Ralph Cousins had been my boss in OP-31. He was OP-03 at that time. Then, when I was OP-95, he was Vice Chief. So I had known Ralph three or four years there and got along very well with him. So I got on the phone about the second day I was in London. I said, "Ralph, I'm on the scene here. Everything's in good shape, and I'm going to make damn sure that things work well with you." On top of that, his deputy was my good friend and classmate, Doug Plate.[‡] We had a love affair there the rest of my time, so we literally cleaned that up in 30 minutes. I don't know why there was this little hate contest between Ralph and Worth. I just don't know why, but there was, and it was not healthy, but we cleaned it up. That was one of the easiest jobs I had over there, just to clean that up. [Laughter]. It took literally a phone call. From then on, almost on a daily basis, either

---

[*] On 1 June 1992 the joint-service U.S. Strategic Command was established.
[†] Admiral Ralph W. Cousins, USN, served as SACLant, CinCLant, and CinCLantFlt from 1972 to 1975.
[‡] Vice Admiral Douglas C. Plate, USN.

Ralph or Doug Plate or I would be on the phone with each other on any little problem that came up that we had to do something about. It worked out very well.

Q: In connection with the British, did you get presented at court and that formal business?

Admiral Shear: No, I did not get presented at court. That was done by the ambassador, and I got along very well with him. You would know him, a great Republican, he has this big place out in Palm Springs.

Q: Annenberg.

Admiral Shear: Annenberg.[*] And I must say Annenberg did a hell of a good job over there.

Q: Which is interesting, because he had no background for it.

Admiral Shear: That's right, but he had unlimited monies; he had unlimited monies. He would throw big parties for the Brits and so forth, and he also did a good official job over there. His office was just across the street. Anytime I had to go over and see him, I went over to see him. I treated him well and had him over to see my place once in a while. It was a very good working relationship.

I'm going to tell you a little story that I had down here to make a note on. Lord Louie Mountbatten was a good friend of mine. I told you about keeping the "Dear Dickie" file as one of my jobs in OP-60. And then, when I went to the Holy Loch, Mountbatten was intensely interested, because they were building Polaris submarines right behind us with all of our help. So he came up and spent a half a day with me. I took him all through the ship and gave him a detailed brief, had him for lunch on board, and he was tickled to death. So that started our personal relationship. Later on and he was sort of a special assistant to the Queen. Of course, he was related to the Queen, and they had a very close relationship

---

[*] Walter H. Annenberg served as U.S. ambassador to Great Britain and Northern Ireland from 1969 to 1974.

with each other. He and Philip had a very close relationship.* Philip sort of idolized the man.

Q: Well, I think his sister was Philip's mother, wasn't it?

Admiral Shear: Yes, something like that. So I would see him in London periodically. So I met the Queen through one of the things that they threw over there, but I was never presented to her. I just met her as the senior military guy on the scene. Lord Louie introduced me to her. Delightful lady, I must say. Tragic ending for Lord Louie.† He was a great man; I thought a great deal of him. It turned out I was the official NATO rep to his funeral, later on when I was CinCSouth.

Q: Did he stop by and visit from time to time?

Admiral Shear: I would go to his headquarters. By that time he was just on the staff of the Queen at that time.

Q: Sort of a gray eminence.

Admiral Shear: Gray eminence, exactly. Gray eminence. First Sea Lord. There were two First Sea Lords when I was there, both of them good men. Terry Lewin was later on, when I was down at Naples.‡ My relationship with the Brits was excellent, across the board. I knew their strengths and weaknesses, and they knew that I knew their strengths and weaknesses.

---

* Prince Philip, the Duke of Edinburgh, is the husband of Queen Elizabeth II.
† Mountbatten was assassinated by Irish terrorists on 27 August 1979. For Prince Philip's memoir on his uncle, see "Lord Louis," U.S. Naval Institute Proceedings, February 1980, pages 26-35.
‡ Admiral Sir Terence Lewin, RN, served as the United Kingdom's First Sea Lord and Chief of Naval Staff, 1977-79. He was subsequently Chief of Defence Staff, 1979-82.

Q: Were there ever any reservations on candor in dealing with the British?

Admiral Shear: None, none. I called a spade a spade, and they would do the same with me. They never had any reservations. We did have a very good intelligence relationship with them too--black intelligence as well as standard intelligence. You know, black programs and things of that nature.

Q: How much were you kept informed on the situation throughout the Navy as a whole? Did the CNO periodically put out information to all the CinCs?

Admiral Shear: Yes, he did. Yes, he did. Even more than that, we would go back every three or four months for a CinCs' conference with the CNO. I would fly back from London. The CinCs would come in from the Pacific and so forth, and we'd have about three days of sitting here with the CNO and going over everything that went on, everything in the Navy. So we were fully up to date, and we had a good exchange going on all the time. Jim Holloway was particularly effective in keeping us well informed.

I had a couple of other things I wanted to tell you here before I left CinCUSNavEur. I told you that the Army and the Air Force were mesmerized over the Central Front. I didn't get much out of them when I had problems in the flanks. Haig understood the picture. Well, I must say his staff didn't. They never understood that the real problems were in the flanks: the Greeks and Turks, things in Africa and so forth. They never got very excited about that. I essentially had that in my own hands. I think Haig appreciated the way I handled those things.

I think I touched on everything that I wanted to touch about. I'll probably go home and forget something. We hit the situation in Teheran, we hit the situation in Iran, we hit the situation all through the Middle East there.

Q: Could you perhaps say a little more about the role of the Middle East Force per se?

Admiral Shear: The Middle East Force was a flag-showing force. It traditionally had been two destroyers and some sort of flagship for the staff. The <u>La Salle</u> was out there for many years. Tom Bigley was ComMidEast Force as a rear admiral while I was there.[*] He later on became vice admiral here in Washington. Tom Bigley was a very good man, a submariner. I'd known him before, and every time I went out there, I stayed in his quarters.

He was very close to the Emir of Bahrain, and he was also very close to the U.S. ambassador there in Bahrain. Through him I met both of them and became well acquainted with them. He had kind of a kooky ambassador out there, kooky guy. Wasn't much help, but he was there. Bigley got along all right with him, but he was not the best ambassador we had seen. But he was there in Bahrain, and you had a strong ambassador in Saudi Arabia. You had a strong ambassador in Iran. I forget who was the ambassador in Kuwait, but I visited him and he was a good man. Bigley's job was essentially to show a flag, and he'd make the rounds periodically, visit all the ports, and have the leaders on board for dinners and things like that. And he would be entertained by them. The British had left a vacuum out there. That was British territory, and they abandoned ship east of Suez. They just abandoned it. That was part of their retraction. That was part of their just becoming a minor power.

Q: That was from the late '60s on.

Admiral Shear: That's correct. They just pulled out. Well, we had to fill that vacuum, or else the Russians were going to fill it. Wasn't any question about that. The U.S. Middle East Force had been out there for many, many years, but their role expanded, even though we didn't increase the size much more. The role expanded because the British had gone, and the vacuum was there. So we had to fill that as far as the Western presence is

---

[*] Rear Admiral Thomas J. Bigley, USN, served as Commander Middle East Force from 20 February 1975 to 30 June 1976.

concerned, and they did a good job. There was a series of these force commanders, one after another. Bill Crowe had that job as a two-star.*

So the Middle East Force paid its way without question, and they did a good job. They had a series of good commanders. This was all before the Gulf War and things of that nature.† They were on the scene, and, of course, as I told you, the Russians moved in there, strengthened Ethiopia and Somalia and other parts of Africa. About all they could do was steam up and down and count the number of Russian ships there. They had no offensive capability against them. But their presence was there, and they showed it.

Q: One other thing I wanted to ask you about. In 1972 there had been the negotiations with the Soviets on the Incidents at Sea agreement to cut down on the harassment. What did you see in the wake of that agreement?

Admiral Shear: I had been on the edges of that. John Warner was the principal negotiator, and he did a pretty good job of it. As you know, we'd had these shouldering incidents, close-aboard ships, and things that were just unseamanlike. They were unnecessarily unseamanlike. I'm not sure that we weren't maybe 50% at fault as the Russians. We always alleged that it was the Russian thing, but, as a matter of fact, I know we pulled some of it ourselves.

I don't recall that we had any major problems in the Med when I was there as far as incidents at sea. We watched them like a hawk, and we knew where every ship was practically all the time. We knew their anchorages, we knew where they were operating, and we had forces either close around them or right with them. And we watched them going in and out of the Black Sea. We had very close intelligence on anything that took

---

* Rear Admiral William J. Crowe, Jr., USN, served as Commander Middle East Force from 30 June 1976 to 4 July 1977.
† In January 1991 U.S. and Allied Coalition forces attacked Iraq to get it to retreat following its August 1990 invasion of neighboring Kuwait. The resulting conflict became known variously as Operation Desert Storm and the Gulf War. Coalition forces won the war in February 1991.

place there. I can't say that I had, when I was there, any major problems with the Soviet afloat forces.

Q: It sounds as if the agreement worked.

Admiral Shear: Yes, I think it did pretty well. I think both sides realized it was kind of dumb to get involved in these things.

Q: When Jerry Miller was Sixth Fleet Commander, he made deliberate attempts to cultivate the Soviet Navy and put it on a professional sailor basis rather than the political so much.

Admiral Shear: Yep. I don't think he had any success. I can't say that I had any problems there.

I'm just looking here to see if there is anything else I wanted to mention about the Sixth Fleet. When I talk about CinCSouth, I want to talk about Haig and Stan Turner. Haig didn't trust Turner as far as he could throw him. I want to get into that later.

Let's move on. My next job was Vice Chief. Worth Bagley decided to retire early. I got a call from Jim Holloway one day. He said, "Worth's going to retire, and I want you to come back and take the job."

Q: Did he say why he had picked you?

Admiral Shear: No. He just said, "I want you to come back and take the job." It had to be either a destroyerman or a submariner. It couldn't be another aviator.

So I said, "Good gosh, Jim, I thought I was going to be over here for three years and retire when you retire."

He said, "Well, things have changed, and I want you to come back and take this job."

I said, "Well, you honor me, and, of course, I'm delighted to come back and take it." My wife almost shot me on the scene. [Laughter] She wanted to be over there for three years in Europe.

Q: I can't blame her.

Admiral Shear: Yes. Well, I worked hard in that job, and he knew I worked hard at it. He said, "Look, I want you to come back and take the Vice Chief job."

I said, "All right, Jim, I'll come back. When you do want me?" He gave me a date. It was right around the corner. So in less than a year I went back there and took the Vice Chief job. I must say that I could not have worked for a better man than Jim Holloway. I think the world of him. There was some feeling there. I don't know why Worth retired early, but I got a pretty good idea. Because he was Zumwalt's boy. Hands down, he was Zumwalt's boy. Although I'm sure he worked conscientiously for Jim Holloway, he was not Holloway's boy; he was Zumwalt's boy. So I could see where that relationship was not going to be the strongest in the world, and I think Worth saw it. He stayed there for a year and retired. So I went back in the summer of '75. I went over to London in May of '74 and came back in May of '75 and took over from Worth and became the Vice Chief.

Vice Chief is a good job, and it's a tough job. The Vice Chief runs the Navy. The CNO is part of the Joint Chiefs. He's the point of contact to the White House and point of contact with the Hill.* The Vice Chief runs the Navy. And I ran that Navy with a very firm hand, a very fair hand. Anyone will tell you that I ran the Navy with a firm hand. I was tough when I had to be, but I was never nasty tough. I enjoyed that job tremendously, and I think Holloway had full confidence in me; we got along very well. Of course, whenever he was out of town, I'd go down and represent him at the Joint Staff and never had any problems there. George Brown was chairman at the time; I got along very well with

---

* The Hill refers to Capitol Hill--the Congress.

George Brown. He was relieved by Davy Jones; Davy Jones was a disaster.[*] You've probably heard something about Davy Jones.

Q: No, I hadn't heard that term used to describe him.

Admiral Shear: He was probably the weakest Chairman we've ever had. Who do you suppose put him in there? Jimmy Carter put him in there because he wanted a "yes" man, which was what he got. I'd seen Davy Jones in action as the Chief Staff of the Air Force. I'd seen him in action in the Tank on JCS matters.[†] I didn't think much of Jones. You could see he was by far the weakest of his compatriots. He just wasn't a man of their stature. He wasn't like Holloway, wasn't like Brown, wasn't like the Chief Staff of the Army. He just wasn't that caliber man, but he got the job because I think Carter knew that he wasn't going to give him any trouble. I'll just pass that on. I'd see him in action periodically then. I had him pretty well spotted, as did everybody else.

    I had that Vice Chief job for two years. And I'm going to tell you something--that probably the most important thing I did in 42 years of active duty was to get the Navy pulled together and back to battery after Zumwalt. I had been on Zumwalt's staff four years. I worked with him closely, and I liked him, and I supported him, but I didn't like some of the things he was doing. And he did some great things. What he did with regard to racism, to blacks, and to women and so forth was absolutely positive. All the other things he did were not good for the Navy. Something that Holloway and I had to do was quietly and firmly get the Navy back to battery. We never put out anything that said that we were getting the Navy back to battery, but we just slowly and calmly just took a round

---

[*] General David C. Jones, USAF, served as Air Force Chief of Staff from 1 July 1974 to 20 June 1978. He was Chairman of the Joint Chiefs of Staff from 21 June 1978 to 18 June 1982.

[†] "Tank" refers to the room in the Pentagon in which the Joint Chiefs of Staff meet on a regular basis.

turn, just took a round turn.* Squeezed the ratchet a little bit, and it became obvious in a matter of months that we were getting the Navy back where it ought to be.

Q: This was not the sort of thing that Admiral Bagley would have been inclined to work on, given his loyalty to Zumwalt.

Admiral Shear: Quite the opposite, quite the opposite. But we never put out anything, and you ask either one of us what we were doing while we were turning all this thing around, we never said anything. We just did it--very, very quietly and very, very gently. But in a matter of months you could see that the Navy was changing for the better.

Q: Did you have a list of things made up as an agenda? Did you deal with them on an ad hoc basis? How did it come about?

Admiral Shear: Holloway and I never sat down and made up a list of things we should do. We just in our own mind knew what had to be done, and we did it.

Q: Do you have a number of examples that you might mention?

Admiral Shear: Well, yes. Appearance. The Navy had gotten sloppy. We just quietly got the word out to the fleet commanders and others that we were going to tighten up. Did we put something in writing like that? Absolutely not, no. We just got the word out.

Q: Did you have the sense that they welcomed this directive?

Admiral Shear: Absolutely. I guess we did put out written directives on a couple of things, but mostly it was just very quiet verbal information that things were going to change. We

---

* In nautical phraseology, taking a round turn means putting two loops of line over a bitt or bollard, thus restraining the ship at the other end of the line. In a figurative sense, it means restraining unwanted behavior.

didn't have any row. It wasn't any big publicity that, "By golly, we're dropping Zumwalt, we're changing things in a different way." Nothing like that ever took place. But we just very quietly, by actions--or inactions, in some cases--we just made sure that the Navy was changing.

Q: Well, this was really a contrast with Admiral Hayward's approach later. He put a label on it: "Pride and professionalism."*

Admiral Shear: Yes, yes, and we were doing the same thing. I don't think we ever put a label on anything we were doing, but, as I say, I think it's the most important thing I ever did in 42 years of active duty.

Q: Were these mostly personnel-type issues that were involved?

Admiral Shear: I don't know that I'd say mostly; I'd say operations and personnel. I think personnel was probably one of the most obvious ones. Because the Navy had gotten very sloppy. Discipline. Tailhook would never have occurred with Holloway and Shear.† It would never have happened. We'd have been on that just like that. [Snaps fingers] We would have had people relieved the next day. I don't know if you ever heard about the Cat Futch situation.‡

---

* Admiral Thomas B. Hayward, USN, served as Chief of Naval Operations from 1 July 1978 to 30 June 1982.
† Following the Tailhook Association's 1991 convention in Las Vegas, a number of women complained of being mistreated by naval officers in attendance. There were other allegations of inappropriate behavior. A long, largely inconclusive investigation followed. The upshot was damage to the Navy's overall reputation and to that of naval aviation in particular. For a detailed analysis, see "Tailhook: What Happened, Why & What's to be Learned," U.S. Naval Institute Proceedings, September 1994, pages 89-103.
‡ On 10 July 1975 Commander Connelly D. Stevenson, USN, permitted stripper Cat Futch to dance topless on the deck of the USS Finback (SSN-670) as the nuclear submarine sailed out of Port Canaveral, Florida. Stevenson was removed from command and subsequently received a disciplinary letter.

Q: Yes, she was a stripper on USS Finback.

Admiral Shear: Yes. We handled that in about 30 minutes. We got the skipper off the ship, had him relieved. We got that out of the press; it was in the press about a day. We killed that. I picked up the phone to my good friend Ike Kidd and said, "Ike, we've got to do something about this fast."[*]

He said, "Don't worry, I'm already ahead of you. I told ComSubLant to get that skipper out of there today."[†] And it was done. Now, we could have done the same thing in Tailhook, exactly the same thing. We'd have hurt some three stars, and we'd have hurt a bunch of squadron commanders, perhaps some of them unjustly, but the thing would have been killed right there. Now it's dragged on for a year and a half, and it's still not killed.

Q: Well, another argument that might be made is that you would not have let an environment develop that would have permitted it in the first place.

Admiral Shear: Exactly, exactly. That's right. So in due course we got the Navy turned around, quite quickly.

Q: One initiative I remember was the return to bell-bottom uniforms.[‡]

Admiral Shear: Yes, uniforms, and haircuts, and beards and all that stuff. We quietly turned that stuff off. And the Z-gram situation--we killed that, of course. Don't misunderstand me now. I worked for Bud for four years, a year as OP-31 and three years as OP-095. I liked Bud, and Bud was very good to me. And we worked well together,

---

[*] Admiral Isaac C. Kidd, Jr., USN, served as Supreme Allied Commander Atlantic, Commander in Chief Atlantic, and Commander in Chief Atlantic Fleet from 1975 to 1978.
[†] ComSubLant--Commander Submarine Force Atlantic Fleet.
[‡] On 1 August 1977 the Navy announced that the uniforms for enlisted personnel below chief petty officer would return to the bell-bottom trousers, jumpers, and white hats that had been traditional prior to 1971 when Admiral Zumwalt introduced coat-and-tie uniforms with visored caps.

particularly in the professional business of hardware and things like that. When I disagreed with Bud, of course, I never did so publicly; I just disagreed with a lot of his letting down the bars in the personnel area. I agreed with him wholeheartedly in what he did with regard to blacks and the women. I think it was long, long overdue. These were things that I had done as a matter of course with my own ships. Hell, I was way ahead of the Navy as far as treatment of blacks and so forth. But Bud made it Navy-wide, and I give him great credit for that, great credit for that.

Q: Well, it has to be done Navy-wide, because just doing it in an individual ship doesn't provide the billet opportunities.

Admiral Shear: Exactly correct. So I give him great credit for that, but on other things we part company.

Q: What do you remember about drugs as a developing problem during those years?

Admiral Shear: We had drug problems. We put out very strong directives against it. And when it occurred, we were ruthless in taking immediate action. I don't recall exactly what directives we put out, but I know we put out a number. I think drugs really developed out of the Vietnam War. But I don't think we've wiped out drugs. We made an impact. I think what Tom Hayward did as a follow-on was very, very good. He probably did more than we did.

Q: My sense is that Admiral Hayward's tenure was when the drug problem really got knocked off in the Navy.

Admiral Shear: We were working hard on it, but I think Tom finished it up.

Q: He had the zero-tolerance approach.

Admiral Shear: That's right. That's correct. That's so. If I had thought of it, we would have done the same thing. But I give him credit for it. We did what we could; we didn't do enough. But we did turn the Navy around.

Q: What do you remember about operations in the post-Vietnam era?

Admiral Shear: It was short of petty officers. On occasion we had to cross-deck, which is always bad in order to fill up one ship before she deploys.* That's bad on morale, that's bad on continuity, it's bad on status quos, and it's bad on keeping people for any length of time. Moving men from ship to ship is always bad. We had some of that in the '70s because we had shortages everywhere. I guess the cause for that was demobilization after the Vietnam War.

Q: Had Admiral Zumwalt's initiatives improved the retention picture? That was one of his big concerns.

Admiral Shear: I don't know. Enlistment rates were down. I forget exactly how much we picked them up. There wasn't any question, we had shortages.

Q: Well, another issue was the all-volunteer force so that there was no longer the threat of a draft to bring people into the Navy.

Admiral Shear: That's correct. And the all-volunteer force clearly showed itself over the years as the way to go. Drafting people for two years, you can't really get them trained. In time of war you've got to do that. I had a lot of two-year sailors in my ship out there in Vietnam. But any time you can get a volunteer four to six years, you can start making a real petty officer out of him.

---

* Cross-deck means to transfer personnel from one ship to another, generally used to refer to beefing up the crew of a ship that is about to make an overseas deployment.

I'm just trying to think of any specifics in the personnel era that we did. Some of the Sixth Fleet ships, some of the Atlantic Fleet ships, some of the Pacific Fleet ships had severe shortages. We kept track of CasReps, including personnel CasReps, as closely as we could.* I can't say what things were at the start of Jim Holloway's tour, versus what they looked like at the end of his tour in numbers. I just don't recall. Things get too hazy. But he was a hell of a good CNO.

Q: Well, please tell me about your personal relationship with him.

Admiral Shear: My personal relationships were excellent. I saw him on a daily basis. We had a regular morning briefing every day, and we had a senior conference, either just before or just after the briefing. I think he had complete confidence in me. I know I had complete confidence in him. We knew each other well. We lived right beside each other over there in that little oasis across the street from the State Department on 23rd Street. Any time he was out of town, I'm sure he didn't have any qualms about my being here running things on the local scene, just as I had complete confidence in Don Engen when I was in London. On a daily basis and on a long-term basis, I think we worked very well together.

Q: What do you remember about his personality?

Admiral Shear: Jim Holloway is a hell of a good guy. Do you know Jim Holloway?

Q: Not well, but I've certainly met him on a number of occasions.

Admiral Shear: Hell of a good guy, got a sense of humor.

Q: Very smooth.

---

* CasReps--casualty reports cover problems that diminish the readiness of a ship or other unit to carry out its mission.

Admiral Shear: Very smooth, very smooth. He can go into a crowd, for example, and work that crowd. He was very competent working the Hill. He had good contacts over there; many he knew personally. He could go over to the Hill with a problem and people like Senator Stennis and others he just handled very, very smoothly, very effectively.* I think he was a great CNO; I think he was a great member of the Joint Chiefs. We didn't have too much contact with the White House. We'd go over there periodically.

Once or twice I went over when he was out of town. The Carter White House didn't call the military over there very often. I think Holloway might have felt--I really can't say this to be a fact--that the White House really didn't really pay as much attention to the military as they should have. As far as the selection of flag officers, that's one of the responsibilities of the Secretary and CNO. He always brought me into the review of who was going to go to what job and so forth. I think he always accepted my input to those deliberations. Sometimes you have to take some very tough action when you move flag officers around. And sometimes it was not the most pleasant thing, but we worked very well, very well together on that, and I think he paid attention to my recommendations to him and, of course, his recommendations to the Secretary.

We had two Secretaries. The first Secretary was Bill Middendorf.† A lot of people thought Bill Middendorf was a stumblebum. Let me tell you, Bill Middendorf was not a stumblebum. He was a smart guy. He had great political influence. He was wealthy, and he kept out of the CNO's hair. He made a point of keeping out of the CNO's hair. He was very effective with the Hill. He'd go up to the Hill, and, Christ, we'd get a half dozen ships. Not too many people thought that Bill Middendorf was a good Secretary. I believe he was a very good Secretary. If he had done nothing else but keep out of the CNO's hair, he'd have been a good Secretary. And he did that. He never questioned anything that Jim Holloway wanted to do with regard to moving flags around or anything of that nature. He never got in his hair nor hung over his desk or anything like that.

---

* Senator John C. Stennis (Democrat-Mississippi) had an interest in military affairs for many, many years. The aircraft carrier John C. Stennis (CVN-74) is named in his honor.
† J. William Middendorf II served as Secretary of the Navy from 1974 to 1977.

He just ran his own show, and he was great at the things he wanted to do. Sometimes he'd grab me and say, "Well, Hal, I want you to come and greet this bunch of friends of mine. What's going on?" Middendorf and I had--as well as Holloway--had a very good working relationship. He got to know me when I was CinCUSNavEur. He came over and spent a week with me once, and I did everything with him. I took him all around the British people and the London area. I had a couple of big dinner parties for him. I found that he liked to work out. So every morning I'd get him up and jog him. A couple of times I jogged him so that I just about wore him out. I was in pretty good shape. I jogged every day myself. So I got to know him well, and he liked me. So when I went back as Vice Chief we got along very well there. He was always hitting me up for some little chore that he wanted done, and I always took care of it in a simple way, and he liked that.

Q: Why do you think he got this reputation in some quarters as a stumblebum?

Admiral Shear: He looked like a stumblebum. You know, he was kind of a big fellow, kind of wandering around a bit off center and so forth. And I guess some of his political cohorts didn't think he was the hottest guy in the world. As far as I'm concerned, he did a damn good job as the Secretary of the Navy. And he was relieved by Graham Claytor.[*] And with Claytor in came Jim Woolsey.[†] Jim Woolsey was kind of a not-dry-behind-the-ears liberal type, and he knew absolutely nothing about the military. Jim Holloway said, "Okay, Hal, the Under Secretary is yours. You take him and you educate him." Well, I did. Woolsey didn't think much of the military, and I rubbed his nose in everything. I really rubbed his nose in everything.

Of course, any decision I always took the issue to him and explained it to him, and in due course he learned to respect us. But he came in with lots of reservations about anybody in a blue suit. I worked hard to make him understand that, by golly, we have some

---

[*] W. Graham Claytor, Jr., served as Secretary of the Navy from 1977 to 1979.
[†] R. James Woolsey served as Under Secretary of the Navy from 9 March 1977 to 7 December 1979.

pretty damn good people, and we knew what we were doing. Holloway knows to this day that I educated Woolsey; it took some doing.

Q: But to give Woolsey his credit, he's a sharp guy.

Admiral Shear: He's sharp as hell. And I like Woolsey; I like him today as a friend. But let me tell you, when he came into that office he was green as grass. He didn't know anything, and he had his mind made up. He had to get a lot of education quick.

Q: Well, it sounds as if he had an open mind, though, in this education process.

Admiral Shear: He had a open mind, and it took some doing. I must say, he absorbed things pretty quickly. Because when Holloway gave me that job, he said, "You educate the Under." And I did. By God, I kept my finger on him every minute.

Q: Claytor was not green; he was very experienced.

Admiral Shear: He was very experienced, and he'd had an excellent war record. He had command of a DE. He was the guy that found the Indianapolis and the survivors in the water.* And he was a nice guy, very experienced. He had been head of that big railroad. Knew his stuff around Washington. Knew his stuff around industry. He was a very competent man, and I liked him. He came over and visited me a couple of times in Europe. He was a little bit of a no-nonsense type, but that's all right, nothing wrong with that. I don't think that he gave Holloway quite the free hand that Middendorf did as far as flags were concerned. Although I must say that I don't think he gave Jim much difficulty either.

---

* As a lieutenant commander, USNR, Claytor was commanding officer of the USS Cecil J. Doyle (DE-368) in early August 1945 when she rescued survivors from the heavy cruiser Indianapolis (CA-35), which a Japanese submarine had torpedoed and sunk a few days earlier.

Q: What do you remember of Harold Brown, who was Secretary of Defense under Carter?

Admiral Shear: Harold Brown was a very good technical man.[*] I had quite a bit of contact with Harold Brown. He had a guy named Fubini, who was sort of his--he was a jumpy and excitable former Italian who was a brain, a whiz brain.[†] He had entrée into Harold Brown's office any hour of the night or day. I had quite a bit of contact with Fubini, who was then working as a civilian. Anything I had to do and I had to get through, if I could get Fubini convinced, it was done.

Q: You talked about some of the problems involved in flag slating. What were those problems?

Admiral Shear: Well, when you go through the selection process, the Secretary of the Navy writes the precept, which is presented to the board. That precept may say, "Well, you must select an officer with this background and so forth." That's perfectly legal. And I must say that neither Middendorf or Claytor ever violated selection boards. Lehman, on the other hand, did--the son of a bitch.[‡] I don't know any naval officer who doesn't despise Lehman. But they never got in and changed the system. It has always been inviolate that the selection boards get a precept, and then they make a selection, and no one ever challenges their selections. They take the best suited. There are hairline differences, and sometimes if you have 30, you'd like to have 32, squeezing in a couple of good, good extra hot-shot captains, but you can't always do that.

Then, of course, you had to assign these officers. And that is basically the CNO's job, and he always keeps the Secretary informed. When it's a three- or four-star assignment, I guess he would always make sure that the Secretary is in full agreement as to

---

[*] Harold Brown served as Secretary of Defense, 1977-81. He had previously been Secretary of the Air Force, 1965-69.
[†] Eugene G. Fubini was chairman of the Defense Science Board.
[‡] John F. Lehman served as Secretary of the Navy from 1981 to 1987.

why they selected this officer and what he is going to do and so forth. I must say that both Middendorf and Claytor were very good about paying attention to the CNO's decisions.

Q: How much personal knowledge did you have of those three and four stars?

Admiral Shear: Well, the people involved in the selection process were basically the CNO, the Vice Chief, and the Chief of Naval personnel. At that time Jim Watkins was Chief of Naval Personnel.[*]

Q: But you probably knew all of these people.

Admiral Shear: We knew them well. At that time the three of us were the principal selectors, and we knew them well. The CNO always made the last selection, but he always paid attention to what either Watkins had to say or what I had to say. Then he would take it to the Secretary and say, "These are my choices. I recommend these people for such and such reason." Unless there was some reason otherwise, the Secretary would go along with it. Once in a while you would get a little political pressure. Stennis was not adverse to putting a little pressure on from time to time, and I guess Mel Laird was the same way.

Q: Apparently, Means Johnston got that CinCSouth job from his Stennis connection.

Admiral Shear: You said that; I didn't say it. I think that's correct.

One thing that Jim Holloway told me was, "Now, sometimes the chaplains can be problems, and I want you, Shear, to make damn sure that you keep the chaplains happy."

I said a cheery, "Aye-aye, I'll keep the chaplains happy." The Chief of Chaplains was a superb guy named John O'Connor.[†] He's now Cardinal O'Connor in New York. I struck up a relationship with O'Connor to make damn sure that I knew what he wanted, and

---

[*] Vice Admiral James D. Watkins, USN, served as Chief of Naval Personnel from 10 April 1975 to 21 July 1978. He later served as Chief of Naval Operations, 1982-86.
[†] Rear Admiral John J. O'Connor, CHC, USN.

in any possible way I'd give him what he wanted. So about once a month or six weeks, I would have O'Connor over for an inner sanctum luncheon in my office. I'd set up a little two-man table there, and we'd have a nice lunch together. I'd keep him informed on what was going on in the Navy, and I'd ask him to let me know how things were going with the chaplains. I'd ask him how many black chaplains he had and if he had any problems anywhere in the chaplain area and what I could do to help him. I kept this relationship going, very closely, and we never had the slightest problem with chaplains. Every once in a while chaplains can be a problem, just as doctors can be a problem. I think Jim always appreciated that I kept the chaplains in pretty good shape.

Q: O'Connor was a real activist as the Chief of Chaplains. He initiated a number of changes.

Admiral Shear: Yes, but it wasn't anything that was bad for the Navy there.

Q: Oh, no.

Admiral Shear: Of course, he's very active in New York, where some things are quite controversial. But I established a very good relationship with O'Connor, and I worked well. He was happy, and we never had the slightest problems with the chaplains.

  I also did as much as I could with the Surgeon General, a good working relationship with him. We'd had some problems with the doctors, and Arentzen was the Surgeon General.[*] We'd had a guy before who wasn't too sharp.[†] Arentzen took over, and Arentzen was a very good professional top-notch doctor. He did a good job. We had some shortages with doctors after Vietnam. We did the best we could to clean that up.

---

[*] Vice Admiral Willard P. Arentzen, MC, USN, served as the Navy's Surgeon General from 1976 to 1980.
[†] Vice Admiral Donald L. Custis, MC, USN, was Arentzen's predecessor.

As far as the day-to-day routine of running the Navy, that went on well. At a moment's notice I could have CinCLantFlt on the phone or CinCPacFlt on the phone. We kept each other fully informed, and we ran a good show.

Q: The CNO and VCNO are not in the operational chain, but they certainly have an impact. Could you describe that impact?

Admiral Shear: On the operational chain they worked for the Joint Chiefs, but the service commander, whether he is Army, Navy, or Air Force has a great deal of impact, a great deal of responsibility as far as the forces are concerned. He's responsible for training and things of that nature. And the fleet commanders, even though they ostensibly work through their CinCs--CinCLant or CinCPac--they also work very closely with the CNO. That's the kind of contact that Holloway and I kept with the fleet commanders, and that worked well; we never had any great problems.

We had the usual problems of the manning levels, which were inherent at the time, true in all forces. We did what we could to improve them, and gradually we built up numbers of career people the best we could. It took a number of years to do that. I guess it took a couple of CNOs before it really got that in shape, after that drawdown after Vietnam.

As far the subordinates in OpNav--the three-star barons for surface forces, submarine forces, air forces, and logistic people--I would have a conference with them at least once a week. Sometimes I'd have to do a little bit of dictating to the barons as to who was going to get what and where, forces and so forth. I guess some of them thought that I was pretty arbitrary, but I always tried to be as fair as I could. We had good people. Bob Long was OP-02 at the time; Jim Doyle was OP-03, surface; and Fred Turner was OP-05.[*] He'd been with me in the Sixth Fleet.[†] We had good working relationships, and we all knew each other well. We were all aimed at doing a good job and keeping the CNO out of

---

[*] Vice Admiral Robert L. J. Long, USN; Vice Admiral James H. Doyle, USN; Vice Admiral Frederick C. Turner, USN.
[†] Vice Admiral Turner commanded the Sixth Fleet from September 1974 to August 1976.

trouble, and we did just that. I didn't have to knock heads together very often, but they knew I was quite capable if I had to do it. So we had good working relationships.

Q: How much did you get involved in the budgetary process and program planning?

Admiral Shear: Quite a bit. OP-090 was sort of a Mr. Big there. And, of course, I had been deeply involved in that as OP-095, where I had to make sure that I had adequate cuts from all three of the barons--surface, submarine, and aviation. So I had a lot of experience in running with the budget people. We had Red Dog Davis as OP-090 then.[*] He became a four-star. Good man. Good man. Quite an individual.

Q: Well, you had capable people in all of these jobs, so it was probably a case of monitoring in many instances.

Admiral Shear: Yes, monitoring, but at the same time you've got to give them some guidance, because they've got to have some guidance. And then the money is a big part of it. OP-090 has to work very closely with the CNO and the Vice Chief before he lays out monies that, for example, OP-05, aviation, can have. How much they can count on, how much money the submariners can have. I guess you sort of manipulate, and you're limited by the total budget. You never have everything you want, so you have to divide what's available. And, of course, the budget process is always presented to the CNO as it goes along in a series of presentations. The actual handing out after the decisions are made is done by OP-090, which incidentally was Worth Bagley's job for Bud Zumwalt. He ran that job very, very tightly. And Red Dog Davis did the same thing for Jim Holloway. I think very highly of Red Dog; I think he did a good job. I don't even know his first name. All we ever called him was "Red Dog." [Laughter]

Q: Did you get into any cases of refereeing among these various claimants?

---

[*] Vice Admiral Donald C. Davis, USN.

Admiral Shear: Yes, frequently.

Q: Any examples that come to mind?

Admiral Shear: Frequently, frequently, and even more in OP-095 than I did as Vice Chief. By the time Red Dog Davis had to actually allocate funds, we'd had a few knock-down, drag-out sessions. And the three-stars, in the presentations to the CNO in the budget reviews, always had the opportunity to make their cases. Sometimes you had to make the decisions right there. They had to be reviewed by the CNO. It was something that Davis or I might do, but they'd always have recourse with the CNO. But we didn't have any major problems as far as divvying up money. You never had enough. That's just the nature of the beast; you never had enough. But everybody had to get a fair share.

As Vice Chief I kept out of the hardware as much as I could. As OP-095 I was in the middle of hardware decisions daily--monitoring the various programs and making sure what things we wanted to stress. For example, in the ASW area, it was towed arrays and helicopters, P-3 aircraft and S-3 aircraft, electronic countermeasures, and so forth. All of those I kept right at my fingertip. As Vice Chief I didn't have to do that; as a matter of fact I couldn't do that, because there was just too much going on. But I made sure that the three-stars were on top of all those programs, because that was their responsibility; that's what they had to do. And, of course, Red Dog had to know in general terms what all the programs were, because he had to have some sort of feel for the emphasis and the amount of money to be put in.

But I must say that we had a good working team in the individuals in all those three-star areas and most of the two-star areas. I look back now, and I can't see anybody that was below par, was not competent at handling his job. We knew that when we put them in there. We knew we had good people.

Q: Did you sit on any selection boards in this period?

Admiral Shear: Yes, I did.

Q: What do you remember about those?

Admiral Shear: Well, I'd been on a number of selection boards, both as a member and as president. In my earlier days I was on boards for commanders and captains. Later on I was member and president of flag boards. That's always a humbling experience. For example, a typical flag board you're looking at 300 or 400 or maybe 500 captains. You're able to select maybe 20 or 25, maybe 25 to 30, 31, 32. That's a typical selection year.

Well, you've got lots of people who can fill those billets that are worthy of selection, and it's always a process where you have to make sure you get the best man and a good man is not left out. You're going to pick one out of ten, something like that, one out of 20. It's a very demanding task, because you have talent coming up the line you wouldn't believe. It's always that way; it's always been that way. That's why the Army and Air Force look at our system with envy. We've got the best selection system of anybody.

Q: How is the Navy system better than those?

Admiral Shear: Well, we have boards that look closely at everybody. Everybody has got a fair shake, and there's a lot more individual selection in the Army and the Air Force. They now have more boards similar to ours, but until just recently there was a lot of input from individual four-stars, "I want this guy," or something like that, you see. It's never been that way in the Navy. The Navy selection board system has been absolutely fair. You can't quibble with it except once in a while. Frequently you run out of numbers before you run out of talent. When a board looks at a group, you've got a section at the bottom, and you know that they're not going to make it. Then you've got a section at the top, and you know that a number of those are going to make it. Then you've got this big section in the middle, and there's a lot of good people in that section. You have to get a few out of that section.

Let's say you've got 30 openings that year. First of all, you have to pay attention to your precept to see whether there's any particular categories that have to be selected. Then you have to look at those categories and get the best of that particular one. Then maybe you get ten people who are so outstanding that they're shoo-ins to be selected. Then you have to look at this big group in the middle and see where the good guys are for the numbers left to fill. That's where you have to do some picking and choosing, which is very, very tight.

One thing we've always stood by is that the selection process is always held as a secret thing, and it's not discussed. You don't discuss individuals, you don't discuss how many votes one guy got. That's always kept strictly within the limits of the board. That was inviolate until that son of a bitch Lehman came along and tried to dictate who was going to be selected. Thank the Lord we knocked him down on that, and we've got Bruce DeMars to thank for that.* He stood up and was counted, said, "I will not do this."

Q: I interviewed Admiral Lawrence, who was Chief of Naval Personnel when Lehman was the Secretary, and he was extremely frustrated in that role.†

Admiral Shear: That's right. Well, we survived Lehman. [Laughter] That's one of the great things about civilian secretaries--they come and they go.

Q: You were talking about sometimes having problems in the slating process once people were selected. What kind of problems could come up?

Admiral Shear: Well, once the selection was made, of course, the CNO would have to take the selections up the Secretary and say, "Mr. Secretary, this is what we plan to do." Unless the Secretary had some reason to object, and normally he didn't, we'd go ahead with the

---

* As president of a selection board, Vice Admiral Bruce DeMars, USN, resisted what he perceived to be Secretary Lehman's efforts to manipulate the results of the board.
† Vice Admiral William P. Lawrence, USN, served as Chief of Naval Personnel from 28 September 1983 to 31 December 1985. His oral history is in the Naval Institute collection.

selections and promulgate them. We'd always have to review the individuals for the CNO to nominate to the Secretary to make sure we had somebody who was capable of doing the job. That was never a problem. We always had more than enough good people coming up the line. That's one of the truly great strengths of the Navy selection process today, whether you're looking at lieutenant commanders or commanders or captains or flag officers. You've always got just numbers of all the young officers coming up the line, and that gives us great depth, tremendous depth. It's always been that way.

Q: And, of course, as you say, sometimes the difference is not much. If you select 32 for rear admiral, there can't be much difference between number 32 and number 33.

Admiral Shear: That's right, hairline differences, and it breaks your heart. It breaks your heart sometimes. You know that this officer who didn't make it versus the one who did is just a hairline difference. One of the things that is always a factor is his performance across the board, and then experience in Washington is always a factor. You've got to know your way around Washington.

Q: I wonder if wives ever serve as a tie-breaker in a situation like that.

Admiral Shear: I wouldn't comment on that. [Laughter]

Q: I think you've commented by the fact that you don't comment.

Admiral Shear: No comment on that. Navy wives as a group are damn fine women, damn fine ladies.

What else do I have to tell you about the VCNO duty?

Q: Well, I would be interested in the role that your own wife played in this, the social side of the job, living in the quarters, and what have you.

Admiral Shear: My wife is a jewel. She's a gourmet cook. She likes to entertain. She's an expert seamstress. She can sit down in an afternoon and make a $500.00 dress, literally. She just fit into Navy life right from the start. We were married when I was serving in my first ship, shortly after leaving the Naval Academy. It's been a great marriage. My wife has always fit into the social scene very nicely. She entertains beautifully; she's always been active in the Navy wives' activities. She's been a tremendous asset to me. And she enjoys every bit of it.

Over there in Europe sometimes she'd have to entertain 100 to 150 people; she can do it hands down. She was always a better cook than the best of the stewards. She could tell them what had to be done and give them directions, and take care of things just as a matter of ease. So I've been very, very fortunate, and she just had a great time doing all of this. I couldn't have had a better partner. And you'll find that most Navy wives are like this, but you won't find any that can cook and entertain like my wife can. She just loves it.

Q: Well, I suppose for those who don't like it, they persuade their husbands to get out before they get promoted too far.

Admiral Shear: Unfortunately, that happens to be the case. I've lost some superb young officers because of wife pressure. Just superb young officers who didn't want to leave the Navy, but their wives just wanted them home more, and they put the pressure on them.

Things we did as VCNO. I said I didn't get involved in hardware. I left that to the three stars. But the F-18 became a big issue.[*] We had to select a cheaper version of the F-14; that was to be the F-18. That aircraft was supposed to be delivered--with spares--for about $3 million. It was a dream.

---

[*] The F/A-18 Hornet has a dual role as both a fighter and attack aircraft. It first flew in 1978 and first entered fleet squadrons in 1981. For details on the program, see Orr Kelly, Hornet: the Inside Story of the F/A-18 (Novato, California: Presidio Press, 1990).

Tom Jones was head of the Northrop Corporation.* They had the prime contract, and he would come into my office about once a week and bang on me as to why we had to select the F-18 from his company. I'd throw him out and send him down to talk to OP-05. Within a week later he would be back banging on my desk. Normally I didn't let the vendors in. I'd turn them over to three-stars. But this guy was persistent, and we could see in a matter of months that there was going to be a lot of cost growth in that program. We knew it was a good aircraft, but we knew it had a lot of cost growth. So he'd came in banging on me about how he was going to keep cost growth under control, and it was going to be a great aircraft.

Well, it did turn out to be a great aircraft, but it became ungodly expensive. We were as tough with them as we could. Toward the end he kept banging on me so hard, I just threw him out and said, "You go down and talk to Bill Houser or Fox Turner."† They had the basic responsibilities. I just use that as a typical example. Once in a while he would just bang on my door, and I'd see him, whereas he should have been dealing with the three star. That one particularly sticks in my mind. Tom Jones was a very persistent guy, and eventually he got into trouble with the company years later. I forget exactly what the circumstances were, but he had some problems.

Q: Do you remember having any dealings with Kent Lee, who was Chief of Naval Air Systems Command?‡

Admiral Shear: Yes, a lot of dealings with Kent Lee. Kent Lee is a damn good man. Excellent naval officer, and he ran a very good systems command. Did he talk to you about cost growth?

---

* Thomas V. Jones.
† Vice Admiral William D. Houser, USN, served as Deputy Chief of Naval Operations (Air Warfare) from 5 August 1972 to 30 April 1976. Vice Admiral Frederick C. Turner, USN, held the billet from 6 October 1976 to 30 June 1979.
‡ Vice Admiral Kent L. Lee, USN, served as Commander Naval Air Systems Command from 31 August 1973 to 29 August 1976. His oral history is in the Naval Institute collection.

Q: That was part of it.

Admiral Shear: They had ungodly cost growth.

Q: Well, there was another part of it, that the choice was sort of dictated by Secretary Clements, because they had this big competition among the various alternatives.*

Admiral Shear: Yes, they did have some competition. I don't recall Clements's dictation. I worked closely with Clements. I thought Clements was a damn good man. I must tell you that Kent Lee was a superb naval officer. Anything Kent Lee did, he did well. I've had the highest regard for Kent Lee. I'm glad you've talked to him.

Q: Anything more to say about Clements?

Admiral Shear: Clements's right-hand assistant was Ken Carr.† He was then a captain, and I guess he made two stars in that job. He was very close to Clements, and I knew Ken very well from the submarine days. I would go to Clements periodically on some major problem or another, and Clements thought the world of Ken Carr. He just idolized Ken Carr. And Ken Carr did a great job for him. Have you ever talked to Ken?

Q: No, I haven't.

Admiral Shear: You ought to. So I got to know Clements pretty well through Carr, and then, of course, through my official contacts anyway. I did business with him. Clements had come there as a politician out of Texas, and he had been a big oil development man worldwide. He'd had a big oil development company, prospecting out in the Middle East

---

* William P. Clements, Jr., Deputy Secretary of Defense, 1973-77.
† Captain Kenneth M. Carr, USN, who eventually retired as a vice admiral.

and places like that. He was a very confident, big industrialist, big businessman. Let's see, who was SecDef at the time.

Q: Well, Schlesinger and then Rumsfeld.*

Admiral Shear: Yes. I thought very highly of Schlesinger. I had less contact with Rumsfeld, but I thought he did a good job. He was kind of a political animal. You wouldn't find any more competent man than Jim Schlesinger.

Q: Well, he ran so many different departments.

Admiral Shear: Right. Some of the people that you've talked to may have talked about Schlesinger. I had quite a bit of contact with Schlesinger when I was up in OP-095, because he was keenly interested in ASW.† I'd give him briefings every once in a while. One of the things that I would always do in both OP-31 and OP-095, I'd give some private briefings to members of Congress who had particular interests in those areas. I'd go over there and brief a number of people, individually or collectively, that wanted to know something about a particular program which was sensitive or something of that nature. I forget some of the specific projects that I had with Bill Clements. I think I kept him briefed on some of the black programs. As a matter of fact, I know I did. I'm just trying to think of any other highlights in the CNO and VCNO area that I have missed.

Q: What about the business of allocating your time when you had so many different concerns? What kind of a staff does VCNO have? What opportunities to relieve some of the time pressure?

---

* James R. Schlesinger served as Secretary of Defense from 1973 to 1975. Donald H. Rumsfeld had the office from 1975 to 1977.
† Schlesinger was Director of the Central Intelligence Agency before becoming Secretary of Defense.

Admiral Shear: I'd be in the office before 7:00 o'clock every morning, and my staff would have the important messages highlighted for me. I'd go over those, 15 to 20 minutes, sometimes 30 minutes. Then we'd have a 7:30 meeting with the CNO, which went for about 30 minutes. Then we'd have a morning briefing at 8:00, which was normally attended by the Secretary and most of the three-stars around the building, in a briefing auditorium. We'd have an intelligence brief, and we'd had an operational brief around the world. So by 8:30 you'd have a pretty good picture of what was going on. The CNO would be in the office, put in 30 minutes when I was there.

I had an administrative assistant, two-star. I happened to have two when I was Vice Chief, both of them superb people. And I had a Marine aide and a Navy aide, both good men, very good men and then I had an assistant administrative assistant. My assistant administrative assistant was Paul Miller.[*] He was then a lieutenant commander, and he's now CinCLant.[†] A great guy. I had a two-star who was a great guy. The first one I had was a Coast Guard Academy graduate, believe it or not, aviator. Then the second administrative assistant I had was Jim Service, who later on became president of the war college.[‡] So I had a lot of talent.

They ran the office, and they made sure that I saw everything immediately that needed to be seen. They got all the necessary correspondence in front of me that had to handled that day or that hour. They did everything, except that we had something that we called the "too-hard basket." [Laughter] When we had things we couldn't address without putting some real effort on, we put them in the too-hard basket. Maybe I'd have to work on it that night or something like that. But we had a smooth-working operation.

In addition, I had this damn piano player right behind me there. I'd just push a button, and I could get four-stars around the world, I could get the three-stars in the building just like that. It was a very professional operation. God, I reveled in it; I liked it. I was busy as the devil, and every once in a while I'd have to go to some function at night that

---

[*] Lieutenant Commander Paul David Miller, USN.
[†] As a four-star admiral, Miller served as CinCLantFlt, 1991-92, and as SACLant/CinCLant, 1992-94.
[‡] Captain James E. Service, USN, later a vice admiral.

I couldn't get out of. The working day was a long one. I'd get out and jog at 6:00, be in the office before 7:00. I had to keep in good physical shape because that was demanding. So I was in the office before 7:00 in the morning and rarely got out of there before 7:00 or 8:00 at night, sometimes later than that. If I had to go to a function, I would sneak out an hour to get the dinner or the reception out of the way, and get a few hours of sleep. Then I was back on the job the next day.

Q: Did you lose some of your effectiveness after that demanding a routine month after month.

Admiral Shear: I did my best not to let it affect my effectiveness. One way to prevent losing your effectiveness is your physical condition. Boy, you've got to be in shape. You've got to be in shape, and I think all flag officers recognize that. Once in a while you see one putting on a few pounds, and you say, "Well, you better get a few more rounds of that tennis game or that jog or whatever you're going to do."

I haven't said anything about the Material Command. You mentioned Kent Lee. He was a three-star under Chief NavMat. Chief NavMat was Ike Kidd, and then Michaelis.[*] That was a very important job. It's been disbanded now.[†] You just have NavSea and NavAir and things like that without the hierarchy above. I'm not so sure that that's not the best. It was sort of an extra hierarchy that you had to work your way through to get to the action. NavMat was put in fairly recently and survived as long as I think it should have survived. Michaelis did a great job; poor man's dead now. Ike Kidd, my classmate, did a good job. We had to work very closely with the Material Command, because they had responsibility for all the hardware programs. And we didn't have any trouble doing that.

---

[*] Admiral Isaac C. Kidd, Jr., USN, served as Chief of Naval Material from 1 December 1971 to 18 April 1975. Admiral Frederick H. Michaelis, USN, served from 18 April 1975 to 1 August 1978. Admiral Michaelis's oral history is in the Naval Institute collection.

[†] In 1985, Secretary of the Navy John Lehman disestablished the Naval Material Command and redistributed functions among the various systems commands. For a summary of the reorganization, see Norman Polmar, "The U.S. Navy: Command Changes," U.S. Naval Institute Proceedings, December 1985, pages 156-157.

We had had to keep close contact with them, though. Once in a while they'd be going off on a tangent, but by and large they all played a good game.

Q: One of the operational things that happened while you were in that job was the collision between the John F. Kennedy and the Belknap.* Any ramifications in your office on that one?

Admiral Shear: I thought that was an unnecessary disaster. It was a total screw-up on the part of the CO of the cruiser. He was down watching a movie, as I recall. He had a young JO as officer of the deck who got confused, turned the wrong way, got under the bows of the carrier, and scraped down her side. Essentially wiped the superstructure right off the cruiser. It was just a totally unseamanlike thing and unnecessary thing to have happened. And it showed the lack of responsibility on the part of the skipper. I was irate. I just thought it had made an utter mess of things.

I forget what action we took against the skipper. It was under ComSixthFlt.† Of course, the responsibility for investigating was under ComSixthFlt, and ComSixthFlt at that time was under CinCUSNavEur. It was still in London then. I forget the details, but I recall the incident very well. I thought it was just gross, just gross. Anytime you have a major incident of that kind at sea, you can always poke around and you're going to find a human error. This was 100% human error.

Q: Absolutely.

Admiral Shear: Someone may have told you more details than this, but it was absolutely human error--uncalled for and unnecessary. I'm not sure that the CO of the carrier could have done much to prevent it. With the position that the cruiser put himself in

---

* During exercises in the Mediterranean Sea on 22 November 1975, the guided missile cruiser Belknap (CG-26) ran into the aircraft carrier John F. Kennedy (CV-67). All told, eight men were killed and another 24 injured seriously enough to require hospitalization.
† Com6thFlt--Commander Sixth Fleet.

unnecessarily, there wasn't much the skipper of the carrier could do. There it was; it happened. But there was plenty the cruiser could have done. Everything in the book they did wrong. As I try to recall the details, this poor, rattled young JO had called the CO and asked him to come to the bridge. I guess maybe the captain said, "After the movie," or something like that. Anytime the officer of the deck needs the skipper, all he has to say is, "Captain to the bridge," and, by golly, the captain is up there; he's there in seconds. Even if he's down in the wardroom, he can be there in seconds. That should be in just any ship, but it didn't happen this time.

Right now I can't think of the name of the skipper of the cruiser. I knew a couple of the JOs on the cruiser. They were not involved; they were not on deck; they were not on the bridge, but they performed very heroically in saving the ship. They damn near lost the ship.

Q: They had a terrible fire.

Admiral Shear: Yes, terrible fire. That's right. And as far as damage control was concerned after the, after the fact, the ship's company did a great job of saving her.

Anything else in the Vice Chief area before we shift over to CinCSouth?

Q: Well, one of the big, big events of that period was the national bicentennial in '76. How much did the Navy support that?

Admiral Shear: You mean the big bicentennial in New York Harbor?

Q: Right.

Admiral Shear: We supported it 100%. We supported it 100%, and we had the fleet up there. Ike Kidd was CinCLantFlt at the time, and I must say Ike did a great job. I couldn't go because the CNO went. Any time the CNO was out of town I had to stay in town. So I was holding the fort in the Pentagon, and the CNO went. They had the carrier up there with VIPs by the thousands on board. Ike was the senior guy afloat, and I must say Ike handled that situation beautifully. They got accolades of every description.

Q: Well, he has a flair for that sort of thing.

Admiral Shear: Yep, Ike had a flair for it. And his wife had a flair for it. She was there, and she did a nice job too. She has a real flair for that kind of thing, and Ike had a great flair for it, and he was in his glory. Just in his glory. Have you talked to Ike?

Q: Yes, he wouldn't do an oral history, but I've talked to him on other things.

Admiral Shear: Why wouldn't he do an oral history?

Q: I guess he just didn't want to put it on the record. I talked to his son also, and he said that his dad just keeps his own counsel on a lot of things.

Admiral Shear: Well, he should because he's got a lot of stuff that ought to be on the record.

Q: I wish he would. I talked to him about his dad because I did a book on the Arizona, and he was willing to talk about that.[*]

Admiral Shear: I was not out there for that occasion, but he made one of the principal speeches at that 50th anniversary. The speech he made was a speech talking to his father entombed below. I understand it's one of the most heart-wrenching things that any person has ever made. There wasn't a dry eye in the audience out there. You may have heard this.

---

[*] Rear Admiral Isaac C. Kidd, USN, Commander Battleship Division One, was killed on board his flagship, USS Arizona (BB-39) when the Japanese attacked Pearl Harbor in December 1941. The book is Paul Stillwell, Battleship Arizona: An Illustrated History (Annapolis: Naval Institute Press, 1991).

Q: I don't think that was the occasion, but I've heard about that speech of his.

Admiral Shear: That was the occasion. That was the event out there in Pearl Harbor where he made it. He may have made it before--I don't know--but he made that speech out there at the time. People who were there told me about it. He said later that he would never go back there again, because it took too much out of him.

Q: Well, I know it was difficult for him to talk with me about it. He said it was very painful for him to read the book also.

Admiral Shear: Yes.

Q: How much did you get involved in JCS business in that job? What about times when you would go to the Tank in place of Admiral Holloway?

Admiral Shear: Any time the CNO was out of town, I would take his position as acting member of the JCS. I would go down there, not frequently but regularly. Of course, most of the time when the JCS met, the members of the Joint Staff were there--the Army, Navy, Air Force, and the Chairman. But I went down there a fair number of times when he was out of town, and you always briefed yourself thoroughly on the agenda that was going to come up for that day. I always did that by reading up on it beforehand, and I would be briefed by the people in OP-06. They would normally be responsible for preparation, plans and policy.

I learned a lot about the Joint Staff and how it operates. As I said, I could see Davy Jones in action, and he couldn't carry the briefcase of anybody else down there. He ended up as Chairman, which shows you something about politics in this town. And Holloway had never any cause for concern about my going down when he wasn't there. I know he knew that I was never going to let him down on anything real controversial that we had to talk about beforehand. He knew what my vote would be if we got to a voting situation. It was a very great experience to see how the system worked.

Of course, you always had to scratch to make sure you were thoroughly prepared before you went down there. And I made damn sure that any time that I was acting CNO that I really had my homework done before I went down to the Tank. So whenever I went in down there, I was comfortable with what I had to do and what the agenda was for the day and how thoroughly I was briefed on it. But I made damn sure that I was up to snuff anytime I went down there.

Q: One of the criticisms of the Navy before Goldwater and Nichols was that it had not always sent its best people to joint billets or participate in jointness as much as the other services.* Is that a valid observation?

Admiral Shear: It's a valid observation as far as sending better people down there. We didn't always send our best people down there. You came to Washington, and you got a good job on the CNO staff. That was great, but to give me a job down there in the Joint Staff, God, I didn't want that damn thing. And there was a lot of that. We did not send our best people down there for a long time until we finally got the picture that that was where the decisions were made. We were reluctant to do that. I don't think we were ever particularly reluctant as far as joint operations were concerned. We might have been that way many years ago but not in recent years. But we finally got the picture on sending our best people down there. But in my days around Washington, around the Pentagon, that was not always the case. Many times we'd send mediocre people down there and put our very best people in the Navy staffs around town. That's a valid criticism. You've probably heard that from others.

---

* The Goldwater-Nichols Defense Reorganization Act of 1986 went into effect on 1 October of that year. For details, see "DoD Reorganization," U.S. Naval Institute Proceedings, May 1987, pages 136-145. Among other things, the law mandates joint-service duty as a requisite for promotion to high rank.

Q: Indeed, I have.

Admiral Shear: And I support that. We were dumb to do that, but it took us a long time to learn. But we learned that lesson now, and we've got lots of good people down there.

Q: Well, especially when it's been made mandatory that people get joint duty before they get promoted to flag.

Admiral Shear: We went through that regime about what's joint duty. We had some Navy billets that we sold as being joint duty, but they really weren't quite that joint. But now we've got the picture, and we send in a lot of crackerjack people to the Joint Staff and other joint staffs around the world. It took us a long time to learn that.

Q: Anything else on that job?

Admiral Shear: I'll think of something tonight, but I haven't any notes on anything else.

Q: Well, you spent two fruitful years in Washington and then moved over to Naples for the NATO job.

Admiral Shear: I had a great tour as Vice Chief, as I told you. It was a demanding job, a very satisfying job, and I think I did a pretty good job for Jim Holloway. And I thought he was a superb CNO.

So here I am. I'm finishing up two years as CNO, Vice CNO, and he sent me over to CinCSouth, which is a NATO job and responsibility for the southern flank of NATO. The southern flank of NATO runs from Portugal and from Gibraltar all the way over to the eastern boundary of Turkey and the Soviet Union. Spain was not in NATO then. France was temporarily out of NATO, although they participated in naval exercises. The principal countries full-time were the U.K., Italy, Greece, and Turkey.[*] We had a lot going on for that three years over there, and I'll start right from the start.

When I arrived on the scene, we had a temporary man as CinCSouth. He was an Italian four-star admiral, Admiral Tomasuolo, a fine old gentleman.[†] He was at retirement age or beyond, and he had taken over temporarily from Stansfield Turner, who had been called back by Jimmy Carter to head up the CIA.[‡] So for all practical purposes, the job had been pretty much vacant for four or five months. I'm going to give you some very frank comments here.

SACEur and CinCEur was still Al Haig. Al took over while I was in London, and he was still in the job. That was normally a six-year job, so he was there for the first two-thirds of my tour of three years as CinCSouth in Naples. Al Haig and Stansfield Turner did not get along very well, frankly because Haig never knew what Turner was going to do next. He did not trust Turner, and he was always nervous that Turner was going to pull some stunt on the southern flank of Europe that was not in the best interests of NATO or anybody else. So he told me very frankly when I arrived on the scene that he was glad to see me, because he knew he could trust me. He knew we had worked closely together in the national side in London and Stuttgart and Brussels, and he said he was glad I was taking over the job down there.

Well, I was delighted to be back there with Haig again, because we had worked well before. I knew that he would support me, even though some of his subordinates up there in the Central Front were not necessarily very responsive to the southern flank. Haig was, and Haig knew the importance of it. So we started out on a good footing with each other, and I must say that Haig supported me very well during the remainder of his tour.

Q: What can you say about his personality and your relations with him?

---

[*] U.K.--United Kingdom.
[†] Ammiraglio di Squadra Luigi Tomasuolo.
[‡] Admiral Stansfield Turner, USN (Ret.), served as Director of Central Intelligence/Director of the Central Intelligence Agency from 9 March 1977 to 20 January 1981. The first part of his tenure was on active duty, prior to his Navy retirement on 1 January 1979.

Admiral Shear: Haig was a very interesting fellow and still is a very interesting fellow. I got to know Haig very well. One of the best bits of advice I had from anybody concerning Al Haig was one that Admiral Blackie Weinel gave me.[*] Blackie Weinel was in the four-star senior U.S. NATO billet in Brussels. He was not under Haig's command; he was under the U.S. Joint Chiefs' command. That was a longstanding four-star billet that had been over there, and Blackie was filling it when I took over CinCSouth. Blackie had gotten to know Haig very well, because they were right on the scene together, and they had a lot of contact with each other.

Blackie Weinel's advice to me was not ever to push Haig off center stage. Haig loved attention, and he liked to be on center stage all the time. Well, I'd worked with Haig before, and I knew this pretty well. But Weinel's advice to me was very good, and I pointedly always made sure that Haig was the center of attention. He got all of his due, with nobody pushing him aside. I did not get in his way any time he visited the southern flank. That approach worked to perfection. That's one of Haig's quirks. He is a great egotist, and he always wanted to be the center of attention, and I always gave it to him. I always made sure that he was the guy in front and got the full attention. And that paid off a great deal.

Q: One of the revealing episodes on him was after President Reagan was shot and he went into the White House briefing room and said, "I am in charge now."[†]

Admiral Shear: That's Haig for you. That's Haig backwards and forwards. I remember that incident very well.

So we started off on a good step, having known each other before, worked together before. And we worked well the remaining part of the tour, which I think was two of my three years. Then he was relieved by General Bernie Rogers.[‡] I also got along very well

---

[*] Admiral John P. Weinel, USN, U.S. Representative to the NATO Military Committee.
[†] Potential assassin John Hinckley shot and wounded President Ronald Reagan in Washington, D.C., on 30 March 1981.
[‡] General Bernard W. Rogers, USA, served as Army Chief of Staff, 1976-79, and SACEur/CinCEur, 1979-87.

with Bernie Rogers, having knowing him slightly back in the Pentagon when he was Chief of Staff of the Army.

We had lots of problems on the southern flank. The Greeks and Turks were still at each other's throats. They had been ever since the initial days of Cyprus when I had that responsibility as CinCUSNavEur. Haig was aware of the situation over there, and Haig had a particular liking for the Turks, as did I. I must say, although he treated everybody fairly, he always did everything that he could to make sure that the Turks got a fair shake and got all the credit due them. And I must say of all our allies in Europe, I thought the Turks were the best, hands down.

I thought the Turks were the best allies we had over there anywhere, including the British. They were superb people, they were tough fighters, they knew their stuff, and they were absolutely loyal to NATO and the United States. I cannot say the same thing about our Greek friends; they were opinionated. They thought that the principal enemy was not the Soviet Union but the Turks. They acted accordingly, and they threw every roadblock they could possibly throw into relationships between themselves and us. It was not a pretty picture at all, and it started out that way. I must say, for all my endeavors I don't think I made much of an impression after three years. Haig had a good feeling for this, and he understood it.

Q: Well, wouldn't the Greeks naturally be resentful if they saw a sense of favoritism toward the Turks?

Admiral Shear: Well, we made very sure that there was no favoritism shown, no visible partiality. And I bent over backward to do that, as did Haig. On a number of occasions Haig and I went to Turkey together. Oh, we also went to Greece together a couple of times. But we made several excursions to Turkey, where we personally talked together with the Turkish senior people of all services.

I remember one particular occasion with the Turkish Chief of General Staff, a tough, experienced four-star Turkish Army general, General Sancar.* We had some problems we had to resolve. He met us at Haig's plane, and we had a conference in the back of Haig's plane, four of us sitting around the table, jammed right in about as tight as you could get; Haig and I and the Turkish general and one other.

We talked for four hours, and we got fidgety, but the general wanted to stay there and continue talking. By the time the four hours were up, we didn't have any kidneys left, but we had a very worthwhile experience. We knew where we stood with that general thereafter. He wanted help from us, and we wanted to help him. It was a very worthwhile four hours, but I can tell you that the seat of our pants were sore, and we were all headed for the head in a rush when the meeting broke up. Every time I've seen Haig since, he reminds me of that meeting with the Turks.

Q: Were these discussions all in English?

Admiral Shear: Through an interpreter; the fourth guy was the interpreter.

Q: I see.

Admiral Shear: Sancar was an institution. Every Turkish military man sort of bowed to Sancar as number one. The Turks were right there on the Soviet border. They were tough as nails. They had this border with Bulgaria, and things were very bad in Bulgaria. They had that big eastern boundary of 400 or 500 miles with the Soviets, and they were right under the gun. We had some very, very sensitive intelligence resources there in Turkey, where we were monitoring and reading the Soviets almost to the minute. Intercepts and various assets right on the border, right hard up against them, are critically important as far as good intelligence is concerned.

---

* General Semih Sancar, Turkish Army.

The Turks cooperated with us 100% in the use of those facilities. And they knew that they were under pressure from the Soviets to do everything they could to make it difficult for us. It just rolled right off their backs; they paid no attention to the Soviets. And there they were, right near the shore of the Black Sea. The Russians could have done all kinds of things to really pressure them, but it didn't bother the Turks at all. They just stood up to them, and they moved back and forth through the straits.* Incidentally, we had detailed plans to close those straits. You can bet your bottom dollar that if we'd had any real flaps with the Soviets that got into a shooting war, that we would close those straits hands down. The Turks had the capability to do it, and they were prepared to take action within hours.

Q: With mines?

Admiral Shear: With mines, and various other devices to close it from one end to the other. They had the capability on site; I personally witnessed it a number of times. And they were ready to go. You can bet that if the balloon had gone up, they would have been there and carried out their responsibilities to the T.

Q: Well, that was a symbiotic relationship that was beneficial for both sides, because it undoubtedly gave the Turks a great deal of confidence to have our backing.

Admiral Shear: No question, no question. And they knew they had our backing. We made it very clear to them that they had our backing. I made innumerable trips to Turkey, and I got to know the details of that country all over: the real estate, the geography. I would go out in the field with them, both in national exercises and in NATO exercises. Some of them were right hard up against the Soviet border. I got to know those people in the field--land, sea, and air--and they were totally professional military men. They were damn good, and they knew they were good.

---

* The Dardanelles and the Bosporus provide a link between the Mediterranean and the Black Sea. Warship passage through the area is controlled by international law.

We did everything we could to give them the modern equipment that we could put together. For instance, I got them a number of additional destroyers and I think a couple of submarines, too, when I was in CinCSouth. They were forever grateful for the improving of their fleet. They also wanted to build some ships under U.S. contract. I don't think we ever got that far with them. They had a good in-house capability in their own navy yards for construction of naval vessels. And many of their people had been U.S. educated at MIT and places like that.[*] They knew their stuff. I can't say enough about what a great ally Turkey had been over the years.

When you go back in history a few years, you can see what they did in Korea, where they had a Turkish division out there. Incidentally, General Evren, who was chief of staff after Sancar, had been out there with that division in Korea and covered himself with great valor.[†] Any time you put a Turkish division on the line and you wonder who's the right, or who's the left, you don't need to worry. That Turkish division is going to be there. The U.S. forces that worked next to them out there in Korea understood how good the Turkish were. They did a great job. They were superb, superb military men, and they were damn good and tough as nails. Tough as nails. They brought the people up there right from their recruits.

Q: They were right in the middle of it during the Gulf War too.

Admiral Shear: Oh, yes, they were. Absolutely. They made all of their assets and facilities available to us. We were flying out of there; we were moving cargoes across their country there. I could have told you. If anybody asked me at the start of the Gulf War, I could have just said, "Look, you'll have no problems with the Turks. They'll back you to the hilt." And they did.

Q: They were in a great position geographically for our uses.

---

[*] MIT--Massachusetts Institute of Technology.
[†] General Kenan Evren. In September 1980, Evren announced that the military leadership was taking over the Turkish government.

Admiral Shear: Absolutely critical--right there at the junction of Europe and the Middle East. Geographically and militarily they were in a vital position, and let me tell you, they lived up to their responsibilities right across the board. I can't tell you the high regard in which I hold the Turks.

Right across the Aegean, I don't have that regard for the Greeks. The Greeks knew they had a big lobby in the U.S. They used it for every devious means you could think of. They kept badgering us for more support all the time, and what they were worried about were not the Russians. They were worried about the Turks coming across the border, and they had been worried about them for over 3,000 years. The Turks were not about to start any sort of scrap with the Greek nation, except they were not taking any foolishness on Cyprus. They made that very clear, and they stuck with it. But they were not about to invade Athens or the Greek Islands or anything of that nature. But the Greeks thought they were, and the Greeks were absolutely convinced. I talked to the highest level of the Greeks, and they were absolutely convinced that the enemy was not Russia; it was the Turks.

Q: And you tried to give them reassurances that the Turks wouldn't do that.

Admiral Shear: Oh, innumerable times. Finally, after a couple of years of nonparticipation, we got them to participate in NATO exercises. Some of those were right up there at the northern end of the Aegean, some in Turkish territory and some in Greek territory. We would have amphibious exercises, we'd have aircraft exercises, and exercises ashore. We finally got them to participate and play ball, and then after we had done this for a year or two the Greeks all of a sudden said, "No, we won't play anymore."

I had some vitriolic exchanges with the Greeks on this, how they'd pulled out and weren't being faithful to NATO. I did a lot of it by message, and I went down there and had some had some eyeball-to-eyeball contact with them. They knew very well that I didn't think they were a very good ally. But I never showed any favoritism to the Turks that they could point to and say, "Shear, you're favoring the Turks against us." I bent over backwards not to do that. But I was not impressed with the Greeks in any way as an ally or as a member of NATO. I must say that my successors found out the same thing. And Stansfield Turner before me had found that, although he had not any great difficulty that I did with them, because they weren't playing that much.

Q: The U.S. Navy had cultivated that relationship since just after World War I, when Admiral Bristol went over there.[*] This was when they were having the great struggles with the Armenians.

Admiral Shear: Yes.

Q: I read the oral history of old Admiral Kinkaid, who had been on Bristol's staff back then.[†] He said that Bristol had a talk with one of the top Turkish officials and said, "Why do you keep killing these Armenians?"

He paused for a moment and said, "Well, somebody has to kill them."

Admiral Shear: [Laughter] That sounds like them; that sounds like them. We had very valuable assets ashore in Turkey, and we had very valuable assets ashore in Greece. We had Souda Bay, for example, a magnificent anchorage there. And we had a several very important communication intelligence intercept sites. One was on Crete, and a couple of more were on the mainland of Greece, as there were on the mainland of Turkey. The goal was to keep on the best relationship we could with everybody, and we did. We really worked at it. But deep down I never trusted the Greeks, and I must say that Haig understood that very well.

I can go on and give you a number of instances in NATO exercises where they would throw little roadblocks into things. They had a continual fight with the Turks, which

---

[*] Rear Admiral Mark L. Bristol, USN, Commanding U.S. Naval Forces Operating in Turkey.
[†] The oral history of Admiral Thomas C. Kinkaid, USN (Ret.), is in the Columbia University collection.

goes on to this day, over the ownership for a couple of the Aegean Islands. Particularly the islands which control the approaches to the Sea of Marmara and the Turkish Straits. That went on continuously, and each year they'd try a little stunt. They'd say, "This is my territory, and I can do such and such with it."

The Greeks and the Turks would say, "No, it's not. It's long been our territory, and we own this island."

They'd say, "No, they don't; we own it," and so forth. That was just a continual annual affair.

Q: What did they do to interfere with these fleet exercises?

Admiral Shear: Oh, they would throw military flights over what they considered to be their territory and so forth. They would participate, and then they'd back out. Or they'd have minor participation, and while we had a NATO exercise going on, they would fly strike aircraft in the immediate vicinity, just to show their presence and to be nasty about it. Now, a couple of times [laughter] we did get them to participate fully, but that was the exception rather than the rule.

I remember Jim Watkins was winding up the Sixth Fleet about the time I left there.[*] We departed from there within a couple of months of each other. He said, "Well, when you retire and get back to the U.S., one thing you won't have to do anymore. You won't have to worry about the Greeks and the Turks." Because on the national side he had much the same kind of problems I did.

Well, I must say that even though the people in Stuttgart and Brussels were concentrated on that central front almost exclusively, that the leadership over there, Bernie Rogers and Haig, really understood the problems of the flanks. They understood the importance of the flanks, but I must tell you that never trickled downhill to the staffs. They never understood that the first time they're going to get in trouble was not going to be in

---

[*] Vice Admiral James D. Watkins, USN, commanded the Sixth Fleet from September 1978 to July 1979.

Central Europe; it was going to be in the flanks. History has shown that now, time after time.

Q: How would you explain that? Why wouldn't the commander's viewpoint trickle down?

Admiral Shear: Because throughout the entire organization, except for the CinC himself, they were just dedicated to that Central Front. Now, the number-two man in CinCEur was a U.S. officer. He was called Deputy CinCEur, but he ran the CinCEur staff. When I was there, it was an Air Force four-star, and he was Haig's deputy running the staff. His eyes never moved a quarter of an inch from the Central Front. So even though he got certain direction from SACEur himself, it never really permeated his staff.

Now, I had a good international staff there. It was a representation from all the countries of the southern flank. And I had some very good people, including Greeks and Turks. On the staff level, the Greeks and Turks worked pretty well together. And I had up to two-star level Greeks and Turks and a number of colonels and so forth and men below, and I insisted that they work together as a team. I must say that by and large they worked pretty well. But I say again that the entire military organization in Europe, which was centered in Germany in Brussels, never understood the importance of the flanks. I would hammer on that to Haig every time I saw him.

Then once or twice a year we would have a big NATO conference in Brussels normally, and we would have representatives from all the NATO nations of three- and four-star level people. I would always get up and make a speech about the importance of the flanks. I was there in the southern flank, and the Norwegians would always get up and say, "Yes, by golly, Admiral Shear, you're right. The trouble is not the Central Front; the trouble is in the flanks." And we got the northern flank, and we were worried about the northern flank. Well, I had the southern flank and all that African mess on the other side of me and the Middle East, and I had all kinds of worries. That really never got across.

Q: One example that makes your point was in 1983, when there was a U.S. air strike in Lebanon. The orders came down through that chain of command from SACEur, and it was not well handled because the people on the scene had to follow orders from somebody who didn't understand the tactical situation.*

Admiral Shear: That's absolutely correct. You've already talked to Bob Long, and you'll see what he had to say about that situation in Lebanon when he was sent over to investigate.† Bernie Rogers really didn't know what the hell was going on over there. I won't attempt to give you the details on that because I had retired. Well, I know that Bob felt that they didn't know what the hell was going on in Central Europe. And he was correct. Just the nature of the beast.

Q: You mentioned when you got over to London you had to mend some fences after Admiral Bagley. Did you have to mend any fences after Admiral Turner when you got to Naples?

Admiral Shear: Turner was gone, and Haig just breathed a sigh of relief. He knew me, and I knew him, and he knew that there wasn't going to be any screwing around with the NATO forces in Southern Europe without his approval and okay. We worked very closely together. I kept him fully informed, and he appreciated it. Admiral Tomasuolo was a nice old guy, but he was just sort of in there temporarily waiting for me to arrive.

I must say our relationships with the Italians were superb across the board, and I did with the Italians just like I did with the Greeks and the Turks. I got out in their exercises. I got up in the Alps and in the NATO exercises and naval exercises at sea. I got to know the military organization of Italy backwards and forwards, as well as the political situation. I must say that my respect for the Italians increased with time. They really were good

---

* On 4 December 1983, A-6 Intruders and A-7 Corsairs from the carriers Independence (CV-62) and John F. Kennedy (CV-67) attacked Syrian positions east of Beirut, Lebanon. Two U.S. aircraft were lost in the strike.
† On 23 October 1983 terrorists exploded a huge bomb under the U.S. Marine barracks in Beirut, Lebanon. The explosion killed 241 Marines and wounded 70. Admiral Robert L. J. Long, USN (Ret.), headed the investigation of the incident. His oral history is in the Naval Institute collection.

professional people. They had some very uneasy feelings about their reputation of World War II, and they did their very best to make sure that those days were past.

Q: Well, the government changes so often, how can you have stability there?

Admiral Shear: As my chief of staff, three-star Army general, great guy, Bob McAlister, used to say, "It doesn't make any difference whether the Italians have a government or not. They just keep on going."[*] Pretty close to the truth. I guess we had half a dozen changes of government while I was there.

At that time the Communist Party was still pretty active. Today they've gone and dropped right off in strength. But we had the Christian Democrat, which is the dominant party. Then we had the Communist Party, which was fairly small but very active. Then we had the other party, headed by a politician who was a general. We had two dominant parties plus the Communists. It was awfully hard for any of them to get a majority. Any time you got a majority it was primarily the Christian Democrats. But frequently they would have to make up a composite government, and that was never very successful. They had a half dozen little picayunish parties that were sort of around the edges. Sometimes you had to absorb them into the party of the guy who almost won so he could get a winning majority put together.

Q: Which gives the smaller parties a lot of bargaining power.

Admiral Shear: Gives them a lot of bargaining power, that's right. For example, the mayor of Naples was an out-and-out hard-charging Communist. I can't think of his name now. He was a good guy, but he was a Communist. When we had an official function, I would always invite the mayor of Naples, this out-and-out Communist. He had dinner with me many times, but he was Communist. He never caused any trouble, but anything that went on in an official nature, if there was an opportunity to favor the left, by golly, he favored the

---

[*] Lieutenant General Robert C. McAlister, USA.

left. There was a lot of strength in southern Italy from the leftist regime. And the Mafia was always in there stirring things up. I can't say that he was associated with the Mafia, but a lot of people said he was. That's neither here nor there.

Well, I got to know Italy backwards and forwards. I travelled all over the country, and I got to know it militarily, and I got to know it industrially and geographically. My respect for the Italians climbed steadily all the time I was there. They've got lots of problems, but they are great people, and they'll give you the shirt off their back without turning around and stealing it the next day. They really are a great people.

Q: Well, Naples particularly had that reputation for thievery.

Admiral Shear: Of course, the difference between northern and southern Italy is night and day. You've got a totally different individual up there. You've got the influence of Northern Europe having penetrated there over the centuries. It's a totally different situation from Rome north all the way up to the Alps. They've got a lot of industrial strength over there, and there are very sophisticated engineers and scientists in that part of Italy.

Q: We've been seeing all of the horrors in Serbia and Bosnia. What was the situation in Yugoslavia when you were there?

Admiral Shear: It was very interesting. There was a very tightly controlled border between northern Italy and Yugoslavia. It was very highly fortified on the Italian side, which I was thoroughly familiar with. It was also very highly fortified on the Yugoslav side, which was essentially controlled by the Russians. Tito was still alive then.[*]

About twice a year we would have a major exercise in northern Italy, and it would center on protecting that border between Yugoslavia and Italy and Austria. The NATO and Italian assets there were quite impressive.

---

[*] In 1945 Josip Broz Tito established a Communist government in Yugoslavia. He broke ties with the Soviet Union in 1948. He remained the nation's ruler untl his death in 1980.

We could have held off a major attack there coming down across the flatlands of Yugoslavia. It's what's called the Lyublyana Gap, and it was a significant defense in depth. The Italians had it well manned, and it was very well fortified. They could have held off a major thrust there, all the way along that Yugoslav border, on up into the Austrian border and some of the passes coming down over the Alps. The very best ground forces that the Italians had were the Alpini. The Alpini were the Italian mountain troops in the northern part of Italy. I used to liken them to the U.S. Marines. They were that type of guy--very tough, slick, competent small outfit. They were very, very good; they were just as good as our Marines.

Q: Well, retrospect tells us that Tito did a hell of a job holding that country together.

Admiral Shear: Yes, doesn't it, though? Doesn't it, though? Of course, the Germans never subdued them in World War II; they never got control of that territory. I think it would be disaster if we tried to get in there militarily and do something right now.

Q: Did you enjoy living in Italy?

Admiral Shear: I enjoyed it thoroughly. I had two guards assigned to my quarters all the time. These were the best of their military. I had a sergeant who rode with me in my car, every time I was in my car, with a machine gun across his knees in the front seat. I never felt the slightest qualm about being attacked, and I never ran into a single incident. After I left, things got worse.

Q: Well, they seized that one Army general.

Admiral Shear: We had an U.S. Army commander up there in the north, and they seized him after I left.* I didn't think we would ever see him alive, but the Italian carbinieri, which

---

* On 17 December 1981 members of the Red Brigades kidnaped Brigadier General James L. Dozier, USA. The Italians eventually rescued him on 28 January 1982.

is sort of a state police, got in there and solved that, and we got him back alive. It was a very, very sophisticated piece of work. I had a northern Italian general who was responsible for northern Italy. He was a four-star general, a very good man. Then we had our own Air Force establishment up there at Avellino, which was a U.S. operation. And then, of course, I had a very close working relationship with all the army, navy, and air force in Italy, as well as the forces of other nations.

At that time, skipping around a little bit, Spain was not in NATO. Since they were not in NATO, I really had no responsibility. I did my damndest for three years to find a way to get Spain into NATO. I certainly was not met with much success nor with much support, because the northern European nations didn't particularly want Spain in NATO. Among other things, they were afraid of trading situations. They would lose out in the trading situation, that they'd be undercut by the Spaniards, who would beat them in prices and so forth. So there wasn't a great deal of enthusiasm to get Spain in NATO. I thought that was a big mistake, and I told Haig so a number of times as well as Bernie Rogers. But I was not successful in doing that.

It came about several years thereafter, and it should have come about long before.[*] Portugal, on the other hand, was always a good little member of NATO, and they always participated in the exercises. They'd send a modest number of troops and always several ships to the exercises in the Med, and we got along well with them. My Portuguese language training in Brazil stood me in good stead, because I was able to go over there in IberLant and converse with them in Portuguese, and it made a good impression with them, which was very helpful.[†]

Q: It's intriguing that you faced that kind of reluctance on their part when they were letting us base ballistic missile submarines at Rota.

---

[*] Spain was admitted to the North Atlantic Treaty Organization in a ceremony at NATO headquarters, Brussels, Belgium, on 5 June 1982.
[†] IberLant--NATO includes the Iberian-Atlantic Command.

Admiral Shear: That's right. That was a national situation. I had been instrumental in setting up that base as a captain. As I told you, right after I left the Holy Loch, I went back and ran the show for Dennison in Norfolk, and we set the base up then.

Q: Did you have another strong political adviser when you were in this job?

Admiral Shear: Yes, just as strong or maybe even a little stronger than the one in London. His name was Jonathan Stoddart, and he was outstanding. He knew his stuff. He was highly thought of in the State Department. He knew all the ambassadors, and we got along very well. He gave me all kinds of sound advice, and I always took him with me. Anywhere I went, I would take Jock Stoddart with me. The ambassador to Turkey, Ron Spiers, was a close personal friend of his, and he became a close personal friend of mine.[*]

We had a very close working relationship there. And, of course, we had Bruce Laingen over in Malta; that was very good. We had a kind of a unique situation in Rome. We had a very liberal Columbia professor there named Gardner.[†] He was an appointee of Jimmy Carter's, and I didn't think he was a very good ambassador. And his wife was not an asset. She was a sort of a fluttering social type and hobnobbing with some of the wrong Italians. Not a healthy situation, but I made a point of getting along with the man. He had a good staff, and Jock Stoddart kept in very close contact with staff.

I was blessed with two superb political advisers, and I couldn't have gotten along without them. They did everything right down to the T to make sure we did a good job. They had a great deal of credit for any successes that I had over there.

Q: Was Stoddart sort of the sounding board when you would have ideas to try out?

Admiral Shear: I used him for everything. I used him for advice; I used him for questions; I used him for what should we do next, and that kind of thing. He was highly thought of throughout Europe. As a matter of fact, when he left me, he went up and became Bernie

---

[*] Ronald I. Spiers.
[†] Richard N. Gardner, U.S. ambassador to Italy.

Rogers's polad, so that gives you an idea of what kind of man he was. He was up there for several years, and he retired from there.

Q: Did these political advisers ever have an agenda of their own that they would bring with them--things that might come out from the State Department that they hoped to achieve through the military commander?

Admiral Shear: They had close contacts with State, but they never had any undercover stuff as far as communications was concerned. Anything we got of an official nature always came to CinCSouth. They didn't have any undercover "this is for Polad eyes only" or anything of that nature. If they had, I'd have skinned them, and they knew that very well.

Q: Well, I wasn't necessarily suggesting subterfuge, but just things that State Department wanted you to accomplish that they would work through this man.

Admiral Shear: I guess you could say that the State uses the military. They knew that our relationships with the countries over there in many cases were far better than theirs. I can't say that they used them, but they knew very well that I was working for the best interests of the United States. Anything they wanted me to make an issue of, I would be well briefed on. Ron Spiers was good, and he told me many times that he recognized that his contacts with the Turkish military were nowhere near as good as mine. He appreciated that, and he appreciated me keeping him advised of all my contacts with them.

Q: Well, you must have had a lot of communications if you got to all these different nations to keep up to speed on things.

Admiral Shear: All kinds of communications. One of the things that the Turks always made a point of when I was over there, any kind of official business I would always be seen or seated next to the Chief of Staff. Most of the time there was General Evren, who later became President of the country. It was still run as a military operation in those days. It had been a democracy and then gone back to military and then back to democracy again. During my time it was a military government. Ron Spiers commented to me a number of times that, "Well, I saw you the other day with General Evren. I know he has great respect for you, and I appreciate that and you know him much better than I do." Anything that Evren ever said to me, I always passed immediately on to the ambassador. He knew anything that I had, he would get, and he knew that I wouldn't pull any stunts with Evren that he didn't approve of. Spiers came over and visited me in Naples several times. Had a delightful wife. But we had excellent relationships.

And in Greece, even though we had lots of problems with the Greek military, I had a good relationship with the ambassador. And I had very good relationships personally with the Secretary of Defense of Greece. He's the man who almost singlehandedly at the end of World War II had prevented Greece from going Communist.

This was the time of the Truman Doctrine.* Before the Truman Doctrine had really taken ahold, he was up there in northern Greece fighting those Communists tooth and nail. He was given credit pretty much for preventing Greece from going Communist. I can't think of his name either, but he and I had a close relationship, even over and above his military people. I could go to him and talk to him anytime. Anytime I had a reason to go to Greece and sometimes even by telephone or message--and he had a good command of the English language--I'd make a point of keeping good contact with him. And that paid off. Anything I learned there, I would always pass on to the ambassador. The ambassador knew that I had a good relationship with him, much better than he did, and he always appreciated what I told him. That's the kind of stuff you don't necessarily learn pushing a ship around.

Q: You're exactly right. [Laughter]

Admiral Shear: But I learned a good deal.

---

* On 12 March 1947 U.S. President Harry S. Truman announced a doctrine of international resistance to Communist aggression. It guaranteed aid to free nations that resisted Communism.

Q: Experience is a good teacher.

Admiral Shear: Exactly.

Q: That's why it makes sense to have people in those billets for quite a period of time.

Admiral Shear: Exactly, exactly correct. I learned something every day, and I always was completely open with the U.S. elements in any of those countries.

Q: Well, speaking of U.S. elements, what about the CIA representatives in those various countries? Did they check in with you at all?

Admiral Shear: No. I knew who they were; they were undercover people. They had a State Department moniker in the embassies. That's how they worked throughout the world. The same way in Brazil. I knew who the CIA guy was; he was on the ambassador's staff, but he was there as a CIA operator. That's the way it was throughout there. I knew who they were, and I had modest contact with them, but I didn't have to work that CIA circuit very much.

Q: Well, you presumably had your own intelligence section too.

Admiral Shear: Excellent intelligence section, and an excellent NATO intelligence section. We had all these monitoring systems which are handled by the military and got all the up-to-date information we could from the Soviets and things of that nature.

I mentioned that the French took part in NATO exercises. On a military-to-military level, I had good contact with the French. On the political level de Gaulle had withdrawn. So at my level, in the military level, it didn't make too much difference. There was some unrest down in the interior of Africa while I was there. I didn't get involved in it, but the French did, down there south of Libya in Chad and places like that.

Once I was in Paris, talking to the senior French military people. The French Chief of Staff, who was an Army general, said, "I want you to understand, Admiral, that we understand and know Africa better than you or your people will ever. We know what's going on down there, and we know how to handle it. You've got to trust us and recognize that we have do some things down there that you might not necessarily like, but we've got to do them anyway. Because we've been in there for hundreds of years, and we know how that continent functions." And they had some pretty slick stuff going on in there, putting in special cadres of troops to handle the situation. They went into Chad in particular, which Libya was stirring up in every possible direction.

Q: That Chad situation festered for a long time.

Admiral Shear: A long time, yep.

Q: Well, the French didn't exactly have that kind of expertise in Indochina, it turned out, despite their long presence.

Admiral Shear: Long is right. But they did know Africa. And, of course, they had lots of problems there, look at Algeria.

Q: Exactly.

Admiral Shear: Look at Algeria. That was considered a big part of mainland France. I must say that their military knew what was going on in those countries.

Q: Did you depend on the French there to keep you informed on Africa?

Admiral Shear: I won't say specifically. But anything we got out of them we appreciated. I don't recall that they had any more information on what Qaddafi was doing than we did, except that they knew when he was stirring things up to the south, in Chad and so forth.[*] They knew a lot about that, because they had people on the scene.

Q: What do you remember about the Afghanistan and Iran situations during your watch?

Admiral Shear: Iran fell apart because of Jimmy Carter, hands down. The Carter Administration abandoned the Shah, and it was a tragedy. Even though the Shah was on his deathbed, we abandoned him and the bad guys took over. They eliminated and murdered--in cold blood--many of the senior people of the military that I knew, wiped them out by the hundreds. Then this crazy Khomeini and company and all of that religious group took over the country and became a disaster. In due course, it developed into this big fight with Iraq, which was totally unnecessary.

If we had kept a firm hand there, even though we had a change of government--and taken a very tough stand with the religious nuts, I guess you'd call them--we could have handled that situation. But you weren't going to handle it with the Carter Administration. That was just a flat-out abandonment of the situation out there. We've paid a terrible price since. Everything bad which has happened to the Middle East has come about because of the abandonment of the Shah and the abandonment of Iran under Carter. It was a terrible, terrible tragedy of his administration.

Q: Can you suggest any explanation for why the Carter Administration did that? Was it the human rights concern?

Admiral Shear: No guts. No guts. I think they misrepresented it as human rights. You know, he did the same thing in South America. He turned off our relationships with the South American nations just terribly. He sent his mother down there to represent himself, which went over like a lead balloon. It's taken until about now to get back to a decent

---

[*] In September 1969 power in Libya was seized when a group of young army officers overthrew the government and established a nominal republic, headed by Muammar al Qaddafi. He has been in power ever since.

relationships with the big countries down there. Putting in a bunch of leftist representatives. The ambassador to Chile was a disaster. And Brazil lost all respect for him whatsoever. You look back in history, and you are going find that the Carter Administration was one of the great tragedies in the United States. Even though he's a Naval Academy graduate.*

Q: Well, that Iran situation was his downfall.

Admiral Shear: It was a downfall; it was a downfall. And totally due to his own mishandling. One of my great problems in my last years in Italy and Europe was having to make excuses for the Commander-in-Chief. All of Europe looked down their nose at Carter. But he was my boss; he was my Commander-in-Chief. I never badmouthed Carter with any of the NATO people. I supported him, made a point of supporting him, and I never badmouthed him. But, let me tell you, they had no use for him.

Q: You had to bite your tongue probably.

Admiral Shear: I had to bite my tongue 1,000 times. And I've got to tell you this now. Haig, on the other hand, had no compunctions whatsoever, and he hated Carter--with a passion. He knew that he was tough enough politically so that Carter could never pull him out of there. So he would badmouth and run down Carter and tear him to pieces at every turn, publicly. I used to sit back in utter amazement and hear about this or actually hear him say these things. But I never did that; I backed my boss. But I had to bite my tongue. And it was not an easy time being in Europe with the Carter Administration in Washington.

Q: Well, another issue from that era that you watched from afar was the Panama Canal negotiations.

---

* Carter graduated from the Naval Academy in the class of 1947.

Admiral Shear: Yes. Of course, I had nothing to do with that. It was a long way off. But many people will tell you that was a disaster. Whether it turns out to be that way, I'm not so sure, but it was considered a big giveaway at the time.[*]

Let me see what else I need to hit you on. Spain and NATO, Gibraltar. I had good relationships with the British in Gibraltar. I went back and forth there a number of times. We knew each other well, and we worked together well, and we had no trouble ever getting U.S. ships into Gibraltar or any ships into Gibraltar. The British always sent good people down there. Normally they had only a three-star Brit down there, but they always had a good man. They came over and visited me, and I went over and visited them. And Gibraltar, being right there at the start of my command, more or less, we worked very well together.

Q: Would you have any general comments on the waning of the British influence throughout the world?

Admiral Shear: Yes. It became obvious.

Q: But do you think that had unfortunate consequences, because they were no longer able to play that role?

Admiral Shear: Let me say a little bit about the waning of the British influence. I don't know that the NATO staff, either publicly or privately, ever told me that the British had had it. But they knew the British had had it. The British would always participate in a modest degree in every exercise, just to show the British flag. But if they'd been there or hadn't been there, it wouldn't have made any difference. They would send a ship or two down, just to make sure that there was a British participation in this NATO exercise. It was obvious it was always going to be minimal, a couple of ships or something like that, a handful of Marines.

---

[*] In 1977 the United States and Panama signed a treaty that resulted in the transfer of the Canal Zone to Panama in 1979 and the canal itself to Panama on 31 December 1999.

The British always loved to command anything they could command, and they had damn good staff officers. My Italian Navy, four-star NATO commander, Admiral Baldini, had been a U.S. prisoner of war.[*] He was a great guy, spoke good English, a fine, superb, thoroughly capable naval officer. His chief of staff, because this was a NATO organization, was a British vice admiral, a Scottish officer named Roddy MacDonald.[†] He was there, and he had a lot of good British staff officers on this Italian component commander's staff. We got along all right, but Baldini would tell me periodically that he wasn't thoroughly impressed with MacDonald. MacDonald was a competent officer and a damn good man, because the British always sent good men to those staffs. But he didn't impress the Italians too much. They really didn't like having him there running the staff, because as the chief he sort of ran the thing.

Q: Why would he be on their national staff?

Admiral Shear: No, this was a NATO staff, NATO staff. Well, the British hung right on to the last end. If they couldn't supply forces, they would supply good staff people. This was just one example.

You get down into Turkey--they didn't have much influence down there in those staffs. But they had a very big influence in that Italian NATO staff. Admiral Baldini was a four-star, ComNavSouth. ComNavSouth was a NATO command, and his chief of staff was MacDonald, who was a very good man, but the British influence as a result of that in their own staff assignments sort of permeated that staff, and that never sat very well with the Italians. There wasn't much that they could do about it, because the staff billets were there and the British filled them.

Q: Well, as their forces diminished more and more, wouldn't the quality of their staff officers decline because they wouldn't have that much experience?

---

[*] Ammiraglio di Squadra Aldo Baldini.
[†] Vice Admiral R. D. MacDonald, Royal Navy.

Admiral Shear: I suppose. I suppose, but at that time they still had very competent officers. The old story is that the Brits will command anything, as long as they get the command. Traditionally, over the years they have produced damn good staff officers. Everywhere I've been, they've done well. This was not a major problem, but Baldini and I would get together for a couple of private talks once in a while. He'd make it clear that he wasn't too enthralled having that British influence so close to him. And he himself was an outstanding officer, competent, and thorough, and he had very good staff people of his own, Italians on the staff, as well as the strength of other NATO nations.

By and large, all of my subordinate staffs were good people. ComLandSouth was in Izmir, Turkey, and he was an American general, four-star. They had two of them there, both very good men. One was Bill Knowlton, who had been superintendent at West Point.[*] I wouldn't make a big issue of this, but he gave me a bit of trouble.

I had one slight problem, and I don't know whether you want to put it on the record or not. I had this four-star U.S. Army general as Commander Land Forces Southeast. That was his title, ComLand Forces Southeast, with headquarters in Izmir. Once he tried to go direct to Haig for some guidance. Of course, I learned about it immediately. I hauled him in and said, "Look, you've got one boss down here. His name is Shear, and if you ever go to Haig again direct without going through me, I will fire you. You'll be home, and you'll probably go home as a three-star." And I didn't have any more problem. The guy before him was just the opposite. Well, this general pulled this little stunt just once. He realized and he was chagrined to know that he'd really made a major mistake. So I just pass that on. That's about the only command relationship problem that I can recall of any kind in that period down there, and that lasted about five minutes.

Q: You talked about the 12-hour days you spent in the Pentagon. What was the pace like in Naples?

---

[*] General William A. Knowlton, USA, Commanding General Allied Land Forces Southeastern Europe, 1976-77.

Admiral Shear: Quite demanding. Quite demanding. There was quite a bit of social stuff you had to go through, whether you wanted to or not. I was on the road a great deal. I had an airplane assigned, and I would be all over that entire command range--from Portugal all the way out to eastern Turkey--pretty regularly. Then we would have fairly frequent conferences up in Brussels, and I'd get up to those. About once a year we would have either a Central Front conference or southern flank conference or northern flank conference, either headed by myself or the Norwegians or the Germans and our various sectors.

All the NATO people would always attend all of those--a good chance to see each other, get to know each other, get things off your chest that had to be reviewed and so forth. So I was on the road a lot. When I was on the scene there in Brussels, we had long working days and quite a bit of responsibilities in the evening as well.

My Army three-star chief of staff, Bob McAlister, did a great job for me. He was a thoroughly professional U.S. Army type. He knew his stuff, and he handled the Italians very well. He fitted into that Italian regime very carefully, and he understood the Italian government situation. I couldn't have asked for a better chief of staff. He was a big help to me. He had been there about six months ahead of me, so he had been there at the tail edges of Stansfield Turner, and then he was there for most of my tour. He left there and went out to become number three in USCinCEur in Stuttgart, Germany. He never made four stars, although I did my damndest to get him four stars.

So I always had top-notch staff people. I was awfully lucky. Anywhere I've been, I've been very lucky with staff people, from flag officers right on down.

Q: What were the major satisfactions of that tour?

Admiral Shear: The major satisfactions, I guess, were doing everything I could to improve the military capabilities of the southern flank. Everything I could to demonstrate to the rest of the world that the southern flank was critically important to the peace and stability of the Mediterranean and the Middle East. I did everything I could to a make the world recognize what a great ally we had in Turkey. And, by golly, one thing I did, I got Haig to understand that pretty thoroughly.

And I did everything I could to get additional equipment for any of those countries down there. We had a lot of surplus U.S. equipment, which was still in excellent shape. I got several destroyers for Turkey. I got some aircraft for Greece and Turkey. And we got a number of things for Italy. So I did everything I could to improve their military situation, and I guess my biggest disappointment was the fact that I never could get the goddamn Greeks and Turks working together. And no one else has either.

Q: That's right.

Admiral Shear: But I really worked on that. But everything I came to learn about the Turks, I tell you, has borne fruit. They are just great people.

Q: There was much talk in that era about hollow forces, both in terms of manpower and equipment and armament and ammunition and so forth. Did you perceive that in the Sixth Fleet ships that came over?

Admiral Shear: Sixth Fleet ships were always in pretty good shape. Sometimes you had to cross-deck them to get them up to par. There isn't any question that we had some petty officer shortages and some pay grade differences. We might have to have a second class in a first class billet, things of that nature. But the ships that came over there were prepared to fight; they were kept in pretty good shape. I knew we had terrible problems throughout the Navy, in just numbers and experience level and so forth. But I can't say that I ever felt that the Sixth Fleet was not prepared to go.

Now, when I was in Naples the Sixth Fleet didn't come directly under me as it had in London, but I still had very close contact with them. All those commanders were double-hatted to me in the national side as well as the NATO side. So I had a very close view of what was going on in Sixth Fleet.

Q: Well, undoubtedly you had to keep apprised of their capabilities for your planning staff.

Admiral Shear: Exactly, exactly. I had good U.S. officers in the planning staffs, and they did a good job, and good NATO officers too. I must say that the NATO people who were sent to the staffs across the board were damn good people. They were carefully selected, and they knew their stuff. I didn't have any complaints about the caliber of people I had on my NATO staffs, or that they had on their own staffs. I guess they knew that if they were going to satisfy NATO they had to satisfy Uncle Sam doing so. They always had good people.

Q: Were you involved in any way in that abortive rescue effort to get the hostages out of Iran?*

Admiral Shear: No. It was in 1980, and I had already left. That was very closely held. Harry Train was CinCLant at the time.† He had basically the responsibility, because that was outside of CinCUSNavEur's area, and it was not a NATO job. It was in the Indian Ocean. It was sort of a split situation between CinCLant and CinCPac.

They had some terrible problems. They had to get the right number of helicopters there. They had long ranges for those helicopters. They finally got them landed, and it might have been successful if they hadn't had all those problems in that initial landing in the desert, when they bumped into each other and had a couple of major fires. They had to get the hell out of there in a hurry, before they ever got to Teheran. I think some of that rubbed off on Harry, through no fault of his own. He did everything he could to make it fly, but it was a long shot. It was a long shot, and we didn't succeed.‡

---

* In an effort to rescue American hostages held in Iran, on 26 April 1980 six Air Force C-130 cargo planes and eight Navy RH-53D helicopters flew to Iran with a joint-service commando team embarked. The aircraft rendezvoused at Desert One, a site 200 miles from the Iranian capital of Teheran. Because of helicopter problems, the mission was canceled. Several servicemen were killed in the futile rescue attempt.

† Admiral Harry D. Train II, USN, served as Supreme Allied Commander Atlantic, Commander in Chief Atlantic, and Commander in Chief Atlantic Fleet from 1978 to 1982. His oral history is in the Naval Institute collection.

‡ See Paul B. Ryan, The Iranian Rescue Mission: Why It Failed (Annapolis: Naval Institute Press, 1985).

I think they had one or two of the colonels there that weren't the best guys for the job. They had a couple of rabble-rousing types. One was a great hero out in Vietnam, and he wasn't necessarily the most levelheaded type of guy.* I think they had a little bit of a running-for-cover type of feeling out there when things went to hell. Anyway, it was a disaster; it failed. Tom Hayward by that time was CNO. I think Tom felt pretty badly about that. Have you talked to Tom?

Q: Yes, but we haven't gotten that far in the discussion of his career yet.

Admiral Shear: You should ask him about that.

Q: Did you have much contact with the CNO when you were in that billet in Naples?

Admiral Shear: Yes. Of course, I was there as a NATO commander. But I always thought highly of Hayward. I don't agree with Bob Long on that. And I'll tell you something that I haven't told anybody. Holloway asked me when he got ready to retire who I would put in to be the CNO. I said, "Of all the contemporaries, the guys that are qualified for it, I'd pick Hayward."

I worked closely with him in the Pentagon when he was OP-090, and there were several other people that Holloway asked me about. I said that clearly he was the best selection. And Jim did that with a number of his senior people whom he regarded highly. I think he got the same answer from a number of them. As a matter of fact, I know he did. Then he'd pass that on to the Secretary and so forth. Anyway, Hayward got the job, and I think he did a damn good job. I don't agree with Bob on that.

Q: What do your remember about your dealings with him when you were in that job?

---

* Colonel Charlie A. Beckwith, USA, was leader of the assault team.

Admiral Shear: I didn't pick up the phone and talk to him like I did the CNO when I was in London--because I had no reason to. He made a specific point of coming over to my change of command. He didn't have to do that, but he did. Among other things, I think he knew because I supported him strongly in his billet as CNO. And he came over for several visits to the Sixth Fleet. Whenever he came over, whether it was a NATO visit or a national visit, I always made it a point to get together with him and made sure we had an exchange while he was in the Mediterranean area. But on a daily basis I had no reason to pick up the phone and talk to Hayward. Because I was outside the national chain of command. The guy I talked to most frequently was my boss in Brussels, i.e., either Bernie Rogers or Al Haig.

Q: So you would not get called in for the CinCs' conferences the way you had when you were in London?

Admiral Shear: No, no. Not called in for CinCs' conferences. It would have been improper for me to be called in for CinCs' conferences.

Q: Well, any other recollections of that tour?

Admiral Shear: I was relieved by Bill Crowe, and I thought highly of Bill Crowe.[*] He did a good job out in the MidEast force. He did a good job as OP-06, head of plans and policy. And he did a good job as my relief as CinCSouth. I told him he was going to have the same problems that I had with the Greeks and Turks, and he told me after he had been there, "Yes, I had the same problems you did with the Greeks and Turks."

---

[*] Admiral William J. Crowe, Jr., USN, served as Commander in Chief Allied Forces Southern Europe from May 1980 to May 1983. He was later Chairman of the Joint Chiefs of Staff from 1 October 1985 to 30 September 1989.

I've been terribly disappointed in Bill Crowe since. Number one, he came out for Clinton, which no active duty officer should have done.* Even though he was retired, he still shouldn't have done it. I became even more disillusioned when he came out in support of queers in the military. He put himself on the line with what he wrote, and I think it was for The Washington Post. All of his colleagues have now lost all faith and confidence in Bill Crowe, almost to the man. It's a sad commentary, but it's true. No longer is he a figure to be admired in the U.S. Navy.

I won't say that he's been downgraded as far as Stansfield Turner, but he's lost most respect, most respect. I've been very frank to you about Stan Turner. I must tell you that practically everybody feels that way about him. They may not say so, but that's how they feel. He's not a professional man.

Q: Did you have any options for further active duty after that tour in Naples?

Admiral Shear: No. I reached the statutory age of 62, and I had to retire. Then I went to work for a shipping company in New York as vice president. Fine old shipping company called Norton Lilly.

Q: Did you feel any pangs taking off the uniform after that many years?

Admiral Shear: Oh, I guess you always do. Well, I couldn't go any further. I was 62 years old, and I had a great career and I was happy. I was in that job for less than a year in New York, and they called me down to the White House. They called me one Sunday night and said, "We want to see you tomorrow morning." Out of the blue.

I said, "What do you want to see me for?"

"We'll tell you when you get here."

---

* Crowe supported Democratic Party candidate Bill Clinton for President in the 1992 general election. Crowe was subsequently appointed as the U.S. ambassador to the United Kingdom.

So I called my boss, who was president of the company, and said, "They want to see me in the White House tomorrow morning."

He said, "Well, you better go."

So I went down there, and they said, "We want you to head up the Maritime Administration."

I said, "Who gave you my name?"

They said, "We won't tell you."

I said, "I've got a good job. I've had seven tours of duty in Washington. My wife doesn't want to come back to Washington. I don't want your job."

I went back to work and told my boss what I had said. And he said, "That's interesting."

One week later they called me and said, "We want to see you in Washington next morning." I went down there, and I saw the chief head hunter. He was a guy named Pemberton James, and he had an assistant who was a gorgeous blonde. She'd interviewed me the first time. When I went back there again, there was the same blonde, striking blonde. She said, "We talked to you before, and we still want you to take this job."

I said, "I don't want the job."

She said, "You said that before. The President wants you to take it."[*]

I said, "Who told the President about me?"

She said, "We want you to go over to talk to Drew Lewis." Drew Lewis was then Secretary of Transportation.[†]

I went over and talked to Lewis, and he said, "We want you for this job."

I said, "Why do you want me? Who told you about me?"

He said, "Well, I won't tell you who told me about you, but we want you for this job. We found out you're the toughest son of a bitch around here, the only guy who can make any progress with it." Because it was a mess; they all knew it was a mess. He said, "Furthermore, the President wants you to take it." I don't know whether the President wanted me to take it or not, but that's what he told me.

---

[*] Ronald Reagan had become the President of the United States in January 1981.
[†] Andrew L. Lewis, Jr., served as U.S. Secretary of Transportation, 1981-83.

So I said, "Well, hell's bells, the President asked me to take a job, I've got to take it."

So he said, "I thought you'd feel that way." [Chuckle] So I went back and told my boss they wanted me to take a job, so I said I would take it.

So he said, "How soon do they want you?"

"They said right away." So I had a few weeks to clean up. Went down and took that job. And it was an utterly nasty, thankless job. I told Drew Lewis, "Look, this industry is a mess, and if I take this job you've got to back me to a hilt, or otherwise we'll get nowhere."

He said, "I'll back you." And I must say, Drew Lewis is a rare man. He ought to be President of the United States.

So I went down and took that job. I told Lewis what we had to do. We had to get the unions under control, we had to get the shipbuilders under control, we had to get the operators under control, and we had to get the politicians under control. I knew we were going to have trouble with each one of them. Well, we did have trouble with each one. I tell you, I got bruises all over me, but we finally got the unions under control--halfway. We forced them to cut down on their grossly overstaffed ships. We forced them to cut down their obscene wages: $150,000 a year for six months, for example. We started to get the industry halfway back on its feet, but we never got anywhere near as far as we should.

Then Lewis departed for bigger and better things, running the Northern Pacific Railroad, and Elizabeth Dole took over.[*] Elizabeth was a delightful lady, smart as a whip. Stood one at Duke, stood one at Harvard Law School. Her husband was Bob Dole.[†] She said she would back me, but she said, "Please don't rock the boat." She just didn't want anything to go off kilter. But, hell, you can't get anywhere with an industry unless you really start tearing them to pieces, because it was just a mess. So I stayed there for four years, the first full term of Reagan's.

Then I said, "Look, I've been here four years, and I've made a little progress, nowhere near enough. But I've got to spend a little more time with my wife. I've given her

---

[*] Elizabeth H. Dole served as Secretary of Transportation, 1983-87.
[†] Senator Robert Dole (Republican--Kansas), who ran unsuccessfully for President in 1996.

a life of the military, and I'm not going to stay for the second term." So I quit in '85, but I can give you half a day's discussion of the problems of the U.S. merchant marine.

Q: Well, please discuss some of the progress that you made.

Admiral Shear: The single most important thing that I was able to do was to get the unions to understand that if they did not cooperate and cut back on some of their ludicrous demands, that they weren't going to have any merchant marine per se in three to five years. There were five big unions. I called in all of the presidents within a couple of weeks of my taking over. I told Lewis I was going to do this. And I laid down the law to them. I said, "Look, I want you to make such and such cut in wages. I want you to reduce the size of your crews from 30-odd down to 20-21. And I want you to start being competitive. If you're not, you're going to put all your companies out of business." And they were very reluctant.

Incidentally, I locked the door. I told my secretary to lock the door and turn off the air-conditioning. And I kept them in the office about this size, five or six of them and myself and my deputy and nobody else, not even a recorder. We were in there four full hours. By that time they were taking off their shirts; they were dripping wet and they were very reluctant. They didn't like my approach a bit. Because there had always been a politician in that job, and they never had to talk to the son of a bitch before. I said, "Look, my career is behind me. You aren't going to put any pressure on me. I took this job to help the President out. If you fellows want to cooperate, fine, but you're not going to get any cooperation out of me unless you do. The facts are there. You're going to lose these ships and these ships. Next year you're going to be down so many, and the year after that you're going to be down so many more, and you've got to face up to reality."

Well, they started to face up to it. First one union and then the others caved in. I think the first guy cut back 7% on the wages. I said, "That's nowhere near enough; you've got to do a little better than that."

Then they said, "Well, we'll cut down to so many men per ship in this company."

I said, "That's not enough. You've got to cut down more than that." We finally made some progress, and the industry will tell you today that what they have been able to do in reducing crews is what I forced on them in 1981. They all know that. They don't necessarily give me any credit for it, but they know that I forced it on them.

Is the industry any better today? No, it's worse. We made some progress with the unions. The industry has traditionally been fighting with each other. They sue each other with the drop of the hat. They forget who the real enemy is. The real enemy is the foreign operator who's more efficient than they are.

Then the U.S. shipbuilders throw their problems in the middle of the ring, and they don't want to let anybody build foreign. But if you don't build foreign, you can't get a competitive ship. There's no way in the world it's possible to build a competitive ship in a U.S. yard at a minimum of three times the price of a foreign ship. But they won't admit that, and they throw legal roadblocks in to prevent building abroad. They run to their lobbyists, their buddies on the hill. It's just a tremendous morass, everybody fighting each other with zero progress.

Now, it's gotten so bad that Clinton's just said, "Well, I'm going to withdraw all subsides." Everybody is screaming about that, but I'm not so sure that's not the best thing. It's a way of forcing them to be more competitive. But what's going to happen is they're not going to try to be competitive. The unions are going to say, "Well, the hell with you. Unions, you aren't cooperating. We're just going to shift our companies to foreign flag." And that's happening right now. So I think within a year or two you're going to see just a handful of ships left, and they're going to be what we call the Jones Act Ships. The Jones Act Ships are the ships that run to Alaska, to San Juan, to Hawaii, and they have to be U.S. flags and U.S. built. That's by law, and everything else is going to be foreign.

Q: Well, the construction subsidies went before. Did you have a hand in that, doing away with those?

Admiral Shear: Construction subsidies went during my period. The White House forced that on me, but even if they hadn't it didn't make any difference. Because even with the construction subsides, the cost of a ship was still two to three times in the U.S. versus what it was foreign. We had a one-year window, incidentally, where we were permitted to build foreign. I got 35, 38 ships built foreign by our better companies within this one-year period. We got them under contract within that one year; that's all you had to do. We built ships in Korea. We built ships in Japan. We built ships in Denmark. We built ships in West Germany.

Those 35, 40-odd ships today are the best ships we've got in the U.S. merchant marine. And they are first-rate ships. The American President Line, for example, has just gone out and built some more in West Germany, even though they had to man them with U.S. crews. And Sea-Land, the next biggest line, is going to do the same thing. I think all of our better lines are going to be foreign flag within one to two years.

That was a tough, mean job. The thinking people of the industry knew I was doing my damndest for them, but the unions, boy, they hated my guts. They did everything possible to downgrade me and run me down. Caused me problems with the Congress. Caused me problems with the owners. It was not a pretty time.

Q: Did it ever get to the area of personal threats or vendettas?

Admiral Shear: Well, they never threatened to shoot me or anything like that. But they did everything under the sun to make life miserable for me. They had ways to do that.

Q: Such as?

Admiral Shear: Well, they would run me down with the Congress, and, of course, they would fight me on cutting down on crews and make it very difficult for me to cut down on wages and crews. You had to force that stuff on them.

Q: Well, presumably you could present the logic of the case to these same committees, couldn't you?

Admiral Shear: Oh, yes, but you don't believe the power of the PACs.* That's one thing I learned in that job. They threw around money like it was going out of style, by the bushel basket full. They had many of those committee members right there in the palm of their hands. I hadn't seen that kind of stuff in the Navy. I knew there was a certain amount of activity between shipbuilders and so forth and the Hill, but I'd never seen the PAC system work as effectively as I did then. The PAC system is going to be the end of U.S. democracy if we don't get it under control. It's just a mess. It's not a matter who you elect; it's who you pay off the best. It goes on right before your eyes.

Q: Well, that's going to be a big hurdle in trying to get any kind of a medical care system implemented.

Admiral Shear: Yep, exactly. So that was not a fun four-year period. I worked my ass off. I worked my tail off. It was a challenge. I liked the industry; I always liked shipping and I like ships. I did my best to make them realize that we had a chance to make a good U.S. merchant marine, but overall--except for my success with the unions--my contributions, I think, were minimal. I did my damndest, and I did halfway get the unions under control. That was about it.

Q: Well, maybe you kept the corpse alive a little longer.

Admiral Shear: That's about it. I kept the corpse alive a little longer. Yep. I was talking to somebody the other day, one of the people in the industry whom I had known. He said, "Well, one thing we've got you to thank for, we got our crews down from 33 down to 21, because they were all overmanned. And we got your halfway decent cut in the wages. Still not enough, but we got a start." So I took that as a pretty good compliment.

---

* PACs--political action committees, which funnel campaign contributions to candidates who support the committee's positions.

Q: Well, it was a two-edged sword. The wages were very high for those who could work, but not a whole lot of people could get work.

Admiral Shear: There were dropping; they were dropping ships every year, that's correct. They were extremely shortsighted in their views, for just that reason.

Q: So it was feast or famine.

Admiral Shear: Yeah, feast or famine, exactly. And now, as far as U.S. seafarers are concerned, it's going to be pretty close to famine. And they did it to themselves. Hands down they did it themselves. They'll wring their hands and say, "Oh, what a terrible thing, there are no U.S. ships." Well, you did it, boys; you did it.

Now, let me digress a bit and take us back practically to the beginning. This is one little recall of my Naval Academy days. Roosevelt was President, of course, and he had the Potomac as a yacht.* She had actually been a former Coast Guard patrol vessel used in rum-running campaigns, among other things. He was quite a yachtsman and quite a sailor, and he would take her up and down the coast. She came into the Naval Academy once while I was here when he was on board.

And, of course, the midshipmen were gawking around; we went down and looked her over from the seawall. He was on the after deck with some guests, and I guess they were having drinks or cocktails and conversation. We went by as close as we could get, which was fairly close, a few feet. He waved to all of us and sang out "Hello" and so forth. So that was my sole contact with the President Roosevelt.

Q: What year would that have been?

---

* The Coast Guard ship Electra was completed in 1934 and taken over the following year by the Navy. She was commissioned as the USS Potomac (AG-25) in March 1936. The ship was 165 feet long, 24 feet in the beam, displaced 416 tons, and had a top speed of 13 knots. She was decommissioned 18 November 1945 and struck from the Navy List 25 February 1946.

Admiral Shear: I would say 1939 or '40.

Q: I think later that yacht was replaced, because when they put antiaircraft guns on it, it got so top-heavy it was not safe to go to sea.

Admiral Shear: Well, let me continue the story on the Potomac. This jumps ahead many years. One day, after I became Maritime Administrator, a visitor came in to see me. It was Roosevelt's son James, and he wanted me to get some money to rebuild his father's yacht. I knew about the yacht; she was out in the basin at Alameda--a total and complete wreck: stripped right down, half the hull was gone, ribs were gone. She was just an absolute wreck.

But there was a group put together; I guess they were called the Potomac Society or something like that. They scraped up a couple of hundred thousand dollars to start the rebuilding, and they wanted the Maritime Administration to fund the rest of the project. Well, you'd just have to start with a little chunk of steel and build around it. That's all there was to it. I went out and looked her over. Fortunately, I had looked her over before James Roosevelt came to see me. He wanted me either to fund it with resources which I had, or he wanted me to sponsor a bill in Congress through the Maritime Administration to get the money to redo it. They said at that time that they wanted $5 million. I didn't have any money of that kind at all, but I did say that I would support them as far as saying that it would be nice to restore the vessel.

Some of the shipping companies on the East Coast generated a little bit of interest. The Port of Alameda in Oakland generated some interest. I went out there later on; we got a little bit of money to see how they were doing. The committee that they had working on it was not doing a very good job, so I said there was nothing more I could do about it. After I left the Maritime Administration, they got an appropriation through the Congress. They got a few million dollars and they got some private funds, and they have her now essentially completely rebuilt. I think they're going to use her for a museum out there.

Q: Maybe 10% of the original vessel in this version?

Admiral Shear: Less than 10%, I would say. So that's what happened to the Potomac.

Q: Well, how have you spent your time since '85, when you left that job with the Maritime Administration?

Admiral Shear: Oh, my God, I've been involved in everything. I've got all these freebies that I work on. Then I have this international construction company that I'm working with quite a bit, and that's a fun deal. That's the single thing that I get paid for right now. Everything else I do is free.

Q: Well, you must take great satisfaction out of the Submarine Museum and Library, for example, up at New London.

Admiral Shear: That's a very nice job. We're making a lot of progress. We're putting 300,000 people a year through that.

Q: It's a beautiful museum.

Admiral Shear: Yep, 300,000 a year. The only things that beat us are the Mystic Seaport and the Mystic Aquarium. The seaport gets about 400,000 a year, and the aquarium, believe it or not, gets over 600,000 a year. And, of course, we got that new gambling casino up there, and that's beating everybody, those crazy Indians on that reservation. Who would believe? It opened a year ago February, and it's been open seven days a week every since. It's packed all the time, 24 hours a day.

Q: That's a truly unfortunate commentary on our society.

Admiral Shear: It is, indeed. Governor Weicker realized it, and he did his best to prevent it.* But the federal government said, "You have this right, Mr. Indian. Go ahead and build your casino." It's a sad thing. All the people are up there just losing their shirt.

Q: Well, I've even heard of cases of shipyard workers from Groton retrained as casino dealers or what have you.

Admiral Shear: That's quite correct, right. What's going to happen to Electric Boat, and as far as submarines are concerned is an open question. We're trying to keep enough money in the budget to keep a modest amount of submarine work. This <u>Seawolf</u> class is being debated up and down the line. What comes out of there, we'll know in a few months. Right now Electric Boat's got two or three years' worth of work left in the Tridents and the SSNs. Then they're going to start laying off people, literally by the thousands. They've already laid off people by the thousands. They've gone out from 20-odd thousand workers down to about 17,000. They're going to be down in a couple of years below 10,000. They figure even if they can keep one submarine a year or every two years going, they'll be down about 7,000. So they are in the process of losing 10,000 more jobs around there.

New England today is in pretty dire straits across the board. Of all the states up there, Connecticut is by far the worst. They are in the midst of a major depression right now. Because their defense work has been cut back everywhere, and it's very expensive to do business in the state of Connecticut anyway. They priced themselves out of business with their terrible Democratic bureaucracy which has been built up in that state. They're hurting very badly, very badly. This fellow Weicker is going his best to put the state back on its feet. He's a tough nut. He's the right guy at the right time, but he has a long way to go.

Q: I hope he has more success than you had in the Maritime Administration.

---

* Governor Lowell P. Weicker, Jr.

Admiral Shear: I hope. I hope. But that was a great experience. I enjoyed it, even though it was tough and difficult.

Q: Moving from the professional to the personal, could you please tell me about your children.

Admiral Shear: We have two great kids. Kathleen was born May 20, 1946, at Mare Island, California, and Kenneth was born December 22, 1949 at Bethesda, Maryland. Kathy graduated from the University of Wyoming with a degree in microbiology. She worked at the Salk Institute in San Diego for a few years, then decided she did not like lab work. She shifted jobs and became a flight attendant with TWA. She has been flying throughout the U.S. and Europe for 24 years. It's tough work, but she enjoys it. She lives in New York City and flies from JFK. She is hard-working, very attractive, and independent as hell. She's never been married.

Our son Ken graduated from Windham College in Vermont with a degree in systematics. He worked in Alaska for ten years in the commercial fishing business and in tugboating, supplying the North Slope of Alaska. He holds a master's license for unlimited oceangoing tugboats. He shifted careers a few years ago and is now working with a large British company which aims to improve businesses which are in trouble and get them on their feet. There's a big demand for this type of work. He has contracts in England, the U.S., Saudi Arabia, and South America. He never married. I don't know why. The girls all love him. He has finally found his place in the world and is doing very well.

The only drawback in this is that Betty is upset because we have no grandchildren.

Q: Well, Admiral, I really thank you for the contribution you've made with this oral history. This is something that will be a legacy for years in the future for people who seek to look back and see how things were. So I very much appreciate it.

Admiral Shear: I've enjoyed it. There are a lot of vacancies in spots here, where I'll think of things that I should have told you years ago. When you've been away 10 or 15 years, things tend to get a bit hazy. You never make the notes that you should, you see. You never make enough notes, so you have to sort of pull things out of thin air. So if you think of something you particularly want to, want me to give an answer on, let me know and I will see what I can dig up.

Q: Thank you very much.

Admiral Shear: Okay.

Index To

Reminiscences of

Admiral Harold Edson Shear

U.S. Navy (Retired)

Adams, Lieutenant Commander Alden W., Jr., USN (USNA, 1944)
　　Served as chief engineer and exec of the submarine Trigger (SS-564) in the early 1960s, 127-128

Afghanistan
　　Site of Soviet intervention in 1979, 285-286

Air Force, U.S.
　　Participation in the Armed Forces Staff College in the mid-1950s, 137-138; involvement in a 1955 joint-service war game involving nuclear weapons, 149-152; the Navy wanted to make sure that the Air Force would not take over its nuclear weapons targets in the early 1960s, 191; SAC provided a briefing to Admiral H. P. Smith, CinCLant, in the early 1960s, 210-211; attitude of members of the SACEur staff in the mid-1970s, 282-283

Alcohol
　　Rum runners brought alcohol ashore on Long Island during the Prohibition era of the 1920s, 3-4; in the mid-1960s the fast combat support ship Sacramento (AOE-1) delivered beer to Marines stationed at Chulai, South Vietnam, 231-233

Alden, Dr. Carroll Storrs
　　Long-time Naval Academy professor with the nickname "Sterile Carroll," 36

Alexander Hamilton, USCGC (WPG-34)
　　Coast Guard cutter torpedoed and sunk off Iceland in January 1942, 44-45

Allied Forces Southern Europe (CinCSouth)
　　Relationship in the mid-1970s with CinCUSNavEur, 288; had command of the Sixth Fleet in some situations, 288; in 1983 the U.S. national billet of CinCUSNavEur was absorbed into the NATO billet of CinCSouth, 301-302; scope of the command in the late 1970s, 342-343; Shear's relation with General Alexander Haig, SACEur, 343-344; relations between Greece and Turkey as NATO members, 345-346, 349-352, 369; U.S. diplomat Jonathan Stoddart served as political adviser to CinCSouth in the late 1970s, 358-359; subordinate commanders from various nations, 365-367

Ammunition
　　Provided at sea to warships in the mid-1960s by the fast combat support ship Sacramento (AOE-1), 224

Anderson, Admiral George W., Jr., USN (USNA, 1927)
　　Was Chief of Naval Operations during the Cuban Missile Crisis of 1962, 198, 200; fired as CNO, 201

Anderson, Commander Roy G., USN (USNA, 1940)
　　Selected in the late 1950s to be a Polaris submarine skipper, chose instead to be chief staff officer of Submarine Squadron 14, 157-158, 166

Annenberg, Walter H.
  Served as U.S. ambassador to Great Britain in the early 1970s, 305

Antiair Warfare
  Measures on board the destroyer Stack (DD-406) in 1942, 60, 63-64; in World War II U.S. submarines in the Pacific used extra lookouts to guard against air attack, 103-104

Antisubmarine Warfare
  Limited sonar capability on board the destroyer Stack (DD-406) early in World War II, 46; Allies slow to deal with the U-boat threat in World War II, 46-47; heavy emphasis on ASW in the 1970s because of the Soviet threat, 262-272; specialized ASW carriers were not particularly effective, 267; development of LAMPS, 271; research in non-acoustic detection measures, 271-272

Antisubmarine Warfare and Tactical Electromagnetic Programs (OP-095), OpNav
  Early directors when the division was formed in the 1960s, 262, 268; heavy emphasis on ASW in the 1970s because of the Soviet threat, 262-272; electronic warfare became part of the ASW division in OpNav in the early 1970s, 263

Arco, Idaho
  In 1958-59 prospective skippers of Polaris submarines underwent the nuclear power training program in Washington, D.C., and Arco, 161-163

Argentina
  Relationship with Brazil in the late 1960s, 246-247

Armed Forces Staff College, Norfolk, Virginia
  In the mid-1950s provided joint-service staff training to officers of the different services, 136-139

Army, U.S.
  Attitude of Army members of the SACEur staff in the mid-1970s, 282-283; in 1974 General Alexander M. Haig, Jr., chose the SACEur job even though he could have been Army Chief of Staff, 287; terrorist kidnaping of an Army general in Italy in the early 1980s, 356-357; an Army officer tried an end run on Shear in the late 1970s and was upbraided, 367

Atlantic Command, U.S. (CinCLant)
  In the early 1960s was in the direct chain of command from the JCS to Polaris submarines, 194-196, 204-209; the United States evacuated its Polaris submarines from Holy Loch, Scotland, during the Cuban crisis in October 1962, 198-199; operated a battle staff at Norfolk during the Cuban crisis, 199-200; coordination with ComSubLant on Polaris submarine schedules in the early 1960s, 207-209

Atomic Bombs
Shear felt that the bombs dropped on Japan in August 1945 were unnecessary as a means of inducing Japanese surrender because of all the bombs and mines dropped previously, 106-107

Aurand, Captain Evan P., USN (USNA, 1938)
Was naval aide to President Dwight Eisenhower during a visit to the ballistic missile submarine Patrick Henry (SSBN-599) in 1960, 178-179

B-29 Superfortress
U.S. bomber used to drop bombs and mines on Japan in the final year of World War II, 106-107

Baer, Rear Admiral Donald G., USN (USNA, 1937)
Commanded the naval base at Subic Bay in the Philippines in the mid-1960s, 228

Bagley, Admiral Worth H., USN (USNA, 1947)
After service as CinCUSNavEur, became Vice Chief of Naval Operations in 1974, 275; close relationship with CNO Elmo Zumwalt, 275-276, 290-292, 311, 313, 326; retired unexpectedly in 1975, 277, 310-311; while CinCUSNavEur had a strained working relationship with CinCLant, Ralph Cousins, 304-305

Bahrain
Served in the 1970s as a base for the U.S. Middle East Force, 308

Baldini, Ammiraglio di Squadra Aldo, Italian Navy
As naval commander for Allied Forces Southern Europe in the late 1970s, 366-367

Bangor, Washington
Selection in the early 1970s as a base for Trident submarines, 252-254

Banister, Commander Alan B., USN (USNA, 1928)
Commanded the submarine Sawfish (SS-276) in the Pacific in 1944, 96-98; commanded a wolf pack called Banister's Beagles, 98; was an aggressive skipper, 100-101

Bardshar, Vice Admiral Frederic A., USN (USNA, 1938)
Lost his job as director of electromagnetic programs in the early 1970s because of differences with CNO Elmo Zumwalt, 263

Beach, Captain Edward L., USN (USNA, 1939)
As the top-ranked midshipman at the Naval Academy in October 1938, he took it seriously when Orson Welles's radio broadcast made it seem that Martians were landing on earth, 29-30; impetuous as the first commanding officer of the submarine Trigger (SS-564) in the early 1950s, 122-128; at the launching of the Nautilus (SSN-571) in 1954, 135; skipper of the submarine Triton (SSN-586) in 1959-60, 250

Becuna, USS (SS-319)
Had a relaxed peacetime operating schedule while based in Hawaii shortly after World War II, 112-116; received a Guppy modernization in the late 1940s, 117, 127; operations in the Atlantic in the early 1950s, 128-129; intelligence-gathering surveillance patrols off the Soviet Union, 129-132; visit to Scotland in the early 1950s, 130; ship handling, 132-134; joined a lineup of submarines for the launching of the nuclear-powered submarine Nautilus (SSN-571) in 1954, 135; the British passenger liner Queen Mary dipped her flag to the Becuna during an encounter in the early 1950s, 136; as part of ASW hunter-killer groups, 267

Belknap, USS (CGN-26)
Collided with the aircraft carrier John F. Kennedy (CV-67) in 1975, 337-338

Benham (DD-397)-Class Destroyers
Commissioned in the late 1930s, these ships were capable of great speed, 68-70

Benson, Commander Roy S., USN (USNA, 1929)
Highly respected officer who was on the staff of submarine school at New London early in 1944, 90-91

Beshany, Rear Admiral Philip A., USN (USNA, 1938)
Served as director of the Submarine Warfare Division of OpNav in the late 1960s, 248-249

Bigley, Rear Admiral Thomas J., USN (USNA, 1950)
Did a fine job as Commander U.S. Middle East Force in the mid-1970s, 308

Black Personnel
Black civilians from the South worked in the menhaden fishing industry in the 1930s, 5-7; as CNO in the early 1970s, Admiral Elmo Zumwalt created enhanced opportunities for blacks in the Navy, 316

Blair, Clay, Jr.
Time magazine writer who rode the new submarine Trigger (SS-564) in the early 1950s, 125-126

Boston, Massachusetts
The British troop transport Queen Mary loaded soldiers there in early 1942 for a transatlantic crossing, 54-55

Brazil
Shear learned the Portuguese language in the late 1960s to prepare for a billet as chief of the U.S. naval mission in Brazil, 233-234; the U.S. naval mission there was established in 1922, 234-235, 242; Shear traveled widely in the country, 235-236, 246-247; industrial base, 237, 245-247; the military sometimes takes over the nation's government, 240-241; President Jimmy Carter's approach toward Brazil damaged U.S. relations with the country in the late 1970s, 241, 363-364; Shear was deeply involved

in all aspects of Brazil's armed forces, 241-244; provided intelligence assistance to the United States in the late 1960s, 242-243; Japanese influence in the country, 245-247; shipbuilding, 246-247; relationship with other South American nations, 246-247

Brazilian Army
Distinguished service in Italy in World War II, 236, 247; still had cavalry divisions in the late 1960s, 246-247

Brazilian Navy
Because of the U.S. naval mission established in Brazil in 1922, by the late 1960s the Brazilian Navy had many similarities to the U.S. Navy, 234-235, 242; responsibility for wide-ranging river systems, 236; service in conjunction with U.S. forces in World War II, 236-237; top officials sought U.S. cruisers when they visited Washington in the late 1960s, 238, 240; turned to the British for new ships after the United States declined to cooperate, 241

Brown, General George S., USAF (USMA, 1941)
Opinion of the British armed forces in the 1970s, 302; excellent Chairman of the Joint Chiefs in the mid-1970s, 311-312

Bryan, Lieutenant (j.g.) Clarence Russell, USN (USNA, 1945)
Service as a junior officer in the submarine Becuna (SS-319) shortly after World War II, 114-115

Budgetary Matters
Role of the Vice Chief of Naval Operations in the budget process in the mid-1970s, 326-327

Bureau of Naval Personnel
Work of the training plans section in the late 1940s and early 1950s, 119-121; impact of the Korean War, 120-121; negotiations with Shear in 1965 concerning command of the fast combat support ship Sacramento (AOE-1), 215-216

Bureau of Supplies and Accounts
Made useful inputs to the design of the fast combat support ship Sacramento (AOE-1) in the early 1960s, 222

Burke, Admiral Arleigh A., USN (USNA, 1923)
Headed an anti-Air Force organization within OpNav in the late 1940s, 139; as Chief of Naval Operations in the mid-1950s had his differences with General Curtis LeMay of the Air Force, 144; relationship in the mid-1950s with Britain's Admiral of the Fleet Lord Louis Mountbatten, 144-146; enthusiastic support for the Polaris program, 154, 169; in 1960 observed Polaris tests on board the ballistic missile submarine Patrick Henry (SSBN-599), 169; sent Shear to brief General LeMay about Polaris patrols in 1961, 182-183; didn't want the Air Force to take over Polaris targets, 191; ensured that Polaris submarines were merged into the SIOP, 195

C-47 Skytrain
   Transport plane used by Shear for his travels throughout Brazil in the late 1960s, 235-236, 246

CH-46 Sea Knight
   Helicopter used by the fast combat support ship Sacramento (AOE-1) for vertical replenishments in the mid-1960s, 220; used in the mid-1960s to deliver beer to Marines stationed at Chulai, South Vietnam, 231-233

Canada
   Canadians worked in the U.S. fishing industry in the 1920s, prior to the Depression, 4-5, 10; work with the U.S. Navy on the development of LAMPs helicopters in the early 1970s, 271

Carlucci, Frank C. III
   As a foreign service officer, was a political officer in Brazil in the late 1960s, later U.S. Secretary of Defense in 1980s, 244

Carr, Rear Admiral Kenneth M., USN (USNA, 1949)
   Performed well as aide to Deputy Secretary of Defense William Clements in the mid-1970s, 333

Carroll, Rear Admiral Kent J., USN
   Role in supervising the clearance of the Suez Canal in the mid-1970s, 293-294

Carter, President James E., Jr. (USNA, 1947)
   After the United States did much to build up Iran in the 1960s and 1970s, Shear believes Carter made a mistake in dropping support for the Shah in 1979, 214, 284, 286-287, 363-364; approach toward Brazil damaged U.S. relations with that country in the late 1970s, 241, 363-364; chose David C. Jones as Chairman of the JCS because he wanted a yes-man, 312; didn't pay much attention to the military, 319; disliked by SACEur, General Alexander Haig, 364

Central Intelligence Agency
   Provided a small part of the student body at the National War College in the mid-1960s, 211; had representatives in various eastern European nations in the late 1970s, 361

Chulai, South Vietnam
   In the mid-1960s the fast combat support ship Sacramento (AOE-1) delivered beer to Marines stationed at Chulai, 231-233

CinCLant
   See Atlantic Command, U.S.

CinCSouth
   See Allied Forces Southern Europe

CinCUSNavEur
See Naval Forces Europe, U.S.

Claytor, W. Graham, Jr.
As Secretary of the Navy in the late 1970s, relationship with the CNO, 320-323

Clements, William P., Jr.
As Deputy Secretary of Defense, was involved in the choice of the F/A-18 aircraft in the mid-1970s, 333-334

Coast Guard, U.S.
Attempted to thwart the rum runners who brought alcohol ashore on Long Island during the Prohibition era of the 1920s, 3-4; the cutter Alexander Hamilton (WPG-34) was torpedoed and sunk off Iceland in January 1942, 44-45

Cochran, Lieutenant Commander Schamyl, USN (Ret.) (USNA, 1908)
Headed a Naval Academy cram school at Annapolis in the late 1930s, 11-13, 17-18, 33

Cochran-Bryan Preparatory School
Operated in Annapolis in the late 1930s to prepare students for Naval Academy entrance exams, 11-13, 17-18, 33

Colclough, Rear Admiral Oswald S., USN (USNA, 1921)
Brilliant officer who served as ComSubPac in 1948-49, 117-118

Commercial Ships
See Merchant Ships

Communications
Use of the SJ radar by the submarine Sawfish (SS-276) in 1944-45 to communicate with other submarines, 101; in Submarine Force Pacific Fleet in the late 1940s, 118; methods used by Polaris submarines in the early 1960s, 183-185; between crew members of the ballistic missile submarine Patrick Henry (SSBN-599) and their families while on patrol in the early 1960s, 187; the U.S. Navy lost an important radio station when the Soviets took over Ethiopia in 1974, 278-279

Communist Party
Active in Italy in the late 1970s, 354-355

Congress
Congressmen visited the new submarine Trigger (SS-564) when she went to Washington in the early 1950s, 126-127; approval of submarine building programs in the late 1960s and early 1970s, 249-252, 258-260; influence on Congress in the 1980s by political action committees, 378-379

Convoying
A number of U.S. destroyers were involved escorting merchant ship convoys in the Atlantic early in World War II, 42-49, 53-54; weather conditions that confronted the convoys, 48-49

Cook, Lieutenant (j.g.) Allen B., USN (Ret.) (USNA, 1921)
As a Naval Academy English teacher in the 1930s, enjoyed going on midshipman cruises, 37-38

Cousins, Admiral Ralph W., USN (USNA, 1937)
While CinCLant in the early 1970s, had a strained working relationship with CinCUSNavEur, Worth Bagley, 304-305

Crowe, Admiral William J., Jr., USN (USNA, 1947)
Was serving as CinCSouth in 1983 when the billet absorbed that of CinCUSNavEur, 301-302; relations with Greece and Turkey, 372; Shear considers Crowe's post-retirement activities as disappointing, 373

Cuban Missile Crisis
The United States evacuated its Polaris submarines from Holy Loch, Scotland, during the Cuban crisis in October 1962, 198-199; CinCLant operated a battle staff at Norfolk, 199-200

Cyprus
Mediterranean island that was source of hassles between Greece and Turkey in the 1970s, 288-290, 345

Damage Control
To ward off on-board fires, U.S. warships chipped off a lot of paint following the sinking of four cruisers off Guadalcanal in August 1942, 62

Dare, Rear Admiral James A., USN (USNA, 1939)
Evaluation of his service as Commander South Atlantic Force in the late 1960s, 239

Daspit, Rear Admiral Lawrence R., USN (USNA, 1927)
Lost out on a chance for promotion to vice admiral when he declined to move ComSubLant headquarters from New London to Norfolk in 1960, 204-205

Davis, Vice Admiral Donald C., USN (USNA, 1944)
Did an excellent job as head of Navy program planning in the mid-1970s, 326-327

Demobilization
Use of Navy ships in the Magic Carpet program to bring servicemen home from overseas at the end of World War II, 111-112

Dennison, Rear Admiral Robert L., USN (USNA, 1923)
Headed the Strategic Plans Division (OP-60) of OpNav in the mid-1950s, 139-142, 147-149; personality of, 148; as Commander in Chief Atlantic in the early 1960s, was in the direct chain of command from the JCS to Polaris submarines, 194-196, 204-207, 210; did a fine job as CinCLant during the Cuban Missile Crisis in October 1962, 198, 200-201

Depth Charges
Dropped by U.S. destroyers on Japanese survivors in the water following the Battle of Vella Gulf in August 1943, 73-74, 76-77; damage to U.S. submarines by Japanese depth charges in World War II, 102-103

DeWolf, Lieutenant Commander Maurice M., USNR
Wealthy reserve officer who taught sailing at the Naval Academy during World War II, 21

Diesel Engines
See Propulsion Plants

Dole, Elizabeth H.
Involvement with the Maritime Administration while serving as Secretary of Transportation in the early 1980s, 375

Draemel, Captain Milo F., USN (USNA, 1906)
Made a fine impression as the Naval Academy's commandant of midshipmen in the late 1930s, 39-40

Drugs
As a problem for the Navy in the 1970s, 316-317

Education
Shear attended a small 12-grade school on Long Island in the 1920s and 1930s, 2, 10-11

Egypt
U.S. clearing of the Suez Canal in the mid-1970s, 293-294

Eisenhower, President Dwight D. (USMA, 1915)
Visited the ballistic missile submarine Patrick Henry (SSBN-599) during her sea trials in 1960, 178-180; witnessed missile tests, 179-180

Electric Boat Division, General Dynamics Corporation
Construction of the ballistic missile submarine Patrick Henry (SSBN-599) in the late 1950s, 170-175; construction of the ballistic submarine Maryland (SSBN-738), commissioned in 1992, 254-255; built a mockup of the Los Angeles (SSN-688)-class submarine, 258-259; laying off thousands of workers in the 1990s as submarine construction declines, 383

Electronic Warfare
Emphasis in the early 1970s on electronic intercepts, 264, 270

Engen, Rear Admiral Donald D., USN
Did a splendid job as deputy CinCUSNavEur in the mid-1970s, 278, 299-300

Erskine Phelps
Former sailing ship that was used in 1942-43 as a fuel barge at Purvis Bay, near Guadalcanal, 67-68

Ethiopia
The U.S. Navy lost an important radio station when the Soviets took over Ethiopia in 1974, 278-270

Evren, General Kenan, Turkish Army
Capable officer who served as chief of staff in the late 1970s, later President of Turkey, 348, 359-360

F/A-18 Hornet
Pressure from the Northrop head as this fighter/attack plane developed for the Navy in the mid-1970s, 331-332

Families of Servicemen
Idyllic life for submarine service families in Hawaii shortly after World War II, 113-114; life for families of crew members of the ballistic missile submarine Patrick Henry (SSBN-599) while she was on patrol in the early 1960s, 187-188

Field, Midshipman Henry C. Field, Jr., USN (USNA, 1942)
Brilliant individual who came from a strong academic background and did well at the Naval Academy, 18-19, 40

Finback, USS (SSN-670)
Left port with a topless dancer topside in 1975, 314-315

Fire
To ward off on-board fires, U.S. warships chipped off a lot of paint following the sinking of four cruisers off Guadalcanal in August 1942, 62

Fishing
Shear's stepfather was the master of a menhaden purse seiner that operated off the East Coast in the 1920s and 1930s, 4; description of fishing techniques and boat crews, 5-9; propulsion plants in fishing ships, 8-9; recreation for crew members, 10; fishing ship berthing arrangements, 24

Food
    Excellent chow was served on board the submarine Sawfish (SS-276) in World War II, 108; the submarine Becuna (SS-319) distributed food to needy Britons during a visit to Scotland in the early 1950s, 130; President Dwight Eisenhower's party brought special food for him during a visit to the ballistic missile submarine Patrick Henry (SSBN-599) in 1960, 179; Shear ate a lamb's eye during a visit to Jordan in the mid-1970s, 295

Football
    Pageantry connected with Army-Navy games in the late 1930s and early 1940s, 34-35

Foreign Service Institute
    Provided Shear with Portuguese language training in the late 1960s to prepare for a billet as chief of the U.S. naval mission in Brazil, 233-234

Foster, John S., Jr.
    As Director of Defense Research and Engineering in the early 1970s, made the decision on the number of missile tubes in a Trident submarine, 249-250

France
    Shear made an official visit while serving as CinCUSNavEur in the mid-1970s, 297-298; interests in Africa in the late 1970s, 361-363

French Navy
    Participated in exercises with the U.S. Sixth Fleet in the 1970s, despite French withdrawal from NATO, 296, 298-299

Gambling
    In the state of Connecticut in the 1990s, 382-383

Gantar, Captain Mark M., USN
    Served as the first skipper when the fast combat support ship Sacramento (AOE-1) went into commission in 1964, 216, 222

Gardner, Richard N.
    Served as U.S. ambassador to Italy during the Carter Administration in the late 1970s, 358

Geis, Rear Admiral Lawrence R., USN (USNA, 1939)
    Was not proficient in the Portuguese language while serving as chief of the U.S. naval mission to Brazil in the mid-1960s, 235

Gelber, Don
    U.S. diplomat who served as political adviser to CinCUSNavEur in the mid-1970s, 297-298

George Washington, USS (SSBN-598)
The first Polaris submarine conducted missile tests in the summer of 1960, 167; began her first deterrent patrol in November 1960, 180

General Dynamics Corporation
See Electric Boat Division, General Dynamics Corporation

German Navy
U-boats were extraordinarily successful in the Atlantic during the early years of World War II, 46-47

Germany
U.S. forces in Germany had a great life-style in the mid-1970s, 282

Ghormley, Vice Admiral Robert L., USN (USNA, 1906)
Apparently overwhelmed by the task facing him in the South Pacific in 1942, he was relieved by Vice Admiral William Halsey, 82-84

Gibraltar
The British stationed capable military officers at Gibraltar in the late 1970s, 365

Gill, Lieutenant Daniel J., USN
Mustang officer who did a fine job as ship's boatswain in the fast combat support ship Sacramento (AOE-1) in the mid-1960s, 218-219, 228

Goodpaster, General Andrew J., USA (USMA, 1939)
Relieved by General Alexander M. Haig, Jr., as SACEur in 1974, 280-281

Gould, Inc.
Work on torpedo development in the early 1970s, 264-265

Graham, Lieutenant Commander Roy W. M., USN (USNA, 1920)
As a Naval Academy duty officer in the late 1930s, seemed to have a perpetual brace, 39

Great Britain
In the mid-1970s the U.S. Navy had magnificent headquarters on Grosvenor Square in London, also a country house, 276-277; CinCUSNavEur staff members lived on the British economy, 303; Walter Annenberg as U.S. ambassador, 305; abandoned role east of Suez in the 1960s, creating a vacuum in the Middle East, 308-309; waning influence in the world in the late 1970s, 365-367
See also Royal Navy

Greece
Squabble with Turkey over Cyprus in the mid-1970s, 288-290, 345; CNO Elmo Zumwalt's attempt to homeport U.S. Navy ships in Greece in the early 1970s was not

successful, 289-292; relations with fellow NATO member Turkey in the late 1970s, 345-346, 349-351, 369

Grenfell, Rear Admiral Elton W., USN (USNA, 1926)
As ComSubPac in the late 1950s, was initially an opponent of the Polaris missile submarine program, 154-155, 204; maneuvered himself into the job as ComSubLant in 1960, 196, 204-205; was unhappy with the Polaris chain of command while serving as ComSubLant, 196-197, 202; coordination with CinCLant on Polaris submarine schedules in the early 1960s, 207-209

Guadalcanal
South Pacific island captured by U.S. Marines in the summer and fall of 1942 with support from Navy ships, 59-68

Guam
Japanese holed up in the hills ambushed submariners who got too adventurous when their boat visited the island for a rest stop in 1945, 99; work of black labor battalions of U.S. naval personnel in 1945, 109; facilities for support of the war effort, 109

Guppy
Modernization program applied to U.S. fleet submarines after World War II, 116-117

Gwin, USS (DD-443)
Served on Atlantic convoy duty early in World War II, 43

Haig, General Alexander M., Jr., USA (USMA, 1947)
Relief of General Andrew Goodpaster as SACEur in 1974, 280-281; relationship with Shear, 281-282, 343-344; chose the SACEur job even though he could have been Army Chief of Staff, 287; understood the importance of NATO's flanks better than his staff did, 307, 343, 351-352; had a poor relationship with Admiral Stansfield Turner, who served as CinCSouth in the mid-1970s, 343, 353; personality of, 344; dealings with Turkey, 345-346, 368; dislike of President Jimmy Carter, 364

Hall, Lieutenant Commander Harvey W., USN
Served as navigator of the battleship Missouri (BB-63) before and after her 1950 grounding, 197-198

Halsey, Admiral William F., Jr., USN (USNA, 1904)
Charismatic leader who did an excellent job of recognizing the work of subordinates in the Solomons campaign in 1943, 82-83

Harlfinger, Rear Admiral Frederick J. II, USN (USNA, 1935)
Evaluation of his service as Commander South Atlantic Force in the late 1960s, 239

Hayward, Admiral Thomas B., USN (USNA, 1948)
Programs to square away the Navy while serving as CNO in the late 1970s, 314, 316-317; role in the abortive hostage rescue attempt from Iran in 1980, 371; Shear's assessment of, 371-372

Hazzard, Captain William H., USN (USNA, 1935)
Did a fine job as Commander Submarine Squadron Two in the late 1950s, 156

Higgins, Commander John M., USN (USNA, 1922)
Commanded the destroyer Gwin (DD-443) on Atlantic convoy duty early in World War II, 43

Holloway, Admiral James L. III, USN (USNA, 1943)
While serving as Chief of Naval Operations in the mid-1970s, had Admiral Worth Bagley as VCNO for about a year, 275-276, 290-292, 310-311; persuaded to knock off overseas homeporting in Greece, 290-292; told Shear to improve relations between CinCUSNavEur and CinCLant, 304-305; as CNO worked with Shear to reverse some of the changes introduced during his predecessor Zumwalt's tenure, 311-316; assessment of, 318-319; relationship with Shear, 318-320, 323, 325; attended the national bicentennial celebration at New York in 1976, 338-339; polled senior subordinates on their ideas for his relief as CNO, 371

Holy Loch, Scotland
Served as a base for U.S. ballistic missile submarines in the early 1960s, 181-182, 190-191; protests by Scottish people, 181, 189-190; the United States evacuated its Polaris submarines from Holy Loch, Scotland, during the Cuban crisis in October 1962, 198-199; closed down as a U.S. base in 1992, 303

Hungary
NATO did not take an active part in supporting the Hungarian revolt in 1956, 153

Hyland, Vice Admiral John J., USN (USNA, 1934)
As Commander Seventh Fleet in the mid-1960s, visited the fast combat support ship Sacramento (AOE-1), 221

Iceland
Served as a support base for U.S. ships escorting transatlantic convoys early in World War II, 43, 48, 53

Incidents at Sea Agreement
Concluded between the United States and the Soviet Union in 1972, 309-310

Ingram, Vice Admiral Jonas H., USN (USNA, 1907)
Was highly regarded by the Brazilian Navy while working with it during World War II, 236-237

Intelligence
Advance intelligence warning helped the U.S. submarine Sawfish sink the Japanese submarine I-29 in 1944, 97-98; in the early 1950s the submarine Becuna (SS-319) made surveillance patrols off the Soviet Union, 129-132; in connection with the Cuban Missile Crisis in 1962, 198-200; Brazil provided intelligence assistance to the United States in the late 1960s, 242-243; emphasis in the early 1970s on electronic intercepts, 264, 270; the Royal Navy was candid about intelligence exchanges with the U.S. Navy in the 1970s, 307; Turkey aided the United States in gathering intelligence on the Soviet Union in the late 1970s, 346-347

Iran
After the United States did much to build up the nation in the 1960s and 1970s, Shear believes President Jimmy Carter made a mistake in dropping support for the Shah in 1979, 214, 283-284, 286-287, 363-364; aborted hostage rescue attempt in April 1980, 370-371

Israel
Perceived in the mid-1960s by war college students as being the major problem in the Middle East, 212; Shear made an official visit as CinCUSNavEur, 295

Italy
U.S. warships were successfully homeported in Italy in the 1970s, 291-292; Italian contributions to NATO in the late 1970s, 353-354; political parties, 354-355; concern in the late 1970s for the border with Yugoslavia, 355-356; terrorist incident in the early 1980s, 356-357; Richard Gardner was U.S. ambassador to Italy in the Carter Administration, 358; Italian Admiral Aldo Baldini was the naval commander for Allied Forces Southern Europe in the late 1970s, 366-367

Izmir, Turkey
The ballistic missile submarine Sam Houston (SSBN-609) visited in the spring of 1963, 203

Japan
Shear felt that the atomic bombs dropped on Japan in August 1945 were unnecessary as a means of inducing Japanese surrender because of all the bombs and mines dropped previously, 106-107; industrial influence in Brazil in the late 1960s, 245-246

Japanese Navy
Participation in a night surface action against U.S. destroyers in the Battle of Vella Gulf in August 1943, 72-78; survivors were depth-charged in the water after the battle, 73-74, 76-77; the U.S. submarine Sawfish sank the Japanese submarine I-29 in 1944, 97-98; damage to U.S. submarines by Japanese depth charges in World War II, 102-103

Jarrett, Lieutenant Commander Harry B., USN (USNA, 1922)
Demonstrated a real gift for leadership while a battalion officer at the Naval Academy in the early 1940s, 31

Johnston, Admiral Means, Jr., USN (USNA, 1939)
While serving as CinCSouth in the mid-1970s, had a good working relationship with CinCUSNavEur, 288; may have gotten the job through political connections, 323

Joint Chiefs of Staff
Role of the Strategic Plans Division (OP-60) of OpNav in contributing to JCS positions in the mid-1950s, 141; meetings of in the mid-1970s, 340-341

Joint Staff
Prior to the Goldwater Nichols Act of 1986, the Navy didn't send its most talented officers to the Joint Staff, 341-342

Joint Strategic Target Planning Staff
Role in U.S. nuclear weapons targeting in the late 1950s and early 1960s, 152, 195, 206-207

Jones, General David C., USAF
Weak and ineffective as Chairman of the Joint Chiefs in the late 1970s, 312, 340

Jones, Thomas V.
Northrop Corporation head who lobbied hard for the F/A-18 Hornet in the mid-1970s, 331-332

Jordan
Shear made an official visit to the country while serving as CinCUSNavEur in the mid-1970s, 295

Jupiter Missiles
U.S. agreement to remove Jupiter missiles from Turkey in the wake of the 1962 Cuban crisis, 202-203; initial planning for sea-based ballistic missiles contemplated the possibility of putting Jupiter missiles in merchant ships, 205-206

Jurika, Captain Stephen, Jr., USN (USNA, 1933)
Brilliant officer who served in the Strategic Plans Division (OP-60) of OpNav in the mid-1950s, 139-140, 144; wasn't selected for flag rank, though the Navy's aviation community thought he would be, even without a carrier command, 140, 146; World War II service, 146-147; involvement in a joint-service war game in the summer of 1955, 149-152

Kaltenborn, H. V.
Radio newscaster who was a passenger on a Pan American Clipper flight from Espiritu Santo to Pearl Harbor in late 1943, 89-90

Kaufman, Commander Robert Y., USN (USNA, 1946)
Served on the staff of the first Polaris submarine squadron in the early 1960s, 166; involved in selling the Trident submarine program to Congress in the early 1980s, 249-252, 258

Kennedy, President John F.
Visited a new Polaris submarine during the Cuban Missile Crisis of October 1962, 200-201; agreement to remove Jupiter missiles from Turkey in the wake of the Cuban crisis, 202-203

Kentucky (BB-66)
Never-finished U.S. battleship that supplied half her engineering plant to the fast combat support ship Sacramento (AOE-1), commissioned in 1964, 216-217

Kidd, Admiral Isaac C., Jr., USN (USNA, 1942)
As a Naval Academy midshipman in the early 1940s, 30-31; death of his father in 1941 on board the Arizona (BB-39), 31, 42, 339-340; graduation from the Naval Academy, 42; as executive assistant to CNO, kept in close touch with CinCLant during the Cuban Missile Crisis in 1962, 198, 200; as CinCLantFlt in 1975, fired the skipper of a nuclear submarine that had a topless dancer topside, 314-315; was on hand for the national bicentennial celebration at New York in 1976, 338-339

Kings Bay, Georgia
Selection in the early 1970s as a base for Trident submarines, 252-254

Kinnebrew, Commander Thomas R., USN
Role in antisubmarine warfare developments in the early 1970s, 268

Kissinger, Henry A.
As Secretary of State in the mid-1970s, was interested in strengthening Iran as a U.S. ally, 283-284

Knox, Frank
As Secretary of the Navy, presided at the December 1941 graduation of the Naval Academy's class of 1942, 42

Korean War
Advent of the war in 1950 brought a sharp turn-around in the amount of personnel training the Navy needed, 120-121

Labor Unions
During his tenure as maritime administration from 1981 to 1985, Shear tried to get the shipowners and unions to work together for the betterment of the industry, 375-380

Laingen, L. Bruce
U.S. diplomat who was stationed in Malta in the mid-1970s and was later taken hostage in Iran in 1979, 296-297

Laird, Melvin R.
Had a sympathetic ear for the Navy while serving as Secretary of Defense, 1969-73, 260-262, his aide, Dan Murphy, later became ComSixthFlt, 292

LAMPS
See Light Airborne Multi-Purpose System

Laning, Captain Richard B., USN (USNA, 1940)
Commanded the submarine tender Proteus (AS-19), which arrived in Holy Loch, Scotland, in the spring of 1960 to take care of Polaris missile submarines, 181, 189, 194

Law of the Sea
OP-60's attempts to get other nations to support the U.S. position on territorial waters in the mid-1950s, 141-144

Leave and Liberty
Not many opportunities for the crew of the destroyer Stack (DD-406) in the Solomons during World War II, 85; rest periods between patrols for the crew of the submarine Sawfish (SS-276) in World War II, 99, 108-109; the town of Olongapo in the Philippine Islands had an unsavory reputation for sailors on liberty in the mid-1960s, 228-229

Lehman, John F., Jr.
As Secretary of the Navy in the early 1980s was viewed as trying to manipulate the results of Navy selection boards, 322, 329

LeMay, General Curtis E., USAF
As Commander in Chief Strategic Air Command, had his differences with Admiral Arleigh Burke, the Chief of Naval Operations, in the mid-1950s, 144; involvement in a 1955 joint-service war game involving nuclear weapons, 150-151; as Air Force Chief of Staff in 1961, received a briefing from Shear on a success Polaris submarine deterrent patrol, 182-183; unsuccessful in his attempt to get Polaris submarines put under the Strategic Air Command, 195; parochial about SAC, 211

Lewis, Andrew L., Jr.,
As Secretary of Transportation in the early 1980s, recruited Lewis to serve as maritime administrator, 374-376

Libby, Vice Admiral Ruthven E., USN (USNA, 1922)
Brilliant officer who served as DCNO (Plans and Policy) in the mid-1950s, 139, 147; austere personality, 147-148

Light Airborne Multi-Purpose System
Development work on LAMPS helicopters in the early 1970s, 271

Little Rock, USS (CLG-4)
As Sixth Fleet flagship, made the first transit through the newly cleared Suez Canal in 1975, 294

Logistics
Various forms of support for the destroyer Stack (DD-406) in 1942-43 while she was in the Solomons campaign, 67-68; high level of support provided in the mid-1960s by the fast combat support ship Sacramento (AOE-1), 215-233

London, England
In the mid-1970s the U.S. Navy had magnificent headquarters on Grosvenor Square, 276-277

Long Island
Rum runners brought alcohol ashore on Long Island during the Prohibition era of the 1920s, 3-4

Long, Admiral Robert L. J., USN (USNA, 1944)
Served as first skipper of the gold crew of the ballistic missile submarine Patrick Henry (SSBN-599), commissioned in 1960, 164-166, 169, 181-182, 187; later commanded a second SSBN, 209

Los Angeles (SSN-688)-Class Submarines
Development and design of the class in the late 1960s, 248-249, 258-259

MacDonald, Vice Admiral R. D., RN
Served as deputy naval commander for Allied Forces Southern Europe in the late 1970s, 366

Magic Carpet
Use of Navy ships to bring servicemen home from overseas at the end of World War II, 111-112

Mail
Censorship of on board the destroyer Stack (DD-406) in World War II, 85-86; routing of 86

Majuro Atoll, Marshall Islands
In 1944 provided a base for submarine tenders and other fleet ships, 96, 98

Malta
Was a continuing problem for the United States in the 1970s, 296

Mare Island Navy Yard, Vallejo, California
Role in laying up submarines in the aftermath of World War II, 110-111

Marine Corps, U.S.
In the mid-1960s the fast combat support ship Sacramento (AOE-1) delivered beer to Marines stationed at Chulai, South Vietnam, 231-233

Maritime Administration
As the Maritime Administrator in the early 1980s, Shear had contacts with DoD official Frank Carlucci, 244; process by which Shear was chosen as the administrator in 1981, 373-375; during his tenure from 1981 to 1985 Shear tried to get the shipowners and unions to work together for the betterment of the industry, 375-380; approached in the 1980s about restoring the presidential yacht Potomac (AG-25), 381-382

Maryland, USS (SSBN-738)
The governor of Maryland snubbed the ship's commissioning ceremony in 1992, 254-255

Mayer, Dr. Eugene S.
Except for a short break in the Depression, taught at the Naval Academy from 1918 to 1948, 13, 36

McAlister, Lieutenant General Robert C., USA (USMA, 1945)
Served capably as chief of staff to CinCSouth in the late 1970s, 354, 368

McCain, Admiral John S., Jr., USN (USNA, 1931)
As a Naval Academy physics instructor in the late 1930s, later a flag officer, 36-37

McCann, Ensign Edward F. II, USN (1965)
Did well as a junior officer in the fast combat support ship Sacramento (AOE-1) after graduating from the Naval Academy, 218-219

McCauley, Rear Admiral Brian, USN (USNA, 1943)
Role in supervising the clearance of the Suez Canal in the mid-1970s, 293-294

McDonald, Admiral David L., USN (USNA, 1928)
As Chief of Naval Operations in 1967, patiently explained to Shear why he was being detailed to Brazil, 233-234

McDonald, Commander Harold W., USN (USNA, 1935)
Aviator with a fine record in World War II, served in BuPers in the late 1940s, 119-120

McKee, Rear Admiral Andrew I., USN (Ret.), (USNA, 1917)
A summary of his many contributions to submarine design and development in the 20th century, 170-171; work at the Electric Boat Company in the late 1950s, 171-172

McMullen, Ensign John J., USN (USNA, 1940)
Did an excellent job as chief engineer of the destroyer Stack (DD-406) at the outset of World War II, 50-53, 95; his father ran a machine shop operation to repair ships around New York, 52

Mediterranean Sea
The United States began sending Polaris submarines into the Mediterranean after removing Jupiter missiles from Turkey and Italy following the 1962 Cuban crisis, 202-203

See also Allied Forces Southern Europe; Sixth Fleet, U.S.

Menhaden
See Fishing

Merchant Ships
Convoying of during World War II, 42-54; initial planning for sea-based ballistic missiles in the mid-1950s contemplated the possibility of putting Jupiter missiles in merchant ships, 205-206; North Vietnam was supplied in the mid-1960s by Communist-bloc merchant shipping, 229-230; during his tenure as maritime administration from 1981 to 1985 Shear tried to get the shipowners and unions to work together for the betterment of the industry, 375-380

Middendorf, J. William II
Assessment of as Secretary of the Navy in the mid-1970s, 319-320, 322-323

Middle East
The area was in turmoil as a result of the closure of the Suez Canal in the autumn of 1956, 142-143; toured by U.S. National War College students in the mid-1960s, 212-215; after the United States did much to build up the nation in the 1960s and 1970s, Shear believes President Jimmy Carter made a mistake in dropping support for the Shah in 1979, 214, 283-284, 286-287, 363-364; Britain abandoned its traditional role east of Suez in the 1960s, creating a vacuum in the Middle East, 308-309; aborted hostage rescue attempt from Iran in April 1980, 370-371

Middle East Force, U.S.
Show-the-flag role in the mid-1960s, 214-215; similar role in the mid-1970s, 308-309

Military Academy, West Point, New York
Shear took West Point entrance exams in the late 1930s as practice for those from the Naval Academy, 18; pageantry connected with Army-Navy football games in the late 1930s and early 1940s, 34-35

Miller, Captain George H., USN (USNA, 1933)
In the 1950s pushed the idea of putting ballistic missiles to sea in merchant ships, 205-206

Miller, Vice Admiral Gerald E., USN (USNA, 1942)
As a Naval Academy midshipman in the early 1940s, 30-32; assigned to the Joint Strategic Target Planning Staff in the late 1950s, 152, 195

Mines
Shear felt that the atomic bombs dropped on Japan in August 1945 were unnecessary as a means of inducing Japanese surrender because of all the bombs and mines dropped previously, 106-107; development of the CapTor mine in the 1970s, 273; Turkish willingness to mine its straits, if necessary, in the late 1970s, 347

Missiles
Theoretical use of Soviet ballistic missiles in a joint-service U.S. war game in 1955, 150-151; the Polaris A-1 version had growing pains in the early 1960s, 167-169; test firing of Polaris missiles for President Dwight D. Eisenhower by the submarine Patrick Henry (SSBN-599) in 1960, 179-180; range of Polaris, 185, 250-251; Cuban Missile Crisis of 1962, 198-201; U.S. agreement to remove Jupiter missiles from Turkey in the wake of the Cuban crisis, 202-203; initial planning for sea-based ballistic missiles contemplated the possibility of putting Jupiter missiles in merchant ships, 205-206; long range of Trident missiles, 206, 250-251; in the early 1970s Dr. John S. Foster, Jr., decided Trident submarines would carry 24 missiles each, 249-250

Missouri, USS (BB-63)
Received a new navigator after running aground in January 1950, 197-198

Moorer, Admiral Thomas H., USN (USNA, 1933)
As Chief of Naval Operations in the late 1960s, visited Brazil and tried unsuccessfully to provide U.S. cruisers to the Brazilian Navy, 237, 240

Moosbrugger, Commander Frederick, USN (USNA, 1923)
Served as Commander Destroyer Division 12 during the victorious Battle of Vella Gulf against the Japanese in August 1943, 72-78

Mountbatten, Admiral of the Fleet Lord Louis, RN
Had a good relationship with Admiral Arleigh Burke, the U.S. Chief of Naval Operations in the latter part of the 1950s, 144-146; following World War II arranged for the U.S. Navy to have magnificent headquarters in London, 276-277; visited the submarine Patrick Henry (SSBN-599) at Holy Loch, Scotland, in 1961, 305; relations with the U.S. Navy in the 1970s, 306

Murphy, Vice Admiral Daniel J., USN
Did an excellent job as Commander Sixth Fleet, 1973-74, 289, 292

Music
Crews of fishing boats sang while pulling in their catches off the East Coast in the 1930s, 6-7; drum and bugle corps at the Naval Academy in the late 1930s, 34-35

Naples, Italy
Had a Communist mayor in the late 1970s, 354-355

National War College, Washington, D.C.
Site of a 1955 joint-service war game involving the projected use of nuclear weapons, 149-152; provided a superb course in the mid-1960s for U.S. military officers and members of State Department and CIA, 211-212; students made informative trips to various parts of the world, 212-215

Nautilus, USS (SSN-571)
Launching of in January 1954, 135; power plant, 162

Naval Academy, Annapolis, Maryland
Various preparatory schools operated in the late 1930s so prospective midshipmen could get ready for entrance exams, 11-13, 17-18, 33; summer training cruises in the late 1930s and early 1940s were limited to the East Coast by the war in Europe, 15, 21-28; plebe summer in 1938, 15-16; upper classmen would sometimes hassle lower classmen and vice versa, 16-17; academics, 18-19, 36-38; sailing program, 19-21; training of Naval Reserve officers in the early 1940s, 23-24; receipt of the news in December 1941 of the Japanese attack on Pearl Harbor, 29; reaction to a 1938 radio broadcast suggesting that Martians were landing on earth, 29-30; social life, 33-34; Army-Navy football games, 34-35; leadership structure, 38-41; early graduation of the class of 1942, 42; President Franklin D. Roosevelt visited Annapolis on board his yacht Potomac (AG-25) around 1940, 380-381

Naval Forces Europe, U.S. (CinCUSNavEur)
Had magnificent headquarters on Grosvenor Square in London, 276-277; involvement in the Ethiopia crisis of 1974, 278-279; Rear Admiral Don Engen did a splendid job as deputy CinCUSNavEur, 278, 299-300; relationship in the mid-1970s with CinCSouth, 288; responsible for the clearing of the Suez Canal in the mid-1970s, 293-294; role of the political adviser on the staff, 297-298; quality of staff members, 300; downgrading of the command in 1983 to a three-star billet, 300-301; staff members lived on the British economy, 303

Naval Material Command
Role of in the mid-1970s, 336-337

Naval Reserve
The influx of reserve officers for training at the beginning of World War II led to an end on the two-year ban on marriage for newly commissioned regular officers, 23-24; reserve officers were essential for the Navy in World War II, 49

Newton, Lieutenant Commander Roy A., USN (USNA, 1930)
Was executive officer of the destroyer Ralph Talbot (DD-390) when she was shot up off Guadalcanal in August 1942, 61-62; as skipper of the destroyer Stack (DD-406) during the Battle of Vella Gulf in August 1943, 73-74, 77-78

New York, USS (BB-34)
Was part of the midshipman training squadron along the East Coast in the summer of 1939, 21-25; propulsion plant, 21; ship's boats, 25-26

News Media
　Interviews of U.S. naval personnel when the first Polaris-armed submarine arrived in Holy Loch, Scotland, in 1961, 181-182

Nickerson, Ensign Emery M., USN (USNA, 1942)
　Was the junior officer of the deck in the carrier Wasp (CV-7) when she collided with the destroyer Stack (DD-406) in March 1942, 56

Nitze, Paul H.
　As Secretary of the Navy in 1967, paid a visit to Brazil, 237

North Atlantic Treaty Organization
　Did not take an active part in supporting the Hungarian revolt in 1956, 153; briefings to NATO commanders after successful Polaris patrols in 1961, 182; General Alexander Haig's relief of General Andrew Goodpaster as SACEur in 1974, 280-281; in the mid-1970s many of the SACEur staff members seemed preoccupied with Europe's Central Front to the exclusion of the flanks, 282-283, 307, 343, 351-352; the Sixth Fleet was a U.S. national asset in some situations, NATO asset in others, 288; the French Navy participated in exercises with the U.S. Sixth Fleet in the 1970s, despite French withdrawal from NATO, 296, 298-299; relations between Greece and Turkey as NATO members, 345-346, 349-352, 369; Italian contributions to the alliance in the late 1970s, 353-354; Shear's efforts to get Spain into NATO, 357-358; periodic commanders' conferences, 368

　See also Allied Forces Southern Europe (CinCSouth)

North Vietnam
　Was supplied in the mid-1960s by Communist-bloc merchant shipping, 229-230; additional supplies came in through Cambodia, 230-231

Norway
　Adjacent to the patrol area for the ballistic missile submarine Patrick Henry (SSBN-599) in the early 1960s, 183-186

Norwegian Sea
　Patrol area for the ballistic missile submarine Patrick Henry (SSBN-599) in the early 1960s, 183-186

Nuclear Power Program
　In 1958-59 prospective skippers of Polaris submarines underwent the nuclear power training program in Washington, D.C., and Arco, Idaho, 161-163; discussion of progressive development of power plants, 162-163; H. G. Rickover's role in ensuring quality and safety, 176-178; debate over the power plant for Trident submarines, 177, 250

Nuclear Weapons
Shear felt that the atomic bombs dropped on Japan in August 1945 were unnecessary as a means of inducing Japanese surrender because of all the bombs and mines dropped previously, 106-107; in the mid-1950s the Air Force seemed to think that nuclear weapons were the solutions to all problems, 138; the National War College was the site of a 1955 joint-service war game involving the projected use of nuclear weapons, 149-152; role of the Joint Strategic Target Planning Staff in nuclear weapons targeting in the late 1950s and early 1960s, 152, 195, 206-207; protests by the Scottish people when the ballistic missile submarine Patrick Henry (SSBN-599) arrived at Holy Loch in 1961, 181; the Navy wanted to make sure that the Air Force would not take over its nuclear weapons targets in the early 1960s, 191; crew members of the Patrick Henry were willing to fire nuclear weapons if ordered to do so, 192-193; in the late 1950s Polaris submarines were merged into the nuclear weapons targeting plan, 195; the United States evacuated its Polaris submarines from Holy Loch, Scotland, during the Cuban crisis in October 1962, 198-199; the United States began sending Polaris submarines into the Mediterranean after removing Jupiter missiles from Turkey and Italy following the 1962 Cuban crisis, 202-203; storage on board the fast combat support ship Sacramento (AOE-1) in the mid-1960s, 224

OP-31
See Submarine Warfare Division (OP-31) of OpNav

OP-60
See Strategic Plans Division (OP-60) of OpNav

OP-095
See Antisubmarine Warfare and Tactical Electromagnetic Programs (OP-095), OpNav

O'Connor, Rear Admiral John J., CHC, USN
Had regular meetings with VCNO Shear while serving as Chief of Chaplains in the mid-1970s, 323-324

Olch, Commander Isaiah, USN (USNA, 1922)
Old-school naval officer who commanded the destroyer Stack (DD-406) at the beginning of World War II, 49-51; career probably damaged by the Stack's March 1942 collision with the carrier Wasp (CV-7), 57

Oliver Hazard Perry (FFG-7)-Class Frigates
Design and development of in the early 1970s, 255-257

Olongapo, Philippine Islands
Town that had an unsavory reputation for sailors on liberty in the mid-1960s, 228-229

Oman
Relations with the United States in the mid-1970s, 285

OpNav
   The work of the Strategic Plans Division (OP-60) in the mid-1950s, 139-155

Osborn, Commander James B., USN (USNA, 1942)
   Student at submarine school in 1944, 92; selected in the late 1950s as one of the first Polaris submarine skippers, 157; underwent the nuclear power training program in 1958-59, 161-163

Overseas-Homeporting Program
   Had mixed results in the 1970s--successful in the Pacific and Italy, not in Greece, 289-292

P-3 Orion
   Improvements in ASW capability over the years, 266

Packard, David
   Highly regarded as Deputy Secretary of Defense, 1969-71, 261-262

Pan American World Airways
   Radio newscaster H. V. Kaltenborn was a passenger on a Clipper flight from Espiritu Santo to Pearl Harbor in late 1943, 89-90

Parker, Rear Admiral Edward N., USN (USNA, 1925)
   Involvement in a 1955 joint-service war game involving nuclear weapons, 149-152; assigned in the late 1950s to the Joint Strategic Target Planning Staff, 195

Patrick Henry, USS (SSBN-599)
   Had a superb crew of officers and enlisted men when she went into commission in 1960, 164; relation of blue and gold crews, 164-165; development of shipboard operating procedures, 166-167; missile failures during tests in 1960, 167-169; construction of, 170-175; inspected by H. G. Rickover, 176-177; President Dwight Eisenhower visited the ship during sea trials in 1960, 178-180; deterrent patrols in the early 1960s, 180-186, 192-194; overseas base at Holy Loch, Scotland, during patrols in the early 1960s, 181-182, 189-190; radio communications while on patrol, 183-185; living conditions on board, 184, 187; avoiding detection, 185-186; families of crew members, 187-188; crew members were willing to fire nuclear weapons if ordered to do so, 192-193; visit from Britain's Lord Louis Mountbatten in 1961, 305

Payne, Captain Kenneth H.
   Merchant marine officer who became Shear's stepfather in the 1920s, 2; as master of a menhaden fishing ship in the 1920s, 4, 8, 10; recommended a naval career for Shear, 13

Pearl Harbor, Hawaii
   Base for submarines that had relaxed operating schedules shortly after World War II, 113-116

Personnel
The Navy faced serious shortages of trained manpower in the late 1970s, 317, 318, 369

See also Bureau of Naval Personnel

PERT Program
As a means of tracking progress in the Polaris program in the late 1950s and early 1960s, 175

Petersen, Rear Admiral Forrest S., USN (USNA, 1945)
As a carrier group commander in the Mediterranean in the mid-1970s, was involved in the question of overseas homeporting, 290

Philippine Islands
Subic Bay Provided a logistic support base for U.S. forces involved in the Vietnam War, 217, 219, 227-229; U.S. forces had to leave in the early 1990s, 227-228

Pirie, Vice Admiral Robert B., USN (USNA, 1926)
As OP-05 in the late 1950s, opposed the Polaris missile submarine program, 154

Planning
Early planning for the Polaris program was done by the Strategic Plans Division (OP-60) of OpNav in the mid-1950s, 154; initial planning for sea-based ballistic missiles contemplated the possibility of putting Jupiter missiles in merchant ships, 205-206

Polaris Missile
The A-1 version had growing pains in the early 1960s, 167-169; test firing of missiles for President Dwight D. Eisenhower by the submarine Patrick Henry (SSBN-599) in 1960, 179-180; range capability, 185

Polaris Program
Early planning for the program was done by the Strategic Plans Division (OP-60) of OpNav in the mid-1950s, 154; H. G. Rickover's selection of the first submarine skippers, 157-161; contributions of William Raborn and Levering Smith, 157, 169, 170, 174-175, 180; in 1958-59 prospective skippers of Polaris submarines underwent the nuclear power training program in Washington, D.C., and Arco, Idaho, 161-163; the program was enacted with unusual speed, 174-175; PERT program for tracking progress, 175; initial planning contemplated the possibility of putting Jupiter missiles in merchant ships, 205-206

See also Atlantic Command, U.S., and Patrick Henry, USS (SSBN-599)

Portuguese Language
Shear learned the language in the late 1960s to prepare for a billet as chief of the U.S. naval mission in Brazil, 233-234; Shear used the language, 1967-69 in his dealings with the Brazilian Navy and as an interpreter, 235, 237-238

Potomac, USS (AG-25)
Presidential yacht that Franklin D. Roosevelt brought to the Naval Academy around 1940, 380-381; efforts in the 1980s by Roosevelt's son to have the yacht restored, 381-382.

Prohibition
Rum runners brought alcohol ashore on Long Island during the 1920s, 3-4

Promotion of Officers
Shear learned of his selection for rear admiral while in command of the fast combat support ship Sacramento (AOE-1) in the mid-1960s, 223; work of selection boards in the mid-1970s, 328-330

Propulsion Plants
Coal-fired triple-expansion steam engines were used in menhaden fishing ships in the 1920s and 1930s, 7-9; conversion to more efficient diesels, 8-9; flooding of the plant in the destroyer Stack (DD-406) when she was in a collision in March 1942, 56-57; description of the Stack's capability and operation, 68-70, 78-80; comparison of the General Motors and Fairbanks-Morse diesel engines in World War II U.S. submarines, 94; the submarine Trigger (SS-564) was commissioned in 1952 with unsatisfactory pancake diesel engines, 123-128; in 1958-59 prospective skippers of Polaris submarines underwent the nuclear power training program in Washington, D.C., and Arco, Idaho, 161-163; the plant in the fast combat support ship Sacramento (AOE-1), completed in 1964, came from the incomplete battleship Kentucky (BB-66), 216-217

Proteus, USS (AS-19)
Submarine tender that arrived in Holy Loch, Scotland, in the spring of 1960 to take care of Polaris missile submarines, 181, 189-190, 194; cleared out of Holy Loch during the Cuban Missile Crisis in October 1962, 199

Providence, USS (CLG-6)
Was due to be commanded by Shear in the mid-1960s, but he was selected for flag rank instead, 223

Public Relations
U.S. naval officers made public appearances in Scotland when Polaris submarines began to be based there in the early 1960s, 191

Pugh, Lieutenant Commander Douglas H., USN (USNA, 1938)
Commanded the submarine Sawfish (SS-276) in 1944-45 during war patrols in the Pacific, 98-99, 105

Queen Mary, RMS
British troop transport that loaded soldiers at Boston in early 1942 for a transatlantic crossing, 54-55; dipped her flag to the submarine Becuna (SS-319) during an encounter in the early 1950s, 136

Rabin, Yitzhak General
   Impressive individual as Israeli Army Chief of Staff in the mid-1960s, 213

Raborn, Rear Admiral William F., Jr., USN (USNA, 1928)
   Directed the Navy's Polaris missile submarine program in the late 1950s, 157, 169, 174-175, 180

Radar
   Provided only limited help during a 1942 collision between the destroyer Stack (DD-406) and the carrier Wasp (CV-7), 55; use of the SJ radar by the submarine Sawfish (SS-276) in 1944-45 to communicate with other submarines, 101

Rademaker, Admiral Augusto Hamann
   Brazilian Naval Minister in the late 1960s, good friend of the United States, 237-238, 240

Radio
   Communications methods used by Polaris submarines in the early 1960s, 183-185; communication between crew members of the ballistic missile submarine Patrick Henry (SSBN-599) and their families while on patrol in the early 1960s, 187; the U.S. Navy lost an important radio station when the Soviets took over Ethiopia in 1974, 278-279

Reeves, Captain John W., Jr., USN (USNA, 1911)
   Perceived as having a cavalier attitude when his ship, the carrier Wasp (CV-7), was in a collision in 1942, 57

Refueling
   The Navy used the former sailing ship Erskine Phelps as a fuel barge at Purvis Bay, near Guadalcanal, in 1942-43, 67-68

Rickover, Vice Admiral Hyman G., USN (USNA, 1922)
   Involvement in the selection in the late 1950s of the commanding officers for the first Polaris submarines, 157-161; description of his interviews, 158-161, 257; involved in the training of prospective Polaris skippers in the late 1950s, 161; inspection of the ballistic missile submarine Patrick Henry (SSBN-599), 176-177; Shear's assessment of, 176-178; involvement in the early 1970s in the Trident program, 177, 250; in the early 1960s did not move quickly enough in selecting and training Polaris submarine skippers, 209-210

Rood, Commander George H., USN
   Navy lawyer who accompanied Shear to the Middle East and Far East in 1956 to try to win votes for the U.S. position on territorial waters, 141-142

Roosevelt, President Franklin D.
   Visited the Naval Academy in his yacht Potomac (AG-25) around 1940, 380-381

Roosevelt, James
    Son of President Franklin D. Roosevelt, tried in the 1980s to have his father's yacht Potomac (AG-25) restored, 381-382

Rota, Spain
    In the mid-1960s became a base for deployed Polaris missile submarines, 202-203

Royall, Lieutenant William F., USN (USNA, 1927)
    Taught seamanship and sailing at the Naval Academy in the late 1930s, 20-21

Royal Navy
    Admiral of the Fleet Lord Louis Mountbatten's relationship with the U.S. Navy in the 1950s and 1960s, 144-146, 305-306; the British were reluctant to have the billet of CinCUSNavEur downgraded to three stars, which it was in 1983, 301-303; candid about intelligence exchanges with the U.S. Navy in the 1970s, 307; stationed capable officers at Gibraltar in the late 1970s, 365; provided top-notch staff officers for NATO commands in the late 1970s, 366-367

Rum Runners
    See Prohibition

Russell, Bertrand
    British writer who protested the arrival of a U.S. Polaris submarine in Scotland in 1961, 181

SACEur
    See North Atlantic Treaty Organization

Sacramento, USS (AOE-1)
    Characteristics of, 216; propulsion plant came from the incomplete battleship Kentucky (BB-66), 216-217; underway replenishment operations, 217, 218-222, 224-226; provided a great deal of logistic support to forces involved in the Vietnam War, 217, 221, 227-229; description of crew members, 218-219; demands on the skipper's stamina, 223; in the mid-1960s delivered beer to Marines stationed at Chulai, South Vietnam, 231-233

Sailing
    During his growing-up years on Long Island in the 1930s, Shear was fond of sailboats, 14; program at the Naval Academy in the late 1930s and early 1940s, 19-21

Salvage
    Clearing of the Suez Canal in the mid-1970s, 293-294

Sancar, General Semih, Turkish Army
    Tough, capable professional military leader in Turkey in the late 1970s, 346

Sawfish, USS (SS-276)
   Patrol operations in the Western Pacific in 1944-45, 96-107; sank the Japanese submarine I-29 in July 1944, 97-98; successful patrol in the fall of 1944, 98, 100-101; recovery of downed aviators, 99; role of the diving officer, 103-104; alertness for air attacks, 104-105; shortage of targets at the end of the war, 105-106; quality of enlisted men, 108; good food on board, 108; rest periods between patrols, 108-109

Schaefer, William Donald
   As governor of Maryland, snubbed the commissioning ceremony for the submarine Maryland (SSBN-738) in 1992, 254-255

Scotland
   The submarine Becuna (SS-319) distributed food to needy Britons during a visit to Scotland in the early 1950s, 130; Holy Loch was a base for U.S. ballistic missile submarines in the early 1960s, 181-182, 190-191; protests by Scottish people, 181; the United States evacuated its Polaris submarines from Holy Loch, Scotland, during the Cuban crisis in October 1962, 198-199; Holy Loch closed down as a U.S. base in 1992, 303

Selection Boards
   Role of the Secretary of the Navy in flag selections in the 1970s and 1980s, 322-323, 329; fairness of the Navy system, 328-330

Shear, Elizabeth Perry
   Met her future husband when the battleship New York (BB-34) visited Portland, Maine, in the summer of 1939, 22-23; waited patiently for marriage while her future husband was a midshipman and ensign, 23-24, 33-34; worked in the Com 12 mail room during World War II, 71, 85-86; accompanied husband to sub school in 1944, 90, 96; life in Hawaii shortly after World War II, 113-114; learned Portuguese in 1967 in preparation for living in Brazil, 234; enjoyed living in London in the mid-1970s, 276-277, 311; served as hostess for her husband, 1975-77, 331; reluctance to live in Washington in the 1980s, 374-376

Shear, Admiral Harold E., USN (Ret.) (USNA, 1942)
   Parents of, 1-2, 7, 10, 18; grandparents of, 1-2; stepfather of, 2, 4, 8, 10, 13; boyhood on Long Island in the 1920s, 2-4, 14; education of, 2, 10-11; summer work on a menhaden fishing ship in the 1920s and 1930s, 4-10; preparatory steps in the late 1930s for entering the Naval Academy, 11-13, 17-18; siblings of, 13; as a Naval Academy midshipman, 1938-41, 15-42; wife of, 22-24, 33-34, 71, 85-86, 90, 96, 114, 234, 276-277, 311, 331, 374-376, 384; duty from 1941 to 1943 in the destroyer Stack (DD-406), 42-88; attended submarine school in the early months of 1944, 90-96; duty in 1944-45 in the submarine Sawfish (SS-276), 96-110; duty in 1945-46 in the Submarine Administrative Command, San Francisco, 110-112; served from 1946 to 1948 as executive officer of the submarine Becuna (SS-319), 112-117; children of, 114, 384; service in 1948-49 on the staff of ComSubPac, 117-119; duty from 1949 to 1951 in the Bureau of Naval Personnel, 119-122; served 1951-52 as executive officer of the submarine Trigger (SS-564), 122-127; commanded the Becuna (SS-319) from

1952 to 1954, 128-136; was a student in 1954-55 at the Armed Forces Staff College, 136-139; duty in 1955-57 in the Strategic Plans Division (OP-60) of OpNav, 139-155; as a member of the staff of Commander Submarine Squadron Two in 1957-58, 156; selection and training for the Navy's nuclear power program in 1958-59, 157-163; served as PCO and CO of the ballistic missile submarine Patrick Henry (SSBN-599) from 1959 to 1962, 164-194; duty from 1962 to 1964 on the CinCLant staff, 194-211; as a student in 1964-65 at the National War College, 211-215; in 1965-66 commanded the fast combat support ship Sacramento (AOE-1), 215-233; selection for flag rank in the mid-1960s, 223; service from 1967 to 1969 as chief of the U.S. naval mission in Brazil, 233-248; served 1969-71 as Director of the Submarine Warfare Division (OP-31) in OpNav, 248-262; served 1971-73 as Director, Antisubmarine Warfare and Tactical Electromagnetic Programs (OP-095) in OpNav, 262-274; served in 1974-75 as Commander in Chief U.S. Naval Forces Europe, 275-310; served as Vice Chief of Naval Operations, 1975-77, 310-342; as CinCSouth, 1977-80, 342-373; administrator of the U.S. Maritime Administration, 1981-85, 373-382; post-retirement activities, 382-384

Sherman, Lieutenant Commander Philip K., USN (USNA, 1933)
As commanding officer of the destroyer Stack (DD-406) in late 1943, was reluctant to release Shear for submarine school, 88-89

Shifley, Vice Admiral Ralph L., USN (Ret.) (USNA, 1933)
In the 1970s helped U.S. development efforts in Iran, 284

Shipbuilding
Construction of the ballistic missile submarine Patrick Henry (SSBN-599) by the Electric Boat Division of General Dynamics in the late 1950s, 170-175; Japanese shipyards in Brazil in the late 1960s and beyond, 245-247; merchant ship construction in the 1980s, 377-378

Ship Design
Contributions by naval architect Andrew I. McKee to submarine development during the course of the 20th century, 170-172; design and development of Oliver Hazard Perry (FFG-7)-class frigates in the early 1970s, 255-257; of the Los Angeles (SSN-66)-class submarines in the late 1960s, 258-259

Ship Handling
In the submarine Becuna (SS-319) in the early 1950s, 132-134; during underway replenishments by the fast combat support ship Sacramento (AOE-1) in the mid-1960s, 220, 225-226

Shore Patrol
At Subic Bay in the Philippines in the mid-1960s, 228-229

Shugg, Carleton (USNA, 1921A)
Headed the Electric Boat Division of General Dynamics in the late 1950s when it was building Polaris ballistic missile submarines, 172-174

Simpson, Commander Rodger W., USN (USNA, 1921)
Destroyer division commander who directed the use of depth charges against Japanese in the water following the Battle of Vella Gulf in August 1943, 73-74, 76-77

Simpson, USS (DD-221)
Destroyer used in the summer of 1940 for an East Coast training cruise for midshipmen, 26-27

Sims, Commander William E., USN (USNA, 1942)
Student at submarine school in early 1944, 92; duty in the submarine Sawfish (SS-276) in the Pacific in the latter part of World War II, 96-97, 100, 107; selected in the late 1950s as the skipper of one of the early Polaris submarines, 157; underwent the nuclear power training program in 1958-59, 161-163

Single Integrated Operational Plan
Role of the Joint Strategic Target Planning Staff in U.S. nuclear weapons targeting in the late 1950s and early 1960s, 152, 195, 206-207, 210-211

Sixth Fleet, U.S.
Was a U.S. national asset in some situations, NATO asset in others, 288, 369; Vice Admiral Daniel J. Murphy did an excellent job as fleet command in 1973-74, 289; level of readiness in the late 1970s, 369

Smith, Admiral Harold Page, USN (USNA, 1924)
As Chief of the Naval Personnel in the late 1950s, pushed H. G. Rickover for faster selection of Polaris submarine skippers, 157-158; as CinCUSNavEur in the early 1960s, 182, 198-199; served as CinCLant in the mid-1960s, 196, 201-202, 210-211; was commanding officer of the battleship Missouri (BB-63) in 1949-50, 197-198; speaker at National War College, 212

Smith, Rear Admiral Levering, USN (USNA, 1932)
Did a fine job as technical director of the Polaris missile program in the late 1950s and early 1960s, 169-170; power plant for Trident submarines in the 1970s, 250

Sonar
Limited capability on board the destroyer Stack (DD-406) early in World War II, 46; use of passive sonar by the ballistic missile submarine Patrick Henry (SSBN-599) during patrols in the early 1960s, 186; efforts in the early 1970s to improve passive sonar, 263-264, 269-270

South Vietnam
In the mid-1960s the fast combat support ship Sacramento (AOE-1) delivered beer to Marines stationed at Chulai, 231-233

Soviet Navy
The U.S. services used the capabilities of Soviet ships in playing a 1955 joint war game involving nuclear weapons, 150-151; unsuccessful in locating U.S. Polaris submarines in the early 1960s, 185-186; had surveillance trawlers observing U.S. naval operations in the Tonkin Gulf in the mid-1960s, 226-227; heavy emphasis on U.S. ASW in the 1970s because of the Soviet threat, 262-272; stationed ships in the Red Sea during the Ethiopia crisis of 1974, 278; incidents at sea with U.S. ships in the 1970s, 309-310

Soviet Union
In the early 1950s the submarine Becuna (SS-319) made intelligence-gathering surveillance patrols off the Soviet Union, 129-132; involvement in the Cuban Missile Crisis in 1962, 198-201; went into Africa in great strength in the mid-1970s, 277-278, 308-309; intervention in Afghanistan in 1979, 285-286; joined in Incidents at Sea agreement with the United States in 1972, 309-310; Turkey aided the United States in gathering intelligence on the Soviet Union in the late 1970s, 346-347

Spain
In the mid-1960s Rota became a base for deployed Polaris missile submarines, 202-203; Shear's efforts in the late 1970s to get the nation into NATO, 357-358

Spear, Lawrence Y. (USNA, 1890)
Submarine design pioneer who had a long career with the Electric Boat Company, 171-173

Spiers, Ronald I.
Served as U.S. ambassador to Turkey in the late 1970s, 358-360

Stack, USS (DD-406)
Collided with the aircraft carrier Wasp (CV-7) in March 1942, 24, 54-57; high-speed capability, 42; duty early in World War II on convoy escort in the Atlantic, 42-49, 53-54; installation of radar in 1942, 45; limited ASW capability, 45-46, 81; handling in heavy weather, 48-49; description of the ship's officers, 49-53; escorted the British transport Queen Mary in early 1942, 54-55; early operations in the Pacific in mid-1942, 58-59; support of the Guadalcanal operation in the summer and fall of 1942, 59-68; antiaircraft measures, 60, 63-64; logistic support during the Solomons campaign, 67-68; propulsion plant, 68-70, 78-80; new guns added during yard period at Mare Island, 71; in 1943 operations began moving north of Guadalcanal in the Solomons chain, 71-72; participation in the Battle of Vella Gulf in August 1943, 72-78; dropped depth charges on Japanese survivors after the battle, 73-74, 76-77, sunk after atomic bomb tests in 1946, 81-82; recognition of the work of subordinates, 82-85; rare opportunities for liberty, 85; censorship of the crew's mail, 85-86; participation in the beginning of the Central Pacific offensive in 1943, 87-88

State Department
Role of foreign service officers as political advisers on the staffs of military CinCs in the 1970s, 297-298, 358-359

Steele, Vice Admiral George P. II, USN (USNA, 1945)
Service as a junior officer in the submarine Becuna (SS-319) shortly after World War II, 114-115; as Commander Seventh Fleet in the mid-1970s, 231

Sterett, USS (DD-407)
Operated with the destroyer Stack (DD-406) during escort operations in the Atlantic in early 1942, 54-58; fought in the Battle of Vella Gulf in August 1943, 72-73

Stoddart, Jonathan D.
U.S. diplomat who served as political adviser to CinCSouth in the late 1970s, 358-359

Strat-X Study
Conducted in the late 1960s as a precursor to the development of the Trident ballistic missile submarine program, 249

Strategic Air Command
Involvement in a 1955 joint-service war game involving nuclear weapons, 149-152; in the late 1950s General Curtis LeMay was unsuccessful in his attempt to get Polaris submarines put under SAC, 195; provided a briefing for Admiral H. P. Smith, CinCLant, in the mid-1960s, 210-211

Strategic Plans Division (OP-60) of OpNav
Discussion of the top-notch officers in the organization in the mid-1950s, 139-140, 145-149; involvement in law of the sea matters in the mid-1950s, 141-144; members of the staff took part in a joint-service war game at the National War College in the summer of 1955, 149-152; various issues dealt with in the mid-1950s, 153-155

Stratton, Representative Samuel S.
Congressman who was very supportive of Navy programs in the early 1970s, 259

Subic Bay, Philippine Islands
Provided a logistic support base for U.S. forces involved in the Vietnam War, 217, 219, 227-229; U.S. forces had to leave in the early 1990s, 227-228; liberty in the town of Olongapo, 228-229

Submarine Administrative Command, San Francisco
Had the duty of bringing submarines back from the war zone for decommissioning in 1945-46, 110-112

Submarine Force Atlantic Fleet
The force commander was not happy with a series of critical messages from Commander Ned Beach in 1952, 127-128; in 1960 E. W. Grenfell maneuvered himself into the billet as force commander after Rear Admiral Dan Daspit declined to move from New London to Norfolk, 196, 204-205; coordination with CinCLant on Polaris submarine schedules in the early 1960s, 207-209

Submarine School, New London, Connecticut
Had a three-month condensed course for prospective submarine officers in early 1944, 90-96

Submarine Warfare Division (OP-31) of OpNav
Involved in attack submarine construction program in the late 1960s, 248-249, 258-259; involvement with the Trident program in the early 1970s, 250-255

Suez Canal
The canal was closed as a result of an international crisis in the autumn of 1956, 142-143; the United States did not become involved in the crisis, 153; clearing of in the mid-1970s, 293-294

Terrorism
Kidnaping of a U.S. Army general in Italy in the early 1980s, 356-357

Thebaud, Captain Leo H., USN (USNA, 1913)
Served as Naval Academy commandant of midshipmen in the early 1940s, then commodore of a destroyer squadron, 40-41

Thomas A. Edison, USS (SSBN-610)
New Polaris submarine visited by President John F. Kennedy during the Cuban Missile Crisis in 1962, 200-201

Tomasuolo, Ammiraglio di Squadra Luigi, Italian Navy
Temporarily commanded CinCSouth in 1977 in the interim between two U.S. Navy CinCs, 343, 353

Torpedoes
Development of the Mark 46 and Mark 48 in the early 1970s, 264-265; development of the CapTor mine in the 1970s, 273

Training
Summer cruises for Naval Academy midshipmen in the late 1930s and early 1940s were limited to the East Coast by the war in Europe, 15, 21-28; the submarine school at New London, Connecticut, had a three-month condensed course of prospective submarine officers in early 1944, 90-96; work of the training plans section of BuPers in the late 1940s and early 1950s, 119-121; in 1958-59 prospective skippers of Polaris submarines underwent the nuclear power training program in Washington, D.C., and Arco, Idaho, 161-163; Shear went through Portuguese language training in the late 1960s to prepare for a billet as chief of the U.S. naval mission in Brazil, 233-234

Trident Missiles
The long range of the missiles eliminates the need for overseas basing of ballistic missile submarines, 206, 253; in the early 1970s Dr. John S. Foster, Jr., decided Trident submarines would carry 24 missiles each, 249-250

Trident Program
H. G. Rickover's involvement in during the early 1970s, 177, 250; Strat-X study in the late 1960s, 249; dispute in the early 1970s over power plant, 250; selling of to Congress, 250-252, 262; selection of base sites in Georgia and Washington, 252-254

Trigger, USS (SS-564)
Commissioned in 1952 with unsatisfactory pancake diesel engines, 123-128; went to Washington, D.C., so congressmen could visit, 126-127; had engine trouble during a cruise to Brazil in 1952, 127-128

Triton, USS (SSN-586)
Circumnavigated the world submerged in 1960, 250

Turkey
U.S. agreement to remove Jupiter missiles from Turkey in the wake of the 1962 Cuban Missile Crisis, 202-203; the ballistic missile submarine Sam Houston (SSBN-609) visited Izmir in the spring of 1963, 203; squabble with Greece over Cyprus in the mid-1970s, 288-290, 345; relations with fellow NATO member Greece in the late 1970s, 345-346, 349-352, 369; the Turkish Army was very capable, 346-348; aided the United States in gathering intelligence on the Soviet Union, 346-347; willingness to mine the Turkish straits if necessary, 347; beneficial geographical position, 348-349; military government in the early 1980s, 359-360

Turner, Vice Admiral Frederick C., USN
Was Commander Sixth Fleet when the flagship Little Rock (CLG-4) went through the newly cleared Suez Canal in 1975, 293-294

Turner, Admiral Stansfield, USN (USNA, 1947)
As CinCSouth in the mid-1970s, relationship with SACEur, General Alexander Haig, 343, 353; relations with Greece, 350; held in low repute by fellow senior officers, 373

Tuthill, John W.
As U.S. ambassador to Brazil in the late 1960s, relied on Shear for military contacts, 243-244

U-boats
German submarines were extraordinarily successful in the Atlantic during the early years of World War II, 46-47

ULMS
See Trident Program

Underway Replenishment
Provided by the fast combat support ship Sacramento (AOE-1) in the mid-1960s, 217-222, 224-226

United Nations
> Vote in the mid-1950s on law of the sea negotiations concerning each nation's territorial waters, 141-144

Vella Gulf, Battle of
> Night action in August 1943 that pitted U.S. and Japanese destroyers against each other, 72-78

Vietnam War
> High level of logistic support provided by the fast combat support ship Sacramento (AOE-1) in 1965-66, 217, 221; the Soviets had surveillance trawlers observing U.S. naval operations in the Tonkin Gulf in the mid-1960s, 226-228; North Vietnamese supported by Communist-bloc merchant shipping, 229-231

Vinson, Representative Carl
> Georgia congressmen who visited the new submarine Trigger (SS-564) in Washington in the early 1950s, 126-127

Vossler, Captain Francis A. L., USN (USNA, 1907)
> Made a poor impression as the Naval Academy's commandant of midshipmen in the early 1940s, 40

War Games
> The National War College was the site of a 1955 joint-service war game involving the projected use of nuclear weapons, 149-152

Ward, Vice Admiral Alfred G., USN (USNA, 1932)
> Was Commander Second Fleet during the Cuban Missile Crisis quarantine of October 1962, 198-199

Ward, Captain Norvell G., USN (USNA, 1935)
> In the late 1950s and early 1960s served as the commodore of Submarine Squadron 14, the first with Polaris submarines, 158, 166, 180, 182, 190

Warder, Rear Admiral Frederick B., USN (USNA, 1925)
> While serving in OpNav in the late 1960s, recognized the importance of the Polaris program, 164-165

Warner, John W.
> As Secretary of the Navy in the early 1970s, helped sell the Trident submarine program to Congress, later a senator, 251-252; involved in the 1972 Incidents at Sea agreement with the Soviet Union, 309-310

Warnke, Paul C.
> Assistant Secretary of Defense who refused to provide updated cruisers to the Brazilian Navy in the late 1960s, 240

Wasp, USS (CV-7)
Collided with the destroyer Stack (DD-406) in March 1942, 24, 54-57; delivered aircraft to Malta in 1942, 57-58; sunk while in support of the Guadalcanal operation in the summer of 1942, 59-61

Watkins, Vice Admiral James D., USN (USNA, 1949)
As Commander Sixth Fleet in the late 1970s, commented on the Greeks and Turks in NATO, 351

Weather
Allied merchant ships convoys and their escorts often experienced heavy seas in the North Atlantic in World War II, 48-49

Weinel, Admiral John P., USN (USNA, 1939)
As U.S. representative to the NATO military committee in the mid-1970s, advised Shear on how to deal with General Alexander Haig, 344

Welles, Orson
Radio actor whose October 1938 drama broadcast made it seem that Martians were landing on earth, 29-30

Weschler, Ensign Admiral Thomas R., USN (USNA, 1939)
Was the officer of the deck in the carrier Wasp (CV-7) when she collided with the destroyer Stack (DD-406) in March 1942, 56

Westinghouse
Defense contractor that developed nuclear power plants for submarines in the 1950s, 162-163

Wilkins, Captain Charles Warren, USN (USNA, 1924)
Peacetime submarine skipper who did well in command of the Narwhal (SS-167) early in World War II, 91; had command of a wolf pack in 1944, 97, 101-102; role in demobilizing submarines at San Francisco after World War II, 111

Wilson, Captain James B., USN (USNA, 1947)
Conducted the Strat-X study in the late 1960s as a precursor to the Trident ballistic missile submarine program, 249; served as aide to Deputy Secretary of Defense David Packard during the Nixon Administration, 261-262

Woolsey, R. James
Didn't have much experience with the Navy when he became Under Secretary in 1977, 320-321

World War I
Shear's father, an Army medical officer, died during the influenza outbreak of 1918, 1; Shear's stepfather was involved in minelaying in the North Sea during the war, 8

Wylie, Captain Joseph C., USN (USNA, 1932)
Excellent writer and strategic thinker who served in the Strategic Plans Division (OP-60) of OpNav in the mid-1950s, 140, 145-146; involvement in the mid-1950s in planning for the Polaris missile submarine program, 154-155

Yard Patrol Craft (YPs)
Used for training of Naval Academy midshipmen in the summer of 1941, 27-28

Yugoslavia
NATO concern for in the late 1970s, 355-356

Zumwalt, Admiral Elmo R., Jr., USN (USNA, 1943)
Underwent a tough interview by H. G. Rickover in the late 1950s as part of applying for the nuclear power program, 159-161, 257; involvement in ship development programs during his tenure in the early 1970s as Chief of Naval Operations, 255-257; assessment of his initiatives in the personnel area, 256-257; close relationship with Admiral Worth Bagley, 275-276, 290-292, 311, 313, 326; had mixed results with his overseas-homeporting program in the early 1970s, 289-292; Admiral James Holloway, CNO 1974-78, reversed some of the initiatives from Zumwalt's tenure, 311-316

www.ingramcontent.com/pod-product-compliance
Lightning Source LLC
Chambersburg PA
CBHW080623170426

43209CB00007B/1499